Greenhill Books

FROM THE
BARREL
OF A GUN

'Every Communist must understand this truth: political power grows from the barrel of a gun ... Everything in Yenan has been built up by means of the gun. Anything can grow from the barrel of a gun. Viewed from the Marxist theory of the state, the army is the chief component of the political power of a state. Whoever wants to seize and hold on to political power must have a strong army ... [W]e can even say that the whole world can be remoulded only with a gun.'

— Mao Tse-tung's concluding remarks at the Sixth Plenum of the Central Committee of the Chinese Communist Party, November 1938.

FROM THE BARREL OF A GUN

A History of Guerrilla, Revolutionary and
Counter-Insurgency Warfare, from the
Romans to the Present

JOHN ELLIS

Greenhill Books, London

Stackpole Books, Pennsylvania

From the Barrel of a Gun
first published 1995 by Greenhill Books,
Lionel Leventhal Limited, Park House, 1 Russell Gardens,
London NW11 9NN
and
Stackpole Books, 5067 Ritter Road, Mechanicsburg, PA 17055, USA

From the Barrel of a Gun is revised and enlarged from
A Short History of Guerrilla Warfare, first published
in 1975 (© John Ellis, 1975)

© John Ellis, 1995
The moral right of the author has been asserted

British Library Cataloguing in Publication Data available

ISBN 1–85367–197–5

Library of Congress Cataloging-in-Publication Data available

Typeset by DP Photosetting, Aylesbury, Bucks
Printed and bound in Great Britain by
Biddles Limited, Guildford and King's Lynn

Contents

Chronology of Notable Guerrilla Wars

Date	Insurgents	Incumbents	Place	Major Leaders
516BC	Scythians	Persians	Scythia	
389–338	Volsci	Romans	n. Italy	
195–138	Celtiberians	Romans	Spain	
166–160	Jews	Syrians	Israel	Judas and Jonathan Maccabeus
154–138	Lusitanians	Romans	Spain	Viriathus
80–72	Celtiberians Lusitanians	Romans	Spain	Sertorius
54	Britons	Romans	England	Cassivellaunus
54–51	Gauls	Romans	France	Vercingetorix, Commius
15–16AD	Chatti	Romans	Germany	Arminius
17–24	Numidians	Romans	Africa	Tacfarinas
36	Cietae	Romans	Anatolia	
43	Britons	Romans	England Wales	Caractacus
355–57	Alamanni	Romans	France	
378	Visigoths	Romans	Italy	
900–950	Magyars	Raids throughout Europe		
1070	Saxons	Holy Roman Empire	Saxony	Otto of Nordheim
1070	Anglo-Saxons	Normans	The Fens	Hereward the Wake
1094–5, 1114	Welsh	English	Snowdonia	Gruffydd ap Cynan
1143	English rebels	Normans	The Fens	Mandeville, Earl of Essex
1282	Welsh	English	Snowdonia	Llewelyn ap Gruffydd
1287–92	Welsh	English	Snowdonia	Rhys ap Maredudd
1296–1328	Scots	English	Scotland	William Wallace, Robert Bruce
1363–84	Tuchins	English	Auvergne	
1418–50	French	English	Normandy Maine	Ambroise de Loré
1550	Estonians	Russians Knights of the Teutonic Order	Reval	Ivo Schenkenberg
1576–1601	Muslims	Moghuls	Mewar	Maharana Partap
1597–1694	African slaves	Portuguese	Brazil	
1604–5	Hungarians	Turks, Austrians	Slovakia	Stephen Bocskai
1627–80	Marathas	Moghuls		Shiva Ji
1655–83	African slaves	English	Jamaica	Juan Bolas
1686–1708	Javanese	Dutch	Java	Surapati
1690–1720	African slaves	English	Jamaica	Cudjoe
1703–11	Camisards	French	Cevennes	
1716–68	Sikhs	Persians	Punjab	

Date	Insurgents	Incumbents	Place	Major Leaders
1740–43	Hungarians	Prussians		
		French	Bohemia	
1772	Caribs	English	St Vincent	
1773–74	Bulgarians	Turks	Bulgaria	
1780–83	Americans	English	Carolinas	Francis Marion
				Thomas Sumter
1785–94	Chechens	Russians	Caucasus	
1791–97	African slaves	French	Haiti	Toussaint
				Louverture
1793	French Royalists	French		
		Republicans	Vendée	Charette
				Henri de la
				Rochejacquelein
1799	Italians	French	Naples	Fabrizio Ruffo
1806–10	Italians	French	Calabria	
1808–13	Spanish	French	Spain	Espoz y Mina
1809	Austrians	French	Tyrol	Andreas Hofer
1809–16	Peruvians	Spanish	n. Peru	Miguel Lanza
1810–21	Mexicans	Spanish	Mexico	Vincente Guerrero
1812–13	Russians	French	Russia	
1817–28	Uruguayans	Portuguese		Jose Artigas
		Argentinians	Uruguay	Fructuoso Rivera
1821–9	Greeks	Turks	Greece	
1825	Javanese	Dutch	Java	
1832–47	Arabs	French	Algeria	Abd-el Kader
1833–39	Carlists	Spanish	Spain	Tomás
				Zumalacárregui
1835–42	Seminoles	Americans	Florida	Osceola
1836–59	Murids	Russians	Caucasus	Imam Shamyl
1846–49	Carlists	Spanish	Catalonia	
1847–1900	Mayas	Mexicans	Yucatan	
1849–55	Hungarians	Austrians	Hungary	Sandor Rosza
1853–68	Nien	Manchus	n. China	Chang Lo-Hsing
1855–72	Miao	Manchus	Kweichow	Chiang
				Hsiu-mei
1858–61	Liberals	Clericals	Mexico	Benito Juárez
1860–66	Neapolitans	Piedmontese	Naples	Carmine
				Donatelli
1860–86	Apaches	Americans	Arizona	Cochise
		Mexicans	n. Mexico	Geronimo
1861–65	Confederates	Union	Missouri	William Clarke
			Kansas	Quantrill
			Virginia	John S. Mosby
1863	Poles	Russians	Poland	
1863–67	Mexicans	French	Mexico	Porfirio Díaz
				Benito Juárez
1866–69	Cretans	Turks	Crete	
1868–78	Cubans	Spanish	Cuba	Antonio Maceo
				Máximo Gómez
1870–71	Franc-tireurs	Prussians	France	
1877–78	?	Russians	Daghestan	
1878–81	Bosnian Moslems	Austrians	Bosnia-	
			Herzegovina	
1880–98	Vietnamese	French	Annam	Thon That
				Thuyet
			Tonking	Nguyen Thien
				Thuat
1882–98	Malinke	French	w. Sudan	Samori Touré
1885–86	Cambodians	French	Cambodia	Si Votha
1886–87	Sarrakole	French	Senegal	Mahmadou
			Gambia	Lamine
1886–98	Kachins, Chins	British	n. Burma	
1887–95	Yaos	British	Malawi	Mlozi

Date	Insurgents	Incumbents	Place	Major Leaders
1894–95	Red Beards	Russians	Manchuria	
1894–1911	Senussi	French	Libya	
1896–97	Brazilian Indians	Brazilians	Canudos	
1896–1908	IMRO	Greeks, Turks		Gotze Deltchev
		Bulgarians	Macedonia	Damian Gruev
1897–1902	Filipinos	Spanish		
		Americans	Philippines	Emilio Aguinaldo
1897–98	Pathans	British	N.W. Frontier	
1898	Temne	British	Sierra Leone	
1900–02	Boers	British	S. Africa	Louis Botha
				C. de Wet
1904–7	Nama	Germans	Tanganyika	Jacob Morenga
1910–20	Mexican Revolution		Mexico	Emiliano Zapata
				Pancho Villa
1910–34	Arabs, Berbers	French, Spanish	Morocco	Abd-el Krim
1914–18	Germans	British	Tanganyika	von Lettow-
				Vorbeck
1916–18	Arabs	Turks	Arabia	T.E. Lawrence
1916–21	IRA	British	Ireland	Michael Collins
				Tom Barry
1918–21	Ukrainians	Bolsheviks	Ukraine	Nestor Mahkno
1918–28	Basmatchis	Russians	Turkestan	
1919–34	IMRO	Greeks,		
		Yugoslavs,		Todor Alexandroff
		Bulgarians	Macedonia	Ivan Michailoff
1920–21	Chechens	Russians	Daghestan	
1920–22	Kurds	Persians	Azerbaijan	Aga Simko
1922–32	Arabs	Italians	Cyrenaica	Omar Mukhtar
1926–49	Chinese Communists	Chinese Nationalists,		Mao Tse-tung,
		Japanese	China	Lin Piao
1927–30	Kurds	Turks	Turkey	Ihsan Nuri
1927–33	Nicaraguans	Americans	Nicaragua	Augusto Sandino
1935–41	Ethiopians	Italians	Ethiopia	Orde Wingate
1936–39	Arabs	British	Palestine	
1941	Partisans, Cetniks	Germans, Italians	Yugoslavia	Josip Tito
	Italians	Germans, Italians	n. Italy	
	Slovaks		Slovakia	
	Albanians		Albania	
	Bulgarians	Germans	Bulgaria	
	French		France	
	Poles		Poland	
1945–49	Indonesians	Dutch	Indonesia	
1946–47	Jews	British, Arabs	Palestine	
1946–49	Greek Communists (ELAS)	Greek govt	Greece	
		British		
1946–54	Hukbalahaps	Filipino govt	Philippines	Luis Taruc
1946–54	Viet-minh	French	Vietnam	Vo Nguyen Giap
1948–60	Malayan Communists	British	Malaya	Chin Peng
1948–?	FARC (to 1990)			
	ELN (GNG from 1986)			
	EPL			
	M-19 (to 1990)			
	ADO	Colombian govt	Colombia	
1949	Indian Communists	Indian govt	Telingana	
1949–?	Karens (KNLA)	Burmese govt	Burma	Bo Mya
1951–55	Mau Mau	British	Kenya	
1953–74	Pathet Lao	Laotian govt	Laos	
1954–59	EOKA	British	Cyprus	George Grivas
1954–62	FLN	French	Algeria	
1955–59	Cuban Civil War		Cuba	Fidel Castro
				Ernesto Guevara
1958–75	Viet Cong (NLF)	S. Vietnamese govt		
	North Vietnamese	USA	S. Vietnam	

Date	Insurgents	Incumbents	Place	Major Leaders
1961–74	MPLA	Portuguese	Angola	
1961–75	Kurds (KDP)	Iraqi govt	Iraq	Mustafa al-Barzani
1962–69	MR 13; FAR	Guatemalan govt	Guatemala	
1963–67	Indonesians	Malayans	Borneo	
		British	Sarawak	
1963–73	PAIGC	Portuguese	Guiné-Bissau	
1963–75	PFLO; DLLF; PFLOAG	Omani govt		
		British	Dhofar	
1963–75	Khmer Rouge	Cambodian govt	Cambodia	Pol Pot
1964–74	FRELIMO	Portuguese	Mozambique	Eduardo Mondlane
1964–91	ELF; EPLF	Ethiopian govt	Eritrea	
1966–89	SWAPO	South Africa	Namibia	
1969–?	NPA			
	MNLF; MILF	Philippine govt	Philippines	
1970–83	PLO and Lebanese			
	Shiites	Israelis	Israel	
1974–?	Chakmas (Shanti			
	Bahini)	Bangladeshi govt	Bangladesh	
1975–?	FRETILIN	Indonesian govt	East Timor	
1975–?	UNITA	Mozambique govt	Mozambique	Jonas Savimbi
1975–?	EGP	Guatemalan govt	Guatemala	
1976–?	POLISARIO	Moroccan govt	Mauretania	
1977–79	Sandanistas	Nicaraguan govt	Nicaragua	
1977–?	Tamil Tigers (LTTE)	Sri Lankan govt	Sri Lanka	
1978–89	Afghans	Afghan govt		
		Soviets	Afghanistan	
1978–?	Khmer Rouge	Cambodian govt	Cambodia	Samphan Khieu
1979–91	TPLF	Ethiopian govt	Tigré	
1980–83	FMLN	Salvadorean govt	El Salvador	
1980–86	Bugandans (NRA)	Ugandan govt	Uganda	Yoweri Museveni
1980–?	Sendero Luminoso			
	Tupac Amaru	Peruvian govt	Peru	Abimael Guzman
1981–90	Contras (NDF; ARDE)	Nicaraguan govt	Nicaragua	
1983–?	Hezbollah	Israelis	Israel/	
		South Lebanon Army	Lebanon	
1984–?	Kurds (KDP)	Iraqi govt	Iraq	Massoud Barzani
1984–?	Kurds (PKK)	Turkish govt	Turkey	Abdullah Ojalan
1987–89	JVP	Sri Lankan govt	Sri Lanka	
1989–92	Afghans	Afghan govt		
		(pro-Soviet)	Afghanistan	
1992–?	Afghans	Afghan 'govt'	Afghanistan	

Preface

When this book appeared in its original edition, in 1976, events in Vietnam, Portuguese Africa and Latin America had brought the notion of guerrilla warfare back into prominence. The many books and articles to which this gave rise seemed mainly to be based on the assumption that guerrilla warfare begins with Mao Tse-tung and develops, if at all, from there. I agree whole-heartedly that Mao is of central importance in any analysis of guerrilla theory and practice – indeed, the title of this new edition is inspired by his words – but what too many writers have chosen to ignore is that guerrilla warfare is as old as man himself, and that there are countless documented examples of this kind of struggle throughout history. The variety of times and places in which guerrilla wars have taken place is shown in the Chronology at the front of this book. I have tried to go beyond the standard passing reference to the historical origins of the word 'guerrilla' (a Spanish word meaning 'little war', absorbed into other languages after the war against Napoleon in Spain) and give a reasonably detailed account of some of the occasions on which this mode of warfare has been used, whether it is referred to as guerrilla warfare, *lestrikos polemos*, a little war, a war of detachments, or an insurgency; or whether the fighters themselves are referred to as guerrillas, *guerrilleros*, brigands, bandits, *haiduks*, *klefts*, *fei*, rangers, *franc-tireurs*, partisans or irregulars.

The history of a phenomenon does not necessarily begin with the introduction of the word now in common usage. This is particularly true of guerrilla warfare, the historical extent of which has been masked by the prejudices of long dead administrators and historians. Today concepts like personal and national freedom and the right to resort to armed resistance are more acceptable than they were to the educated classes in the ancient and medieval worlds. For them power was based exclusively upon authority and deference, and there was almost no conception of 'consensus' or 'legitimacy'. Anyone who took up arms against the state was by definition a criminal or bandit, and was referred to as such. But the modern historian, with rather different perspectives on the dividing line between criminality and political protest, must look carefully at these ancient accounts and decide whether the bandits described therein might not more usefully be regarded as guerrillas.

This I have tried to do. Indeed my policy throughout the book has been to keep the exact definition of guerrilla warfare as wide as possible, to show that it is not an absolutely discrete phenomenon, but that it merges into many other types of military activity. During the decline of the Roman Empire, for example, when Europe was being assailed on all sides by the 'barbarians', the Arabs and the Moors, the latter's mode of warfare displayed many guerrilla characteristics. The most cursory examination of the Civil Wars in England during Stephen's reign, the Hundred Years War, the Dutch War of Independence, or the Thirty Years War will also show that during the medieval and early modern periods in Europe even the 'conventional' wars of the time showed such characteristics. Guerrilla warfare can also be a specifically chosen tactic, employed alongside more orthodox measures, during a basically 'regular' war. Such was the case with the employment of light troops during the War of Austrian Succession, of the *franc-tireurs* during the Franco-Prussian War, T. E. Lawrence's Arabs during the Palestine campaign, or Wingate's Chindits during World War II.

Guerrilla warfare is not even to be regarded simply as a military phenomenon. The logic of its very nature often means that it is just as much a political activity as a military one. It is usually the struggle of a weak people against superior numbers and technology. Guerrilla armies have to be built up from scratch, amongst a people whose original military organisation proved inadequate or even non-existent. Because the guerrilla army has to be built from the bottom upwards, its members have to be persuaded to fight rather than being coerced by existing administrative and repressive structures. The guerrilla leaders, therefore, need to show clearly that it is in the people's interest to fight, by appealing either to feelings of nationalism and xenophobia or to the wish for social and economic changes after the war.

When I first wrote this book, I took an almost positivistic view of the history of guerrilla warfare, seeing the Chinese and Vietnamese experiences as models of a newly refined 'people's war' that offered the prospect of genuine social revolution to oppressed peoples. In fact, I still regard politically aware guerrilla warfare as having at least this potential, but have to admit that my implicit expectation that it would become a dominant mode of struggle in the Third World has most definitely not been realised.

My over-optimism stemmed partly from a rather doctrinaire assessment of the Vietnam War, which overrated the autonomous role of the South Vietnamese Viet Cong, and which failed to put the war as a whole in its proper Cold War context, which permitted North Vietnamese regulars to make a vital, long-term military contribution. All this is now dealt with in detail in the revised and expanded chapter on Vietnam. In fact, the emphasis of this chapter has now changed so much that it might be argued that it rather loses sight of the socio-economic dimension of the war and the pertinent political work by the NLF. For this reason I have retained my original conclusion (now the penultimate chapter) to firmly restate my view that up to 1975, at least, the merging of guerrilla warfare with grass-roots political activism and organisation was by far the most significant development in the history of this mode of warfare. Moreover, it was one that led to military victory and significant improvements in the lives of millions of ordinary people.

Usually, of course, these improvements started from a desperately low baseline, whilst very recent history has shown that the political organisation required in a revolutionary movement tends, once victory has been achieved, to induce excessive rigour and later rigor mortis, leading to Party-dominated repression and an inability to create the conditions for economic lift-off. Interestingly, though, China and Vietnam have been the most alert of Communist states in trying to loosen the Party's grip on purely 'economic' levers but whether this can also be achieved without also surrendering political power remains to be seen. Twenty years on, therefore, it has to be admitted that even people's war was no political panacea, and it could well be argued that the very centralised commitment that enabled it to succeed in the first place bore the seeds of eventual bureaucratic sterility and, often, totalitarian excess.

Yet, as the new final chapter shows, nothing in the last twenty years gives any indication of alternative ways in which to fight a genuinely liberating guerrilla war. Indeed, the Eritrean experience might seem to show that full-scale, sustained, popular mobilisation still offers the surest way forward, whilst Afghanistan clearly confirms that mass participation without political focusing will not of itself lead to political stability, even after military victory. That said, however, one can only shake one's head resignedly when trying to assess whether any amount of mass education and discussion could have eased the ethnic and religious tensions that lie behind so many of today's other guerrilla wars, as, for example, in Angola, Peru, Lebanon/Palestine, Sri Lanka, Kurdistan, Guatemala, Burma or Sudan.

Former Yugoslavia is relevant here as it was long assumed that just such tensions had been dissolved through political participation in a national setting. Yet the collapse of Communism throughout Eastern Europe has shattered the 'Yugoslav' facade instantly and completely, presenting terrible evidence of the power and pervasiveness of historical trauma. Nevertheless, despite this similarity with other contemporary conflicts, I have not included the Yugoslav war in the main body of this book. At the time of writing, at least, the blood-letting there does not constitute a guerrilla war and is not likely to become such, unless either the Bosnians are herded into some remote fastness and give up all hope of real substance to UN and NATO assurances, or this substance is forthcoming and is significant enough to force the Serbs to disperse into mobile guerrilla bands. As things stand, however, we are looking simply at a war of sieges, depredations and atrocities in which the drunken pot-shot, be it from a rifle or a modern artillery piece, is the dominant tactic.

I have also persisted in the exclusion from this book of so-called urban guerrilla warfare and terrorism. It is my contention that the very term 'urban guerrilla warfare' is a misnomer. The use of the word 'warfare' implies a certain level of organised violence which is above and beyond isolated acts of sniping, kidnapping and robbery. Certainly many rural insurgencies began at this level. But the reason for referring to such struggles as guerrilla warfare is that they have implicit in them the possibility of raising the level of the struggle to a full-scale military confrontation. The whole point of the Maoist theory of guerrilla warfare is that any revolutionary group must endeavour to turn its peasant irregulars into mobile regular troops, capable of taking on the incumbent forces on equal terms. One of the main reasons they can do this is that the size and terrain of the country in which they are fighting offers the possibility for the creation of sufficiently remote, yet sufficiently large base areas where this kind of force can be trained and assembled. This kind of organisation is simply not possible in a city. Urban revolutionary activity must of necessity be limited to isolated acts of violence. History reveals conclusively that any attempt to operate on a mass scale in the city and to take on a regular army on equal terms is doomed to failure. Paris in 1851 and 1871, Johannesburg in 1922, Vienna in 1934, Canton in 1927, Warsaw in 1944, Algiers in 1961 all demonstrate this fact quite clearly. Successful urban insurrections, such as Paris in 1830 and 1848, are merely the exceptions that prove the rule. The revolutionaries only achieved success because on these occasions the incumbent military forces gave up before battle was joined. Their defeat stemmed from their level of consciousness rather than from a military confrontation.

It is true that the war in Northern Ireland now seems more of a piece with the recent ethnic and religious struggles covered in the new final chapter, but the IRA effort, and Protestant reprisals, have still not risen above the level of isolated acts of terrorism that present no real threat to efficient security forces. As such they do not merit inclusion in a history of guerrilla warfare. If British forces do eventually withdraw from Northern Ireland, the reasons will owe much more to reduced levels of public spending than they will to the IRA.

And they will also owe something to the way such money is spent. As military budgets become increasingly concerned with hugely expensive precision weapons, and the platforms and technicians to carry and service them, they can accommodate fewer and fewer ordinary infantrymen, the companies and battalions that undertake an actual counter-insurgency on the ground. But the precision weapons are themselves too expensive to use on mere guerrillas and, moreover, might have an unacceptable 'collateral' impact on the surrounding population. Thus the more that conventional armed forces prize missiles that can check in at Baghdad hotels, the less likely it is that such forces can effectively intervene, whether to defeat, disarm or deter, in a guerrilla, or indeed any internal war.

And so guerrilla wars will continue to proliferate. But so too, as we know, do nuclear devices and the wherewithal to manufacture them. On what bright day, one wonders, will the two 'extremes' of modern strategy, nuclear and guerrilla/terrorist, actually converge in some low-intensity Armageddon?

John Ellis
Manchester 1995

CHAPTER 1

The Ancient World

The Jews

The Old Testament offers one of the very first accounts, albeit fragmentary, of what was probably, at least in the early stages, an irregular war. In the Book of Joshua there is related the story of the Israelites' conquest of Canaan under the leadership of Joshua.

As Yigael Yadin has written:

'The darkness of night necessary to the laying of an ambush was also required by irregular forces operating against a regular army, both to cover their advance and to launch their attack. The Book of Joshua describes how at times Joshua would advance all through the night in order to surprise the enemy at dawn. Similarly one of the documents of Mursilis, the Hittite king, speaks of the special security orders he gave to his forces for his own safety, when he was compelled to make a night march. The same document echoes the wrath of the regular armies against night attacks and night ambush by the irregulars. "They [the irregulars] did not dare attack me in the daylight, and preferred to fall on me during the night".'[1]

In the Book of Samuel we are told briefly of the existence of a group of insurgents who banded together in the Cave of Adullam under the leadership of David, at that time hiding from the reigning monarch, Saul. If we are to believe the writer, David's band was clearly based around the more under-privileged elements of society. 'And everyone that was in distress, and everyone that was in debt, and everyone that was discontented gathered themselves unto him; and he became a captain over them.'[2] Here is one of the first examples of a phenomenon that will be observed again and again through this book – guerrilla warfare as a reflection of internal economic and social antagonisms.

However, most of the guerrilla activity undertaken by the Jews in this period was inspired by nationalist sentiments. Their aim, throughout the periods of Greek and later Roman domination, was to throw out the foreigner and set up a Jewish state. The first key figures were the Maccabees.

In 200BC Israel had fallen under the sway of the Syrian Seleucids when they, under their king Antiochus III, had defeated the Ptolemaic armies at the Battle of Banyas, on Israel's northern border. In 167BC the Jews were ruled over by Antiochus IV, who had forbidden the practice of the Jewish religion and was insisting that all take part in various pagan rites. Led by the Hasidim, the chief scribes and authoritative interpreters of the Torah, many people left Jerusalem and other cities to set up small, authentic Jewish outposts in the wilderness. In order to facilitate Seleucid control of the Jewish nation, Antiochus had been sending in Greek and Jewish settlers to take over vast tracts of land. This, not unnaturally, created much discontent among the indigenous Jewish peasantry. Thus, by the second half of the century, there existed a large body of Jews willing to revolt against their Graeco-Syrian overlords.

The spark was struck in 167BC when one Mattathias, in the village of Modin, killed a priest sent to officiate at a pagan ceremony. He and his sons were forced to flee into the desert, and there they made contact with the Hasidim. From there Mattathias and his followers undertook raids on surrounding villages, destroying the pagan idols and killing all those who refused to remain faithful to the Jewish religion. In 166 Mattathias died and leadership of the revolt passed to his son, Judas Maccabee (the 'Hammer'). From this date the resistance became much more effective. Judas abandoned the earlier strict insistence that true Jews could not engage in combat, not even to defend themselves, upon the Sabbath. The second Book of Maccabees gives an impression of the rising tempo of his activities:

'Secretly they made entry into the villages, whence they summoned both kinsmen and friends of theirs; ay and rallied many more that were yet true to the Jewish faith, till they had mustered an army of six thousand ... On village or town of theirs he would fall suddenly, and burn it to the ground; by seizing some point of vantage, once and again he put their forces to the rout; going about these forays at night-time for the most part, till the fame of his valour spread far and wide.'[3]

At first the rebels' only arms were slings and various clubs and agricultural implements. But as they became more daring they ambushed small Syrian patrols and began to build up a stock of captured weapons. They went on from success to success and soon 'had spoil to divide in plenty [and] ... cripples and orphans and widows, and aged folk too, must have a share to match their own. Weapons of war they gathered with all care, and bestowed where they were most needed'.[4] This latter quotation from II Maccabees is particularly interesting. It shows that Judas's forces passed beyond the stage of being an isolated marauding band in the mountains, and established intimate links with the inhabitants of the surrounding villages. On the one hand, they looked after the interests of those not able to fend for themselves, and on the other, distributed arms to enable the villagers to protect themselves. Modern Israeli historians are probably right in thinking that Maccabee swelled his forces considerably by establishing some sort of militia system by which the able-bodied males of all the villages, taking up the arms that had been given them, would come together at times of emergency and help fight off any large Syrian offensives. When the crisis was past they would disperse to their villages and resume their normal seasonal activities.

Considerable military successes followed. During 165BC, Judas effectively cleaned out the Syrian forces in the countryside around his base area. One large Syrian force was ambushed in the hills as it was advancing towards the pass of Beth Horon. On another occasion the Syrians attempted to force Judas to fight a pitched battle on the plain of Emmaus. But his forces skirted the enemy positions, through the surrounding hills, and fell upon and destroyed their camp. Their supplies destroyed, the Syrians had no choice but to retreat. In the autumn of that year he cut the Syrian communications between Acra and the sea. But by this time the incumbent forces seem to have learned some lessons, for they themselves simply planted forces to the south of Judas's mountain stronghold and severed his own communications with the villages from whence came his supplies and recruits. He was forced to quit his base and negotiate with the Syrians. An amnesty was arranged and the Jews were granted complete freedom of worship. But it was at best a very shaky truce. In the following year Judas was in arms yet again and eventually he succeeded in capturing Jerusalem. In 164 and 163BC his forces spread over the whole of Palestine defending the Jewish population and attacking Syrian forces and garrisons. He ravaged many towns but always avoided staying in one place for too long. Even by the beginning of 163BC only Acra could be considered a safe refuge for those still loyal to the Seleucid regime. But later in the year Judas decided to lay siege to the city and was forced to fight a pitched battle with the Syrian relieving forces at Beth Zechariah. The Jewish army suffered a crushing defeat, and the Syrians advanced towards Jerusalem, to which they laid siege. But in 162, Lysias, the Syrian king and commander, was obliged to break off the siege to deal with a rival claimant to his throne.

Unfortunately for Judas the Syrians managed to have him replaced as High Priest by Alcimus, who was generally favourable to Syrian rule within Israel. So once again Judas was obliged to take to the wilderness and conduct harrying operations against the Syrians and their Jewish adherents. In March 160 he had become strong enough to defeat a substantial Syrian army at Adasa. He then concluded a treaty with the Romans which finally forced his enemies to send a large, well-armed force of Syrian regulars against him. In the summer of that year Judas gambled everything on the outcome of an open battle. But the bulk of his army fled almost immediately, and Judas was cut down with the few followers who had remained with him.

Leadership of the revolt passed to his brother, Jonathan, who once again took up authentic guerrilla operations, and for the next four years he harried the Syrians ceaselessly, setting up bases now in the wilderness of Tekoa, now in Trans-Jordan. To counter his assaults, the Syrians 'took to fortifying the cities of Judaea with high walls and barred gates, making strongholds at Jericho, Ammaum, Bethron, Bethel, Thamnata, Phara, and Thopo; here garrisons were set up for the harrying of Israel ... Keeping them all well-manned and provisioned; ay, the great men of all the country round must yield up their children as hostages, to be held in Jerusalem ...'[6] Despite all their efforts, however, the Syrians were unable decisively to come to grips with Jonathan. They were actually defeated by him in battle in 160. In 158 the Syrian leader, Bacchides, concluded a treaty with the Jewish resistance forces and for the next 100 years or so the Maccabean dynasty ruled in Israel.

In chronological terms the struggle of Judas Maccabee and his brothers is not the first guerrilla struggle that will be dealt with in these pages, but I chose to begin with it because it demonstrates many of the features of an advanced mode of guerrilla warfare. Two of these can usefully be isolated here. On the purely *military* level one might note the gradual transition from a petty warfare of ambush and swift retreat to an inaccessible base, to a more open type of war in which, as the insurgents become more skilled and better armed, they feel capable of meeting the enemy in pitched battle. As will become increasingly apparent, a guerrilla insurrection is unlikely to succeed in displacing the incumbent regime, be it made up of foreigners or fellow-countrymen, unless it can eventually build up the military capacity to fight out in the open. The other point of importance is the careful attention Judas paid to the *social* and *political* aspects of his insurrection. In other words, he made sure of the loyalty of the surrounding villages to his cause by eliminating pro-Syrian elements, by giving the villagers the means with which to defend themselves, and by looking after their material interests – the attacks on foreign settlers and the aid given to the old and needy. Only by such measures could Judas ensure that he would have the support of the people at large. For without such support – intelligence about enemy movements, its denial to the incumbent forces, food, shelter, and armed assistance – no guerrilla group can hope to be more than a very temporary thorn in the enemy's side. In most cases it is the extent to which a guerrilla force pursues these twin policies, the military and the socio-political, that determines its chances of eventual success.

But the success of the Maccabees was not the end of the story of Jewish resistance to foreign oppression. After ridding themselves of the Seleucids, they soon found themselves facing the fact of Roman occupation. In the last years of the first century BC, Herod, at that time the governor of Galilee, had to cope with an insurrection led by one Hezekiah. It was put down and its leader captured, but in 4BC his son Judas the Galilean himself rose up. His band swooped on the royal palace at Sephoris and there obtained the arms necessary to begin a guerrilla struggle. From this time right up to the great Jewish Revolt of AD66 guerrilla activities were endemic to this part of the Roman Empire. The great historian of this period was Josephus, a Romanised Jew, who has left a full account of the ceaseless struggle against the Romans. Throughout his works *The Jewish War* and, in particular, *Jewish Antiquities*, he constantly dismisses the resistance fighters as mere murderers and bandits. The war of Judas the Galilean he called *lestrikos polemos* or 'a war of Brigands'. But, as Professor Brandon pointed out, bandits do not normally wage wars, and it would be reasonable for us to translate the term as 'guerrilla war', operations of the kind that have often since been carried out against occupying powers.

Judas had his strongholds in the caves and deserts of Palestine and carried on the struggle for at least 10 years. His operations were particularly significant during the year AD6, when the Romans were conducting a census that seemed to threaten increased taxation. In this year also there first appeared a group of dedicated Jewish nationalists known as the Zealots. Judas aligned himself with a radical Pharisee, Zaddok, and the whole group disappeared underground, becoming more of a terrorist organisation than an orthodox guerrilla band. A little later the Zealots seem to have divided their activities between military guerrilla operations on the one hand, and terrorist activities on the other. For 10 years or so, for example, a certain Eleazar, son of Deinaeus, operated in the mountains of Galilee until he was at last captured and executed by the Roman procurator Antonius Felix. In AD44, two years after the Romans had reintroduced direct rule in the province, the procurator Cuspius Fadus had to conduct military operations in Judaea to clear it of brigands. At the same time, one Tholomaios was operating against the Romans in Idumaea and conducted frequent raids into Nabataean Arabia. According to Josephus, the insurgents were also striking at the villages of those Jews who were collaborating with the Romans. In AD46 two sons of Judas the Galilean were arrested and crucified, and it seems safe to assume that they too had been engaged in rebellion against Roman rule. But from AD48 the Zealots were also employing a number of assassins, called *sicarii* or dagger-men, who infiltrated into the cities where they struck down prominent Jewish collaborators.

The *sicarii* continued their activities right through the next 20 years, whilst others carried on the guerrilla struggle from the mountains and the deserts. Josephus tells us that throughout the fifth decade of that century there was continual co-operation between 'brigands' (Zealots) and 'imposters', various figures who claimed to be the Messiah come to free the Jews from Roman domination. He relates how they grouped together in military companies for the purpose of terrorising those who were cautious about the value of open resistance, killing the rich who collaborated with the Romans, and inciting general revolt. In AD63 the guerrillas even entered Jerusalem where they captured the chief assistant to Eleazar, the Captain of the Temple. They only released him after 10 captured guerrillas had been set free by the Romans. The success of this tactic impressed the guerrillas and on several occasions they secured the release of comrades who had been captured by kidnapping members of the Staff of the Temple Guard and holding them to ransom.

In AD66 the guerrillas considered themselves strong enough to seize Jerusalem itself and incite a general rebellion. The revolt began when Menahem, the son of Judas the Galilean, captured Masada and a large stock of arms and moved from there into Jerusalem. The city was besieged by Cestius Gallus but, for unknown reasons, he raised the siege when on the brink of success, and during his retreat through the hills around Beth Horon his army was mercilessly harried by bands of insurgents. But relations between the various resistance groups actually in Jerusalem became strained. Ananus and the State Council of the most prominent Sadducees and Pharisees took over command and the guerrilla leaders were driven out of the city. Among them was Simon Gioras, who had been leading operations in northern Judaea. He fled to Masada where he joined forces with Eleazar, son of Jair, another kinsman of Judas the Galilean. Jerusalem fell in AD67, and between AD67 and 69 the Roman commander Vespasian conducted operations throughout the country, reducing the various Jewish strongholds and cities. In AD70 the fortress of Masada itself fell and the Revolt was effectively over.

The rebellion taught one very important lesson about the conduct of guerrilla operations. Until one is absolutely sure of one's parity with the forces of the incumbent regime it is extremely dangerous to entrust one's fortunes to the defence of fixed points. Certainly the capture of Jerusalem was of immense psychological value in any attempt to raise up the entire Jewish nation, but it was nevertheless clear that, in the long run, superior Roman equipment, discipline and logistics must prevail. Once Jerusalem had fallen it was even more rash for the insurgents to sacrifice their remaining fighters in the futile defence of certain strongpoints. No matter how heroic that defence was, all that could come of it was the eventual liquidation of the fighters.

Nevertheless the tradition of revolt did live on. In 128 sporadic military operations were again taking place as the Romans tried to root out various bands of Jewish guerrillas. In 132 another full-scale revolt broke out which lasted a full two years. It was led by Shimeon bar Kosiba who declared himself the President of Israel. It is interesting to note that one of his uncles came from Modin, the birth place of Judas Maccabee. He had considerable success in inland and upland Judaea, and also for a time held parts of Samaria. Shimeon was clearly trying to set up some kind of alternative Jewish state and recent archaeological discoveries have shown that he nationalised the land under his control, which had formerly belonged to the crown, and leased it out to Jewish settlers.[8] His military tactics were of the classic guerrilla mode. One ancient historian, Dio Cassio, has left the only account of the uprising:

> '[The rebels] did not dare try conclusions with the Romans in the open field, but they occupied the advantageous positions in the country and strengthened them with mines and walls in order that they might have places of refuge whenever they should be hard-pressed, and might meet together unobserved underground; and they pierced the subterranean passages from above at intervals to let in air and light.'

In 133 Hadrian sent Sextus Julius Severus as general to crush the uprising, and he evidently proved himself adept at counter-insurgency operations. According to Dio Cassio: 'He did not venture to attack in the open at any one point, in view of their numbers and their desperation, but by intercepting small groups ... and by depriving them of food and shutting them up, he was able, rather slowly to be sure, but with comparatively little danger, to crush, exhaust, and exterminate them.'[9] Two important principles of counter-guerrilla warfare are in evidence here. Firstly, it is of the utmost value to cut off the guerrillas from their supplies of food and other essentials. Severus did this by building an ever-shrinking ring of new roads and by setting up numerous checkpoints through which Shimeon's men were unable to infiltrate. Secondly, one can only come to grips with the guerrillas themselves if one is prepared to split one's command into small patrols which can take insurgent bands by surprise, or track them to their hiding places. In this latter respect, the Jews' underground hideouts must have proved a severe handicap, for once discovered they would be little more than rat-traps. Even if they were unoccupied when uncovered by the Romans, their discovery must still have entailed the loss of precious supplies.[10]

The Roman Empire

Almost all the other recorded guerrilla struggles of the ancient world were against the Roman Empire. Only on two earlier occasions does one read of a mode of warfare that might usefully be regarded as a type of guerrilla operation. One of these was merely a theoretical formulation, the *Art of War*, by the Chinese scholar Sun Tzu, written in 500BC, and as it can be discussed most usefully in terms of very much later military developments in China, the campaigns of Mao Tse-tung, I shall deal with it at the end of this chapter, as a kind of appendix.

The other pre-Roman campaign was that of the Scythians against the Persian king Darius who attacked Scythia, part of the Balkan hinterland, in 516BC. Darius attacked across the Danube and marched north or north-west across the Moldavian plain. But the Scythians were a nomadic people, needing only pasture for the horses on which they lived almost continually. Their mounts had saddles but no stirrups, and the riders had perfected the technique of firing arrows from horseback rather than relying on the charge and close-quarters combat. They lived in tents which were easily dismantled and packed up, and were thus extremely mobile.

This mobility was the essential characteristic of their tactics against the Persians. Herodotus described their mode of warfare thus:

> 'They have so devised that none who attack them can escape, and none can catch them if they desire not to be found. For when men have no stablished cities or fortresses, but all are house-bearers and mounted archers, living not by tilling the soil but by cattle-rearing and carrying their dwellings on wagons, how should these not be invincible and unapproachable? ... The Scythians ... resolved not to meet their enemy in the open field ... but rather to withdraw and drive off their herds, choking the wells and springs on their way and rooting up the grass from the earth ... So they watched for a time when Darius' men were foraging, and they did according to their plan. The Scythian horse ever routed the Persian horse and the Persian horsemen falling back in flight on their footmen, the foot would come to their aid; and the Scythians, once they had driven in the horse, turned about for fear of the foot.'

The Scythians attacked in this fashion by night as well as by day. These were typical *defensive* guerrilla tactics. The aim is never to engage with your enemy in pitched battle, but merely to harass his forces as one's own retreat draws him in deeper and deeper and stretches his lines of communication to an unacceptable degree. By destroying the wells and the pasture, the Scythians ensured that Darius was entirely dependent upon the flow of supplies from outside. Clearly, the longer the campaign lasted the more desperate would the invader's position become. Herodotus describes how the Scythians quite deliberately sought to lure the Persians as far into their country as possible:

> 'When the Scythians saw that the Persians were shaken, they formed a plan, whereby they might remain longer in Scythia and so remaining might be dis-tressed by the lack of all things needful: they would leave some of their flocks behind with the shepherds, themselves moving away to another place; and the Persians would come and take the sheep and be uplifted by this achievement.'[11]

Unable to find his enemy or to sustain his own army, Darius was eventually compelled to leave the Scythians in peace. In 210 and 209BC they tried these tactics once again, in Parthia, when they were attacked by the Syrian Anti-ochus II. Their king, Archases II, abandoned his capital and fell back on the mountains, fighting harassing rearguard actions all the way. But for reasons which are not clear, perhaps to do with changes in the Scythians' original nomadic state, Antiochus was eventually able to force them to sue for peace. Certainly this type of purely defensive guerrilla warfare can only be successful if the defenders have nothing to lose, in terms of land or security, by being continually on the move, and if the invader lacks the resolve and the logistical ability to maintain his pursuit. If the invader can sustain operations he must eventually be able to bottle up his enemy and either starve him out or defeat him in open battle.

As for the almost continuous series of Roman operations to extend the dominion of their Republic and Empire, it would be impossible to deal with them all in the space of one chapter, even concentrating only on those with a pronounced guerrilla character. For, almost by definition, resistance to Roman rule was likely to assume the form of a guerrilla struggle, simply because no other nation had a military capacity – in terms of manpower, discipline, technique and logistics – that was remotely comparable to that of the Romans. In regular warfare the legions were almost invincible, and their opponents were obliged to rely on whatever advantages could be gained from the nature of the terrain, surprise attacks and superior mobility.

A typical war in the early period of Roman expansion was that against the Volsci, a tribe in northern Italy. It lasted from 389 to 338BC, a full 50 years, though the course of the actual fighting is more of a testimony to the sheer stubbornness and fortitude of the Volsci, than to their tactical sophistication. In this respect it is an example of guerrilla warfare at its most primitive level, more a series of intermittent uprisings than a coherent protracted struggle. Nevertheless the very resilience of the tribesmen shows that there must always have been those willing to keep the spirit of resistance alive. In 389BC it was the Volsci who first attacked the Romans, but they were defeated by Camillus who ravaged their country and slowly razed the series of wooden fortifications which they chose to fight behind. In 386 they were again defeated by Camillus after they had attempted to storm the town of Satricum. They rose up again in 385BC but were defeated by A. Cornelius Crassus, and a colony of two thousand Roman citizens was introduced to try and keep the Volsci in order. In 382 they succeeded in capturing Satricum but were again defeated by Camillus in the following year. In 379 they attacked a Roman army under P. and C. Manlius but, though they captured the camp, the soldiers were able to drive them off. In the following year the Romans decided upon harsh measures. They invaded the region from two directions, via the coast and mountains, and remorselessly laid it waste, cutting down trees, the tribesmen's refuge, and burning the crops. In 377 another attack on Satricum was beaten off and the Volsci gave up the struggle for a while. In 358 the Romans annexed the Pontine plains and formed two new tribes, thus all but hemming in the Volsci.

From 348 to 338BC, attacked from all sides, the Volsci were gradually overcome and forced to submit to Roman rule.

Thus, though the tactics of the Volsci, with their over-optimistic faith in the potential of sieges, pitched battles, and positional defences, were not really those of the successful guerrilla, on a strategic level they were able to fulfil some of the basic requirements of a guerrilla struggle. Firstly, they obviously possessed a fanatical will to resist and a basic hatred of foreign domination. Secondly, through judicious use of the hostile terrain, they were always able to extricate enough men to keep the spirit of resistance alive and build up the forces for another offensive. Thirdly, their mode of social and political organisation was clearly loose enough for the nation as a whole to be unaffected fatally by one decisive defeat in battle, or even by one seemingly devastating campaign. These three factors enabled the Volsci to pursue, albeit unwittingly, a strategy of the *protracted war* through which they were able to give themselves the space and the time to recover to some extent from each Roman blow. For the Volsci it was merely a fortuitous conjunction of physical and social factors that endowed them with this ability, and they were never able to capitalise upon it to build a resistance movement that could more than seriously annoy the Romans. But it will be seen in later chapters that this ability to wage a protracted struggle is one of the foundations of a successful guerrilla resistance, one that can eventually take the offensive with hopes of victory in open battle.

The next important theatre of operations for the Romans was Spain. There, in the last two centuries before Christ, they had to fight four long and hard campaigns. Two of them were against the Celtiberians, between 195 and 179BC and 153 and 133BC, one against the Lusitanians under Viriathus from 154 to 138BC, and one against a rebel Roman, Sertorius, who, between 80 and 72BC, utilised these same Spanish tribesmen to support the Marian cause against the dictator Sulla. The fighting took place in what is now New Castile, much of which consists of bare, waterless deserts, mountains and ravines – perfect terrain for guerrillas. The area also experiences great extremes of climate which were most taxing for the Roman regulars sent against the insurgents.

At least two commentators have left descriptions of the fighting against the Celtiberians. Of the second campaign, Polybius, who referred to it as a 'war of fire', wrote:

'This name refers to the special conditions in which . . . [the war] was fought and the continuous engagements which it occasioned. In Greece and in Asia, a single battle, or, more rarely, two generally suffice to decide the issue in a war and, in these battles themselves, the matter is decided at a precise moment . . . But in that war things were quite different. Generally only nightfall brought an end to the combats . . . The bad season itself only caused a limited lessening of the fighting and of this succession of engagements.'[12]

In other words, the Celtiberians too were fighting a protracted war in which they ensured that defeat in any one battle, always of a minor nature, would never mean that their whole fighting capacity was destroyed. In this, they, like the Volsci, were greatly aided by the political structure of their nation, which was divided into thousands of small communities which could operate quite independently if necessary. These tactics served them well for 36 years of continual warfare, though they were almost defeated in 179BC by Sempronius Gracchus and Postumius Albinus who destroyed about 300 stockades and villages in the last great offensive of the First Celtiberian War. The Romans' tactics have been described by Frontinus who, in his *Stratagems*, put them forward as one model of counter-insurgency warfare:

'Sempronius Gracchus, when waging war against the Celtiberians, feigned fear and kept his army in camp. Then, by sending out light-armed troops to harass the enemy and retreat forthwith, he caused the enemy to come out; whereupon he attacked them before they could form, and crushed them so completely that he also captured their camp.'[13]

They were finally subdued by Scipio Africanus the Younger, who made great efforts to improve the quality of his troops by forcing them to travel light, without baggage wagons, stopping straggling on the march, and getting rid of camp-followers and soothsayers who were undermining morale. His tactics consisted mainly of avoiding any battles and trying to deny supplies to the enemy. As Appian wrote: 'He showed himself more experienced in war than themselves, by refusing to join battle with wild beasts when he could reduce them by that invincible enemy, hunger.'[14]

Unlike the Celtiberians, the Lusitanians were able to offer a more centralised resistance to the Romans for they found themselves an outstanding guerrilla leader, Viriathus. His usual tactic was to offer his enemy the chance of a pitched battle, then to feign retreat, drawing them into an ambush. Appian has left a full description of his tactics. In 148, for example, Viriathus found himself faced by a superior Roman force:

'He drew them all up in line of battle as though he intended to fight, but gave them orders that when he should mount his horse they should scatter in every direction ... He chose a thousand only whom he commanded to stay with him ... Vitelius [the Roman commander] was afraid to pursue those who had scattered in so many different directions, but turning towards Viriathus ... joined battle with him. Viriathus, having very swift horses, harassed the Romans by attacking, then retreating, again standing still and again attacking, and thus consumed the whole of that day and the next dashing around on the same field. As soon as he conjectured that the others had made good their escape, he hastened away in the night by devious paths.'

The Romans nevertheless pursued the Lusitanians towards their capital of Tribola, whereupon 'Viriathus, having first laid an ambush in a dense thicket, retreated until Vitelius was passing by the place, when he turned, and those who were in ambush sprang up.'

The Romans then sent another commander, Plautius, to Spain. He fared no better than his predecessor and the bulk of his army was wiped out in two major ambushes, in 146. Viriathus then set about imposing a strict central control on the whole region. He 'overran the whole country without check and required the owners of the growing crops to pay him the value thereof, or if they would not, he destroyed the crops.' Yet another general was sent, in 142, but he again was no match for the Spanish tactics. 'Viriathus continued to make frequent incursions by night or in the heat of the day, appearing at every unexpected time with his light-armed troops and his swift horses to annoy the enemy, until he forced Servilianus back to Itucca.' The example of the Lusitanian resistance spread, and towards the end of the war, 'emulating the example of Viriathus many other guerrilla bands made incursions into Lusitania and ravaged it. Sextus Junius Brutus, who was sent against them, despaired of following through the extensive country . . . because he considered it extremely difficult to overtake them, while they moved swiftly from place to place as freebooters do . . .'[15]

The last serious opponent of the Romans in Spain was Quintus Sertorius, who had served under Didius, a Roman general, in the Celtiberian Wars. He was a supporter of Marius in the civil war against Sulla and used his Roman supporters as officers in building up a large Lusitanian/Celtiberian guerrilla army. Regarding his tactics, Plutarch has left a very succinct description of the mode of warfare used against one of his opponents:

'Nor did Metellus know which way to turn himself, in a war with such a bold and ready commander, who was continually molesting him, and yet could not be brought to a set battle, but by the swiftness and dexterity of his Spanish soldiery was able to shift and adapt himself to any change of circumstances. Metellus had had experience in battles fought by regular legions . . . [who were] admirably trained for encountering and overcoming an enemy who came to close combat, hand to hand, but entirely unfit for climbing among the hills, and competing incessantly with the swift attacks and retreats of a set of fleet mountaineers, or to endure hunger and thirst, and live exposed like them to the wind and weather without fire or covering . . . Sertorius, though he refused the field, reaped all the advantages of a conqueror. For he hindered them from foraging, and cut them off from water; if they advanced he was nowhere to be found; if they stayed in any one place and encamped, he continually molested and alarmed them; if they besieged any town, he presently appeared and besieged them again, and put them to extremities for want of necessities.'[16]

This is a masterly brief description of the purely military aspects of guerrilla warfare, and of the problems faced by a regular military man when embarking upon counter-insurgency operations. The last sentence, in particular, is a fascinating forerunner of Mao Tse-tung's precis of the basic essentials of guerrilla tactics.[17] But once again it is necessary to recognise that such tactics were not enough to allow the Spaniards to take the offensive and to actually drive the Romans out of the country. With such tactics Sertorius could only act as a very valuable ally to a more conventional drive against Sulla in Italy itself. As it was, he never got the chance to transform his army into one suitable for regular operations. As the years passed his rule in Spain became more and more autocratic and in 72BC he was poisoned, whereupon the resistance movement swiftly collapsed.

But Spain was not the only area in Europe in which the Romans had to face serious guerrilla resistance. The campaigns of Julius Caesar, for example, in Gaul and Britain offer other excellent examples. In 54BC Caesar made his second landing in Britain, on the Kent coast, with 5 legions and 2,000 cavalry. He found himself faced by the Kentish tribesmen united under Cassivellaunus, the king of the Catuvellauni. Resistance to the landing itself was easily brushed aside and Caesar drove inland across the Stour and the Thames, heading for Cassivellaunus's capital at Wheathampstead. The British chieftain soon saw that it was futile to attempt to defeat the Romans in pitched battle and he contented himself with harassing their soldiers on the march, making the most of his superior knowledge of the terrain, and the mobility of his large chariot force. Caesar himself described what followed:

'Cassivellaunus had now given up the idea of fighting a pitched battle. He disbanded most of his forces and followed our line of march with some four thousand chariots. Keeping off the main route under cover of dense thickets, he drove the inhabitants and their cattle from the open country into the woods wherever he knew that we would pass. If our cavalry ranged too far to plunder and devastate the neighbourhood they were in grave danger from the native chariots sent out of the woods to engage them. In face of this threat they could not go far afield.'[18]

Once again we have a perfect example of defensive guerrilla war, in which the defenders limit themselves to harassing operations, hoping thereby to make the enemy's continued presence too costly for him. It is doubtful whether Caesar ever intended to stay in Britain anyway, but he soon withdrew his troops to their ships and returned to Gaul, without having inflicted any extensive damage upon the natives.

For Caesar's main troubles were in Gaul, where a series of major uprisings between 54 and 51 BC almost succeeded in driving out the Romans. At first, as in the earlier Gallic risings in 59 and 58, the Gauls trusted their fortunes to pitched battles with the Romans, but they were easily defeated. In 52 the leadership of the revolt passed to one Vercingetorix, relying mainly upon the support of the Carnutes and the Averni. Vercingetorix adopted a scorched earth policy as he slowly retreated in front of the Romans, attempting to deny them any supplies. Also, as a modern historian has noted, under his leadership the Gallic armies 'for the first time included a large proletarian element, predictably identified by Caesar as vagabonds and robbers.'[19] Such men were not bound by any close ties of loyalty to the chieftains and were thus spared the futility of fighting shoulder to shoulder in pitched battles against the superior legions. Instead they grouped together in small bands and harried the Roman columns as they were racing back to the scene of any emergency. One such band is described in Book VIII of the *Gallic Wars* (actually written by Aulus Hirtius): 'When Vercingetorix first raised the standard of rebellion, the Senorian leader Drappes had collected a random force of desperados made up of bandits, slaves who had been invited to resume their freedom, and outlaws from every tribe. With these he began raiding our convoys, and had been doing so ever since.'[20] Despite the aid Vercingetorix received from such bands, he himself was eventually forced back upon his fortress at Alesia, in the marshland around Bourges. Though he constantly harassed the besiegers with small parties of horse and foot his fortress was eventually stormed and he himself captured. In 51 leadership of the revolt passed to Commius of the Atrebates, who held out for a while, limiting his operations to attacks on convoys and patrols. Aulus Hirtius tells us that 'he supported himself and his adherents by organising a troop of horsemen, with which he infested the woods and intercepted a number of Roman convoys.'[21]

Hirtius goes on to refer to the Atrebatean guerrillas as 'these bandits', and this whole latter period of the Gallic Wars raises an interesting general point about guerrilla warfare. Although the classification of the partisans as mere brigands has a basically pejorative intent, it is not without a certain social validity. Indeed it is a common feature of wars of resistance to foreign occupation that those who are not bound by kinship ties, oaths of allegiance, or the ownership of property, particularly land, are more able to cut themselves off from a particular area or community and take to the hills and forests. Such men are necessarily at the lower end of the social scale – landless labourers, slaves and outlaws – and thus it is not particularly surprising that it is they who are often at the heart of guerrilla movement, especially in its early stages. Similarly, because such men are on the margins of the community they are not bound by any ties of respect or obligation to its leaders. Thus they do not feel it necessary to share the tactical preconceptions of these leaders, whose notions of honour and tradition often force them to meet the enemy head on, irrespective of his technical superiority.

Throughout this period the Romans also had to deal with periodic outbreaks of rebellion amongst the German tribes. At first they used to attack in family bands, under an elected chieftain, and would recklessly, and usually in a quite unconnected fashion, assault the Roman positions in loose wedge-shaped formation. They had few swords, wickerwork shields, and lances which were a considerable encumbrance in hand-to-hand fighting. Naturally enough such tactics made little impression upon the Roman ranks. But they seem to have learnt some lessons. Of German tactics in the first years of the first century AD, Tacitus writes that, for the tribesmen, 'to give ground, provided that you return to the attack, is considered good tactics rather than cowardice.'[22] This remark speaks volumes about the different cultural attitudes that either discourage or encourage a resort to guerrilla tactics, and breed the regular's contempt for those that adopt them.

Their new tactics consisted of attacking the Romans in an open plain that was surrounded by woods or marshes, from which the Germans would emerge in short, sharp attacks from all directions. One major campaign in which such a policy was pursued was that of Germanicus against the Cherusci and other German tribes under Arminius. Tacitus wrote an account of it. In AD15, for example:

'Arminius retreated into pathless country. Germanicus followed. When an opportunity arose he instructed the cavalry to move forward and rush the flat ground where the enemy was stationed. Arminius first ordered his men to fall back on the woods in close order. Then he suddenly wheeled them round and a force he had secretly posted in the forest was given the signal to charge ... [Throughout the following year] Germans of every rank and age launched sudden and daring attacks against the Romans on the march.'[23]

In AD83 Domitian led a Roman army against the German tribes and he too was faced with a similar mode of resistance. Here one is dependent upon Frontinus for the following examples of the nature of the fighting. He speaks of various occasions 'when the Germans, in accordance with their usual custom, kept emerging from woodland pastures and unsuspected hiding places to attack our men, and then finding a safe refuge in the depths of the forest ...' Frontinus also tells how Domitian made some attempt to hit back at these lightning forays:

'When the Chatti, by fleeing into the forests, again and again interfered with the course of a cavalry engagement, [he] ordered his men, as soon as they should reach the enemy's baggage train, to dismount and fight on foot. By this means he made sure that his successes should not be blocked by any difficulties of terrain.'[24]

In AD43 the Emperor Claudius decided that another attempt should be made to add Britain to the Empire, and an invasion force was dispatched there. Between AD43 and 47 the Roman commander, Vespasian, did not have too much difficulty in overcoming the resistance put up by the British tribes. During operations in the south-west in this period, Vespasian stormed some 20 hill-forts where the British chose to make their stands. After this British resistance moved to north-east Wales and began to take on the character of a guerrilla war.

Under the influence of the Druids of Mona, whose role in this stage of the resistance was somewhat analogous to that of the Hasidim in the Maccabean revolt, the Welsh tribes chose Caractacus, a chief of the Belgae, as their war leader. Between AD47 and 51 the Romans, under Ostorius Scapula, were engaged in constant hostilities with Caractacus. Tacitus described these operations: 'Their lands were ravaged and booty was collected on all sides. The natives did not venture on a pitched battle, and ... they tried to harass the column from ambush.'[25] In the campaign of AD50 Caractacus simply allowed Ostorius to march aimlessly about the countryside without attacking him at all. In 51, however, he took the chance of meeting the Romans in open battle and was easily vanquished. Though he himself escaped he was handed over to the invaders by Queen Cartimandua of the Brigantae, and sent off to Rome in chains. On hearing of this treachery the Silures rose up, and they too conducted an effective long guerrilla campaign. In 52 they were brought to battle by Ostorius but managed, at the last moment, to get away with slight loss. Tacitus has described their usual tactics: 'They crept through the glens and swamps like bandits – each man as chance offered or courage led, accidentally or deliberately, for booty or revenge, at the command of their leaders – or sometimes without their knowledge.'[26] The campaign in fact dragged on until the year 60, when Boadicea hastened the end of British resistance by attempting to defeat the Roman legions on the open field of battle.

But the greatest guerrilla campaign of this period took place some years earlier, and in a different part of the Empire. This was in North Africa, in parts of what are now Algeria and Morocco. There the Numidians, led by Tacfarinas, held off Roman punitive expeditions for almost eight years, from AD17 to 24. The story of this campaign is told by Tacitus, and his account brings out all the essential points about African and Roman tactics:

'His first followers were vagabonds and marauders who came for loot. Then he organised them into army units and formations, and was finally recognised as the chief... of the Numidian people ... Their army was in two parts. Tacfarinas retained in camp an elite force trained in Roman fashion, which he instructed in obedience and discipline ... while light-armed troops burnt, killed and intimidated.'

In AD19 Tacfarinas overrated his strength vis-à-vis the Romans and prematurely engaged them in open battle. He was defeated but escaped with enough of his men to take up guerrilla operations again: 'After normal raids – too swift for reprisals – he began destroying villages and looting extensively . . . Since the Numidians were . . . impatient of siege warfare, Tacfarinas conducted a guerrilla campaign, giving way under pressure and then attacking from the rear. The tired Romans, frustrated and ridiculed by the tactics, could not retaliate.'

But once again Tacfarinas over-optimistically assessed his strength and set up a stationary base within reach of the Romans. They soon located it and attacked, driving Tacfarinas once again into the inaccessible desert areas. In 21 he was once more in action and had the temerity to suggest that if the Romans wished for peace they must provide land for all the members of his army. 'As the alternative he offered endless war.' In the following year, Quintus Julius Blaesus, the governor of the province offered an amnesty to all those who would give themselves up. Tired of the ceaseless warfare many of Tacfarinas' followers took advantage of this offer. But others stayed on:

'Since . . . [Tacfarinas's] army was inferior in fighting power but superior in raiding capacity, he operated with independent groups, avoiding engagements and setting traps. So the Romans, too, attacked with three separate formations . . . By planting forts and defences at appropriate spots . . . [Blaesus] cramped and harassed the enemy. In whatever direction they moved, they found part of the Roman army on front, flanks, and often rear. By these methods many rebels were killed and taken prisoner.

'Then Blaesus split up his three formations into smaller bodies, each under a company commander of distinguished record. It had been customary to withdraw the troops when summer was over, and quarter them in winter camps . . . Blaesus abolished this custom. Instead he established a chain of forts – the usual procedure at the beginning not the end of a campaigning season. Then, employing mobile columns with desert training, he kept Tacfarinas in a continual state of movement . . . [In 24 the next governor, Publius Cornelius Dolabella], since several expeditions had proved that a single, heavy-armed force could never catch so mobile an enemy, . . . mobilised Ptolemy [the king of Mauretania] and his compatriots as well. Four columns were organised under Roman generals or colonels; and Mauretanian officers were selected to lead raiding parties. Dolabella himself attended and directed the different units in turn.'[27]

Some weeks later Tacfarinas and the bulk of his force were captured whilst resting in a ruined fort. With the loss of their leader Numidian resistance very soon crumbled.

Tacitus's account raises several very interesting points. On the African side the most remarkable feature of the campaign was that Tacfarinas went beyond the usual organisational levels of guerrilla forces at this time and set up his army on a two-tier system. The bulk of his forces remained as roving guerrillas but the best of them were transformed into disciplined regulars. This type of organisation was to be the basic feature of all later guerrilla armies that managed to move beyond the stage of defensive harassing tactics, and themselves take up the offensive. As has already been said, without such a development few guerrilla armies can hope for more than a limited number of transitory successes. Unfortunately Tacitus gives no details of how this regular force was used, though his brief reference to it seems to imply that it was a kind of elite bodyguard used to defend the base area and the leader himself. If this was the case then Tacfarinas's version of the two-tier system has only formal similarities to later guerrilla armies. For his employment of it was directly the reverse of, for example, the Maoist strategy, where the regulars are used as a mobile striking force, and the guerrillas for support operations in the base area.

It is also instructive to note that the Romans were quite capable of altering their military orthodoxies to take account of the quite different characteristics of guerrilla warfare. In this respect they showed far more flexibility than has been shown in this century by many Western military establishments. The most important lesson they learnt, and one that it is basic to a purely military counter-insurgency campaign, was that it is vital to split one's forces into small, self-sufficient units which can penetrate deep into enemy territory and keep the guerrilla on the move at all times, never allowing him time to halt and regroup or reprovision. The use of forts and strongpoints to block off escape routes, and the extension of the campaigning season were both important refinements to this basic technique. In this way the Romans were able to put their opponents on the strategic and the tactical defensive, robbing them of the initiative, and so tiring them that eventual capture or death was only a matter of time.

Usually Roman counter-insurgency methods were of a more plodding nature. In AD26 Caius Poppaeus Sabinus began operations against rebellious Thracian hill tribes:

> 'Sabinus ... hoped that the natives might be tempted ... to risk battle. But they would not leave the fortress and its surrounding hills. So he proceeded to hem them in by strong-points, which – conveniently enough – he had already begun to construct. Linking these by a ditch and breastwork four miles in circumference, he gradually narrowed and tightened the loop, to cut off the water and fodder.'[28]

Very similar tactics were used against the Cietae, in south Anatolia, in AD36. They fortified a mountain base and from it sent forth raiding parties who attacked cultivators and travellers. They fought on foot, and the rough nature of the terrain prevented either infantrymen or cavalrymen from being able to pursue them:

> '... withdrawing to the heights of the Taurus mountains, ... aided by the nature of the country, they held out against the prince's unwarlike troops. But ... Marcus Trebellius, sent by ... the governor of Syria with four thousand regulars and picked auxiliary forces, constructed earthworks round two hills held by the natives ... After killing some who attempted to break out, Trebellius forced the rest to surrender.'[29]

Both these campaigns indicate the danger for a guerrilla force that takes up a fixed base, and resolves to defend it to the end. In the face of a technically superior enemy, a guerrilla army must always be able, when absolutely necessary, to evacuate one position and move to another, no matter how distant. But neither the Thracians nor the Cietae had the foresight or, more importantly, the room for manoeuvre, to effect such a move. The regions in which they fought were too circumscribed for them to be able to effect their own version of Mao's Long March or of Tito's endless peregrinations around the Balkans. For, as will be seen later, a *big country* is a vital prerequisite of effective long-term guerrilla operations.

China

Little is known about guerrilla operations in ancient China, though some of the numerous large-scale peasant revolts during the period must surely have thrown up guerrilla bands, particularly in those areas in which banditry was rife.[30] But this period did produce a theoretical work that is of considerable interest to the student of guerrilla warfare and throws an interesting light on the long-standing Chinese military traditions upon which the later Maoist doctrine was based. The work in question is Sun Tzu's *Art of War*, probably written between 400 and 320BC. Though the book is written for the guidance of those commanding regular armies, many of the strategic and tactical principles enunciated therein have much in common with those that underlay later advanced theories of guerrilla warfare.

The crucial feature of Sun Tzu's philosophy of war was that he saw no virtue in seeking out the opportunity for a large, bloody pitched battle. For him war was rather a matter of fighting as few battles as possible, and then only when it was quite clear that the balance of forces was overwhelmingly in one's favour. The essential purpose of any campaign was to ensure that such a balance did exist, primarily by misleading the enemy about one's dispositions and strength:

> '... the general must create situations which will contribute to ... [the]

accomplishment [of his plans]. By "situations" I mean that he should act expediently in accordance with what is advantageous and so control the balance. All warfare is based upon deception. Therefore, when capable, feign incapacity; when active, inactivity. When near, make it appear that you are far away; when far away, that you are near. Offer the enemy a bait to lure him; feign disorder and strike him ... When he concentrates, prepare against him, where he is strong avoid him. Anger his general and confuse him ... Pretend inferiority and encourage his arrogance ... Keep him under a strain and wear him down ... Attack where he is unprepared; sally out when he does not expect you.'[31]

He goes on:

'... the art of using troops is this: when ten to the enemy's one, surround him; when five times his strength, attack him ... if double his strength, divide him ... If equally matched you may engage him ... [But] in these circumstances only the able general can win. If weaker numerically, be capable of withdrawing ... And if in all respects unequal, be capable of eluding him, for a small force is but booty for one more powerful.'[32]

Such precepts, with their emphasis upon the conservation of men and resources, and the retention of the initiative are, for obvious reasons, most relevant for any leader fighting a guerrilla campaign, in which his men are under-trained, under-equipped and numerically inferior. Yet in one respect, this great concern for minimising contact in battle led Sun Tzu to very different conclusions from those reached by most guerrilla leaders. As a corollary to his arguments he points out:

'Victory is the main object in war. If this is long delayed, weapons are blunted and morale depressed ... When the army engages in protracted campaigns the resources of the state will not suffice ... While we have heard of blundering swiftness in war, we have not yet seen a clever operation that was prolonged ... For there has never been a protracted war from which a country has bene-fited.'[32]

In terms of conventional warfare such strictures have some validity, but as regards guerrilla warfare the significance of a *protracted war* is ambivalent. For the incumbent regime it is almost always disadvantageous for the war to go on for any length of time, as it acts as a drain on the economy and increasingly alienates the support of the people. But for the guerrillas its protracted nature has two distinct advantages. Firstly, it undermines the position of the incumbent regime, in the ways just mentioned. Secondly, it allows the guer-rillas time in which to build up their forces, and slowly bring their troops up to an adequate level of combat efficiency. Certainly the length of the war is a great burden on the guerrillas and their supporters; unfortunately, however, there is no such thing as a short, successful guerrilla war. This was as true in the ancient world as it will be seen to be in the succeeding centuries.

1. Y. Yadin, *The Art of Warfare in Biblical Lands*, Weidenfeld & Nicholson, 1963, p111
2. I Samuel: 22; 1
3. II Maccabees: 8; 1, 6, 7
4. *ibid:* 8; 30, 31
5. See M. Pearlman, *The Maccabees*, Weidenfeld & Nicholson, pp72–75, and V. Tcherikover, *Hellenistic Civilisation and the Jews*, The Jewish Publication Society of America, Philadelphia, 1959, p223
6. I Maccabees: 9; 50–53
7. S. G. F. Brandon, *Jesus and the Zealots*, Manchester University Press, 1967, p55
8. See Y. Yadin, *Bar-Kokhba*, Weidenfeld & Nicholson, 1971, p111
9. M. Grant, *The Jews in the Roman World*, Weidenfeld & Nicholson, 1973, pp252–3
10. cf Roman operations in Armenia under Cnaetus Domitius Corbulo, in AD59–60, where 'the natives according to their dispositions, offered submission or evacuated their villages and withdrew into the wilds. Some hid themselves and their families in caves ... Those in hiding ... [Corbulo] ruthlessly burnt out after stuffing the mouths and exits of their caves with bushes and faggots.' Tacitus, (trans M. Grant), *The Annals of Imperial Rome*, Penguin Books, 1971, p325
11. Herodotus (trans A. R. Godley), Heinemann, 1921, Vol 2, pp 247, 321, 329, 331
12. Polybius, *Histories*, Book 35; i–v (my translation)
13. Frontinus (trans C. E. Bennett), *The Stratagems*, Heinemann, 1925, p135
14. Appian (trans H. White), *The Wars in Spain*, Heinemann, 1912, p293
15. *ibid*, pp 235, 237, 239, 245, 249
16. *Plutarch's Lives* (trans A. H. Clough), Dent, nd, Vol 2, pp 317–18
17. See below p186
18. Caesar (trans J. Warrington), *The Gallic Wars*, Dent, 1953, p78
19. M. Grant, *Julius Caesar*, Weidenfeld & Nicholson, 1969, p134
20. *Gallic Wars, op cit*, p172
21. *ibid*, p179
22. Tacitus (trans M. Grant), *Germania*, Penguin Books, 1971, p106
23. *Annals, op cit*, pp 68 and 85
24. Frontinus, *op cit*, pp 25–27 and 123
25. G. Webster and D. R. Dudley, *The Roman Conquest of Britain*, Batsford, 1965, p148
26. *ibid*, p171
27. *Annals, op cit*, pp 103, 130, 154–55, 169
28. *ibid*, p182
29. *ibid*, p221
30. The biggest revolts were those led by Chen Sheng, Wu Kuang and Liu Pang in 209BC, the Red Eyebrows Rebellion of AD18, and the Yellow Turbans Rebellion in AD184. This latter group held out in east Szechwan for 20 years.
31. *Sun Tzu: the Art of War*, (trans S. B. Griffith), Clarendon Press, Oxford, 1963, pp 66–9
32. *ibid*, pp 79–80
33. *ibid*, p73

CHAPTER 2

The Medieval World and the Ancien Régime

The Defence of Europe

From the third to the twelfth centuries European military history was dominated by a continuous series of invasions by various peoples who had remained outside the sway of the Roman Empire. In some instances these offensives took on the character of guerrilla wars, but before going on to these in detail it might be useful to list the major waves of invasion.

(1) From very early times in the centuries after Christ there had been a steady but peaceful infiltration of nomadic tribesmen into the border regions of the Empire. These were usually welcomed and used as defenders of the frontiers (*feoderati*).

(2) In 257 the Alamanni and the Franks invaded north Italy and Spain.

(3) In 276 and 277 there was a major Germanic invasion of Gaul.

(4) In 410 the Visigoths sacked Rome and then moved on into Spain, forcing the Vandals into North Africa.

(5) Throughout the fourth century the Huns ravaged Austria, Bavaria and Gaul until they were defeated by a Roman–German army at Chalons in 451.

(6) In 476 northern Italy was invaded by the Herulians, who were defeated by the Ostrogoths in 493, advancing from Hungary in the name of the Eastern Roman Empire.

(7) During the fifth century England was invaded by Picts and Jutes.

(8) In the sixth century Vandals, Alans and Suevi attacked into Gaul and Spain. In Gaul they were followed by Franks and Burgundians.

(9) Between 534 and 535 Italy was invaded by Lombards from Germany, and between 754 and 766 by Franks from Gaul.

(10) In 793 the Vikings began their raids on England and the Frankish-Frisian coast.

(11) From the middle of the ninth century the Moors and the Spanish began

the long series of wars, known as the *Reconquista*, which eventually drove
out the Moors. The crucial battle was on the Plain of Tolosa in 1212.

(12) By 900 the Magyars were established in Hungary. They threatened Paris
in 937, and between 938 and 943 overran the Balkans. In 955 they were
decisively defeated at Lechfeld by the Holy Roman Emperor, Otto the
Great.

(13) Throughout the tenth century, and beyond, the Byzantine Empire was
fighting against the Arabs.

It is in no way my intention to suggest that all these invasions should be
regarded as guerrilla wars. But by outlining the general history of this most
confusing period, I hope to have made the reader able to place a specific
campaign within some sort of historical context.

Nevertheless, certain of these incursions took a form that makes them at
least comparable to more well-known guerrilla campaigns. The tactics adopted
by the defenders, in particular, often had much in common with what we
should today describe as counter-insurgency operations.

In one respect, of course, they differ markedly from anything that has been
discussed so far in that they were always offensive campaigns. For this reason I
have chosen to describe this type of attack as *predatory guerrilla warfare*. Unlike
the earlier defensive campaigns against the Romans, those of the migratory
tribesmen of central and eastern Europe were concerned only with obtaining
plunder and food, and later on with actually driving out the original inhabitants so that the invaders could themselves settle down. As soon as they did
manage to find the necessary *Lebensraum* the invaders quickly forgot their
original guerrilla methods, based as they were on the necessity to be constantly
on the move in search of fresh supplies. But in the early stages of an invasion
their tactics were very much of the guerrilla mode.

They usually attacked in numerous small bands because only thus could
they hope to feed themselves from the scanty resources to be found in a particular town or village. But this proliferation of small, fast-moving groups of
horsemen could quickly throw the defenders off balance and spread panic
through the population. E. A. Thompson has described the impact of the
Alamanni invasion of Gaul in 355:

'... these bands of Alamanni, roving over enormous areas of the province,
penetrating everywhere, and making their appearance at unexpected places
without warning, could reduce a country to chaos ... It was exceedingly difficult for the Romans to move small detachments of their troops with any
feeling of security, for in the general confusion they could not see at what
moment the troops might be surprised and cut to pieces, when every road and
every bridge might conceal an ambush.'[1]

The effect of this on the Romans is evidenced by the fact that, in 357, Julian was persuaded by his men to go into battle with the Alamanni because they threatened to mutiny if they had to go back to hunting the small bands.

The Alamanni, like all the other German tribes, were usually footmen. Thus it can be understood that the Hun invasions of Europe, in which the attackers were mounted on small, swift horses, caused even greater alarm and confusion. As Jerome wrote at the time: '... swarms of Huns ... filled the whole earth with slaughter and panic as they flitted hither and thither on their swift horses ... They were at hand everywhere before they were expected: by their speed they outstripped rumour.'[2] They were absolutely superior to the Romans in terms of mobility, and could always disappear completely out of the way of any advancing punitive force. In fact, so outclassed were the Romans, that they only once, both in the east and the west, mounted an offensive against the Huns. On the whole they were helpless, and could only hope that the nomads would be foolish enough to risk a pitched battle. Because the Huns adopted the guerrilla mode from force of circumstance, rather than as a deliberate, consciously chosen tactic, they did in fact sometimes face the Romans in open battle, as at the River Utus in 447, around Constantinople in 443, and at the disaster before Châlons in 451.

Against the barbarian tribes fighting on foot, the Romans did manage to devise some kind of tactical response. Sometimes they were able to starve them out by withdrawing the population and the harvest into fortified towns which the invaders could not storm. When this proved impossible the Romans would sometimes use small units of crack troops, often foreign auxiliaries more accustomed to this type of warfare, to hunt down the individual barbarian bands. One general, Sebastian, used 2,000 such troops in operations against the Visigoths in Italy in 378. They tried to 'lay ambushes continually for the scattered bands of the enemy, to make lightning sallies, to cut off their supplies, and to score a rapid succession of victories over their foraging parties. This is what Sebastian did in the year or two preceding the battle of Adrianople. This is how Charietto helped Julian to overcome the Chamavian Franks in 358.'[3] In other words, the Romans managed to some extent to use the invaders' own tactics against them and to rob them of the initiative. Once again they were forced to learn the lesson taught by the campaign against Tacfarinas, in North Africa, and which, through the centuries, a whole succession of conventional military establishments were destined to have to learn over and over again.

Another group of invaders who adopted guerrilla tactics were the Magyars, more nomadic horsemen, who were almost identical to the Huns. By 900 they had almost completely taken control of Hungary, and for the next fifty years launched devastating raids into all parts of Europe. In 915 they were at the gates of Hamburg. In 937 they were before Paris, and between 938 and 943 they overran the Balkans. In 933 they were defeated by the Germans near Merseburg, and thereafter they avoided the German heartland. In 955 they suffered another crushing defeat at Lechfeld, at the hands of Otto the Great, and this virtually ended their raids westward. Sometimes, then, the Magyars did commit themselves to fighting pitched battles, where the size of their small horses and their lack of armour was a severe disadvantage. Usually, however, they adopted tactics that made the most of their capabilities as very mobile horse archers. In the great raids of 910, 924, 926 and 954 they avoided hand-to-hand combat as much as possible preferring to pick off their opponents at a distance before fleeing. Often these retreats were merely a decoy to draw the enemy after them to some spot where a larger force was waiting in ambush. In 910, the army of Ludwig the Child was almost completely destroyed in such an ambush on the River Lech.

German history at this time was a constant record of irregular border warfare and internal civil wars. Between 500 and 1000, one group of early Germans, the so-called Old Prussians, were continuously defending themselves against the raids of Vikings, Poles and Lithuanians. We know very little about the Old Prussians, but the very persistence of their resistance seems to indicate that they had adopted some kind of guerrilla strategy to stave off annihilation by their more powerful neighbours. They also had to fight off invasions from the west, by the Knights of the Teutonic Order. Between 1248 and 1266 they launched six crusades against the Old Prussians, who threw up some very successful resistance leaders. One of them, Herkus Monte, managed to keep his forces intact for 11 years. The social and political structure of the Old Prussian nation was undoubtedly of great importance in explaining the extent of their resistance. They were mostly free farmers and fishermen, ruled over by numerous petty chieftains, and 'despite the manifold pressure of their enemies ... the Old Prussians never developed any recognisable political structure'.[4] But an organised political structure is not necessarily an advantage in such circumstances, and the very atomisation of their nation must have been an important factor in the resistance movement, as it enabled each small community to operate independently, relatively unaffected by reverses in other areas. Certainly the more organised a state becomes, the more capable it is of effectively mustering all its resources to fight off foreign aggression. Yet this is not necessarily an advantage, for by the same token the state is more likely to succumb in the event of its suffering just one severe defeat on the field of battle. Then it will experience all the disadvantages of having put all its eggs in one basket. In a totally decentralised state, however, one defeat or even a series of them will have much less impact, and each small community will be able to conduct its own harassing operations against the enemy and deny him any major target against which to launch his forces.

Of the rest of German history in this period, and the great series of civil wars that wracked the area between 900 and 1300, almost nothing is known, particularly in the military sphere. All we do know is that in some instances the petty fighting did take on a guerrilla character. For example:

> 'It would be instructive to know more about the guerrilla campaign waged against Henry IV by Otto of Nordheim in 1070. Otto's operations were centred in the wilderness of the Thüringer Wald and eventually led to more formal civil war. Vast stretches of uncultivated land made irregular operations a practical alternative for the weaker side in any struggle to an extent that was seldom possible in France or England.'[5]

Border warfare was also endemic in northern Spain for some 400 years, as the rulers of Aragon, Navarre, León and Castile tried first to stem the Moorish advance and then to drive southwards themselves. On both sides the ultimate aim was to decide the issue in pitched battle, and in Castile, in particular, the armed forces were made up predominantly of noble, heavy knights, intended to steamroller through the opposition. But such troops could only be brought to bear after the Spaniards had driven down to the plains, notably those of the Douro and the Ebro. In León and Castile this happened in the ninth century, in Aragon during the eleventh. Later as Castile became dominant, heavy knights were developed in large numbers, and in 1212 they defeated the Moors on the Plains of Tolosa. In the years between, however, the mountainous nature of the terrain in northern Spain, and the general insecurity of life in the Spanish Marches, led to a very irregular type of warfare. Campaigns usually took the form of raids and counter-raids by small groups of men. At first only infantry were used, and later, with the accent always on mobility, a special type of light cavalry was developed, who adopted a style of riding known as *a la jinete*, employing short stirrups, a low saddle, and neck-reining to direct the horse. 'Eventually the riders developed into the celebrated light cavalry (*genitours*), who were admirably suited to the hit-and-run tactics of frontier warfare.'[6]

Yet another precarious frontier, where fighting was nothing more than a series of fast-moving raids and withdrawals, was that between the Byzantine Empire and the Arabs. In the Taurus mountains and Cappadocia, where the Romans had earlier fought against the Cietae, the Byzantines during the tenth century were constantly on the defensive against Arab raiders. Their experiences compelled one of their Emperors, Nicephorus II Phocas (963–69), to write what is perhaps the first work on irregular warfare, *A Treatise on Border Wars*. The defensive tactics prescribed by Nicephorus involved the maintenance of a long line of small strongpoints on the frontier in which were garrisoned units of fast-moving Turkish cavalrymen from Trezibond. Each post communicated with its neighbours by signal, and upon hearing of a raiding party all the troops in that section of the line would swiftly converge upon the threatened area. They were instructed to travel with their weapons covered so that their presence should not be revealed to the enemy by the metal glinting in the sunlight. Whilst the cavalry attempted to pin down the raiders, infantry and regular cavalry would gather in the rear and the inhabitants of the area would take shelter in various fortified emplacements.

The British Isles

This period of predatory guerrilla warfare was, however, exceptional in terms of the overall history of this mode of warfare. As should already be apparent, guerrilla warfare is usually a *defensive* response to political repression and/or economic exploitation. Thus it appears most frequently as the mode of resistance adopted by those peoples struggling against imperialist encroachments by another great power. Thus in the ancient world, as has been seen, almost all of the notable guerrilla campaigns were conducted by tribes and leaders seeking to throw off the yoke of Roman imperialism. Whether Roman rule was or was not repressive and exploitative is not at issue here. All that is important is that the Britons, the Gauls, the Spaniards, the Germans etc felt it to be so, or likely to be, and thus felt it their duty to try and drive out the Romans. The history of the British Isles during the Middle Ages is another striking proof of this correlation between guerrilla warfare and the reactions of smaller nations or communities to the expansion of a larger power. Even now there are many in Scotland, Wales and Ireland who do not take rule from London for granted. As yet they have not resorted to guerrilla warfare to advance their aspirations, but in all three countries, at one time or another, resistance to English rule has taken this form.

Nowhere was this resistance more doggedly maintained than in Wales, where there was a strong resurgence of the fighting spirit that had earlier enabled Caractacus to hold out against the Romans. In the 1040s there was chronic border warfare between the English and the Welsh led by Gruffydd ap Llewelyn and Gruffydd ap Rhydderch. In 1049 the latter lured the shire levies of Gloucester and Worcester into an ambush and inflicted a severe defeat upon them. In 1062 Harold led an expedition into Wales, and after isolating Gruffydd ap Llewelyn in Snowdonia, the traditional retreat of Welsh guerrillas, he managed to hunt him down. In 1094 Gruffydd ap Cynan led a revolt against William Rufus. 'After the end of some months 160 men had joined him, and they wandered from place to place in Gwynedd [Snowdonia], doing damage ever to Earl Hugh, like King David ... in the land of Judaea in the time of Saul.'[7] Twice, in 1095 and 1097, Rufus led expeditionary forces into Wales but failed to bring Gruffydd to battle. According to the Welsh chronicler, Rufus waged counter-insurgency campaigns of extreme ruthlessness, combining the now well-known techniques of defoliation and mass slaughter:

'[He] intended to abolish and utterly destroy all of the people until there should be alive not so much as a dog. He had purposed also to cut down all of the woods and groves so that there might not be shelter nor defence for the men of Gwynedd henceforth ... When Gruffydd heard this he assembled the host of the whole kingdom and went against him to create obstacles for him in narrow places when he descended from the mountains.'[8]

In 1114 yet another expedition was led against Gruffydd by Henry I, but he too was baulked by the effectiveness of the former's tactics and the impenetrability of his mountainous base area. 'Gruffydd came up against him according to his usual custom, and placed his possessions and his multitude of villeins with the women and children in the recesses of the mountains of Snowdonia, where they did not suffer a single peril.'[9]

After these abortive invasions the Normans adopted other tactics in an effort to minimise Welsh depredations without having to try and actually engage them in combat. They started on a large-scale campaign of castle-building, hoping to contain the Welsh within the upland areas. For two main reasons this campaign was fairly successful, reasons which stem from the nature of Welsh society at this time. It was a non-agricultural society, based around clan and tribal rights over grazing lands for the cattle that were the mainstay of Welsh social and economic life. Because of this the Welsh armed forces were made up of loosely organised part-time infantry whose usual activities were feuding and cattle-raiding. Such troops, inherently mobile because of their lack of ties to the land, and well-rehearsed in the tactics of the ambush and the lightning raid, were natural guerrillas. But 'when the Normans began to emphasise defensive works, they changed their military objectives from success in open combat to success in positional warfare. The Welsh were both militarily and socially incapable at this time of competing with the Normans in any such struggle. Their economy and customs were those of a pastoral people, and it was extremely difficult for them to maintain continuous occupation and control of any given area.'[10] The castles were also very useful because of the Welsh reliance on the seizure of plunder. For as soon as the news of a party of raiders was received, all movable wealth could be swiftly taken into the castles. There it was quite safe, for the Welsh had neither the time nor the equipment to attempt to lay siege to any solid fortification. Even if the raiders had managed to seize some booty before it could be transferred to a safe place, the castles would still have represented a considerable stumbling block. They were usually situated around the most important exits from the Welsh uplands, and though they might not prevent a raiding-party from slipping round them at the beginning of a foray, they made a considerable difference at the end. Then the Welsh band would be loaded down with plunder, both treasure and livestock, and it would be considerably more difficult for them to try and bypass the castles, which overlooked the most feasible routes back into the hills.

The next serious resurgence of Welsh nationalism was in the reign of Edward I, between 1282 and 1295. Between 1257 and 1267 Llewelyn ap Gruffydd slowly recovered power in Wales and united the bulk of the population under him. In 1282 his brother, David, organised a revolt, and in June ambushed the Earl of Gloucester and his forces at Llandeilo Fawr. Then Llewelyn himself appeared to lead the revolt and he continued to harry the English until the autumn. Once again the English found it almost impossible to track down the guerrillas. Most Welshmen were able, within a matter of hours to pack up their belongings and leave their crude huts to take refuge in the most inaccessible parts of the countryside. For the Earl of Montgomery it seemed that the only way the English could hope to stamp out this revolt was by starving out the rebels: 'The greatest damage that can be done to them from this time onwards is to guard the March carefully so that supplies do not pass to them ... for much supplies enter the March without anyone's knowledge.'[11] Though Llewelyn was eventually defeated, Welsh resistance was far from stamped out, and it flared up twice more during the reign of Edward I. In 1287 Rhys ap Maredudd led a revolt which began with the launching of surprise attacks on English castles. He captured them but was soon driven out, for this was one mode of warfare in which the English were fairly proficient. Rhys then took to the woods and maintained a guerrilla resistance until 1292. In 1294 the Welsh rose up yet again under Madog ap Llewelyn and scored some impressive successes. In January 1295 they managed to ambush the king's baggage train, whilst it was travelling from Bangor to Conway.

One notable result of this long period of guerrilla warfare was that it prompted one scholar to attempt some theoretical formulations concerning this type of conflict, and to suggest ways in which it could best be countered. In the *Description of Wales*, written in 1194, its author, known to us as Gerald of Wales, came up with an analysis which often has an astonishingly modern ring to it. It is worth quoting this little-known work at some length, for it, more than anything else, helps to underline the point that guerrilla warfare is far from being a recent phenomenon. Firstly Gerald describes the tactics of the Welsh:

'In war this nation is very severe in the first attack ... swift and rapid in their advances and the throwing of darts ... They cannot bear a repulse ... and they trust to flight for their safety ... Their courage manifests itself chiefly in the retreat, when they frequently return, and ... shoot their arrows behind them ... Their mode of fighting consists in chasing the enemy or in retreating. This light-armed people, relying more on their activity than on their strength, cannot struggle for the field of battle, enter into close engagements, or endure long and severe actions.... Though defeated and put to flight one day, they are ready to resume combat on the next, neither dejected by their loss, nor by their dishonour, and though, perhaps, they do not display great fortitude in open engagements and regular conflicts, yet they harass the enemy by ambuscades and nightly sallies. Hence, neither oppressed nor cold, not fatigued by martial labours, nor despondent in adversity, but ready, after defeat, to return immediately to action, and endure again the dangers of war, they are not easy to overcome in a single battle, as difficult to subdue in a protracted war.'

Here are several already familiar themes. The phrase 'relying more on their activity than on their strength', for example, is a brilliant encapsulation of the nature of guerrilla warfare, in which the resistance fighters try to wear down their opponents by ceaseless harassing operations rather than by decisive battles. The author goes on to describe in full the character of these operations, with their reliance on 'ambuscades', 'nightly sallies' and swift retreats. With regard to the latter, however, Gerald is unable to permit his obvious respect for the advantages of this type of fighting to outweigh his prejudiced notions of what warfare should be like. Thus for him these retreats, though singularly effective, are a source of 'dishonour' for the Welsh, even though it was patently obvious that if the Welsh had stood their ground, they would have been cut to pieces. This kind of attitude has already been noted in the writings of Tacitus and has continued to bedevil regular military men right up to the present day. In a way, one of the main differences between guerrilla and regular military operations is of a cultural nature, in that for the guerrilla the retreat is an essential tactical ploy, whilst for the regular it is often thought to be better to fight to the last man, or even surrender honourably, rather than give ground temporarily.

In his next chapter Gerald goes on to outline how an English ruler might best set about trying to break Welsh resistance. Once again his remarks have a surprisingly modern ring to them:

'The prince who would wish to subdue this nation and govern it peaceably, must use this method ... Let him divide their strength and by bribes and promises endeavour to stir up one against the other ... In the autumn let not only the marshes, but also the interior part of the country be strongly fortified with castles, provisions and confidential families. In the meantime the purchase of corn, cloth and salt, with which they are usually supplied from England, should be strictly interdicted; and well-manned ships placed as a guard on the coast ... Afterwards, when the severity of winter approaches ... and the mountains no longer afford hope of pasturage ... let a body of light-armed infantry penetrate into their woody and mountainous retreats, and let these troops be supported and relieved by others; and thus by frequent changes, and replacing the men who are either fatigued or slain in battle, this nation may be ultimately subdued.'[12]

The last major guerrilla campaign in Wales was that led by Owen Glendower from 1400 to 1415. The revolt began over a dispute between Reginald, Lord of Ruthin, and Glendower, himself a Lord of the March of substantial means. From 1402 to 1404 the revolt had an essentially guerrilla character. Supported mainly by those Welsh peasants who were labouring under increased baronial exactions and gradually becoming more and more impoverished, Glendower flitted about Wales with remarkable rapidity. By 1404 almost the whole of the country was cleared of the English and their supporters. For two years Glendower reigned supreme, basing himself around the two great castles of Aberystwyth and Harlech. But then the English counter-offensive began, and Glendower, trusting his fortunes to the retention of the castles and the staging of pitched battles, was slowly overcome. By 1408 he had to resume his guerrilla tactics, sallying out from various bases in the mountains of Merioneth and Caernarvon. By 1410 he was a hunted outlaw, and though his presence was always sufficient to rally a small band of fighters to him, he never again aspired to being anything more than an isolated bandit leader.

Another major campaign for national independence, of which Edward I again bore the brunt, was that conducted by the Scots between 1296 and 1328. Again much of the campaign displayed marked guerrilla characteristics. Like the Welsh, the Scots were no match for the English army in open battle, at least in the years before Bannockburn, in 1314, and their leaders assiduously avoided being forced to fight one. The lesson was painfully underlined by the experiences of William Wallace. He had risen up against the English in 1296 and within a few months had gathered a sizeable force around him, based in the forest of Selkirk. But his successes as a guerrilla gave him a false sense of security and by August 1297 'he was bestriding the land not in secret, as before, but openly', seeking to engage the English in open battle.[13] He had some success at Stirling Forth, in the following month, but in July 1298 he was routed by Edward's army at the Battle of Falkirk.

In 1306, Robert Bruce, who had earlier been crowned king of Scotland but had been forced to flee the country, returned and began the long process of trying to drive out the English. He made his base in the hill country of Carrick and Galloway and began gradually to build up his forces, with the eventual aim of breaking out to the country north of the Forth. With the lesson of Wallace in mind he limited himself to guerrilla tactics. 'Speed, surprise, mobility, small-scale engagements, scorched earth and dismantling of fortresses – these were to be the hall-marks of his campaigns'[14]

'[His tactical principles] were laid down in what the Scots called "gude King

Robert's testiment". In these verses his troops were advised to fight "by hyll and mosse" (morass). They should have woods for their "wallis" (walls); that is they should not try to fortify themselves behind walls, but should make their keeps and strong points in the forests. They should keep their stores "in strait placis" (in places hard to get at). And they should go in for the scorched earth tactic, and burn the plains: they should "byren ye planeland thaim before". King Robert advised his soldiers to raid at night: "with wyles and waykings of the night and mekill noyis maid on hytht.'[15]

Right up until 1314 Bruce was loth to fight a pitched battle and concentrated upon merely harassing the occupying forces and their supporters. As an English observer of the time remarked: '[He] did not believe he was able to meet the king's forces in a plain field.'[16] One area of his activity that at first sight does not seem to have much to do with guerrilla warfare was his continuous effort to capture castles. In this he was extremely successful but his methods had little in common with the classic medieval siege, with its emphasis upon heavy siege-weapons or starvation, but were much more akin to modern commando methods. Castles would be taken by stealth, at night, as a picked band of soldiers would infiltrate some badly guarded section of the walls by throwing up rope ladders and silently climbing in. The garrison would then quietly be overcome and the gates opened for the rest of the attacking force.

Another key feature of Scottish policy was the mounting of frequent raids into England. These were, on the one hand, an attempt to prove to the English that it would be too expensive for them not to come to terms with the Scots. On the other, they were a means of obtaining supplies and raising money from the land-owners and communities that were blackmailed into paying the raiders not to completely destroy their property. This policy was kept up even after the battle of Bannockburn, and continued right up to 1328 and the eventual peace treaty. The raids were usually led by Sir James Douglas or Thomas Randolph, Earl of Moray, Bruce's most skilled commanders. The Scots were mounted on sturdy, light horses called hobins, from which came the word hobelars that was applied to the raiders. They wore little armour and lived rough, usually eating oaten bannocks cooked on iron plates, all of which they carried with them. They were able to fight on horse or foot and were extremely mobile, almost always being able to elude their English pursuers.

After Bannockburn the English launched occasional operations against the Scots but without much success. The invasion of 1322 ground to a halt because the Scots simply retreated before the advancing English, laying the countryside bare behind them. In Lothian, usually a very fertile region, the English found but one solitary cow. This is reputed to have induced Tranent, Earl of Surrey, to remark: 'This is the dearest beef that I ever saw; surely it has cost one thousand pounds and more.'[17] As the English retreated, driven out by famine, they were ambushed by Douglas and his men, who had been hiding in nearby woods. In 1327, during the reign of Edward III, the English attempted to track down a particularly destructive raiding-party. They pursued them relentlessly into Weardale and thought that they had finally managed to bring them to battle. But as the English lines prepared for combat they found that the Scots, as ever, had silently slipped away.

In Ireland such a concerted campaign for national independence did not come until centuries later. There were chronic outbreaks of guerrilla activity throughout the period under discussion in this chapter, but they were more a form of banditry than of deliberate guerrilla warfare. Nevertheless they were a serious obstacle to the full imposition of English rule and they merit some attention.

The kind of problems the English were to face were clear even in 1392, when Richard II led an expedition across the Irish Sea. At one stage the famous chronicler, Froissart, had a conversation with Richard's interpreter, Henry Cristall, and he left an account of what the latter had to say about the operations against the Irish:

'Ireland is one of the worst countries to make war in or to conquer, for there are such impenetrable and extensive forests, lakes and bogs, there is no knowing how to pass them and carry on war to advantage ... Whenever the Irish perceive any parties advancing in hostile array, they fly to such narrow passes, it is impossible to follow them. No man at arms, however well-mounted, can overtake them, so light are they of foot. They have pointed knives [skenes], with broad blades, sharp on both sides, with which they kill their enemies.'[18]

Here is a typical example of the guerrillas' use of difficult terrain to render enemy offensives relatively ineffective. The woods, in particular, were of great help to Irish rebels as sanctuaries from which to stage ambushes and to which they could flee if hard-pressed. A recent Irish scholar has maintained that the sustained policy of cutting down these forests was a commercial rather than a counter-insurgency operation, but it is nevertheless clear that on occasions English motives were of a strategic nature. In 1399, for example, when McMorough, the king of Ireland, was hiding with his forces in a wood west of Kilkenny, Richard II ordered the mobilisation of 2,500 men to cut down and burn the trees. During the revolt in Munster in 1579 and 1585, the idea of cutting down the woods was twice suggested, though this time nothing was actually done about it. In 1601 an observer noted that: 'the woods and bogs are a great hindrance to us and help to the rebels.'[19]

But the Irish never presented any united front against the English and never co-ordinated the activities of the various bands. Thus they were looked upon more as bandits, a social inconvenience rather than a serious political or military threat. Nevertheless, they were very difficult to eradicate and plagued the English right up until the middle of the eighteenth century. At first they were known as woodkernes, but from the mid-1640s they were generally referred to as tories (from the Gaelic *tóir*, to search) or Rapparees. Some of them were mere murderers or highwaymen, but most of the leading tories were members of the dispossessed Gaelic aristocracy, and their motives had a political as well as an economic basis. One historian of the last century wrote of them:

'Ejected proprietors ... might be found in abject poverty hanging round the land which had recently been their own ... and still receiving a secret homage from their old tenants. In a country where the clan spirit was intensely strong ... these impoverished chiefs naturally found themselves at the head of the discontented classes ... and for many years ... they and their followers ... waged a kind of guerrilla war of depredation upon their successors.'[20]

A pamphleteer of the time described how in one district 'where the Papists outnumbered the Protestants by 900 to 1, a band of twenty or thirty or sometimes even a hundred tories moved up and down the country and at the approach of the army dispersed and concealed themselves in the glens and fastnesses.'[21] Describing the Rapparees Macaulay had this to say about their tactics:

'The English complained that it was no easy matter to catch a Rapparee. Sometimes, when he saw danger approaching, he lay down in the long grass of the bog, and then it was as difficult to find him as to find a hare sitting. Sometimes he sprang into a stream, and lay there like an otter, with only his mouth and nostrils above the water. Nay, a whole gang of banditti would, in a twinkling of an eye, transform itself into a crowd of harmless labourers. Every man took his gun to pieces, hid the lock in his clothes, stuck a cork in the muzzle, stopped the touch-hole with a quill, and threw the weapon into the next pond ... When the peril was over ... every man flew to the place where he had hid his arms, and soon the robbers were in full march towards some Protestant mansion.'[22]

This ability to merge with the population at large is another important consideration in any general analysis of the nature of guerrilla warfare. As will be seen it has long been a complaint of counter-insurgency forces that they are unable to distinguish guerrillas and civilians when attempting to round up those actually fighting against them. Guerrillas are almost always part-time fighters who have important duties to fulfil in the fields and the villages. They have regularly to return to those villages, and therefore it would be rash of them to wear distinctive uniforms that would guarantee their arrest in the event of an enemy sweep.

It must be admitted, however, that this consideration was not of paramount importance in Ireland. One reason for referring to the tories as *bandit-guerrillas* is that they did not maintain intimate links with the population at large. Though they had their tacit support, and were satisfying *symbols* of resistance for the oppressed peasantry, they did not consciously do much to actually help them. The tories tended to live together in their own bands, away from the rest of the population, and supported themselves by plunder and robbery. Thus, whilst they were a constant annoyance to the English colonists they never went far towards trying to mobilise a genuine national resistance to English rule. Consequently, they never had any chance, even assuming they wished it, of actually driving out the English. It was this basic separation of people and rebels, and of one tory band from another, that dictated the English tactics in trying to bring them under control. Basically they tried to set the Irish against each other, hoping the dissident elements might wipe themselves out. In 1697 a law was passed by which any tory who could show that he had killed two others was to be granted a pardon. Between 1717 and 1776 the statute books included the provision that any tory who brought in the head of just one other was also to receive a pardon.

The Nature of 'Conventional' Warfare in Europe

A concept is defined as much by reference to what it is not, as to what it is. This is particularly true of the definition of guerrilla warfare, which is negatively defined by subsuming under that heading all those types of military and para-military operations which cannot usefully be regarded as 'regular' or 'conventional' warfare. As military science developed and as states became more capable, through administrative, financial and technological advances, of keeping a large standing army in the field, this contrast between regular and guerrilla operations became increasingly marked. The development of large battle formations, close-order drill, more efficient weapons, uniforms, and standardised systems of tactics, as well as positional doctrines of 'decisive' battles and 'standing one's ground', all contributed to the emergence of a recognisable mode of 'conventional' warfare. Compared to it, guerrilla operations, with their lack of formal military organisation and the explicit avoidance of pitched battles, were obviously a quite distinct phenomenon. But warfare as a whole has not always been so easily separable into regular and irregular categories. During the Middle Ages, and right up until 1648, the most sophisticated type of warfare, even on an international level, showed features akin to what today would be regarded as irregular operations.

The history of the British Isles once again offers adequate testimony to this point, particularly during the troubled reign of King Stephen. The various campaigns that constituted the civil war of this period were all small-scale, localised affairs, and the desultory pace of the fighting reduced many of them to the level of guerrilla conflicts. The war waged against Stephen by the Earl of Chester is a particularly good example. An account of it is to be found in the *Gesta Stephani*, one of the prime documentary sources for the period:

'... he began ... everywhere to rage cruelly with plunder and arson, violence and the sword, sometimes against his opponents, sometimes even against his own side ... In one district he seized the king's castles by stratagem or broke into them by assault ... [and] he passed rapidly from one region to another with his unbridled army and by his ravages turned everything into a desert and bare fields. In front of the town of Lincoln ... in which the king had ... stationed the flower of his troops, he made frequent raids with an armed force ... The king arrived escorted by a fine and numerous body of knights ... and fought a number of engagements with the earl, who laid ambushes for him at the most difficult points on his journey.'[23]

The ubiquity of the Earl's operations, the use of 'stratagems' to take castles, the destruction of the enemy's resources, the launching of 'frequent raids' and the use of 'ambushes' are all typical of the period, and are clearly very akin to what would now be described as guerrilla warfare.

The reliance on raids, already seen as a basic tactic of Robert Bruce during the War of Scottish Independence, dominated tactics and strategy and tactics in Europe right up to the end of the Thirty Years War. English military policy during the Hundred Years War (1337–1453) offers a good example of this. Though the war is only generally known by reference to such rare occurrences as the pitched battles at Crécy, Agincourt or Poitiers, most of the campaigning was undertaken with no thought of coming to grips with the enemy in such a dramatic fashion. The most usual tactic was the launching of a raid or *chevauchée* (from the French 'to ride'), the main object of which was to devastate enemy territory, and thus undermine his economic and psychological capacity for further fighting. The raids varied in size, smaller ones being led by freebooters like Sir John Chandos, the larger ones by such eminent leaders as John of Gaunt, the Black Prince, or the Earls of Cambridge and Buckingham. But none of them were particularly large expeditionary forces whose aim could realistically be construed as the complete destruction of the French armed forces. Their 'business ... was not to seek and defeat the enemy army, but to bring military pressure on the enemy's country ... Military pressure consisted in inflicting *damnun* (loss), or working havoc by the destruction of the means by which life was maintained – houses, barns, stables, mills, stores, vehicles, boats, and such ... Fire was the chief agent of destruction. It was widely used and wholly effective.'[24]

One of the best organised of these raids was that led by the Black Prince in Armagnac, between 1355 and 1357. Once arrived in France the English set up bases in the region, in captured castles, and from these sent out a series of small raiding-parties to harass the French and devastate the countryside: 'The disposition of the Anglo-Gascon forces in 1356 reveals widespread, small-scale campaigns directed largely against the region which Jean d'Armagnac had to defend. The army has been broken into groups: the earls are leading their men on separate or combined enterprises; the prince's following is divided into several independent or associated commands ...' As a contemporary commentator remarked, these groups 'from the places entrusted to them (which they skilfully organised for defence) ... went out frequently on expeditions, accomplished great exploits and carried away much booty ...'[25]

But such a mode of warfare must inevitably have a profound effect on the social and economic fabric of the regions in which it was waged. In some parts of France, it threw up groups of impoverished Frenchmen who were forced to become marauders or guerrillas out of sheer desperation. Some of these, like the tories in Ireland, were destitute noblemen who formed bands of freebooters that preyed upon French and English alike. One French chronicler, Enguerrand de Monstrelet, wrote:

'Because of these misfortunes many of the nobility and common people alike ... were reduced to a state of doubt and misery. Those bands of Frenchmen known as the skinners [écorcheurs] were operating on the borders of Burgundy, where they caused considerable damage by taking castles, seizing prisoners, killing men and ravishing women of all classes, just as if they had been the enemies of France.'[26]

The Anglo-Gascons also had their bands of freebooters who were not very choosy about whom they attacked. They were known as *routiers*, and under such leaders as Arnaud de Cervole, Guilhem Valette, and Rodrigue de Villandrando their bands terrorised Auvergne and Languedoc. In Auvergne, in the period between 1360 and 1390, resistance forces sprang up, known as the *tuchins* who operated in bands of about 30 men to counter the depredations of the *routiers*. In 1427 a pardon was granted to one such man who had cited the following facts to support his case:

'Many good and honest men ... [because] no-one knew what to do, what to take up ... and ... had no refuge in a fortress or place to which they could retire, except to the woods, the rocks, the quarries or the caverns ... [and] this suppliant applied himself to making war on our enemies, always sticking to our side ...'[27]

In north-western France such anti-English guerrilla activity was quite frequent, though historians recently have disputed the extent to which it should be regarded as mere brigandage or a conscious desire for national liberation.[28] Whichever interpretation is more correct, and it would certainly be dangerous to place too much emphasis upon the purely political motives of any outbreak of popular violence in this period, it is certainly true that the activities of such men were very much of the guerrilla type. They had their bases in the forests and rocks alongside the main roads and limited themselves to attacking English travellers or very small groups of soldiers. They were usually peasants, and even when they had quit their villages they almost always remained in contact with those who had stayed behind, receiving supplies and information from them. Notable leaders were such men as Pierre le Porc, Jean de la Haye, Ambroise de Loré, Roger Christofle, and Guillaume Hallé. Most of the bands operated in their own localities and rarely strayed beyond a few kilometres from home during operations.[29] Their war was thus of a very defensive nature, with neither any thought nor possibility of co-ordinated operations actually to drive out the English. Nevertheless, according to one French historian of the Maine, there were certain more militarised bands that harried the English very successfully:

> 'The captains of Charles VII, each one leading his own partisan war and based around several fortresses, accomplished some brilliantly audacious *coups de main*. There were several of these bold leaders in the Maine ... The story of Ambroise de Loré is one of implacable partisan warfare, over twenty years, which never allowed the English to feel secure ... and which was a great comfort to the oppressed population.'[30]

On the whole, then, though the Hundred Years War is usually examined in terms of the confrontation between knights in armour and the redoubtable English archer with his trusty longbow, its conduct has much in common with wars of a more acknowledged guerrilla nature. As a recent French historian has put it: 'Even though history has above all retained the names of a few pitched battles, the Hundred Years War is much more characterised by a multitude of local engagements, often unlooked for, which created in the kingdom a state of permanent insecurity.'[31]

One could well make a similar judgement about two other major wars of the period after the Middle Ages. In the War of Dutch Independence, from 1560 to 1640, the fighting of the first years, at least up until 1590, was very much of this petty localised type. Much of it was carried out by freebooters (*vrijbuiters*) comparable to the *routiers* and *écorcheurs* in France, and consisted mainly of small parties of soldiers fighting ceaselessly, with no fixed fronts, for the control of small villages. As Blaise de Monluc, a French contemporary, observed, the war was a matter of 'fights, encounters, skirmishes, ambushes, an occasional battle, minor sieges, assaults, escalades, captures and surprises of towns.'[32] For the Duke of Alva, one of the principal Spanish commanders of the period, this emphasis upon surprise and skirmish, what the English called 'actions', demanded troops that were particularly tough and well-trained, the equivalent of today's paratroopers or commandos. '[He] always insisted that some trained troops were indispensable for success in the Low Countries Wars because "one cannot fight any 'actions' with other troops – unless it comes to a pitched battle where entire formations are engaged".'[33]

The Thirty Years War, too, followed a similar general pattern, with very few large-scale battles and an endless succession of skirmishes, ambushes, and precipitate retreats. As a recent historian of the war remarked: 'Concerted planning nearly always failed, and the majority of the campaigns were little more than large-scale raids with limited tactical objectives; moreover they always petered out when the immediate aim had been, or had failed to be, achieved.'[34] So much had these military operations in common with guerrilla warfare that General Davidoff, a nineteenth-century Russian writer on partisan tactics, included four of the indefatigable German leaders amongst his list of great partisans. These were George, Margrave of Baden; John, Duke of Brandenburg; Christian, Duke of Brunswick; and Ernest, Count of Mansfield. It is a little extreme, I feel, to regard these men as authentic guerrillas, but the point is well made that their style of warfare, with their endless swift marches and ambuscades, had a great deal in common with genuine guerrilla wars, at least in the purely tactical dimension, and very little with the more formalised positional wars of the following three centuries.

In the Czechoslovakian period of the war, in the 1620s, certain of the campaigns were very definitely examples of guerrilla operations. In his history of the Thirty Years War, one Czech writer took the example of the town of Zlin, in Moravia, as a microcosm of the social and political tensions that lay behind the whole European conflict. Zlin was part of the Vlach, or 'Wallachian' lands, and the Vlachs, hill-colonists of Latin descent, put up a protracted resistance to Hapsburg presence along the Moravian-Slovakian frontier. They were a pastoral people, mainly shepherds, and were thus well-suited to the impermanence and continued movement of the guerrilla's life. A preacher of the time wrote that they 'are a warlike people; even after the defeat of Frederick in 1620 they refused to accept the Hapsburg yoke and for three whole years defended their freedom with the sword.' In 1624 they repulsed a pacification expedition of 1,000 men, led by Colonel Strojnowski, and few of the assaults on their territory met with much success. Another contemporary wrote: 'The inhabitants of the lordship of Vsetin and the mountains thereabouts ... continued to resist with arms and could not be brought to deny their faith ... although several times the Germans, the Italians and the Polish

Cossacks, falling upon them through the narrow defiles in those mountains, sought to destroy them. Thus it was that these Moravian mountains served as a refuge for many men.'[35]

In various ways that I have already mentioned, warfare in Europe after 1648 became progressively more regularised. Campaigns and wars as a whole lost their inchoate guerrilla characteristics and became formalised, tightly organised set-pieces, always aiming at the battle that would destroy the enemy's capacity to resist. But, and this fact is overlooked by many military historians, there was still considerable interest in the potential of guerrilla operations as an *ancillary* to conventional warfare. During the War of Austrian Succession, for example, when the Empress Maria Theresa was assailed by the combined armies of France, Prussia and Saxony, she mobilised the Hungarians in support of the Empire. Under the dashing leadership of men like Mentzel, Frenk, Moratz and Frankini, the Magyar and Croat light cavalry, fighting in fast-moving guerrilla bands, were a constant menace to the French and Prussians.

In 1742, for example, the French general, Bellisle, was investing Prague with 22,000 men. He was obliged to lift the siege, and by the time he had crossed the Egra, a journey of 22 miles which took him all of 10 days, the guerrillas harrying his flanks had reduced his army to 9,000 men, without once giving Bellisle the opportunity to fight a pitched battle. Writing in 1756, about these and other operations, one French writer noted: 'It was this multitude of men, distinguished by bonnets and capes of every kind and colour, that forced us in 1744 and the following years to raise the regiments de Grassin, de la Morlière, des Cantabres, Breton-Volunteers, ... de Guesreick, and several free (partisan) companies, aside from countless detachments that daily set out from the lines.'[36]

Frederick the Great, too, suffered greatly from the activities of the guerrillas, particularly during the campaign of 1742, and has himself left a record of his troubles. From a man who is largely remembered for his influence on regular tactics, it is interesting to note the emphasis that he placed upon the role of guerrilla groups. Referring to his operations in Bohemia he wrote:

'The enemy's light troops operated with such activity and success, that all food supplies were cut off, and for four weeks the Prussian army was without news from Prague ... The Austrian government ordered the inhabitants to abandon their homes as soon as the Prussians should approach, to hide their grain and to flee to the woods, promising to indemnify them for all losses ... The difficulties increased yet more on the arrival of the Hungarian troops who cut off all communications ... The Prussians ... dare not venture out of the camp, and when one attempted to make reconnaissance, one almost always had to suffer certain losses. Eventually, the royal army, trapped in camp, unable to obtain forage, and without any supplies at all, was obliged to retreat by the same road which it had taken when entering Bohemia.'

Frederick marched into Bohemia again but was severely harassed by Frankini in the forest region known as the Royaume de Silvie, and the latter cut all roads from Brosnau and Trotenau. Frederick was forced to retreat to Staudentz, via the forests again, and he suffered many losses. Writing of this second campaign, he noted:

'When one sent out foraging parties, in order that the troops should not be partially destroyed it was necessary to protect them with detachments of 3,000 cavalrymen, and up to 7,000 or 8,000 infantry. Every bundle of hay cost blood. Moratz, Frenk, Nadesty and Frankini were indefatigable, and one can say that they gave the first lessons in the art of the little war.'[37]

Nor were the lessons wasted. During the Seven Years War, Frederick raised 23 battalions of partisans which were known as *Freibataillone*. But these units were always meant to act in conjunction with the regular forces, rather than to pursue independent guerrilla operations. By 1807, indeed, they had been absorbed into the line army, as fusilier battalions on the regular list. The experiences in central Europe had their effect throughout the continent. In the mid-eighteenth century books began to appear on the subject of 'little wars' or guerrilla operations, and by the end of the century at least 50 such titles had been published. Many of these books went through several editions and were translated into other languages. As Peter Paret has justly commented: 'It is remarkable that during the years when the theory of tactics and of grand operations was pushed to the extremes of almost geometric precision ... irregular warfare for the first time became a common concern of military thinkers ...'[38]

The Balkans

It still remains to deal in this chapter with the other major onslaught on Europe in this period. This was the Turkish occupation of most of eastern Europe, which had begun in 1396 when they occupied Bulgaria. In 1453 they captured Constantinople. In 1459 they occupied Serbia, and in 1467 Herzegovina. A few years later they conquered Albania, and in 1526 their victory at the Battle of Mohacs secured for them the domination of Hungary. During these campaigns and the centuries that followed there were numerous wars of resistance fought by Serbs, Hungarians, Montenegrins, Bulgarians and others, and these generally took the form of guerrilla operations.

In Hungary, for example, between 1591 and 1606, a war was fought against the Turks that had many of the characteristics already noted in the Dutch War of Independence and the Thirty Years War. In the later stages, particularly between 1604 and 1605, the Hungarian operations were of a definite guerrilla type, but even before that campaigning was always on a petty level and there were no decisive battles: 'The great strategical principle of the epoch, that of avoiding battles in which the armies could be destroyed, was scrupulously observed.'[39]

But the most common type of guerrilla warfare in the Balkans was that waged by the *haiduks*, a type of bandit-guerrilla similar in many respects to the tories in Ireland.[40] They were patriots in that they fought against the Turks and, in Hungary, the Hapsburgs, but they always operated in small bands and kept themselves apart from the population as a whole. Certainly they had the sympathy of the people at large, and their activities had much symbolic value, but there was rarely any thought of trying to arouse the whole population against the foreigner. In most cases the fact that their targets were foreign travellers was simply a convenient way of legitimising their murders and robberies rather than a preliminary tactic in a war of national liberation. The *haiduk*'s main loyalty was to his own band, and had there been no foreigner to attack they would doubtless have preyed upon their own countrymen.

In Hungary they first appeared in the mid-sixteenth century along the Transylvanian frontiers. The first ones were ex-cattle-drivers, or *hajtóks*, who refused to become serfs. Once again one notes that it is those men without fixed roots who are most able to adapt themselves to the insecurity and movement of the guerrilla's life. At first they fought against the Turks, but during the seventeenth century, as their numbers increased, they began to offer their services as mercenaries, and to receive certain privileges in return. By the end of the century there were some tens of thousands of them, living in small colonies along the frontiers. Even so, they did on occasion form the basis of revolt against foreign domination. In 1604–5, Stephen Bocskai, a Transylvanian prince, organised the *haiduks* in a rebellion against the Hapsburgs and had soon taken control of much of the Hungarian highlands, basing himself in west Slovakia and the Valley of the Vag. As well as the *haiduks* Bocskai also had units of Turkish and Tartar light cavalry, and in 1605 such troops conducted raids into Moravia. Bocskai had gained the *haiduks'* support by ennobling their leaders and granting them areas of land. Thus, by the end of the wars, the men who had once been marauding guerrillas, without social roots, were now landowners with a vested interest in giving up their old way of life and settling down as peaceful petty noblemen.

But there were always those who were unable to settle down, and from the 1660s there grew up new bands of rival *haiduks*, known as the *kuruc* and the *labanc*. The former were anti-Hapsburgs, and took their name from the cross worn by the peasant rebels who had followed George Desza in 1514. The latter were Hapsburg supporters, the word *labanc* simply meaning 'foot soldier'. Both groups took to the woods in the Partium, between Hapsburg Hungary, the Turkish zone, and Transylvania proper. There they conducted a long and bloody warfare, often descending to mere banditry. An important *kuruc* leader was Imre Thokoly, and until 1680 this particular faction received financial aid from Louis XIV, always on the lookout for means of undermining the power of the Hapsburg Empire. Unfortunately very little is known of the origins of each group, but it would be interesting to know whether allegiance to the pro- or anti-Hapsburg bands had any socio-economic basis. As it is, one can only tentatively suggest that perhaps the rivalry between *kuruc* and *labanc* had something in common with that between Cetnik and Partisan in Yugoslavia, during World War II.[41] The *kurucs* were still in existence at the beginning of the eighteenth century, and between 1703 and 1704, Francis Rakoczi organised them in an anti-Hapsburg revolt. He started with only 300 men but soon rallied most of the country to him and built up an army of 30,000 men. 'The officers he had brought with him, and to whose advice he listened, were mostly survivors of Thokoly's campaigns, whose ruling ideas were to avoid decisive encounters, to set Austrian pitfalls everywhere, and to roam over the country and take booty.' The ordinary soldiers, too, were more suited to guerrilla warfare than to regular operations. As one of their leaders wrote: 'The Hungarian has the soul of a volunteer, and will never be nailed down, neither by monthly pay nor by regulations ... To whatever discipline and order we may try to break Hungarians, they will never get accustomed to fight otherwise, they will either pursue or run away ... It is all no use, if they do not win they get tired, if they do they want to carry their gains home.'[42] But Rakoczi soon ceased to listen to the advice of his officers and tried to turn his men into a regular army. He formed 11 regiments of infantry and 8 of cavalry, and gave them uniforms and regular training. But neither he nor his subordinates had any particular military talent and all the pitched battles he insisted on fighting ended in defeat. In 1711 he was forced to sue for peace.

Haiduks were also important in the region that is now Yugoslavia, and again they seem to have first appeared during the fifteenth century, their numbers slowly growing in the years that followed. The most notable example of guerrilla resistance was that which took place in Montenegro, from the fifteenth to the eighteenth century. The name was first used in 1435. It means 'Black Mountain' and refers to the mountainous inner core of the Zeta region. On account of the nature of the terrain it remained largely independent of the Turks, whose numerous expeditions always ended in disaster. As one writer has put it: 'Its history for ... three centuries was that of a protracted resistance movement.'[43] One of the biggest Turkish offensives took place in 1713 when they sent an army of 120,000 men against a region whose total population could not have been more than 30,000. The structure of Montenegrin society also helps to explain how they were so able to conduct endless guerrilla operations against the Turks. Because of the nature of the terrain, and the difficulty of agricultural production, the Montenegrins were nearly all stock-rearers, who supplemented their incomes by continual raids into the lowlands. Their chief social unit was the *bratstvo*, or brotherhood, an extended kinship group with an elected chief. They also received much practice in petty warfare through the blood feuds which were a constant feature of their existence. It is perhaps not surprising that during the Yugoslav War of Liberation, from 1941–45, the Montenegrins, some 3 per cent of the population, supplied 17 per cent of the officers in Tito's army.

Haiduks were also very important in Bulgaria, where they first appeared in the early sixteenth century. They lived in bands of 20 to 30 men under a leader, the *voivoda*, and a second-in-command known as the standard-bearer, or *bairaktar*. The *voivoda* was almost always elected, usually after some sort of trial of physical prowess. They operated in the mountains, but only whilst there were leaves on the trees. In winter, when the mountains became uninhabitable, they returned to their villages. They usually wore some exaggerated kind of national costume and were liberally armed with swords, pistols and muskets. In theory at least, 'they had a high code of behaviour: no *haiduk* stole, troubled women or plundered innocent people; no *haiduk* ever deserted a wounded comrade.'[44] Some of the more important leaders were Chardar in the Rila Mountains, Manush of Strandzha and Strashil of the Pirin. From time to time they took part in quite extensive anti-Turkish operations, as in 1688 when there was an abortive rising in north-west Bulgaria, around Chiprovets, led by Georgi Peyachevich and Bogdan Marinov. In 1773 and 1774, during the Russo-Turkish War, hundreds of Bulgarians fought for the Russians in volunteer detachments and partisan units. After the Treaty of Kuchuk Kai-nardji, when the Russians left Bulgaria, hundreds of frustrated patriots took to the mountains to further swell the *haiduk* ranks. The Bulgarian experience is also of interest as regards Turkish methods of trying to put down revolts. Their usual response after a *haiduk* attack was to impose a collective punishment on the inhabitants of the nearest village. They would either be fined or more likely the village would be destroyed and the inhabitants transported to Asia Minor to be sold or forcibly Turkicised. Depopulation and reprisals are counter-insurgency techniques that will become increasingly familiar as the history of guerrilla warfare is unfolded.

The Americas

I have already stressed the importance of the social structure of a particular group or nation in determining its ability to undertake effective guerrilla warfare. One group whose rootlessness and sense of social alienation made it very easy for it to adapt to the insecurity of guerrilla warfare was the African slaves of North and South America and the Caribbean. In the United States the slaves never seem to have found the freedom of manoeuvre to take their revolts beyond a few isolated acts of protest or flights, but in other regions it did sometimes assume a much more widespread and protracted form.

Some of the earliest large revolts were in Brazil, in the seventeenth century. The first slaves had arrived there in 1552, and already by 1580 there were some 10,000 of them. Because of the vastness of the country and the inaccessibility of many areas there were always individual escapes and subsequent acts of banditry. From the 1630s, however, the movement assumed a wider dimension, and in certain areas whole colonies of escaped slaves grew up, which defended themselves against Portuguese retaliation by constant harassing operations and achieving a mastery of jungle warfare. These colonies were known as *quilombos*, and 10 major ones were formed before the end of the eighteenth century. Those set up in 1632, 1636, 1646, 1650, 1731, 1758 and 1796 were all destroyed within two years of their formation. But in Minas Gerais one lasted from 1712–19, and in the Matto Grosso there was one that managed to survive from 1770 right through until 1795.

The longest lived of all, however, was the quilombo in Palmares, in Pernambuco, which first began around 1597 and lasted almost 100 years until its final destruction in 1694. It took shape as a state in its own right in 1605, when the various Bantu-speaking Africans chose for themselves a king. They grew crops and made frequent raids upon nearby Portuguese plantations. Based around two large population centres and numerous other smaller ones, the insurgents totalled perhaps 10,000 men and were a constant thorn in the Portuguese side. An official wrote in 1612: 'Some thirty miles inland there is a site between mountains called Palmares, which harbours runaway slaves ... whose attacks and raids force the whites into armed pursuits which amount to little for they return to raid again.'[45] Between 1640 and 1654 the Dutch occupied Brazil, and they too mounted expeditions into Palmares in 1640 and 1645. But the slaves refused to be drawn into any major confrontation, even though many of their villages were destroyed, and the Dutch achieved very little. Between 1672 and 1694 the Portuguese mounted an average of one expedition every 15 months, and very gradually they began to wear down the insurgents. In the last one 6,000 troops were involved. They managed to encircle the bulk of the negroes and destroy their state after a siege of 42 days. After this success the Portuguese tried, though not always successfully, to crush slave-gatherings in the bud. To this end they established special units of troops, experienced in jungle fighting, and led by picked veterans known as *capitaes-do-mato*, or bush captains.

There were also important outbreaks of slave insurgency in the West Indies. In Jamaica, for example, escaped slaves, known as Maroons, began in the middle of the seventeenth century to establish their own form of home rule in remote villages, and to protect themselves by resort to guerrilla techniques. In 1655 the British captured Jamaica from the Spanish. But for a short time certain of the slaves, most of them tough cattle-herders, took to the hills and actually aided the Spanish in trying to throw the British out. A prominent leader was Juan de Bolas who based himself in the mountains of Clarendon. In 1660 the Spaniards surrendered to the English, in return for grants of land, but certain of the Africans stayed up in the hills and became exceptionally skilful fighters, armed usually with lances and bows, though they also had a few captured firearms.

In 1683 Bolas was killed in an ambush and the confrontation between the English and the escaped slaves became somewhat less violent. But the Maroons were always there and, after another slave revolt in 1690, their bands began once again to assume menacing proportions. Again the insurgents were based in the Clarendon mountains, though by this time the original Maroons had moved away into the north and east of Jamaica. The most important leader on this occasion was known as Cudjoe. The war against him and his followers continued until 1720, and even in 1730 the British were obliged to mount three expeditions against the Maroon bands. The latter were now armed with cutlasses, or whatever firearms they had managed to capture from the English. They fought in small bands, and used horns, known as *abengs*, to warn each other of the approach of the enemy. Then they would either retire or, if the enemy group was not too large, concentrate for an ambush. Their mastery of the tactics of elusiveness and surprise was described by the Governor of the island in 1764:

'With amazing ability they ran, or rather rolled, through their various firings and evolutions. This part of their exercise indeed more justly deserves to be styled evolution than any that is practised by regular troops, for they fire stooping almost to the very ground, and no sooner are their muskets discharged than they throw themselves into a thousand antic gestures, and tumble over and over, so as to be continually shifting their place; the intention of which is to elude the shot as well as to deceive the aim of their adversaries which their nimble and almost instantaneous change of position renders extremely uncertain.[46]

Eventually, however, the British were able to wear them down. They embarked upon a programme of constructing advanced fortified posts from which parties would be sent forth for a full 20 days to search an area thoroughly. Each post had its own pack of tracker dogs and was manned by a specially trained ranger squad. In the bigger offensives they would be aided by the militia, and at all times they made it one of their highest priorities to seek out and destroy those areas in which the negroes were secretly growing or storing their provisions. In 1739 the Maroons gave up the struggle and signed a treaty with the British by which, in return for some measure of autonomy, they themselves became the hunters of escaped slaves and rebels.

Although slave revolts never attained the proportions of guerrilla warfare in North America, there were other campaigns in which it had a role. The chronic warfare against the Indians, for example, revealed many of the characteristics of petty guerrilla operations. The accent must be put on the word 'petty', however, for the usual Indian tactics were to limit themselves to dawn attacks on an isolated cabin or very small settlement. Only occasionally did they venture to attack bodies of soldiers, and even then the activities of one tribe were hardly ever co-ordinated with those of others. One of the few exceptions to this rule was in 1711, in North Carolina, when five tribes made a concerted attack on all the settlements in the state. They achieved perfect surprise and came within an ace of eliminating the white presence there. By 1713 most Indians had some firearms, and by 1740 nearly all had horses. But these latter were very rarely used, and the Indians thus denied themselves a very important element of mobility. According to Colonel Henry Bouquet, a Swiss officer in British service, and one of the chief theoreticians of Indian warfare, they fought according to three main principles. Firstly they always remained scattered; secondly their chief offensive tactic was to try and surround their enemy; thirdly they were always ready to give ground when harassed, and to return when the pressure eased.

From the middle of the eighteenth century the British and Americans gradually worked out ways of containing the Indian threat and themselves taking the offensive. In certain states, chains of forts were established and special units of rangers were used to plug the gaps in the chain. Probably the most famous of these were Rogers' Rangers, whose commander left behind a pithy summary of the basic tactical principles of this type of warfare; it consists of a list of 19 essential rules for a Ranger, but I shall only cite a few of them here:

(1) Don't forget nothing.

(3) When you're on the march, act the way you would if you was sneaking up on a deer. See the enemy first.

(4) Tell the truth about what you see and what you do. There is an army depending on us for correct information.

(11) Don't ever march home the same way. Take a different route so you won't be ambushed.

(13) Every night you'll be told where to meet if surrounded by a superior force.

(17) If somebody's trailing you, make a circle, come back onto your own tracks and ambush the folks that aim to ambush you.

(18) Don't stand up when the enemy's coming against you. Kneel down, lie down, hide behind a tree.

(19) Let the enemy come till he's almost close enough to touch. Then let him have it and jump out and finish him up with your hatchet.[47]

But such special troops usually demanded very special rates of pay and many states were unable to raise the necessary taxes. They preferred instead to induce the provincials to join light infantry units which were nonetheless on the regular list, and were paid accordingly. Bouquet, Brigadier George Augustus and Lord Howe were important innovators here. They concentrated upon training the men very hard, forcing them to travel light, without camp-followers and servants, and to be able to disperse and rally swiftly, and to shoot from all positions. As one correspondent wrote to Pitt, in 1756:

'[Such troops] require no exercise but to be perfectly acquainted with the use of their arms, that is to load quick and hit the mark, and for military discipline but this one rule: if they are attacked by French and Indians to rush to all parts from where their fire comes ... It is an unpardonable neglect of duty to be surprised ... when a few brisk men scattered for two hundred yards on each side will prevent it: keep them from surprising you and they are an easy conquest.'[48]

The key offensive method of the whites was to threaten an Indian village and its crops, thus forcing them to stand together and fight. Such a tactic was greatly facilitated by the unfortunate Indian habit of never posting sentries. When the Indians were thus caught *en masse* the superior discipline of the regular troops, particularly their offensive use of the bayonet, almost always brought them to victory.[49]

The traditions of Indian fighting were to some extent carried over by the Americans into the War of Independence, from 1775-83. Such tactics were used mainly during the campaigns in North and South Carolina, from 1780–83. On May 12, 1780, General Lincoln surrendered Charleston to the British, and all organised military strength in the area collapsed. In August General Gates took a small force of Continentals and militia to engage the British, but his over-optimistic assessment of his chances brought a crushing defeat for the Americans at the battle of Camden. In December the command of the southern theatre was given to General Nathaniel Greene who twice defeated the British, under Cornwallis, at the Cowpens and Guildford Court House. For most of the time, however, Greene refused to face the British in open battle, but contented himself with wearing them down by continual marching across the Carolinas and even into Virginia. In October, the British general surrendered at Yorktown.

Throughout this period Greene was supported by guerrilla bands operating in the swamps of eastern Carolina, between Camden and the coast. The guerrilla leaders included such men as Thomas Sumter, Maurice Murphy, Andrew Pickens, but perhaps the most successful of them all was Francis Marion. He was known almost everywhere as the 'Swamp Fox' because it was in such areas, at Snow's Island, for example, or Peyre's Plantation, that he made his base. He and his horsemen would emerge from their hideouts around sunset and ride swiftly towards their target which they would fall upon in the very early hours of the morning. Having accomplished their mission they would ride back as swiftly. When his men were acting as one unit, as at the battles of Black Mingo or Tearcoat Swamp, they would attack in three groups, one assaulting frontally and one on each flank, after quietly stealing up on their enemy. But at all times Marion kept some of his forces on the move, in groups of 5 to 10 men, who would gather information, comfort rebel families, and harass isolated Loyalists and English soldiers. If ever Marion's base was threatened by a powerful force of the enemy he had no compunction in retreating to another base area:

'[He was] the scourge of the British. He seemed ubiquitous, lurking everywhere: hiding in an unknown rendezvous, creeping stealthily along on a raid, or leading a midnight attack. To add to the enemy's alarm he kept his patrols constantly moving up and down the Santee Road. British waggoners were afraid to cross at Nelson's ford, but took the longer more tortuous route to Camden.'[50]

British counter-insurgency tactics were particularly crude in this theatre. Generally they were little more than savage reprisals against all those suspected of supporting or merely being related to any of the rebels. The Loyalists were particularly brutal in this respect, and in one offensive they burned a swathe 15 miles across and 75 miles long through rebel territory. Looms, grist mills and blacksmiths shops were broken up, houses burnt, and even the milk cows and sheep were shot or bayoneted. But such tactics were in the end counterproductive, as is usually the case with any counter-insurgency campaign based purely upon terror. On the whole Marion gained more recruits than he lost supporters, for reprisals cease to be effective if one completely destroys the livelihood of a suspect. Then he has nothing left to lose and might just as well join the guerrillas as starve to death.

The American War of Independence is also of interest in that it reveals many *strategic* similarities with other guerrilla wars. I have already shown how Greene based much of his southern campaign around the notion of avoiding disastrous pitched battles and concentrating simply upon tiring out the British. Sometimes he was forced to fight rearguard actions, but even then he concentrated upon extricating enough of his forces to remain a threat. As he said after the Battle of Hobkirk's Mill: 'We fight, get beat, rise and fight again'. Most of the great American spokesmen and leaders also saw the war in this perspective. In 1776 Washington told Congress that: 'We should on all occasions avoid a general action, and never be drawn into a necessity to put everything to the risk.'[51] Alexander Hamilton, then Washington's aide-de-camp, observed: 'It may be asked, if, to avoid general engagements, we give up objects of the first importance, what is to prevent the enemy from carrying every important point and ruining us? My answer is that our hopes are not placed in any particular city or spot of ground, but in ... [trying to] waste and defeat the enemy by piece-meal.'[52] Thomas Paine's description of the war as a 'war of invasion' offers a concise early definition of the nature of a guerrilla strategy:

'The conquest of America by arms ... is not within the compass of human practicability, for America is too extensive either to be fully conquered or *passively* defended. But she may be *actively* defended by defeating or making prisoners of the army that invades her. And this is the only system of defence that can be effectual in a large country. There is something in a war carried on by invasion that makes it differ in circumstances from any other mode of war, because he who conducts it cannot tell whether the ground he gains, be for him, or against him, when he first makes it.'[53]

But the interesting point about the War of Independence is that, although it was fought according to a guerrilla strategy, by and large, and here the experience of the Carolinas is not really typical, guerrilla tactics were eschewed. For guerrilla tactics demand that the troops themselves be allowed a large amount of independence and initiative, as well as a genuine commitment to the cause for which they are fighting. Without such a commitment few troops will long be willing to endure the rigours of guerrilla life. The more they feel that their cause offers some real prospect of political and social emancipation, the deeper their commitment will be. But Washington and the American leaders were exceptionally wary of letting the war become in any sense a social revolution. For them the ideal peace treaty would guarantee a *status quo ante bellum*, except without the British. Therefore all manifestations of grass-roots independence by the troops were to be vigorously suppressed. Because of this, guerrilla units and many of the egalitarian militia units were frowned upon, and at the tactical level the American leaders concentrated on turning their troops into well-disciplined regulars with a suitable respect for authority. In 1775 Benjamin Thompson noted the fearful contradiction inherent in the resort to a war of national liberation that somehow hoped not to upset the *status quo*. He found cause to 'lament the existence of that very spirit which induced the common people to take up arms and resist the authority of Great Britain ... [because it induces] them to resist the authority of their own officers, and by that means effectually prevents them ever making good soldiers.'[54] Alexander Hamilton was quite explicit about how this contradiction should be resolved: 'Let officers be men of sense and sentiment, and the nearer the soldiers approach to machines, perhaps the better.'[55] But machines do not make good guerrillas, and the Americans found themselves in the unique position of fighting a war according to a guerrilla strategy, but with regular troops who were almost indistinguishable from the British and Hessian opponents.[56]

1. E. A. Thompson, *The Early Germans*, Clarendon Press, Oxford, 1965, p 146
2. E. A. Thompson, *Attila and the Huns*, Clarendon Press, Oxford, 1948, p 27
3. Thompson, *Germans, op cit*, pp 148–9
4. H. Schreiber (trans J. Cleugh), *Teuton and Slav*, Constable, 1965, p 27
5. J. Beeler, *Warfare in Feudal Europe 730–1200*, Cornell University Press, Ithaca, 1971, p 239
6. *ibid*, pp 170–71
7. A. Jones (trans), *The History of Gruffydd ap Cynan*, Manchester University Press, 1910, p 135
8. *ibid*, p 141
9. *ibid*, p 153
10. L. H. Nelson, *The Normans in South Wales*, University of Texas Press, Austin, 1966, pp 116–117
11. Sir M. Powicke, *The Thirteenth Century, 1216–1307*, Clarendon Press, Oxford, 1962, p 423
12. Gerald of Wales (trans T. Wright), *The Historical Works of Geraldius Cambriensis*, H. G. Bohn, London, 1863, pp 511–12 and 517–18
13. W. D. Dickenson, *Scotland from the Earliest Times to 1603*, Nelson, 1966, p 157
14. G. W. S. Barrow, *Robert the Bruce*, Eyre & Spottiswoode, 1965, p 243
15. 'Yank' Levy, *Guerrilla Warfare*, Penguin Books, 1941, p 19
16. Barrow, *op cit*, p 267
17. *ibid*, pp 344–45
18. C. M. Yonge, *Cameos from English History: the Wars in France*, Macmillan, 1874, p 192
19. E. McCracken, *The Irish Woods Since Tudor Times*, David & Charles, 1971, p 28
20. W. E. H. Lecky, *A History of England in the Eighteenth Century*, Longmans Green, 1890, Vol 2, p 346
21. E. MacLysaght, *Irish Life in the Seventeenth Century*, Dublin, 1939, pp 274–75
22. Gann, *op cit*, p 8
23. K. R. Potter (trans), *Gesta Stephani*, Nelson, 1955, pp 130–32
24. H. Hewitt, The Organisation of War, in K. Fowler (ed), *The Hundred Years War*, Macmillan, 1971, p 87
25. H. Hewitt, *The Black Prince's Expedition of 1355–57*, Manchester University Press, 1958, pp 88–89
26. P. E. Thompson (ed), *Contemporary Chronicles of the Hundred Years War*, Folio Society, 1966, p 323
27. P. S. Lewis, *Later Medieval France*, Macmillan, 1968, p 286
28. See, for example, B. J. H. Rowe, John Duke of Bedford and the Norman 'Brigands', *English Historical Review*, October 1932, and R. Jonet, *La résistance à l'occupation anglaise en Basse-Normandie*, Musée de Normandie, Caen, 1969
29. See Jouet, *op cit*, p 81
30. A. Bouton, *Le Maine, histoire économique et sociale aux XIV, XV et XVI siècles*, CNRS, Paris, 1970, p 49
31. P-C. Timbal, *La Guerre de Cent Ans ...*, CNRS, Paris, 1961, p 105

32. G. Parker, *The Army of Flanders and the Spanish Road, 1567–1659*, Cambridge University Press, 1972, p 12

33. *ibid*, p 13

34. S. H. Steinberg, *The 'Thirty Years War' and the Conflict for European Hegemony 1600–1660*, Edward Arnold, 1966, pp 101–2

35. J. V. Polisenŝky (trans R. Evans), *The Thirty Years War*, Batsford, 1971, pp 147 and 159

36. P. Paret, Colonial Experience and European Military Reform at the End of the Eighteenth Century, *Bulletin of the Institute of Historical Research*, 1964, p 54

37. Gen Davidoff, *La Guerre des Partisans*, J. Correard, Paris, 1841, pp 29–31

38. Paret, *op cit*, p 57

39. D. Sinor, *A History of Hungary*, Allen & Unwin, 1959, p 176

40. The spelling of 'haiduk' has numerous regional variations, eg *hajdu, hayduk, hajtok, hajdut, hajdutin*

41. See below pp 168–69

42. L. Hengelmuller, *Hungary's Fight for National Existence*, Macmillan, 1913, pp 160 and 229

43. M. Heppel and M. B. Singleton, *Yugoslavia*, Ernest Benn, 1961, p 91

44. M. Macdermott, *A History of Bulgaria 1393–1885*, Allen & Unwin, 1962, p 50

45. R. K. Kent, Palmares, an African State in Brazil, *Journal of African History*, 1965, p 164

46. C. Robinson, *The Fighting Maroons of Jamaica*, William Collins & Sangster, Jamaica, 1969, pp 35–6

47. F. Sully, *Age of the Guerrilla*, Avon, New York, 1968, pp 198–99

48. Paret, *op cit*, p 47

49. See J. K. Mahon, Anglo-American Methods of Indian Warfare, 1676–1794, *Mississippi Valley Historical Review*, 1958, pp 254–275

50. R. D. Bass, *Swamp Fox*, Alvin Redman, 1960, p 79

51. E. Robson, *The American Revolution 1763–83*, Blatchworth Press, 1955, p 97

52. *ibid*, p 161

53. S. Hook (ed), *The Essential Works of Thomas Paine*, Signet, New York, 1969, p 37

54. H. Commager and R. Morris, *The Spirit of '76*, Bobbs-Merrill, New York, 1958, Vol 1, p 155

55. B. Mitchell, *Alexander Hamilton: Youth to Maturity 1755–88*, Macmillan, New York, 1957, p 177

56. For a more detailed treatment of this point see J. Ellis, *Armies in Revolution*, Croom Helm, 1973, pp 45–73

CHAPTER 3

Revolution and Empire 1791–1815

The Vendée

In the light of the experience of guerrilla warfare in this century, it is often tempting to associate that type of conflict only with radical left-wing ideologies. In certain cases, however, guerrilla struggles have been undertaken in the name of counter-revolution, often with a most reactionary attachment to the symbols of the old order – king, aristocracy and clergy. European history from 1793 to 1815 is particularly full of such examples, as the peasantry of the more backward regions struggled against the imposition of Revolutionary and Imperial rule. The first notable uprising took place within France itself, and represented a more serious threat to the Revolution than the conventional, if rather half-hearted responses of the European *ancien régimes*.

It took place in the Vendée, an area of some 800 square miles, bounded on the north by the Loire and the west by the sea, and containing not more than two per cent of the French population. Many of the peasants in this region had not suffered the same oppressive aristocratic exactions as had the rural population in other parts of France, and felt no particular hostility towards the nobility. They were also fanatically attached to their local priests and reacted strongly to revolutionary attempts to undermine the role of the Catholic religion. In August 1792 there were localised outbreaks of popular discontent in Châtillon and Bressuire, when news spread of a decree ordering the banishment of all refractory clergy. But the final straw for the peasantry of this region was the promulgation of the *levée en masse*, demanding that all Frenchmen put themselves at the service of the country, ready if need be to be transported to the frontiers to fight off foreign aggression.

On March 10, 1793, the signal was given for general revolt and the first move was made at Machecoul, when the little town was seized by thousands of the local peasants. From then on, for the next nine months, the forces of the First Republic found themselves engaged in a bitter guerrilla struggle which, combined with the aggression from abroad, almost brought it down. As one French general said of the Vendéan guerrillas: 'I assure you nothing was wanting to the soldiers save the uniform ... To me this war of peasants, of

brigands, which has been so greatly ridiculed and treated with contempt ...
has always seemed the great test of the Republic.'[1] There is no space here for a
complete narrative of the bitter fighting, and I shall merely attempt to sketch
in some of the more important aspects of the struggle.

One of the great strengths of the insurgents was the nature of the terrain. In
the Lower Vendée, the coastal region, it was mostly marshland, whilst in the
Central and Upper Vendée it was what is known as *bocage*, a labyrinth of
narrow roads and paths cutting through tangled high hedgerows. Taking
advantage of such difficult terrain, the Vendéans were able to wage a classic
guerrilla war of ambush and swift withdrawal. One of their Republican
adversaries, General Thurreau, has left an excellent description of the nature of
the fighting:

> 'The Vendéans possessed a hitherto unknown style of fighting and an inimitable
> one, in that it was solely appropriate to the country and the genius of the
> inhabitants ... The rebels ... employ their own particular tactics ... Assured of
> the advantages derived from their method of attack, they never allow them-
> selves to be surprised. They only fight when and where they wish. Their skill in
> the use of firearms is such that no known people ... make better use of [them]
> ... than the poachers of the *bocage*. When they attack, their onslaught is terrible,
> sudden and almost always unforseen owing to the difficulty in the Vendée of
> reconnoitring the ground and protecting oneself against surprises ... Before you
> have time to know what has hit you you find yourself over-whelmed by a rain of
> fire more massive than anything we can produce under our regulations. They do
> not wait for the word of command before firing, and have nothing like volley-
> firing by battalions, ranks or squads ... If you can stand up to the violence of
> their attack they will seldom dispute the victory with you, but this will profit
> you but little, because they retreat so swiftly, that it is very difficult to catch
> them up as the terrain is almost always unsuited to the use of cavalry. Their
> forces disperse and they escape through fields, hedges, woods and thickets. They
> know all the paths, by-ways, gullies and ravines, and all the obstacles capable of
> impeding their flight and how to avoid them ... When they are winning they
> surround you and cut into your troops everywhere. They pursue you with
> inconceivable fury and speed. They run, when attacking or pursuing, as fast as
> they do when they are fleeing, but they continue firing all the time. They load
> their muskets as they march or even at the double and their constant movement
> does not detract from the briskness or the accuracy of their fire. Generally
> speaking warfare in the Vendée possesses such singular characteristics that it
> needs long experience to master them.'[2]

The insurgents also possessed two other major advantages. In the early weeks
of the rebellion, in particular, they were aided by the fact that the Republicans
could only muster a very small force against them, most of these being

untrained levies. Throughout the campaign the bulk of the veteran forces were kept on the frontiers, whilst only a small proportion of the troops available to the revolutionary leaders could be mobilised against the Vendéans. With or without the external aggression the suppression of the insurgency would have been a bloody and tedious task, but it is undeniable that the Prussians, Austrians and Spanish had much to do with its protracted nature. The other major advantage was the significant degree of class unity within the counter-revolutionary areas. There was hardly any of the tension between aristocrat and peasant that was so important in other parts of France. The peasants were eager and willing to call upon the military experience of men like Charette de la Contrie, de Bonchamps, Sapinaud de la Verrie, marquis d'Elbée, marquis de Lescure, and marquis de la Rochejacquelein. Conversely, these aristocrats were also willing to work hand in hand with lower class leaders like Cathelineau, an artisan, Stofflet, a gamekeeper, and Joly, a surgeon.

But the insurgents also suffered several major disadvantages. Most important, perhaps, was the fact that the sheer force of numbers was against them, in the long run. Whilst the insurgents in the Upper Vendée, the main theatre of operations, could never muster more than 50,000 to 60,000 men, the Republicans were able, from September, to put more than 100,000 men in the field, a number that gradually increased as they encircled the rebel area. The Vendéans were also at the mercy of one of the greatest weaknesses of peasant guerrilla armies – their *parochialism*. Although the peasants would speedily assemble when the alarm was given, they were loth both to travel far outside their immediate surroundings and to remain under arms when the immediate danger seemed to have passed. Once a victory had been won, it was very difficult for the leaders to keep a large force together, and so maintain the offensive. This fact was of particular help to the hard-pressed Republicans after the fall of Saumur in early June.

The rebel effort was also seriously undermined by weaknesses and splits within the leadership. In the early days, the struggle was fragmented into quite separate bands: Royrand and Sapinaud de la Verrie in the Centre, Charette in the Lower Vendée, Cathelineau in Anjou, and de Lescure and de la Roche-jacquelein in Poitou. Even though some of these groups did later join together to form the so-called Grande Armée, Charette always remained isolated from the main effort, and there were even further divisions within this one area. In September, Charette's Council of War explicitly laid it down that henceforth each chief would act singly and independently in defence of his own district. A little before this decision, one leader was driven to complain that although they had just captured munitions and money:

'What good has this been to us? The chiefs of the country have done this separately, without giving anyone ... notice. Had there been notice blows might have been struck at ... the low country towns. Monsieur Charette proceeds with as much secrecy as the army of Anjou. Nothing that he undertakes is known. He never goes to the help of his neighbours, notwithstanding their demands ... Safety will lie in combination alone.'[3]

The movement also suffered from lack of adequate co-operation between the military and the civil leadership. In late May, a Superior Council of Administration was set up in Châtillon, but it was dominated by civilians who seemed unable to take measures attuned to the military demands of the situation. On July 12, one of its members wrote to the military chiefs:

'There ought to be more officers amongst us. They would possibly shorten discussion. We never arrive at the end of it; and often, though without desiring to do so, we go against your decisions. We have amongst us honest but timid men, who will not recognise the fact that events sometimes require prompt and revolutionary methods of treatment. The best course is to put an end to the Council and to adopt military measures. We discuss, and you act; but in the long run the men who discuss might dominate the men of action, and in civil war this must be avoided or all will be lost ...'[4]

Here is one of the most pressing problems facing all guerrilla armies, and one that has come more and more to the fore with the increasing sophistication of insurgency techniques. A guerrilla force must set up machinery to look after the political and economic interests of the population at large. But the operation of this machinery must at all times be geared to the military demands of the situation, to prevent a weakening of the war effort. Without such a co-ordination it is impossible to mobilise fully the material and human resources of the insurgent area, or to make emphatic enough the fact that armed resistance is done in the defence of real socio-economic interests. Not until one comes to discuss such organised political *parties* as the Bolsheviks or the Chinese Communists will it be seen how important this close integration of military and political functions can be.

The government's counter-insurgency methods became more and more stringent as the months elapsed. At the end of March all those who had taken part in the rebellion were outlawed and military tribunals set up to try suspects. Each tribunal was composed of five officers who were to judge a case on the evidence of two witnesses and bring judgement within 24 hours. Later, legalistic methods made way for more direct attacks on the rebels' means of livelihood. According to a directive of the Convention, in July: 'The Minister of War will dispatch to the Vendée combustible materials of all kinds, for the purpose of burning the woods, the copses, the undergrowth. The forests will be cut down, the dens of the rebels destroyed, the harvests will be cut, and the cattle seized. The property of the rebels will be declared to belong to the Republic.'[5] By mid-September over 100 rebel hamlets and villages had been razed to the ground.

On the purely military front the Republicans managed to overcome some of their more serious difficulties by the simple tactical expedient of never sending out isolated expeditions. Instead of deploying numerous small columns to engage the rebels wherever they were heard of, they tried to keep their forces together and to attack *en masse*. This was mainly the idea of Vergnes, General Canclaux's chief of staff, who noted that the Vendéans would muster men quickly from many districts to attack a particular small Republican column, and this force could easily disperse before reinforcements were brought up. 'Let us profit by our faults and abandon the plan of thus attacking the rebels by means of columns at a distance of several leagues from one another, under the pretext of surrounding them ... The Vendée must be attacked *en masse*.'[6] The generals were slow in applying this principle, but as they got stronger they were increasingly able to do so. By October one Vendéan leader was lamenting that: 'The enemy has at length learnt the secret of victory since they are forming in masses to overwhelm us.'[7]

Certain republican leaders, fired by the new revolutionary faith in the potential of science, felt that technology must defeat the Vendéans. One proposed the use of mines, another invented a combustible compound which would release asphyxiating fumes, while yet another claimed that he had produced a solution which would infect the whole countryside. None of them were successful, but it is interesting to see that the Americans in Vietnam were not the first to be carried away by technological fetishism as a solution to their military problems.

What finally defeated the Vendéans was the sheer pressure of numbers. They chose to fight a large pitched battle at Chollet, on October 17, and were decisively defeated. Rather than disperse to their ravaged villages, many of them chose to cross the Loire into Brittany, hoping to bring the population there over to their side. But, though they won a few more victories, the Bretons never rose up. Cut off from their home base, the rebels were gradually worn down by vastly superior numbers and by December the revolt was as good as over.

Spain

During his futile attempt to dominate Europe, in the early years of the nineteenth century, Napoleon had to face two major guerrilla uprisings, both of which made substantial contributions to his eventual downfall. The first of these was in Spain, between 1808 and 1813. This particular campaign is worthy of special note in any history of guerrilla warfare, if only because it gave us the actual word 'guerrilla'. It means 'little war' and the actual Spanish word for one who participates in this type of conflict is '*guerrillero*'.

In October 1807, French troops first entered Spain. Although certain groups there, led notably by Godoy, the Chief Minister, and Ferdinand, the heir to the throne, had been courting Napoleon for their own ends, the crowns of Portugal and Spain respectively, Napoleon lured them to Bayonne and put his own brother, Joseph, on the throne, in June 1808. But already the Spanish people had suffered terribly under French rule, and in May there had been an abortive insurrection in Madrid in favour of Ferdinand. Attacks were also made on the occupying forces throughout the country, and numerous local *juntas*, committees of resistance, sprang up. On May 25, the Assembly of the province of Asturias took leadership of the revolt and declared war on Napoleon. In September a Central Junta was established at Aranjuez, but after a disastrous defeat at the battle of Ocaña, in November of the following year, it broke up and fled, to be replaced by a conservative Regency of Five.

In the early years the Spanish attempted to base their war of liberation around the regular army. In July 1808, they won a convincing victory at the battle of Bailén, but their success was in large part attributable to the appalling quality of the French troops on that particular field. Unfortunately the Spanish leaders failed to acknowledge this fact and Bailén created a positive mania for pitched battles, and a quite unwarranted faith in the capabilities of the Spanish regulars. They suffered defeat after defeat, most notably at Ocaña and Medellin, in March 1809. Luckily, Spanish resistance had two other long-term factors in its favour. Firstly, in 1808, the English had dispatched a force of 10,000 regulars to the Iberian peninsula, under Sir John Moore. Even though he was driven out the English were determined to maintain a large presence in the area, and they returned again in 1810. Secondly, the Spaniards' own war effort did not entirely depend on the regular army. There were also far more numerous forces of guerrillas all over the countryside. These did much to pin down substantial numbers of French troops, who might otherwise have been used against the English.

By 1809, many of the regular troops, especially those around Madrid, under Venegas and Cuesta, were acting as guerrillas. They remained for the most part holed up in the mountains of the Sierra Morena and made only occasional forays. At the same time, however, many of the organisers of the Spanish resistance were mistrustful of the anarchic spontaneity of the guerrilla movement proper and made great efforts to organise it along more regular lines. Fearful of any weakening of their already dubious authority, 'throughout the war, the government, whether Junta or Cadiz Regency, did everything in its power to maintain its authority over the guerrilla armies, to subordinate them to the armies in the field, and to give them regular military organisation.'[8] On December 2, 1808, an order was issued by the Central Junta which it was hoped would regularise the guerrilla struggle. The *partidas*, or guerrilla bands, were to have a fixed complement of 100 men, 50 if mounted; pay was to be given, and all troops were to submit to a regular military discipline. Also all guerrilla leaders were to take their orders from the generals commanding the regular units in a particular zone of operations.

For their part, the French were not particularly impressed. In 1810, as the tempo of guerrilla activity increased, Marshal Soult issued the following proclamation: 'There is no Spanish Army apart from that of His Catholic Majesty, Joseph Napoleon. All factions now in existence anywhere in the country, whatever their size and whoever leads them, shall therefore be treated as gangs of bandits ... All individual members of these groups caught sword in hand shall be summarily tried ... and shot.'[9] Nor did Napoleon himself think much of the guerrillas. One of his generals recalled him saying: 'As for the war in Spain itself, it is now little more than a matter of guerrilla contests. On the day the English are driven out of the Peninsula, there will be nothing left of the war but isolated bodies of rebels.'[10] But, despite the brutality of the French counter-insurgency operations, the revolt continued to grow. There were bands almost everywhere. In Andalusia there was El Montequero; in Aragon, Villacampa; in Asturias, Ballasteros; in Cantabria, Porlier and Longa; in Catalonia, Baron de Eroles; in Old Castille, Julian Sanchez; in Galicia, Marquerito; in Guadalajara, El Empicinado; in León, Capuchino; and in Navarre, Mina, the 'Student', and his uncle Espoz y Mina. In 1811 Joseph was moved to complain that: 'There have never been so many guerrilla bands as there now are in northern Spain.'[11]

By and large the war was of a minor guerrilla nature, in which the various bands concentrated on falling upon isolated French scouts, messengers and stragglers. Between 1810 and 1812, according to General Bigarré, the Spaniards killed an average of 100 Frenchmen every day. In some cases it required a couple of hundred cavalry men to take a message from one place to another, and that in a country where forage was extremely scarce. These constant attacks on their communication hampered the French very badly. Massena, in Portugal, went for three months without ever receiving any orders or news from Madrid, and the French regional commanders rarely had any idea of what their counterparts in other areas were doing. The Spanish, on the other hand, were always very well informed about the enemy's movements, and were able to disperse or advance accordingly. As a French soldier wrote in his memoirs: 'To carry messages or news they employed agile and vigorous young men, whom they placed near every inhabited place and in a suitable spot. There was always one of them at his post, eyes open and ears cocked, and as soon as he had received a message he would dart across fields to hand it to a comrade ... These messengers never fell into our hands.'[12]

Though most of the war was fought on this petty level of assassination and ambuscade, a few bands did go some way towards making the transition from guerrilla to mobile regular warfare, able to face small French forces in open battle. Perhaps the most successful leader in this respect was Espoz y Mina. For one thing he had greater financial resources than other guerrilla chiefs, and had a substantial revenue which was raised by levying a customs duty on all goods imported from France which had to pass through his zone of control. His commissariat too was surprisingly effective. As one Spaniard noted: 'Everywhere uniforms were secretly made for his soldiers, and the highest mountains as well as almost impassable defiles were the seat of arms manufactories, munitions dumps and hospitals. His sick and at times his wounded were cared for in villages and hamlets, and quite a few in the very houses where those who had caused their wounds were lodging.'[13] At the peak of his activity, he had some 8,000 men under his command and on at least one occasion, at Aibar in 1810, he defeated a French force in open battle. The more organised guerrillas were sometimes used as an auxiliary force during regular operations. One such occasion was in 1812 when Porlier and Longa struck from the mountains at several French coastal forts, in support of a British landing under Sir Brooke Popham.

In terms of English and Spanish historiography, the actual effectiveness of the Spanish guerrillas is a vexed question. For the English the guerrillas were of little importance, whilst for most Spanish writers Wellesley's effort was but a sideshow. It is perhaps safest to conclude that both sides have often seriously overstated their case. Without a doubt, Wellesley's task would have been much more difficult without the guerrillas, who pinned down thousands of French soldiers. On the other hand, had it not been for the existence of the English army – and, in the broadest strategic terms, the Russian, Prussian and Austrian armies – the Spanish effort would never have been adequate to the task of actually driving out the French. So far as one can judge, the weakness of the central leadership, and fragmentation of the struggle would have been serious handicaps had the Spanish been left completely to their own devices. But in a way such speculation is pointless. The Spanish struggle was taking place within the context of a broader continental conflict, and in this context it was sufficient for them to try simply to preserve what they could, in terms of self-respect as much as of property, and to wait for other powers to deal the actual death-blows. There seems to be little profit in criticising the Spaniards for not being able to put many of their men on the field of open battle, when all they had to do was to wait for other countries to fight those battles for them.

Prussia

The Spanish experience is also important in that it prompted some early theoretical speculation about the nature of guerrilla warfare. In 1810 and 1811, Karl von Clausewitz gave a series of lectures at the War Academy in

Berlin, in which he outlined the virtues of this type of warfare. In 1812, in his *Bekenntrusse*, he drew up a scheme for a Prussian partisan force in which all male citizens between the ages of eighteen and sixty, who were not serving with the regular army, would be armed with muskets, scythes and pitchforks. With their only uniform some kind of padded hat and provincial insignia, and carrying with them a bag of supplies, they were to devote themselves to 'hindering French officials, capturing detachments and attacking convoys, conducting ambushes and lending support to the regular army.'[14]

The most mature formulation of his views on guerrilla warfare is to be found in his *On War*, published posthumously. One of the chapters is entitled 'Arming the Nation', and in it Clausewitz was one of the first to note that guerrilla warfare was a unique means of harnessing the nationalistic fervour of a whole people, offering many inherent military advantages:

> '[with people's wars] the people who make judicious use of this means will gain a proportionate superiority over those who despise its use ... But the opinion may be advanced, that the resources swallowed up in people's wars might be more profitably employed, if used in providing other military means; no very deep investigation, however, is necessary to be convinced that these resources are for the most part not disposable, and cannot be utilised in an arbitrary manner at pleasure. One essential part, that is the moral element, is not called into existence until this kind of employment for it arises.'

For Clausewitz the key variable for determining the chances of success for a guerrilla war was the size of the country. Usually, guerrilla forces operate in small bands, scattered about the countryside. Thus: 'It follows from the very nature of the thing that defensive means thus widely dispersed, are not suitable to great blows requiring concentrated actions in time and space ... The more [the incumbent] Army spreads itself out, so much greater will be the effects of arming the nation. Like a slow, gradual heat it destroys the foundations of the enemy's Army.' He then goes on to make a list of the other key factors that will be favourable to the pursuance of a guerrilla strategy:

(1) That the war is carried on in the heart of the country.
(2) That it cannot be decided by a single catastrophe.
(3) That the theatre of war embraces a considerable extent of the country.
(4) That the national character is favourable to the measure.
(5) That the country is of a broken and difficult nature, either from being mountainous, or by reason of woods and marshes, or from the peculiar mode of cultivation in use.'

The rest of his remarks make up a description of the actual nature of a guerrilla war:

'[In a] people's war ... the principle of resistance exists everywhere but is nowhere tangible ... Armed peasantry cannot and should not be employed against the main body of the enemy's army ... They must not attempt to crack the nut, they must only gnaw on the surface and the borders ... Armed peasants are not to be driven before us in the same way as a body of soldiers who keep together like a herd of cattle ... When broken [they] disperse in all directions, for which no formal plan is required; through this circumstance, the march of every small body of troops in a mountainous, thickly wooded, or even broken country, becomes a service of a very dangerous character, for at any moment a combat may arise on the march ... The enemy has no other means to oppose the action of national levies except of detaching numerous parties to furnish escorts ... etc. In proportion as the first efforts of the national levies are small, so the detachments sent out will be weak in numbers, from the repugnance to a great dispersion of forces; it is on these weak bodies that the fire of a national war usually first properly kindles itself ... According to our idea of a people's war, it should, like a kind of nebulous vapoury essence, never condense into a solid body; otherwise the enemy sends an adequate force against this core [and] crushes it ... Another ... leading principle in the method of using such levies ... is that as a rule, with this great strategic means of defence, a tactical defence should seldom or never take place ... They may, and should ... defend the approaches to mountains, dykes, over marshes, river-passages, as long as possible; but when once they are broken, they should rather disperse, and continue their defence by sudden attacks, than concentrate and allow themselves to be shut up in some narrow last refuge in a regular defensive position.'

Clausewitz also made some allowance for the possibility of guerrilla forces being able to make at least some of the transition to a more regular mode of warfare. Referring again to his conception of the 'vapoury essence', he points out:

'Still it is necessary that this mist should collect at some points into denser masses ... These points are chiefly on the flanks of the enemy's theatre of war ... There the armament of the people should be organised into greater and more systematic bodies ... so as to give it the appearance of a regular force ... From these points the irregular character in the organisation of these bodies should diminish in proportion as they are employed more in the direction of the rear of the enemy, where he is exposed to their hardest blows.'

But it is most important to be clear that Clausewitz never foresaw the possibility of guerrilla alone being able to bring any war to a decisive conclusion. For him they could never be more than an ancillary to the operations of regular troops, organised along conventional lines. After comparing the growth of a guerrilla struggle to the spread of a moorland fire, he nevertheless felt it necessary to point out that:

> '[For] the flames of the conflagration [to] envelop the enemy's army, and compel it to evacuate the country to save itself from utter destruction ... we must suppose either a surface extent of the dominions invaded, exceeding that of any country in Europe except Russia, or suppose a disproportion between the strength of the invading army and the extent of the country, such as never occurs in reality. Therefore, to avoid following a [chimera], we must imagine a people's war always in combination with a war carried on by a regular army, and both carried on according to a plan embracing the operations of the whole.'[15]

It was this kind of ancillary guerrilla struggle that the Prussians hoped to wage against Napoleon during their War of Liberation. In October 1806, the Prussian Army was decisively defeated by the French at the battles of Saalfeld, Jena and Auerstadt. In July of the following year, after the Russian defeat at Friedland, the Prussian king was forced to sign a humiliating peace-treaty with Napoleon, at Tilsit. But the Prussian national spirit still burned in certain quarters, and a small group of prominent soldiers and statesmen attempted to rebuild the army and create a new will to resist. A Military Reorganisation Commission was set up and certain political reforms were enacted which it was hoped would give the people at large some stake in the country's future. Finally, in 1813, all Prussian citizens were declared liable for military service, and the line army was bolstered by the creation of *Landwehr* units, a type of militia.

The regular army and the *Landwehr* were also to have the support of the *Landsturm*, a guerrilla force of the whole people, very similar to that envisaged by Clausewitz in the *Bekenntrusse*. Other Prussian leaders had advocated some kind of guerrilla resistance to the French. In 1808 Gneisenau had stated that Prussia's only hope lay in a national insurrection and he consistently advocated this form of resistance. In 1811 Scharnhorst submitted a plan to the king which recommended the use of widespread guerrilla warfare, backed by existing regular forces in the fortresses. Boyen also called for such a mode of fighting, although he did acknowledge that it might need support from the Prussian regulars.

But the most distinctive feature was not simply that it envisaged the use of guerrillas merely as an auxiliary force to the regular units, but that the very formation of the guerrilla force was decreed from above. In this it was almost unique, as one of the most distinguishing features of a guerrilla insurgency, indeed one of the main reasons for this mode of warfare, is that it is the *spontaneous* resistance of an oppressed people. Thus, by definition, a guerrilla war can usually find enough popular support to sustain itself. But the Prussians did not necessarily have that support and embarked upon the contradictory course of trying to create a popular guerrilla army by decree.

On April 21, 1813, they enacted the creation of the *Landsturm*. All able-bodied men aged between 18 and 60 who were not already in the regular forces were to serve in it. They were not to wear uniforms as these would cause them to be recognised by the enemy. When the enemy approached, the inhabitants of a particular area were to flee their villages, organise under previously nominated officers and take refuge in the woods. From there they were to harass the enemy. As they retreated they were to carry off the corn, smash the casks, burn the mills, bridges and boats, and fill in the wells. 'For', in the words of the decree, 'it takes less to rebuild a village than to feed the enemy.' Gneisenau had an even more far-reaching notion of true guerrilla warfare. According to him, every male over the age of 17 should be armed, local officials of dubious loyalty were to be suspended, the property of cowards and traitors should be redistributed to war victims, and titles of nobility should lapse unless merited by distinguished war service.

But the effectiveness of these guerrilla forces was seriously undermined by their very creators. Because they were members of the ruling elite, they only wished, at the end of the war, for a return to the *status quo*. Thus they had no time for any popular struggle that would reveal explosive class tensions or provoke undue disrespect for authority and property. So from the beginning the *Landsturm*'s operations were hampered by numerous qualifications and regulations. The guerrillas themselves were to be under the command of the provincial authorities, civil and military. Only local units could be mobilised on the initiative of the local commander, and his appointment had to be endorsed by the governor of the province. Gatherings of several local units could only be sanctioned by army or corps commanders, or provincial military governors. Any assembly of the *Landsturm* without authority was to be punished as mutiny. On top of this all members had to swear to abide by the following articles of war: 'Any attack on, robbery or looting of, property in friendly territory, without orders from commanding generals and military governors, any attempt to evade taxes, duties, compulsory labour, or due obedience to local authorities resulting from or aided by, the arming or mobilisation of the *Landsturm*, will be mercilessly punished by death.'[16] After the first three months of its existence, the captains of the local units were to be chosen by the troops, but the decree also laid down that only landowners, state and local officials, and teachers were eligible to apply. It is small wonder that such a force, hamstrung by a total denial of local tactical initiative, a fanatical sense of respect for property, and the suppression of possible gifted local leaders, should last for barely three months. During its brief existence it represented a futile attempt to wage guerrilla warfare without true guerrillas, people's war without the people.

Russia

On June 24, 1812, Napoleon and his *Grande Armée* crossed the Niemen and marched into Russia. He failed to encircle their army around Vilna, as he had intended, but nevertheless managed to drive them out of old Poland. On September 7 he defeated the Russian army at Borodino, and on October 15 he entered Moscow. Even before this, however, some Russian soldiers had come to the conclusion that the surest way to drive out the French was to allow them to overextend their lines of communication, to limit their retreat to the route they had already devastated during their advance, and to harass them continually with guerrilla detachments. Like the Prussians, certain Russians had drawn lessons from the Spanish experience. In 1812, during the early stages of Napoleon's invasion, General Chuykevich wrote a book called *Reflections on the War of 1812*, in which he cited the Spanish resistance as a model resistance struggle:

'The rapid successes of the French arms in Spain are explained by the fact that the inhabitants of that country, burning with desire to take revenge on the French, relied too much on their personal bravery and the justice of their cause. Hurriedly mobilised recruits were opposed to the French armies and were beaten by an enemy superior in numbers and experience. These disastrous lessons induced the brave Spaniards to change their methods of fighting. They magnanimously chose a protracted struggle that would be to their advantage. Avoiding general battles with the French forces, they divided their men into small units ... frequently interrupted communications with France, destroyed the enemy's supplies, and exhausted him with ceaseless marches ... In vain did the French captains cross Spain from one end to the other, conquering cities and entire regions.'[17]

Others, notably General Pfuhl and Barclay de Tolly, were in favour of a prolonged retreat that would overextend the French communications. As the latter noted: 'If I were commander-in-chief I would avoid a decisive battle, and would carry out a retreat in such a way that the French would find in place of victory a second Poltava.'[18] Eventual Russian policy combined the two strategies. After falling back for some months, drawing the French deeper into Russia, they counter-attacked, but Kutuzov, the Russian commander, chose to avoid a full-scale pitched battle. Between November 14 and 18, for example, as the French were falling back, he chose to fight 10 separate minor engagements rather than risk concentrating all his forces for one decisive encounter.

But he was also forced to use guerrilla bands to help him in his policy of continually harrying the enemy. One of the most famous guerrilla commanders, General Davidoff, had suggested the use of such troops five days before

Borodino, and a few days after that battle he had raised his own unit. Other important bands had fought under Colonel Kudashev and Captains Seslavin, Figner and Naryshkin. Their record was a fine one, and they undoubtedly contributed much to the eventual Russian victory. As Davidoff wrote, some years later:

'[The] partisans, destroying wagon-loads of food and ammunition, struck most effectively at the enemy and . . . going in front of and surrounding the French army during its retreat from Moscow to the Niemen, fought day and night, destroyed bridges, cut passes, and by continual forays disturbed the rest periods that were so important to troops worn out by hunger, cold and forced marches.'[19]

Nor did the guerrilla activity cease when the French were driven out of Russia. In Poland, Saxony and Prussia, during 1813, leaders like Chernyshev, Benckendorf and Tettenborn continually harried the French. In Saxony, in August and September, General Tilleman led a flying column of guerrillas who operated in close conjunction with the regular forces.

Indeed the relationship of almost all the guerrilla bands with the regular forces is the most important characteristic of the Russian experience. In this respect it has much more in common with what happened in Prussia than with the Spanish resistance, which it was supposedly emulating. For, from the very beginning, the Russian leaders, notably Kutuzov, were very worried about the partisans and the evils inherent in their freedom from central control. Throughout the war the Russian commander rarely explicitly included them in his strategy. When Davidoff's idea was first suggested to him he only allowed the former to detach a mere 130 men with which to form a guerrilla band. Kutuzov was even more afraid of Davidoff's other plan which was to use the small bands of Cossacks and light cavalry taken from the line army as the foci of general peasant guerrilla warfare. To the Russian commander there seemed too much doubt about what these armed groups of peasants would do after the French had been expelled. For him it was more than likely that they would use these arms to turn upon their landlords and attempt to throw off the bondage of serfdom.

In some areas the peasants were successfully mobilised. Even before Borodino there had been isolated incidents of peasant bands turning on the invader. After the battle, one soldier, Private Chetvertakov, single-handedly organised the peasantry in the Gzhatsk region. He kept up a permanent detachment of 300 men and for large-scale raids was sometimes able to put as many as 4,000 other peasants into the field. But he was a known troublemaker within his regiment and the authorities looked on his activities with the deepest suspicion. In November he was obliged to return to his regiment.

Another guerrilla commander who successfully mobilised the peasants was Captain Naryshkin, in charge of a band of light cavalry around Klin. He soon began to distribute arms to the surrounding population and they became enthusiastic participants in his operations. But once again the central authorities were fearful, as Naryshkin himself wrote later:

'[I] received an order, inspired by mendacious reports and base slander, to disarm peasants and execute by firing squads those convicted of rebellion. Surprised by this order, so unworthy of the magnanimous conduct of the peasants, I replied that I could not disarm hands I had myself armed and who were seeking to destroy my country's enemies, nor treat as rebels men who sacrificed their lives to defend their freedom, wives and homes.'[20]

On the whole, then, despite the frequent spontaneous enthusiasm of the peasantry and a widespread desire to participate in the liberation of their country, the Russian leaders severely repressed their efforts. The only guerrilla activity they were prepared to tolerate, and that most grudgingly, was the use of bands taken from the regular military establishment, commanded by regular officers, and as much under the control as possible of the high command. This characteristic of the Russian experience is brought out by Davidoff, who some years later wrote a short book entitled *An Essay on Partisan Warfare*.

Throughout the book Davidoff treats guerrilla warfare as a mode of combat to be undertaken by particular types of *regular* troops, detached specially for this purpose. For him the ideal guerrilla unit was one of about 1,500 Cossacks accompanied by two light horse-artillery pieces. Moreover, these troops, although allowed certain tactical flexibility, are to operate within areas previously assigned to them, and are at all times to keep in touch with the nearest regular army headquarters. There is hardly any mention of guerrilla operations carried on by the population at large, and in this book Davidoff seems rather to have lost sight of his original vision of using the detached regulars to raise up the peasantry. His only reference to the population as a whole is when he makes the point that it is important to maintain good relations with them and not indulge in plundering. At one point he speaks of the necessity to set up forward observation posts in the villages, and notes that for this it is vital that there exist 'friendly relations with the inhabitants, and the exercise of the most impartial justice should conflicts arise between them and the Cossacks.' Later he says that on occasions it might be useful to send out small groups of guerrillas to attack stragglers and couriers. 'But as these small detachments are no longer under the eyes of their leader and could commit many crimes, or even show cruelty to the inhabitants, [this could] upset the countryside and [deny] the advantages which one gets from maintaining a good understanding with them.'[21] This is a crucial point for all guerrilla forces, and Davidoff might have done well to dwell on it in more detail.

In fact, Davidoff largely ignores all the social and political factors implicit in any resort to guerrilla warfare and his book is only of interest as a discussion of the technical aspects of this type of struggle. In this respect he brings up several points that are already familiar. One of the most interesting of these is his assertion that an effective guerrilla war should be both *offensive* and *defensive*. In other words, whilst the bulk of one's activities should be aimed at harrying the enemy's own army, there should also be sufficient guerrilla units kept in reserve to be used to defend one's own lines of communication and guard against guerrilla-type attacks by the enemy's light cavalry. For the rest Davidoff deals with tactical principles that have already been touched upon.

For him, the principal aim of the guerrillas is always the disruption of the enemy's supply lines. 'Parties of light troops, ceaselessly harassing the enemy's lines of communication, slipping between his units, fall upon the artillery parks, which they destroy, along with the convoys of food, ammunition etc ...'[22] Because they are only acting as an auxiliary to the regular army, another of their most important tasks is 'to send to the army prompt and accurate information about the movements and dispositions of the enemy.'[23] The other duties of a guerrilla group consist of the following:

> 'To destroy ... the detachments moving to rejoin the enemy army; to stop couriers and free prisoners; to burn all the magazines, hospitals, pharmacies and other establishments in the rear of the enemy army; to give prompt notice of the enemy's partial or general retreat, of reinforcements that are arriving, of the location of his supply dumps and the places where he is regrouping those ... [units] which have suffered excessive casualties in battle; of the new magazines he has set up ...; to increase the obstacles which could slow the enemy's retreat; to avoid the attacks of the enemy, and to attack him at those points where he is least expecting it.'[24]

Guerrilla units should only attack when they are superior in numbers and in an advantageous position, bearing in mind 'the simple truths that "ten men are stronger than one", and that, because of human nature itself, a man is braver when he is facing to the front rather than to his rear or his flanks.'[25] But guerrillas should never participate in pitched battles for 'the strength of the guerrilla consists more in his skill and talent than in his shock-value, and his most certain ally is surprise.'[26] They should not allow themselves to be tied down to any fixed base, however useful this might seem for the storing of provisions and booty, and the care of the wounded. For the enemy will eventually be able to locate and destroy such a base.[27] Rather the guerrilla leader should chose a series of temporary bases 'where the sick and wounded will be left for a time, [and which] will only serve as an intermediary link between the band and the army, and will in no way be regarded as a base of operations.'[28] Finally, all the movements of the various guerrilla bands are to be co-ordinated by a central authority:

'Many people will blame me for having limited the guerrilla's freedom of action, and will tell me that complete freedom is the very essence of any action which, at the mercy of circumstance, calls for vigorous, swift movements and speedy decisions by the commander ... But these limits on the freedom of action of the bands only apply to the choice of ... the theatre of operations, and in no way affect their mode of warfare ... How can one give the activities of the bands any common purpose, if they are neither linked one with another, nor with those of the army? Without such a common purpose, partisan warfare will bring no glory to the leaders of the bands, no articles for the journalists, nor any booty for the soldiers.'[29]

Haiti

One outbreak of guerrilla warfare in this period spanned both the Republic and the early years of the First Empire. It was another slave revolt and set in motion a train of events that eventually led to the island's independence. The full story of the war years, from 1791 to 1802, is rather complex, involving national rivalries between the French, British and Spanish, tensions between the various racial groups, whites, mulattoes and blacks, and even divisions within each group. There is no space here to examine these shifting alignments in any detail and I shall risk oversimplifying things a little by dividing the war into three main phases.

The first phase began in August 1791 when there was an insurrection of negro slaves against the plantation owners and the white ruling elite in St Domingo, then part of the French empire. A hundred thousand slaves were involved, and within two months over a thousand plantations had been destroyed. At the beginning the revolt was a simple mass uprising, characterised more by pillage and brutality than any kind of tactical method or central direction, and as the French got over their initial panic they succeeded, by setting up a fortified cordon, in confining the revolt to the North Province. Then the slaves themselves began to produce their own leaders and organisation. Notable amongst these were Jean-François, Biassou and Toussaint Louverture. During this phase the negroes' mode of warfare still centred on the pitched battle, though even so it had more in common with the tactics of Arminius against the Romans than with those of the European armies of the eighteenth century. As an anonymous contemporary wrote: 'The negroes never mass in the open: a thousand blacks will never await in line of battle the attack of a hundred whites. They first advance with a frightful clamour ... When they have arrived just out of gunshot ... [they] range themselves in such a manner that they appear six times as numerous as they really are.'[30] They achieved this effect by arranging themselves in separate groups, wherever possible taking advantage of the cover of the woods. Their basic aim was to surround the whites and then overwhelm them in one swift rush. If the enemy remained unshaken, the negroes would swiftly retreat.

But, from the very beginning, Louverture was keen to build up a small, disciplined regular army rather than have to rely on achieving overwhelming numerical superiority. To this end he took only the best recruits, and in July 1792 his army numbered only some 500 men.

Louverture largely succeeded in his purpose. During the second phase of the fighting, from 1794–98, when he allied himself with the French revolutionaries against the British and the Spanish, the core of his army was composed of very competent troops. A British officer described them, and one is reminded of a kind of regularised Jamaican Maroon:

'Each general officer had a demi-brigade ... They performed, excellently well, several manoeuvres applicable to their method of fighting. At a whistle a whole brigade ran three or four hundred yards; and then, separating, threw themselves flat on the ground, changing to their backs and sides, and at all times keeping up a strong fire; after this they formed in an instant again into their wonted regularity. This single manoeuvre is executed with such facility and precision, as totally prevents cavalry from charging them in bushy or hilly country.'[31]

But Louverture always deployed these units within the context of a general guerrilla strategy. His troops were able to move extremely quickly, as they took no baggage with them, nor even much clothing. On one occasion they covered 64 kilometres in a single day, through mountainous territory and with only a rough trail to guide them. In the first few months of the operations against the British, Louverture fought over 200 encounters, driving the enemy from the greater part of the North and West Provinces. As one of his new French allies wrote:

'He disappears ... as if by magic. Now he reappears again where he is least expected. He seems to be ubiquitous. One never knows where his army is, what it subsists on, how he manages to recruit it, in what mountainous fastness he has hidden his supplies and his treasury. He, on the other hand, seems perfectly informed concerning everything that goes on in the enemy camp.'[32]

In July 1795 the Spanish signed a peace treaty with the French, and by early 1798 the British were confined to a narrow coastal strip in the west. And this though they rarely had less than 20,000 men on the island, whilst Louverture had only 10 demi-brigades of 1,600 men each. A few months later the British held only Môle St Nicholas in the north and Jérémie in the south. In October 1798 the British quit the island altogether, contenting themselves, some months later, with signing a commercial treaty with the victors.

The third phase of the liberation struggle began in 1802 when Napoleon decided to reclaim the island and re-impose slavery. The French troops were commanded by General Leclerc, who launched a three-pronged attack on the blacks, forcing Louverture to take refuge in the Arborite range, at Crête-à-Pierrot. One of his most important subordinates was Dessalines who on one occasion outlined the benefits of the new resort to guerrilla tactics:

'The French will not be able to remain long in St Domingo. They will do well at first, but will soon fall ill and die like flies ... If Dessalines surrenders a hundred times he will deceive them a hundred times ... You will see that when the French are few we shall harass them, we shall beat them, we shall burn the harvests and retire to the mountains. They will not be able to guard the country and they will have to leave.'[33]

This proved substantially to be the case. The blacks retreated into mountain bases and various important guerrilla bands sprang up under leaders like Macaya at Limbé, Sylla in the mountains of Plaisance, Sans-Souci at Ste Suzanne, Belair at the entrance to the Grand Cahos mountains. As an early historian of the movement wrote:

'In proportion as the French army forced its way into the interior of the country, which was broken by gorges, mountains, and defiles, the conflict became more and more difficult. The soldiers were vexed and harassed at having to do with a flying enemy, who, constantly fighting in ambush, inflicted wounds or death as if from an invisible cause, with perfect impunity to themselves ... from the speed with which they flew into well-known retreats.'[34]

Harassed by these tactics, and by raging disease, the French had little hope of defeating the resistance movement. But then, for reasons which are by no means clear, Louverture decided to enter into negotiations with them. This he did, but was then betrayed by several of his important generals, notably Dessalines, and Leclerc was able to arrest and imprison Louverture. These generals then took over the task of suppressing any blacks who still attempted to fight against the French, and under the guidance of Leclerc's successor, Rochambeau, a veritable reign of terror was instituted against them.

1. A. Taylor, *The Tragedy of an Army: La Vendée 1793*. Hutchinson, 1913, p 318
2. G. Plaissier and F. Pernoud, *The French Revolution*, Secker and Warburg, 1960. pp 298–99
3. Taylor, *op cit*, p 92
4. *ibid*, p 138
5. *ibid*, p 148
6. *ibid*, pp 166–67
7. *ibid*, p 198
8. G. H. Lovett, *Napoleon and the Birth of Modern Spain*, New York University Press, 1965, Vol 2, p 675
9. W. N. Hargreaves-Mawdsley (ed), *Spain under the Bourbons*, Macmillan, 1973, p 233
10. M. Glover, *Legacy of Glory*, Leo Cooper, 1972, p 263
11. ibid p 209
12. Lovett, *op cit*, p 681
13. *ibid*, p 717
14. R. Parkinson, *Clausewitz*, Wayland, 1970, p 135
15. K. von Clausewitz (trans Col J. J. Graham), *On War*, Routledge and Kegan Paul, 1966, Vol 2, pp 341–9
16. W. M. Simon, *The Failure of the Prussian Reform Movement 1807–19*, Cornell University Press, Ithaca, 1955, p 170
17. E. Tarlé, *Napoleon's Invasion of Russia 1812*, Allen and Unwin, 1942, p 246
18. A. A. Lobanov-Rostovsky, *Russia and Europe 1789–1825*, Duke University Press, Durham, 1947, p 202
19. Davidoff, *La Guerre des Partisans*, J. Correard, Paris, 1841, pp 38 and 50
20. Tarlé, *op cit*, p 252
21. Davidoff, *op cit*, p 96
22. *ibid*, p 50
23. *ibid*, p 55
24. *ibid*, p 70
25. *ibid*, p 85
26. *ibid*, p 99
27. *ibid*, pp 71 and 94
28. *ibid*, p 82
29. *ibid*, pp 64–65
30. R. Korngold, *Citizen Toussaint*, Gollancz, 1944, pp 67–68
31. *ibid*, p 74
32. *ibid*, p 93
33. C. R. L. James, *The Black Jacobins*, Secker and Warburg, 1938, p 261
34. J. R. Beard, *The Life of Toussaint Louverture*, London, 1853, p 181

CHAPTER 4

The 19th Century: Europe and America

Resistance to the Turks

Throughout the preceding years sporadic resistance to the Turks by the *hai-duks*, *pandours* (in Roumania), and *klefts* (in Greece) had continued, within its traditional limits of small-scale banditry. But in the nineteenth century certain of these groups were subsumed within more ambitious, and self-consciously political movements of national liberation, and the anti-Turkish struggle occasionally flared up into full-scale guerrilla warfare.

One such occasion was the Greek War of Independence, from 1821 to 1829. During the eighteenth and early nineteenth centuries there had arisen in Greece various types of irregular bands, who were engaged in continuous internecine warfare. There were the *klefts* who, like the *haiduks*, were bandits preying upon the Turks and their supporters. There were the *kapi*, who were irregulars employed by the Greek primates to counter the depredations of the *klefts*. Finally, there were the *armatoli*, employed by the Turks for the same purpose. By 1821, however, the rivalry between these various groups had become secondary to a common hatred of Turkish rule. In March of that year, Konstantinos Ipsilantis led an insurrection against the Turks in the Greek Principalities. He insisted on meeting the enemy in open battle and was thus easily defeated, but his example was sufficient to rouse the leaders of the bands elsewhere in Greece to widespread revolt.

From 1821 to 1825 they waged a successful guerrilla campaign and resisted all Turkish attempts to subdue them. Geography and terrain dominated the campaigning. The Turks had to enter Greece by Makrinoros in the west or Thermopylae in the east and communications across the northern half were severely hampered by the Pindus mountains. Similarly, if the Turks wished to drive south into the Peloponnese (Morea), they had to cross the Gulf of Corinth or force the mountainous defiles of the Corinthian isthmus. Their navy was not adequate to the former task, whilst the latter, like operations in Thessaly, was always hampered by the activities of the Greek guerrillas.

'The immediate cause of their successful resistance ... is to be found in the peculiar nature of the country; in the sufficiency of the Greek troops to the defence of their mountains against an enemy who had no infantry of a similar kind; ... in the unfitness of cavalry alone ... to retain the country which it overran, and to keep up the communication between the districts to the southward of Mount Oeta and the positions in Thessaly, where alone they had any magazine; but above all, it was derived from the great defensive strength of the approaches to the Peloponnesus ...'[1]

However, although the guerrilla bands had the perfect terrain for their activities, their mode of organisation was a great handicap. Though they could keep up harassing operations *ad infinitum*, it was almost impossible either to keep the bands in the field long enough, or bring sufficient men to one point to inflict a decisive defeat on the Turks. One Englishman who visited Greece at this time gave a succinct analysis of the weaknesses inherent in this reliance upon numerous autonomous bandit-chiefs. Though operations were nominally under the command of the most important *kleft* leaders, or *Kapitanei*, 'the inferior commanders ... [were] elected by the voluntary suffrage of the provincial militia that served under them. Thus each village had its petty chief who was allowed to command while he made himself agreeable and no longer.' In a report of September 1823, to the Greek Committee in London, he noted that:

'Although nearly the whole male population ..., capable of carrying arms, is provided with pistols and attagans, the number which can take the field is very limited, depending almost entirely on the means possessed by the leaders, each of whom has hitherto been unable to employ more followers than he could provide for out of his personal resources, and the scanty and precarious aid of the government ... There is not more than a third of the number ... supplied with sufficient clothing to shelter them from the inclemencies of mountain warfare ... They often march forty miles a day, almost invariably sleep in the open air, and frequently pass two or three days without any other food than the herbs of the field ... The Greek army receives no pay whatsoever. The general mode, adopted by the chiefs, is to advance a small sum to each soldier previous to entering the field: with this he provides himself with bread, tobacco and whatever other necessaries he may require, as far as the supply will go.'[2]

Thus, throughout the war, the Greek effort was seriously undermined by rivalries between the individual leaders, which sometimes became open civil war, and by the inability to raise a force that was capable of fighting sustained operations. In 1826 the eminent British soldier, Sir Charles Napier, pointed out that guerrilla warfare of this type had its limitations. He suggested that they raise a force of regulars and take up prepared positions in Sparta:

'If beaten at Sparta I would go to Malvasia and abide a siege ... The enemy ... would find it very difficult, as I would leave all the irregular troops under an active partisan in the mountains. They would terribly infest his supplies ... Thus you may always oblige the enemy to attack you in your own position with your back to a fortress, thus uniting offensive war with defensive positions, which is the secret of mountain warfare – a warfare that requires more science and better-drilled troops than any other. Peasants may maintain a long war in their mountains without science, but no results are produced.'[3]

As the war progressed the Greek leaders made some attempts to regularise their forces but the administrative and financial weaknesses of the government, coupled with the fierce independence of the guerrilla chiefs, made things very difficult. The first line regiment was set up in 1822, and there was also a Philhellene Legion, of European volunteers, under the command of a German, General Normann. But these were isolated efforts and it was not until 1828 that Kapodistrias began to regularise the mustering, pay and supply of the guerrillas. In February 8,000 of them were summoned to Troezene where they were divided into Chiliarchies (regiments) of 1,000 men. Officers were named by the President and a regular commissariat and paymaster's department were introduced. In the autumn of 1829 further reorganisation took place under the guidance of a French soldier, Colonel Gérard.

But by this time the war was over. This raises a very important general point about the ability of guerrilla forces to wage a successful liberation struggle. Although the Greeks had been unable to take the war beyond the stage of uncoordinated harassing operations, and were thus unlikely to have succeeded by their own efforts in driving the Turks out, the very existence of their struggle brought them the recognition of various European powers. A combination of the respect for ancient Greek culture and the geopolitical significance of this part of Europe, prompted France, Britain and Russia to take an interest in the struggle. In July 1827 the three countries signed the Treaty of London, which demanded an armistice in Greece, and that the country should be accorded autonomy, though still as a tributary state within the Turkish empire. A little later the Turkish fleet was destroyed at Navarino by the Allied fleet under Admiral Codrington. In April 1828 Russia declared war on Turkey and the latter was forced to withdraw her troops from Greece. After the Turkish defeat the three powers again debated the future of Greece, and by a Convention signed in May 1832 it was established as an independent kingdom, with an imported king. Thus, though the Greeks had severely embarrassed the Turks with their protracted guerrilla war, in the last analysis their success is only to be explained in terms of the diplomatic and military pressure that the other great powers of Europe were able to bring to bear.

Resistance to the Turks continued in other parts of Eastern Europe. *Haiduk* activity was prevalent throughout the Balkans at all times. In Serbia, in 1802, there was a very significant movement to the woods and mountains, and guerrilla activity increased considerably. In 1804 the standard of revolt was raised in the forests of Šumadija, south of Belgrade, and the stock-rearer George Petrović (Black George) was elected as the leader. But the Serbians became over-ambitious and attempted a too precipitate transition to regular military operations. They won three pitched battles in 1806 and captured Belgrade. But in 1809 they attempted a four-pronged offensive which failed disastrously. The Serbs were forced to rely again on minor harassment and the movement was effectively quelled by a major Turkish offensive in 1813.

There was also considerable *haiduk* activity in Bulgaria. In that country there were also certain leaders who wished to transform this sporadic resistance into a national uprising, and throw out the Turks once and for all. One such was Georgi Rakovsky who came to prominence after the Crimean War. He admired the *haiduks* but wanted to bring their *četi* (*četa* – armed band) within the framework of a centralised revolutionary organisation. This would recruit and train a band of picked guerrillas, on foreign soil, who would then be sent into Bulgaria to try and stir up revolt. In 1861 he drew up a *Plan for the Liberation of Bulgaria*, which envisaged a band of 1,000 men, of whom 100 were to be cavalry, and who would also take along two small cannon and two surgeons. Once in Bulgaria it was expected that the band would soon attract followers and eventually a force of some 50,000 men would be built up. In 1867 he issued a *Law on the Četi*, which 'strongly reflects the romanticism of the *haiduk* ideal ... On joining the *četa* its members were to eschew drunkenness, lying, stealing from one's comrades, and fornication; always to obey the *voivoda* and standard-bearer ... and to be content with whatever pay the *voivoda* thought fit to give.'[4] On three occasions the Bulgarians attempted to put this strategy into effect. In 1862 a *četa* under Panaiot Khitov was sent into the mountains between Sliven and Turnovo. In 1867 two *četi* under Khitov and Filip Totyu crossed into Bulgaria. Each had between 30 and 40 men, and the Turks dismissed them as mere 'bandits'. In 1868 a *četa* was set up under the ex-*haiduks* Hadzhi Dimiter and Stefan Karadzhata. It entered Bulgaria with 120 men, but in the course of a series of small skirmishes with the Turks almost all of them were killed. This unsuccessful attempt to raise the people by importing revolution from outside prompted Vasil Levsky, a future leading Bulgarian nationalist, and a member of one of the 1867 *četi*, to write:

'We encountered great difficulties in the mountains last summer because the people ... did not want to help us ... No-one has taken the trouble to prepare [them] – that is why they do not know what to do – To prepare the people with *četi* is both dangerous and useless; it alerts the Turks and creates even greater difficulties for the people's cause.'[5]

It is a pity perhaps that Ernesto Guevara had not heard of Levsky when he undertook his suicidal mission to Bolivia, for this statement is a fascinating fore-runner of the kind of arguments that centred around his and Regis Debray's theories about the prospects for guerrilla warfare in Latin America.[6]

In 1876 the nationalists changed their tactics and began infiltrating agents into Bulgaria, who were secretly to prepare the people for a swift, nationwide insurrection. The Gyurgevo Committee organised the population of four separate mountain regions, and managed to attract a good deal of popular support. They manufactured their own arms, and in one region even had their own secret postal service, police force and night patrols. The important question, however, was what exactly to do with this secret organisation. A conference was held at Oborishté, and one of the participants has described the debate over tactics:

> '[Some held] that the best course would be to form bands of resolute men who would take refuge in the mountains and from there descend, as opportunity offered, and harass the enemy, while the population at large remained peaceful ... But the majority ... advocated the *levée en masse* of the whole population [and] maintained that if the bands took to the Balkans the Turkish authorities would have an excellent pretext for regarding them as mere brigands, and would send large forces of regular troops against them, and so each band would be pursued and destroyed piecemeal.'[7]

So the conference decided against guerrilla warfare and opted for a national insurrection in which the whole people would mobilise at certain points and fall upon the key towns of their region. This they did in April 1876, but after a few initial successes the Turks were able to pin down the insurgents in the towns they had seized and annihilate them at their leisure. Like the Greeks, the Bulgarians owed their eventual independence more to the efforts of the European powers than to the efficacy of their revolutionary methods. In 1878, by the Treaty of Berlin, Bulgaria was made a vassal principality and eastern Roumelia an autonomous province. In 1885 the two were united in a bloodless coup.

Towards the end of the nineteenth century the policies of the new Greek and Bulgarian governments came into conflict over another Balkan region that was seeking to throw off the Turkish yoke. This was Macedonia that had sizable numbers of Greeks and Bulgarians within its borders, and to which both countries laid claim. It was the Bulgarians and the Bulgarian Macedonians who made the first significant moves towards translating the discontent of the people into full-scale guerrilla warfare. In 1895 the so-called Officers' Organisation in Bulgaria sent 800 *haiduks* and others over the border into Macedonia to initiate guerrilla operations. The attempt failed and in 1896 certain

Bulgarians decided that it would be necessary to organise the people before trying to start an open war. Gotzé Deltchev and Damian Gruev set up the Internal Macedonian Revolutionary Organisation (IMRO), with the aim of building a state within a state, and undermining the Turkish administration. By the turn of the century they had achieved remarkable success. IMRO members were recruited in each village, usually in groups of about 10. Each group sent its representative to the local committees who in turn sent someone to the district committees. These were all elective and received their instructions from the central committee. Also, 'independent bands of *haiduks* submitted to IMRO's control, becoming its police force, protecting arms convoys, punishing malefactors and executing spies condemned by secret revolutionary tribunals ... Soon there were regular couriers, guides, a revolutionary postal service, and half a dozen hectographed news sheets.'[8] IMRO's initial aim had been to stop short of offensive military operations and concentrate upon laying the foundations of a future independent Macedonian state. But in the first months after its foundation the very existence of the organisation was threatened by betrayals to the Turks, and their discovery of certain arms caches and administrative records. The revolutionaries were forced to adopt an overt military posture to protect themselves from the Turks:

> 'New duties and functions were added to the chetas until gradually they became the mobile centres of the county and district revolutionary committee. Finally they became the axis around which all revolutionary activity revolved ... The whole structure of IMRO changed ... It changed into a military machine that took possession of the forests, revolutionised the villages ... and openly shared authority with the Sultan in Macedonia.[9]

These aspects of IMRO's organisation raise two points of great significance for the future development of guerrilla warfare. Firstly, IMRO paid a good deal of attention to the building up of a solid organisational base among the people. They constituted what was almost a state within the state, by subverting people's loyalty to the Turkish regime and effectively removing them from Ottoman administrative control. Fifty years later, French counter-insurgency theorists were to note the importance of this technique, the establishment of what they called *parallel hierarchies*, in explaining the success of the Chinese, Vietnamese and Algerian guerrillas. The second point concerns the way in which the military struggle came to be integrated with the political, and the bands emerged as the foci of all activity, their military successes laying the foundation for further political development. Again, it will be seen how this type of revolutionary strategy has been basic to more modern successful guerrilla movements.

At first IMRO had substantial military success. It was engaged in constant engagements with the Turks and inflicted severe casualties.[10] In 1903 a widespread uprising was organised in an attempt completely to overwhelm the Turkish presence. The local bands were grouped together in units of 70 to 100 men and upwards of 15,000 insurgents were mobilised. In one district, Bitolje, it was estimated that one in every six adult males was in arms. Between August 2 and November 1 the guerrillas fought 203 engagements, in which they killed over 3,000 Turks for the loss of 948 of their own men. Unfortunately this massive outburst of revolutionary violence forced the Turks to take vigorous counter-measures. Over 250,000 men were poured into the area and a judicious mixture of terror and extensive military operations quelled the uprising before the end of the year. But guerrilla activity did not cease completely, and the Turkish authorities were involved in continual skirmishes and ambushes for the next six years. One American left a record of his adventures with a band of IMRO guerrillas, or *comitadjis* (committee men) as they were often known. At one stage he describes the clothing and equipment of a typical *comitadji*:

'We wore two sets of underclothing ... It is extremely cold in the mountains after dark, and woollen underwear is an absolute necessity ... Each man carried a cartridge belt containing 150 rounds of rifle ammunition; a web belt carrying 50 rounds of revolver cartridges; a French seven-shooter and a Männlicher carbine and knife-bayonet. The revolvers were hung round the neck on a cord, so that in close hand-to-hand fighting a man could drop his revolver and apply both hands to his bayonet.'

Later on the writer describes the laying of a typical ambush of a small Turkish patrol:

'We descended the mountain to a clearing on the road ... It was ... covered with fallen tree-trunks and tangled underbrush. Along the edge, we constructed a series of rifle-pits, each large enough to contain one or two men, and so placed that the fire from one pit enfiladed that of another ... It was a very deadly ambuscade. The pits were hollows scooped out of the ground with a bayonet, and reinforced by logs and small boulders. These, in turn, were masked by branches and scrub pines.'[11]

But if IMRO was in many respects a very modern type of guerrilla movement, it was also bedevilled by the most traditional and vicious Balkan rivalries. Not only did it have to tackle the Turks, but it was also engaged in continuous hostilities with other guerrilla bands. Up to 1903 these were mainly Bulgarian, sent into Macedonia by those Bulgarians who were totally opposed to the idea of an independent Macedonian state. In 1903 the Bulgarian Supremists, as they were known, and IMRO, or the Internalists, came to some kind of truce. At this moment, however, the Greeks began to intervene because of their total opposition to Macedonia either achieving independence or being absorbed into Bulgaria. Under the guidance of men like Lambros Koromilas, Pavlos Melas and Konstantinos Mazarakis, bands were sent into Macedonia to seek out and destroy the IMRO guerrillas. They were almost always led by Greek officers, but the rank-and-file were usually Greek Macedonians or IMRO deserters. There were 11 major bands, which could be split into smaller groups when necessary. Their basic strategy was to carve out a salient in the west of Macedonia and from there set out on long-term raids. Between 1905 and 1908 they gradually established a supremacy over the IMRO guerrillas. Whilst they lost about 650 fighting men, IMRO 'casualties were certainly many times larger than the Greek.'[12] The pressures on the *comitadjis* were increased in 1909 when the Turks renewed their campaign of repression and terror. They set about a systematic disarming of the population and declared all Macedonian adult males liable for compulsory military service. Attacked by both Greeks and Turks, deprived of arms and new recruits, IMRO almost completely collapsed.

The Carlist War in Spain

In 1823 King Ferdinand returned to Spain from exile. He ruled until his death 10 years later but his vaccillating policies had offended many of the arch-reactionary churchmen in Spain, the so-called Apostolic party, and even during his reign many of them began to form a clique around Ferdinand's brother, Carlos. When the former died the throne passed to his young daughter, Isabel, under the regency of his wife, Christina. But this represented a break with traditional notions of succession, previously based upon the Salic Law, and Carlos and his party insisted that he was the rightful heir to the throne, and on this pretext rose up in rebellion.

The centres of revolt were the Basque provinces, Navarre and Catalonia, particularly the Maestrazgo, the rocky foothills of the Pyrenees. Until 1835 the Spanish government underestimated the seriousness of the revolt and did not bother to dispatch an army to the north. At first this policy seemed fairly justified in that Carlist activities were limited to a few raids and risings in the smaller towns. But the insurgents soon began to set up rudimentary administrative machinery, as well as an officers' academy and several small munitions factories. Even more importantly, the Carlists acquired the services of a brilliant guerrilla tactician, Tomás Zumalacárregui. He had served under Mina during the war against Napoleon, and it is clear that his experiences then had taught him much about effective guerrilla warfare. When he arrived in the Carlist camp he found a mere 800 men for him to command. By the time of his death in June 1834, his army contained 35,000 soldiers. They were, moreover, disciplined soldiers, for Zumalacárregui was insistent about the value of training and the necessity for orders to be instantly obeyed. Many of the soldiers even had crude uniforms, which were turned out at the rate of 300 a day from small workshops in the Carlist base areas. But the troops always travelled light. Instead of the usual shako they wore the traditional Basque red beret. Instead of a cartouche they wore a cartridge belt around their waist, and kept all their personal supplies, one shirt, a pair of sandals, one day's food and a pipe, in a small canvas knapsack.

But his tactics were of the classic guerrilla pattern. An Englishman who fought with the Carlists while Zumalacárregui was alive wrote an account of his experiences, and included several interesting descriptions of the Carlist's mode of warfare:

'[Zumalacárragui] began by organising and augmenting, day by day, his army, leading them by mountain roads through the most inaccessible territory ... away from the enemy, and there training them ... by bringing them into skirmishes ... and ambuscades ... never at first attacking but where he could not compromise their safety ... He adopted the plan which has been proved decidedly the best for a mountainous country – distributing his force by battalions, each commanded by a colonel, instead of by regiments. Well aware that it could only be by the rapidity of his marches ... that he could hope to struggle with the fearful odds ... he equipped [his men] as lightly as possible.'

A little later he tells how:

'When a column came out, messengers were immediately sent off, and Zumalacárregui in an incredibly short time was informed of it ... Three or four dozen [guerrillas] would fire from a distance on the column ... When a company was sent out to dislodge them they disappeared among the rocks like chamois, loading and firing as they fled ... Members of one partida ... would follow the column, hovering around and cutting off stragglers until they were relieved by the partida of another station ... The nature of the roads ... left it entirely at the option of the Carlists to fight or fly, and to form their combinations accordingly.'[13]

Basically then Zumalacárregui's tactics were much like those of the other guerrilla leaders already mentioned. But what is worth taking special note of is the fact that he clearly wished to go beyond the purely defensive guerrilla stage and train his men to be able to stand up to the regular forces of the Spanish government. It was with this end in mind that he gave his men uniforms, competent officers, and thorough training in small-scale combat situations. We also know that Zumalacárregui wanted to march on Madrid at an early stage and try and force the government troops into a decisive battle.

But his wishes were ignored, and instead the Carlists laid siege to Bilbao, in 1834. Here Zumalacárregui received a wound in the leg from which, to his great surprise, he soon died. The loss of this great commander proved to be the turning point of the war, even though it dragged on for another six years. The siege was lifted and the Carlists returned to the mountains. But the poverty of this area, with a population of only half a million, made it impossible for the Carlist forces to sustain themselves. In 1837 they set off on a full-scale raid on Madrid, known as the Royal Expedition, but were beaten back. In 1839 the government commander-in-chief, Espartero, had 100,000 troops at his disposal on the northern front. In April he took Morella, the central base of Ramón Cabrera, the Carlists' only other effective guerrilla leader. In the next few months Espartero drove deeper into Carlist territory, and in August 1839 the whole movement collapsed.

The Risorgimento

The *Risorgimento* is the name given to the long and confused series of events that led to the liberation of the various Italian states and to the eventual unification of Italy as one nation. The tactics of the nationalists varied greatly from place to place, and from period to period. Some placed their faith in the creation of secret societies and the planning of insurrections within the most important cities. Some wanted to enlist the support of the Italian monarchies, notably Piedmont, and use their regular troops to drive out the occupying powers. Others put their trust in high-level diplomacy and the rivalries of the great powers. But there were those who put their faith in guerrilla warfare as the most effective means of resisting the enemy's armed forces.

In the early stages of his career, one of the key figures of the Risorgimento, Giuseppe Mazzini, advocated just such a mode of resistance. In the *Instructions for the Members of Young Italy*, the secret society which he founded in 1831, he wrote: 'Insurrection by means of guerrilla bands is the true method of warfare for all nations desirous of emancipating themselves from a foreign yoke. It forms the military education of the people and consecrates every foot of the nation's soil by the memory of some warlike deed.' Later he wrote a set of *Rules for the Conduct of Guerrilla Bands*, and there we read that:

'Guerrilla warfare opens a field of activity for every local capacity; forces the enemy into an unaccustomed method of battle; avoids the consequences of a great defeat; secures the national war from the risk of treason, and has the advantage of not confining it within any defined and determinate base of operations. It is invincible, indestructible.'[14]

It seems that during this period of his life Mazzini was greatly influenced by his friend Carlo Bianco, who had himself taken part in the Carlist Wars. But his interest in the potentialities did not last, and by 1840 he had stopped advocating this type of tactics.

But there were others, like Carlo Piscane and Francesco Milo Guggino, who perisisted in thinking that guerrilla warfare was the correct mode of resistance for the Italian nationalists. Another such was Enrico Gentilini, a Savoyard, who had been involved in the revolutionary movement since 1833. In 1848 he wrote a pamphlet called *Partisan or Guerrilla Warfare*, in which he laid out quite detailed instructions on the way the *stracorridori*, or guerrillas, should conduct their operations. Most of them are of a specifically tactical nature, concerning the best way to lay ambushes, where to set up camp etc, but there are also some more general points about the nature of guerrilla warfare. Thus:

> 'The principal objective of this warfare is to fall upon the enemy in those places which he cannot garrison with considerable numbers of men; to torment him continually, tire him and deny supplies, without exposing oneself to serious risks ... The main aim is to surprise the enemy's posts, throw his camp into disarray, assault him at night in his tents, attack him from above whilst he is on the march, surprise his convoys, cut his communications, be the first to occupy those places which one is almost sure the enemy wishes to take; destroy his arms and powder workshops and other military establishments ... eliminate unsympathetic generals, suspect authorities, and hold to ransom that part of the population known to support the enemy, intercept the couriers, burn the magazines ... to keep intact ... the communications of our regular army ... to watch over the enemy so that he does not take us by surprise, and finally to reconnoitre ... his positions.'

Though Gentilini never makes it explicit, he does seem to assume that all guerrilla activity will be carried out in conjunction with the operations of regular forces. For him guerrilla warfare is essentially based around the use of the ambush:

> 'It is a war of surprise: that is why one should occupy gorges and sunken roads; one should place one's forces in hidden, inaccessible spots, behind hills, rising ground, hedges; in valleys, on mountains, amongst rocks, in thickets, behind clumps of trees, along river-banks, on the edge of forests and woods, in places in which it is easy to conceal oneself, so that one can attack the enemy at will and bring off minor successes.'

Gentilini acknowledges the need for good intelligence through the use of spies, and keeping in regular touch with the population at large. He is particularly insistent upon the need to maintain good relations with the inhabitants of the guerrilla areas:

'It must be made a very serious offence for any guerrilla to enter their homes and disturb the peace of the occupants, show rudeness or shamelessly steal anything ... By committing such an infamous act you will bring down upon yourselves the hatred of the inhabitants, and you will have many more enemies to contend with; and as well as being unable to carry out your own plans, you will put yourself into the very difficulties which should afflict the enemy.'

Deception is also a basic tactic of the guerrilla: 'An enemy taken by surprise is virtually defeated ... In one's operations it is necessary to keep the enemy guessing, hiding one's intentions as much as possible, so that he has no suspicions as to what you will do and is unable to frustrate your plans ... Make mock attacks, seeming to be attacking on one side whilst actually making the assault on the other.' Finally, the guerrilla force should always remain mobile. Whilst it should choose appropriate terrain for its base area – 'Mountainous areas and plains dotted with forests, woods, hills, lakes, swamps etc' – it should never lose sight of the fact that 'there would be no greater error for a guerrilla force than to limit its operations to one single area and to become enslaved within a particular stretch of terrain.'[15]

However, during the Risorgimento, this admirable theory was hardly ever put into practice, and never on any extensive scale. In 1843, after an abortive rising in Savigno, in the Papal States, a band of 80 men fled to the hills. They made one raid on Savigno, in which they captured six hostages, and retreated back into the hills. But they were pursued by Papal troops who caught up with the band and killed or captured all its members. The main exponent of guerrilla methods in practice was Giuseppe Garibaldi, though even he never achieved any notable successes with this mode of warfare. His most famous achievements, in 1860, in Sicily, were made with volunteers prepared to take on regular troops in open battle.

Nevertheless, he did sometimes undertake more irregular operations. In 1848 he came to the aid of Charles Albert of Piedmont and his regulars by seizing several paddle-steamers on Lake Maggiore. These he used to transfer his troops from spot to spot, to make swift raids into Austrian territory and cut their communications. He started with a force of 1,000 men, but when Charles Albert came to terms with the Austrians most of these volunteers melted away, leaving Garibaldi with a mere 30 men. In 1849 he took part in the siege of Rome, and after its failure decided to take to the hills, remarking that 'wherever we are, there will be Rome'. Four thousand men went with him and a substantial part of them eventually reached San Marino. But the operation should be regarded more as a 'Long March' than as a guerrilla campaign in itself. Though he brilliantly evaded three pursuing armies, by a judicious use of cavalry screens and the spreading of false rumours about his intentions, he never represented much of an actual military threat to his pursuers. In 1859 he fought against the Austrians yet again. He raised a force known as the *Cacciatori delle Alpi*, composed of 3,000 infantrymen, 50 scouts and 40 sharpshooters. He defined his purpose as the 'disorganisation of the Austrian army by disrupting their lines of communication, blowing up bridges, cutting telegraph wires and burning stores.'[16] Though defeated by the Austrians in a minor battle at Laveno, Garibaldi went a long way towards realising his intentions. He made a successful attack on Corno, and managed to keep 11,000 Austrian regulars constantly occupied. Unfortunately his very success was an embarrassment to those nationalists who hoped for a diplomatic solution, and their most prominent spokesman, Cavour, packed Garibaldi and his force, now 12,000 strong, off to remote Valtellina to 'guard' the Stelvio Pass.

Ironically, the only major guerrilla war of this period was fought *against* the forces of the Italian nationalists. In 1860 Garibaldi and his 'thousand' landed in Sicily and marched through Naples, winning victory after victory over the forces of the Bourbon king, Francis II. At first Garibaldi received substantial aid from the bands of brigands that had long infested southern Italy. The most important of these was 'Crocco' (Carmine Donatelli), and his band did valuable work cutting water supplies, destroying flour-mills, cutting telegraph wires and ambushing stragglers. But the brigandage was a symptom of widespread peasant unrest, mainly among the farm-hands and day labourers, though the petty landholders also began to take exception to the new efforts of the southern landlords to enclose their properties.[17] Thus, while the northern liberals might welcome purely military support from the brigands, they were utterly opposed to any outbursts of peasant protest. Even in 1860 Garibaldi dealt very severely with any such outbreaks, and the southern peasants soon began to turn against the invaders. Right up until 1866 the various bands waged a vicious war against the nationalists that was only put down with the utmost difficulty and the greatest savagery. 120,000 troops were involved in its suppression, as opposed to perhaps 80,000 brigands, and more troops were killed than in all the wars of the Risorgimento put together. Terror was the main weapon of the counter-insurgents. One of General Cialdini's first orders after taking command in 1860 was that anyone found bearing arms was to be shot at once. The records for 1863 show that 1,038 people were executed for this reason. At the same time nearly 2,500 southerners were killed in the continuous fighting, and over 2,700 were imprisoned.

The American Civil War

Most of the next two case-studies concern wars in which the bulk of the fighting was done by regulars. But as is often the case in major conventional struggles, in which the whole resources of a particular country are called into play, guerrilla forces sprang up in certain theatres to supplement the activities of the main armies. The most notable example of this during the American Civil War was the campaign waged by John Singleton Mosby, between January 1863 and April 1865.

Mosby joined the Confederate Army in early 1861, in Virginia. In January 1863 he accompanied Jeb Stuart on a successful cavalry raid into North Virginia, and when the main body of troops pulled out he asked to be left behind with just six men to operate behind the enemy lines. His raids on the Union outposts were so successful that Stuart increased his force to 15 men. Within a few months he had 100 men under him, and by the end of the war this number had increased to 200, split into two separate commands. In January Mosby crossed the Rappahannock. As he himself wrote later: 'In general my purpose was to threaten and harass the enemy on the border and in this way compel him to withdraw troops from his front to guard the line of the Potomac and Washington.'[18]

Throughout his operations Mosby used pretty much the same tactics. His guerrillas were all cavalrymen who had abandoned the conventional sabre, and used carbines for ambushes and two Colt revolvers for hand-to-hand fighting. The men, known as the Partisan Rangers, were split into small groups for minor operations, but would occasionally come together for a concerted attack on a supply convoy, railway train, or enemy unit. In such a case the usual method of attack was to dash through the enemy, seize whatever wagons and horses were within reach, and dash off almost at once. Mosby later proudly pointed out that his men never received anything from the Confederate headquarters but the grey jackets they wore. Otherwise they lived off the country, taking food, horses, guns and other supplies from their enemies. Until June 1863 Mosby operated in support of the Confederates engaged in the Gettysburg campaign. From then, until August 1864, he harassed various Union commanders, including Grant after his crossing of the Rapidan. After August 1864 he was engaged in continuous hostilities with Sheridan's forces and his command was not disbanded until April 20, 1865. Sheridan was particularly distressed by Mosby's activities. After he had left the Shenandoah Valley to go into winter quarters, '[Mosby] kept up a desultory warfare on outposts, supply trains and detachments ... Unable to exterminate the hostile bands by arms, Sheridan had applied the torch and attempted to drive us from the district in which we operated by destroying everything that could support man or horse.'[19] On the whole, the Partisan leader seems to have avoided the temptation to indulge in counter-terror. A letter written by one of his ex-prisoners, in 1910, throws an interesting light on the low esteem in which guerrillas were still held by regular soldiers: 'You kindly gave us our horses to ride ... which was the act of the highest type of man, and should bury deep forever the name of a "guerrilla" and substitute "to picket lines a bad disturber".'[20]

In another part of the United States, however, a rather different type of campaign was fought, which in many respects can be regarded as a full-scale, autonomous guerrilla war. This was in Kansas and Missouri, which saw few regular operations but which were the scene of constant guerrilla activity, throughout the war. The seeds of the struggle had been laid even before the war. The inhabitants of Missouri were nearly all from the southern states whilst those in Kansas were nearly all abolitionists, encouraged to settle there by northern anti-slavery groups. Border warfare had begun between the two groups in 1854, and right up until 1860 the situation along the border was anarchic.

In 1861 Union troops seized much of Missouri and installed their own administration there. In the winter of that year numerous bands of Missourians installed themselves in the southern and central areas of the state and began to promote guerrilla warfare throughout the area. Up until the spring of 1862 the guerrillas were backed by Confederate regulars, led by General Price, who tried to incorporate the irregulars' efforts within the general southern strategy. By April, however, all Confederate troops had been pushed out of the state, and the guerrillas were left essentially to their own devices. They did, however, receive the official endorsement of the Confederate leaders. Jefferson Davis was opposed to guerrilla warfare on principle, regarding it as mere banditry, but on April 21, 1862 the passing of the Partisan Ranger Act authorised him to commission the formation of guerrilla units, wherever appropriate. An advocate of this mode of warfare, among the regular soldiers, was General Hindman, and on July 17 he issued his own orders for the raising of guerrilla bands:

(1) 'For the more effectual annoyance of the enemy upon our rivers and in our mountains and woods all citizens in this district who are not subject to conscription are called upon to organise themselves into independent companies of mounted men, or infantry, as they prefer, arming and equipping themselves, and to serve in that part of the district to which they belong.

(2) When as many as ten men come together for this purpose they may organise by electing a captain, one sergeant, one corporal, and will at once commence operations against the enemy without waiting for special instructions. Their duty will be to cut off Federal pickets, scouts, foraging parties, and trains, to kill pilots and others on gunboat and transports, attacking them day and night and using the greatest vigour in their movements . . . All such organisations will be reported to these headquarters as soon as practicable. They will receive pay and allowances for subsistence and forage for the time actually in the field . . .

(3) These companies will be governed in all respects by the same regulations as other troops. Captains will be held responsible for the good conduct and efficiency of the men, and will report to these headquarters from time to time.'[21]

Certain Confederate officers, such as Colonels Porter and Poindexter, were sent into Missouri to take charge of bands already there or to try and raise new ones. Nevertheless, on the whole the guerrilla movement was of a spontaneous nature and the most prominent leaders came from the indigenous Missouri population. Probably the most famous of these was William Clarke Quantrill, who led a large band of his own which in turn spawned leaders like Bill Anderson, George Todd, William Gregg and David Pool.

Quantrill operated in much the same fashion as Mosby. His band never exceeded 20 men and usually operated in several much smaller formations. The men were always mounted on the very best horses, usually captured, and their chief weapon was the Colt revolver, of which some guerrillas had as many as eight. They concentrated upon destroying the enemy's communications and laying ambushes. Occasionally they made lightning raids on small townships in Missouri or Kansas. The most notorious of these was against Lawrence (Kansas) in August 1863, when Quantrill's men cut down over 150 soldiers and civilians. By October 1863 Quantrill had begun to lose control of his men and was inactive all that winter. But in April 1864 he reorganised his followers and remained a very real threat to the Union administration until his capture and death in June of the following year.

These guerrillas had a quite significant impact on the Union war effort in the western theatre. In 1862, for example, a mere 3–4,000 guerrillas were holding down 60,000 Union troops. In 1863 General Curtis, in St Louis, wrote that:

> 'Guerrillas may be defined as troops not belonging to a regular army, consisting of volunteers, perhaps self-constituted, but generally raised by individuals authorised to do so . . . by their government. They . . . take up arms or lay them down at intervals, and carry on a petty war chiefly by raids, extortion, destruction and massacre, and . . . cannot encumber themselves with many prisoners, and will, therefore, generally give no quarter. They are particularly dangerous because they easily evade pursuit, and, by laying down their arms, become insidious enemies, because they cannot otherwise subsist than by rapine, and almost always degenerate into simple robbers or brigands.'[22]

This estimation of the guerrillas as mere bandits was a constant theme of contemporary reports and orders. Even certain Confederate generals felt little sympathy for their supposed allies. In February 1864 one wrote of Quantrill and his band: 'They will only fight when they have all the advantages and when they can run away whenever they find things too hot for them. I regard them as but one stage better than highwaymen.'[23] After their first depredations in the winter of 1861–2, the Union General Halleck pointed out the legal consequences of the guerrillas' peculiar military status:

'It is a well-established principle that insurgents, not militarily organised under the laws of the State, predatory partisans, and guerrilla bands are not entitled to [any] exemptions; such men are not legitimately in arms, and the military name and garb which they have assumed cannot give a military exemption to the crimes which they commit. They are . . . mere free-booters and banditti, and are liable to the same punishment which was imposed upon guerrilla bands by Napoleon in Spain and by Scott in Mexico.'[24]

But the purely military measures of the Union forces against the guerrillas themselves had little effect. They maintained small cavalry units in all towns, which were sent out on constant patrols, though usually without much success. On top of this the severest measures were taken against the guerrillas they managed to capture. At one stage an order was issued that two guerrilla prisoners were to be shot for every Union soldier killed by them. Nevertheless, in 1864, one Kansas newspaper was compelled to admit:

'What is the condition of the truly loyal people of the border counties of Missouri south of the river? Simply one of siege. Outside of the military posts and their immediate vicinity, no man of known and open loyalty can safely live for a moment. The loyal people are gathered in scattered towns and military posts, while to all practical intents and purposes the rebels hold possession of the county.'[25]

So the Union military authorities also extended their repressive measures to include the whole population of the insurgent areas. In August 1861 martial law was declared and was not revoked until March 1865. From January 1862 all cases involving any kind of 'subversive' activity were tried by military tribunals. Shortly after this, Committees of Public Safety were set up in the towns which were held collectively responsible for any destruction caused by the guerrillas and were required to pay compensation for such acts. In the summer of 1862 General Schofield laid down that: 'During active operations in the field in pursuit of guerrillas, the troops of this command will not be encumbered with transportation of supplies, but will, as far as possible, obtain subsistence from the enemy and those who aid and encourage the rebellion.'[26] Whilst it certainly makes sense to require counter-insurgency forces to travel as light as possible, to ensure maximum mobility, it was an act of criminal stupidity to allow these forces to forcibly requisition their supplies from the surrounding population. This could only drive hundreds more people into the arms of the guerrillas. Schofield's next measure had a similar effect when, in October, he attempted to draft the whole able-bodied male population to put down the guerrillas. Also in 1862, the Union authorities in certain towns adopted the expedient of demanding loyalty oaths and good behaviour bonds from certain individuals. These bonds were generally for $1,000, and by April 1863 it was claimed that all in all they were worth as much as $27 million. In November 1862 mass arrests were made in those towns suspected of sheltering and aiding guerrillas. Often over 200 people at a time were arrested, and in December the authorities endowed themselves with the right to banish any such arrestee without trial. In late May 1863 General Ewing proposed that all guerrilla families and their friends should be deported wholesale to Arkansas. In August a selective removal of the population was authorised, although the order included the quite unrealistic stipulation that the authorities must 'discriminate as carefully as possible between those who are compelled, by threats or fears, to aid the rebels, and those who aid them from disloyal motives.' A few days later an order was issued for the complete removal of all people in Jackson, Cass, Bates and Vernon Counties who lived more than one mile from an army post. Thus the war in this part of the United States was in every sense of the term a war against an insurgent people rather than simply against a few isolated bandits and terrorists.

The Franco-Prussian War

On July 19, 1870, the French declared war on Prussia. Between August 4 and 6 they were defeated at the decisive battles of Wissembourg, Froeschwiller and Firbach. On September 2 Napoleon III surrendered at Sedan. Following these humiliating events a Government of National Defence was established, and the Third Republic proclaimed. This government attempted various last-ditch measures to try and recoup the fortunes of French arms. Under the guidance of Léon Gambetta the entire male population between the ages of 21 and 40 was called up, as well as the provincial *Garde Mobile* and *Garde Nationale*. The government also encouraged the formation of bands of *francs-tireurs*, or guerrillas who were to carry out a war of ambuscades against the German invader. Indeed, to many of the French leaders this stage of the war was to be entirely conducted as a guerrilla war. On September 21 Admiral Fourichon, the Minister of the Navy, advised that the role of the *Mobiles* themselves 'is less to fight than to harass the enemy . . . to obstruct him in his requisitions . . . Above all to carry out *coups de main* . . . to capture convoys, cut roads and railways, destroy bridges . . . These troops must wage real partisan war.'[27] In a proclamation issued in October Gambetta expressed a similar conception of the war at this stage:

> 'We must . . . increase partisan warfare and, against an enemy so skilled in ambush and surprise, ourselves employ ruses, attack his flanks, surprise his rear – in short inaugurate a national war . . . Tied down and contained by the capital, the Prussians, far from home, anxious, harassed, hunted down by our reawa-

kened people, will be gradually decimated by our arms, by hunger, by natural causes.'[28]

At Tours one Frenchman called for the formation of small groups 'which will cut off convoys, harass the enemy and hang from trees all they can take well and truly by the neck ... I suggest the type of war which the Spaniards waged against us under the First Empire and the Mexicans under the Second.'[29]

It has been estimated that at the height of their activities there were some 300 partisan bands operating throughout France, incorporating over 57,000 men. As early as September 6 Gambetta had sent out orders to all prefects of the departments threatened by invasion to defend their territory as best they could with the National Guard and bands of *francs-tireurs*. On October 14 he issued an order commanding that all departments within 100 kilometres of the Prussians were to be declared in a state of war. Military committees were to be set up, led by local notables, livestock and crops were to be evacuated, and everyone capable of bearing arms was to repel the invader.

These measures had considerable success. A German commentator noted that the National Guard, in particular, was a threat to German supply lines and detachments:

'[They] were charged locally with harassing the Germans as much as possible, and rendering the lines of march insecure. For this purpose the State had supplied all the towns and villages with a number of smooth-bore muskets and a quantity of ammunition ... [They] wore no uniforms and kept their arms concealed in woods and thickets. There they lay in ambush waiting for the Germans. They never came to close quarters, but struck from a distance with firearms ... They were wont at need to assume the appearance of inoffensive peasants ...'

He goes on later to state: 'The guerrilla warfare never ceased; some attacks were always being made on small bodies of infantry, on single horsemen, on small patrols, on some travelling detachments, mails of the field post-office, posts or patrols at stations on the lines of communication or along the railway, and railways and telegraphs were being destroyed.'[30]

The railways were particularly vulnerable to the attacks of the guerrillas. There were only three lines crossing the Franco-German frontier and the bulk of German supplies had to pass along them. One of these was denied to the Germans throughout the war because it was overlooked by the fortresses of Belfort and Langres. Another was threatened by the fortress of Mézières, which the Germans did not reduce until January 2, 1871. On January 22 a group of guerrillas blew up the viaduct at Fontenoy-sur-Moselle, on the third line, and had this coup been carried off before the capture of Mézières, 'it is hard to see how the German supply system could have been saved from total, if temporary, collapse.'[31]

One of the most successful guerrilla groups was led by Giuseppe Garibaldi, a figure already familiar to us. It was based upon Autun and conducted operations throughout the Côte d'Or. During the last fortnight of November and the first of December, 1870, its members conducted a particularly effective harassing campaign against one German corps, based upon Dijon, that was for the moment wholly responsible for guarding German communications against attacks from the south. During this period, as the Corps historian wrote, Garibaldi achieved great success by:

'restricting the zone of its free operations, and, what was still more important, the area from which its supplies were drawn ... Nothing decisive could be done to destroy this nuisance; the enemy force consisted mostly of flying columns, which, marching only at night, appeared each day at some different point in the line of outposts, attempting surprises of patrols, and attacks of small parties.'[32]

But all this activity never had any chance of becoming the authentic war of national liberation for which the Republican leaders hoped. For one thing there was no common political basis for the struggle. The Republicans only attempted to invoke the xenophobia of the French populace, rather than integrate the struggle into a far-reaching call for real economic and social reforms. Thus men were only called upon to repel the invader, and as most people realised that the Prussians were not likely to remain in France after the cessation of hostilities, it seemed pointless to risk one's life for a goal that was already inevitable, and in the forseeable future. Thus all that the bulk of the French peasantry wanted was for the war to end as quickly as possible. Waging a guerrilla war seemed one sure way to defer this event, without it bringing any other concrete gains.

German counter-insurgency measures also contributed to this reluctance of the average Frenchman to compromise himself in the name of some vague nationalist ideal. The measures took two main forms. On the purely military level the Prussians made use of small flying columns, usually of two *Landwehr* battalions and a cavalry squadron, which attempted to track the guerrillas down or discourage them by the speed and frequency of their movements. On top of this the Germans made much use of selective terror. Moltke had been clear on the necessity of this from the very beginning. At the start of the counter-offensive by the Government of National Defence he declared that *franc-tireurs* had no belligerent status and were liable to be shot out of hand. Later he told one corps commander that: 'The very severest treatment of the guilty as regards life and property can alone be recommended ..., whole parishes being held responsible for the deeds of individual members when these cannot be discovered.'[33] After a successful guerrilla attack on a provisions column, around Rethel, in October 1870, one parish was required to pay a 10,000 francs fine and six guerrilla prisoners were summarily executed. A month or so later a German flying column was operating in the region of Montereau and Nogent. 'It marched upwards of 130 miles in six days. On the way a fine of £1,080 was levied upon Provins. Wholesome [sic] terror had been inspired throughout an extensive tract of land, and a heavy blow dealt against the arming of the populace.'[34] Such measures, combined with the frequent burning-down of property and an attempt to completely disarm the populace, did much to increase the apathy of the French peasantry and undermine the possibility of widespread guerrilla warfare.

1. W. M. Leake, *Historical Outline of the Greek Revolution*, John Murray, 1826, p68
2. E. Blaquière, *The Greek Revolution*, London, 1824, pp 358–59
3. G. Finlay, *History of the Greek Revolution*, London, 1861, Vol 2, pp 391–92
4. M. Macdermott, *A History of Bulgaria 1393–1885*, Allen & Unwin, 1962, p189
5. M. Macdermott, *Apostle of Revolution*, Allen & Unwin, 1967, p130
6. See below pp 216–20
7. M. W. Potter (trans), *Zachary Stoyonoff: Pages from the Autobiography of a Bulgarian Insurgent*, Edward Arnold, 1913, p141
8. J. Swire, *Bulgarian Conspiracy*, Robert Hale, 1939, p79
9. S. Christowe, *Heroes and Assassins*, Gollancz, 1935, pp 55–56
10. See Swire, *op cit*, pp 87–88 and 103
11. A. D. H. Smith, *Fighting the Turk in the Balkans*, Putnams, New York, pp 46–47 and 254–55
12. D. Dakin, *The Unification of Greece 1770–1923*, Ernest Benn, 1972
13. C. F. Henningsen, *The Most Striking Events of a Twelve Months Campaign with Zumalacárregui*, John Murray, 1836, pp 105–6 and 113–14
14. E. Kedourie, *Nationalism*, Longmans, 1960, p98
15. M. Bravo (ed), *Les Socialistes avant Marx*, Maspéro, Paris, 1970, Vol 3, pp 205–27
16. C. Hibbert, *Garibaldi and his Enemies*, Longmans, 1965, p148
17. See E. Hobsbawm, *Bandits*, Pengiun Books, 1971, p31
18. C. W. Russell (ed), *The Memoirs of Colonel John S. Mosby*, Indiana University Press, Bloomington, 1959, pp 149–50
19. *ibid*, p333
20. *Ibid*, p189
21. R. S. Brownlee, *Grey Ghosts of the Confederacy*, Louisiana State University Press, Baton Rouge, 1958, p78
22. *ibid*, p112
23. *ibid*, p140
24. *ibid*, p26
25. *ibid*, pp 191–92
26. *ibid*, p85
27. M. Howard, *The Franco-Prussian War*, Fontana, 1967, p249
28. *ibid*, p240
29. *ibid*, p250
30. Col G. C. von Widdern, 'The Guerrilla Warfare in the Districts in the Rear of the German

Armies', in Maj-Gen J. F. Maurice (ed), *The Franco-German War 1870–71*, Swan Sonnenschein, 1900, pp 546 and 548

31. Howard, *op cit*, p377
32. *ibid*, p409
33. *ibid*, p378
34. Widdern, *op cit*, p555

CHAPTER 5

The 19th Century: Resistance to Imperialism

As must be clear by now, guerrilla warfare is usually the mode of resistance adopted by small people and nations when faced with the overwhelming military might of a foreign power seeking to dominate that particular area. The expansion of the Roman, Napoleonic and Turkish empires, for example, have all been seen to be the cause of numerous outbreaks of guerrilla warfare, as militarily weak peoples struggled to assert their political and economic independence. It is hardly surprising, therefore, that the great upsurge of imperialist activity that characterised European history during the nineteenth century should also have sparked off a parallel explosion of guerrilla resistance movements. It will be impossible to give more than the sketchiest coverage of all such movements within this chapter. Moreover, few of them contributed any significant innovations to guerrilla methods, and I shall, therefore, only deal at any length with those that provoked important advances in *counter*-insurgency techniques. For until the twentieth century it was only in this sphere that any systematic attempts were made to raise the level of military competence. As far as the methods of the guerrillas are concerned, most of the nineteenth century struggles are simple repetitions of those dealt with in previous pages.

The Americas

The first anti-colonial revolts of the nineteenth century were not in fact responses to the renewed vigour of European imperialism, as typified by the British, French and Germans, but rather to the decay of an old empire whose metropolitan centre was now incapable of meeting its financial, military and administrative obligations. This was Spain, whose South American empire suddenly fell apart in the first two decades of the nineteenth century.

The most important components of the military resistance cannot really be regarded as guerrilla forces. These were the armies of Simón Bolívar and José de San Martín, which were built up with the express purpose of meeting the small Spanish armies in open battle. But the first outbreak of insurrectionary violence, in Peru, in 1809, was of the guerrilla mode. There were six main centres of resistance among the mountainous terrain of upper Peru, and there small groups of guerrillas formed around some local leader or *Caudillo*. 'Each valley, each mountain, each village had its partisan group and its petty *caudillo*, who made their locality a minor zone of insurrection, a *republiqueta*, whose local patriotism burgeoned into local independence.'[1] But the extent of their nationalist fervour should not be overestimated. Like the *haiduks* and others discussed above, these Peruvian guerrillas were as much bandits as authentic freedom fighters. They were mainly held together by their allegiance to the local *caudillo* and always expected some kind of financial return from their operations. As often as not they were prepared to make a deal with the local Spanish commander in return for some degree of immunity.

In 1816 all the major bands, except that of Miguel Lanza, between La Paz and Cochabamba, were destroyed in a large Spanish offensive. However, this operation involved the diversion of 15,000 troops from Chile, and this greatly aided San Martín during his campaign there. This latter operation was of a semi-regular nature and the issue was decided at the small but crucial battles of Chacabuco and Maipú, in 1817. San Martín had in fact spent three years in Argentina preparing his army for this struggle, and he avoided all contact with the Spaniards until he felt that his troops were ready. When in Chile he did make use of small numbers of Chilean guerrillas, but these were an insignificant factor in terms of the whole campaign. From Chile San Martín eventually led an expeditionary force to Peru, in 1821. In July he took Lima, but never felt himself strong enough to face the main Spanish army which had taken refuge in the mountains. Later in the year San Martín was overthrown by a coup in his absence, and he quit South America for good.

The task of liberating Peru was left to Simón Bolívar who entered the country in 1824. He defeated the Spaniards at the battles of Junín and Ayacucho and in the following year the country was granted its independence. Bolívar's career as a militant revolutionary had begun in 1812 when he was operating along the Magdalena river with a small force of guerrillas and succeeded in seizing several small towns and winning a few skirmishes. In 1813 he decided to move north into Venezuela and attempt to drive out the Spaniards. He had some preliminary successes, but was himself driven out in the following year by the Spanish general, Boves, who organised a backlands counter-revolt amongst the wild, cowboy lancers, known as the *llaneros*. Bolívar fled to Haiti, but in 1816 he returned and began a new struggle against the Spanish, sometimes known as the War to the Death, which went on until 1820. This time Bolívar had the *llaneros* on his side, particularly those under the command of José Paez. He avoided a frontal assault on Caracas and seized the estuary of the Orinoco, from whence groups of men were sent out, on horseback or in boats, to operate on the enemy's flanks and in his rear.

The only other country in South America proper in which there was any significant guerrilla activity was Uruguay, which waged a continual war not only against the Spanish, but also against the Portuguese and the new Argentinian leaders, all of whom were loth to allow the emergence of a separate Uruguayan state. The leading nationalist here was José Artigas who was forced, in 1817, to surrender Montivideo and initiate a stubborn guerrilla campaign in the interior. In 1820 he was obliged to retreat to Paraguay, but the bare bones of a resistance movement did survive. In 1825 it was reactivated by Juan Lavajella, who soon isolated the Portuguese in the larger towns. In 1828 Fructuoso Rivera recruited another guerrilla force, and, taking advantage of a war between Argentina and Brazil, he won independence for his country in August of that year.

Mexico won her independence from the Spaniards in 1821. The struggle had begun in 1810 with an Indian uprising led by a Creole priest, Miguel Hidalgo. The revolt was simply a bloody insurrection rather than an organised insurgency and it collapsed within months, upon the death of its leader. The standard was picked up by others, notably José Morelos, who kept resistance alive until 1815. But again there was little military organisation and the whole uprising was crushed quite easily by General Félix Cajella. From then until 1820, whatever opposition there was to Spanish rule found its only expression in the activities of a few gangs of bandits who were more interested in plunder than in the cause of Mexican nationalism. They lived by raids on the surrounding Spanish *haciendas*, or by exacting contributions from local towns and villages. When not in the field they holed up in some fortress built in a particularly inaccessible piece of terrain. Among these bands, only that of Vincente Guerrero could really be regarded as a guerrilla force rather than just a gang of freebooters. He himself later went on to become the President of the Republic.

But the constant raiding and skirmishing, terror and counter-terror, that characterised the last years of Spanish rule did irreparable harm to the social and economic fabric of the country. This in turn created chronic political instability, and the years until 1863 were characterised by constant coups and changes of government. In its turn this completely obviated any possibility of an improvement in the socio-economic situation and created a permanent bandit problem in the country. But many of the bandits were more than just cynical murderers, and in times of particularly acute political crisis they were often led, by a mixture of political opportunism and ideological commitment, to throw their forces behind one political leader or another. This was the case between 1858 and 1861, during the so-called War of Reform. Then the Mexican 'Liberals', led by Benito Juárez, were assailed by the forces of reaction, spearheaded by certain clerics and army officers. In the three years of bitter fighting many of the bandits, and other Mexicans rendered destitute by the ceaseless warfare, rallied to the Liberal guerrilla leaders in the hills. Prominent among these were Santos Degollado in Jalisco, Marcos Pérez, and Santiago Vidaurri in the north-east.

It was these same reactionary clericals who decided to bring some sort of stability to Mexico by involving a European power in their struggle. In 1863 a French army, under Marshal Forey, landed in the country to prepare the way for the arrival of an Emperor, Maximilian. In October General Bazaine took over from Forey and over the next few months he managed to clear central Mexico of the disorganised Juárista forces. Juárez was forced to flee to the north, but Bazaine's 'victory' was merely the signal for the appearance of scores of guerrilla bands. One of the most important of these was that of Porfirio Díaz, in Oaxaca. In 1864 Bazaine led a force of 10,000 men against this fortress and Díaz was forced to surrender. However, in September 1865, he escaped, and began building up a new guerrilla force in Guerrero. For the next two years the guerrillas slowly nibbled away at the French forces, and bit by bit forced them into the larger towns. For Maximilian's wife, Carlotta, the guerrillas were nothing more than bandits:

'No-one can foresee whence guerrilla bands may spring up. Theirs is a kind of spontaneous generation. As I understand the matter, a man leaves his village with a horse, a weapon, and a firm determination to prosper by any means except work ... The only thing he cares about is lucrative adventure. Such a fellow as this has little trouble recruiting others of the same kidney.[2]

Certainly there was a strong tradition of banditry in Mexico, but it seems a little sweeping thus to write off the whole massive guerrilla resistance to this ill-fated Imperial experiment. As has already been seen, the Mexican guerrillas were not immune to a certain naive political idealism, and it seems more than likely that their level of consciousness was considerably heightened by the fact that in this case they were fighting against foreign invaders. But whatever the relative importance of mercenary, liberal or nationalist feelings, the guerrillas' tactics were of the classic pattern, to which the French had no adequate response. Various observers described the Mexican tactics. One of Carlotta's retinue noted that:

'By the time one town is freed from the insurgents ... by the time that messages of victory [have been] broadcast far and wide – the guerrillas have mastered some other important place, and the troops leave the conquered town to hunt them from their new acquisition. But scarcely are the troops out of sight when one hears the ring of the guerrilla cavalry, which surrounds the deserted town.'[3]

There was also, inevitably, an Englishman at the scene of the fighting, and he left a record of his experiences there. The unfortunate French, he observed, 'soon discovered the impossibility of catching their straggling bands, who, besides, had the great advantage of knowing the country perfectly ... [and] who ... when once in the mountains, were almost sure to escape, dispersing and meeting again, days after, in another part of the country'. The guerrillas were well aware of their limitations and made it a policy 'never to engage in a doubtful affair if it could possibly be avoided, and to keep up a constant system of intercepting couriers, occasionally annoying the weaker posts of the Imperialists, whenever they happened to be somewhat isolated from immediate support.'[4]

French counter-insurgency methods were of two main types. On the one hand they made some attempt to adapt their forces to the demands of this type of warfare. Forey set up a force of 'contre-guerrillas', under the command of one Colonel du Pin. It consisted of two squadrons of cavalry, four companies of infantry and two light artillery pieces, and was recruited from amongst the Mexicans and certain foreign adventurers. The emphasis was upon mobility. It took no baggage train but carried all its supplies on pack mules. Later the French began to organise one company in every battalion in this way.

But their main emphasis was upon terror. On October 3, 1865, the so-called Black Decree was enacted, which imposed the harshest penalties upon anyone who even sympathised with the guerrillas. All members of guerrilla bands, 'if found guilty merely of such membership, shall be condemned to death and executed within twenty-four hours after passing of sentence.' Anyone who gave information to the guerrillas, sold them horses, ammunition, failed to inform the authorities of their passage, and even 'those who did not resist bands of guerrillas' were liable to heavy fines and imprisonment. By the terms of Article 9, the standard expedient of collective punishment was also introduced. If any male citizens between the ages of 18 and 55 failed to come to the defence of a threatened town, and if the authorities felt it necessary, 'a fine ranging from 200 to 2,000 pesos may be imposed, to be paid by all who being aware of this decree disregarded it.'[5]

But none of these measures had much effect. The French forces were soon forced to pull back into the main towns and leave the countryside to the mercy of the guerrillas. On top of this, the whole venture was very unpopular in France itself and Bazaine was aware that his troops might be recalled at any time. This made him reluctant to fritter them away in futile missions. In 1867 they were recalled, and Maximilian was left alone with a ragged force of Mexicans and a few European volunteers. Within a few weeks the ramshackle Empire was overthrown and Maximilian was shot on the orders of Juárez.

Shortly after this Díaz was made President and began a long dictatorship of increasing repressiveness. Once again the regime brought into being numerous bands of bandits and guerrillas, and once again, at the beginning of the next century, these groups formed a loose union to overthrow the oppressor. But before I come to the anarchic period known as the Mexican Revolution, it is necessary to take note of another guerrilla struggle not typical of the usual Mexican pattern of politicised banditry. This war, usually known as the Caste War of Yucatán, involved the remnants of the Maya Indians, fighting against ruthless exploitation by Spanish and Creole Mexicans. The war began in earnest in 1847, with a surprise Maya attack on the small town of Tepich. Two small Mexican columns were sent out to retake the town, and one of them was ambushed on the way and routed. The war lasted until 1901, a full 54 years. Although little is heard of this conflict outside Mexico, it in fact represents one of the best and most successful examples of a defensive guerrilla war. In the end the Mayas were defeated, but the organisation and tactics they developed during the years of resistance showed a sophisticated appreciation of the demands of guerrilla warfare.

The war fell into two main phases. The first lasted until 1848, during which time the Maya operated from their traditional villages and made frequent raids outside their own domains. In the early stages they concentrated upon storming Mexican towns to seize plunder and massacre the inhabitants. After sacking a town they would immediately return to their villages. If the Mexicans sent a column in pursuit it would inevitably fall into a Mayan ambush, or rearguard action. Often the Maya would throw up makeshift limestone barricades to slow the Mexicans down. 'At first the barricades simply blocked the trails, but ... they were capable of many refinements – flanking walls for enfilade, carefully masked strongpoints, support lines, and pitfalls bristling with pointed stakes.'[6] A prominent leader at this time was Cecilio Chi who dominated the area around Valladolid. He attacked the local *haciendas*, hamlets and villages, taking as much plunder as possible, which was sent south, to the British Honduras, to be traded for weapons. He never waited long enough in one place for the Mexicans to lay siege to him. His bands communicated with each other by means of a *tunkul*, a hollow log drum which carried for miles. If a column was too large to attack, Chi would simply let it wander around aimlessly. If small enough, he would wait until it was strung out along a jungle trail and then his machete-swinging troops would emerge from cover.

In 1848, however, the resistance movement collapsed temporarily. The Mayas had been extraordinarily successful, taking vast amounts of loot and killing hundreds of their enemies. In their eyes they had won a great victory and, like all peasants, they wished to be allowed to simply return to their fields. They had no conception of the strategic demands of their struggle, and were unable to visualise the possibility of a Mexican recovery and counter-offensive. Many years later, a descendant of these Indians described their feelings to an American scholar:

' "Eheu! The time has come for us to make our planting, for if we do not we shall have no Grace of God to fill the bellies of our children." In this way they talked among themselves and argued, thinking deeply, and then when morning came, my father's people said ... "I am going" – and in spite of the supplications and threats of the chiefs, each man rolled up his blanket and put it in his food pouch, tightening the thongs of his sandals, and started for his home and his cornfield.'[7]

This reluctance of the peasant to let the fighting interfere with the perennial tasks of harvesting and sowing is one of the most important considerations for any leader wishing to go beyond purely defensive harassment.

By June, however, the Mexicans had rallied their forces and the war began again. By December the rebels were very much on the defensive, contained within the dense rain forests along the eastern coast, an area without villages or roads and completely unknown to the white man. But from this base the Indians fought on, sowing secret corn fields, sniping at convoys and rushing isolated outposts. By the end of 1849 the whole Maya nation had retreated into this inaccessible region. Their migration was greatly facilitated by their abject poverty. A more developed people would find it almost impossible to move lock, stock and barrel to another region, and would be much more likely to come to terms with their enemy, no matter how humiliating those terms might be. But the Maya needed only their machetes, rifles and a little food. Everything else, from their crude huts to their bowls, jars and hearthstones, could be made anew when they found fresh refuge.

At first they fought a rather fragmentary struggle, each rebel feeling that his loyalty was to his village company, usually between 50 and 300 men, rather than to the people as a whole. From 1852, however, the Mayas found a potent unifying force in the form of the so-called Speaking Cross. Around this was developed a religious creed compounded of Catholic and Maya traditions and rituals. This creed was of crucial importance in giving the Maya a spiritual basis for their endless struggle. It also provided the organisational base. At the head was the high-priest, or *Tatich*, and his two assistants. Beneath him were the military leaders – the supreme commander, or *Tata Chikiuc* (General of the Plaza) and the various company commanders. There was also an intelligence officer, or *Tata Nohoch Zul* (Great Father Spy) who kept regular agents among the Mexicans, and also kept his eye on over-ambitious commanders. Finally, the Maya went some way towards creating a permanent force of regulars. This was the *Guardia*, or Guard of the Saint, which was charged with the protection of the cross itself. It was made up of several companies of 150 men and all the rebels did one month's service in it, living in barracks at Chan Santa Cruz, the capital of the insurgent area. In fact very few of the Maya were permanent residents there. One of the most pressing problems was food, and all able-bodied people, including the generals and company commanders, were obliged to assist with the work in the corn fields, in the surrounding villages.

But ultimately time was not on the side of the Mayas. 'They lived at subsistence level, at the mercy of the dry year, corn fungus, hail and hurricanes,
with no reserves to fall back on, under the recurring lash of small-pox, cholera
and whooping cough.'[8] Their numbers dwindled. In 1855 there were 40,000
of them, in 1870 20,000, and by 1895 there were no more than half that
number. What the Mexicans were unable to achieve in their numerous raids,
was done for them by natural causes. In 1900 they decided that they were in a
position to finish with the problem once and for all. Under the command of
General Ignacio Bravo they began to lay a railway line right across the rebel
region. Moving at about 10 miles a month, the engineers and soldiers methodically hacked their way through the forest, never giving the Indians a small
enough target for them to attack. Unable to resist effectively, the rebels
scattered for ever and the Caste War was finally ended.

In 1910 Mexico was convulsed by yet another revolution. It began inno-
cently enough, in November, when Francisco Madero assumed the provisional
presidency, from Díaz, and called for certain limited constitutional reforms.
But the fall of Díaz revealed the deep-seated grievances of the whole Mexican
people, grievances which had gradually been growing up over the years. What
was intended as a swift *coup d'état* soon turned into a long and bloody social
revolution. By and large this great upheaval took the form of a guerrilla war,
and as such it can be divided into two basic parts. One was the war waged in
northern Mexico by Pancho Villa (Doroteo Arango), the other the much more
dogged struggle led by Emiliano Zapata, in Morelos in the south. The two
wars offer interesting insights into the significance of the *social base* of a guerrilla
war, and the way in which different social groups are more or less fitted to wage
this type of struggle.

Villa's force had certain very important military advantages. His base,
Chihuahua, was a region of vast ranches and the bulk of its population was
landless and rootless. Thus the cowboys, muleskinners, bandits, peddlers and
refugee peons that made up his army, the so-called Division of the North, were
completely mobile, able to advance, retreat and regroup at will. As a hard-
hitting force of irregular cavalry they were almost without parallel. One of the
soldiers fighting against them sent back a report which contains a delightful
summary of the problems of waging war against guerrillas: 'I have the honour
to inform you that according to all information that is true and verified, Villa is
at this moment in all parts and none in particular.' But this very rootlessness
had important drawbacks. The Villistas had no concrete social aspirations, no
vested interest in a particular form of social or political organisation, that could
give their struggle any specific point. Thus they had no incentive to carry on
their struggle if faced by severe setbacks, nor any strategic ambitions that could
give their endless *galopades* some unified coherence. Moreover, this lack of class
interests made them much easier to bribe. Though Villa gave some nominal

support to the demands of the land-hungry peasantry of the south, and even confiscated certain large *haciendas* in this region, many of his lieutenants regarded the war simply as a means of enriching themselves. Many of the estates seized soon passed into their hands and these men became petty warlords, bitterly opposed to the agrarian radicalism that threatened their new acquisitions. In the last analysis, the inchoate Villista struggle was a case of every man for himself, and no guerrilla war can long maintain itself when built upon such shaky foundations. This lack of social coherence seems to have affected even the Villistas' tactical conceptions. In 1915 Villa attacked the Constitutionalist forces under Alavara Obregón, but he seems to have taken no account of the vastly superior Constitutionalist firepower. At this battle, at Celeya, Villa's massed cavalry charges were cut to shreds by Obregón's machine-guns, protected by trenches and barbed wire. From this date the Villista movement began to decline and was never again a significant force in the revolution.

Emiliano Zapata's struggle lasted much longer, and was not finally ended until his death, in an ambush, in 1919. The basic reason for his ability to lead a more protracted struggle was the solid support given by the peasantry of Morelos, fighting to protect their communal village lands against the encroachments of the sugar plantation owners. The specific nature of this objective, and the fact that it was the common goal of almost the whole population of that state, gave Zapata's movement more resilience than that of Villa in the north.

He began operations in 1911, with his base behind the line between the towns of Jojulta and Yecaptixla. Though a supporter of Madero, his demands and his growing influence in his own state soon alienated the clique of generals around the new president, notably Victoriano Huerta, and by the end of the year Zapata was a hunted outlaw. He fled into the mountains on the Puebla-Guerrero border and there began to rally other guerrilla chiefs to his side. By the middle of 1914 his supporters controlled much of Morelos, and from then until autumn 1915 he was left in peace to organise his own regime within the state. Another series of offensives against him lasted until 1916, but by the end of the year he was again in control of the region. At the end of 1917 the Government began to put pressure on him yet again, and in 1919, having lost control of all the towns and with his support fast dwindling, he was murdered in a treacherous ambush.

Zapata's actual tactics are of little especial interest, being based mainly on swift hit-and-run raids and occasional concentrations to take the larger towns. But what is of exceptional importance, in the light of later developments, is his emphasis upon the maintenance of amicable civil-military relations. From the beginning Zapata realised that to survive his movement must have the whole-hearted support of the people, and that his policies must be designed to alienate that support as little as possible. Thus, in 1912, he began to charge the main cost of his campaigns not to his supporters in the pueblos, but to the local sugar planters. In November a *junta* of guerrilla leaders decided that a weekly tax was to be levied on each *hacienda*, and the various chiefs allotted each other a zone of collection. A letter was sent to each planter in which it was pointed out that if he refused to pay up his cane fields would be burnt. In this way Zapata removed the financial burden from the villagers and ensured himself a much larger source of revenue.

The various series of instructions that Zapata issued to his officers also reveal his intense concern with the maintenance of popular support. Those of May 1913 stipulated that the officers should 'levy forced loans on prosperous merchants and landlords, replace local officials "in accordance with the will of the people" ... and lend their "moral and material support" to villages presenting titles and filing reclamations' in support of claims for the restitution of common lands.[9] In October Zapata had to face up to the problems of trying to take the struggle beyond the guerrilla stage and initiating conventional, positional operations. Fresh instructions were issued to the officers:

> 'These rules greatly elaborated the formal structure of the army. Chiefs were to name corporals and sergeants ... "so that they ... may mobilise their troops with more exactitude and rapidity". Any subordinate was to obey any superior, whether he belonged to his outfit or not. Soldiers in combat or on march were to stay in their assigned units and not mingle with others ... Any soldier who left his post in battle or retreat was a deserter, and on missions requiring them to abandon their units soldiers had to carry written orders.'[10]

The rules on collecting forced loans and the prohibitions on pillage and other abuses to the villagers were made just as strictly, but there was a distinct weakening of the powers of officers to initiate or promote land reform, or replace local officials. Here Zapata and his advisers had been brought face to face with the problems inherent in an attempt to raise a guerrilla struggle to a higher level. Because of the increased military and logistical demands of regular warfare it was essential that the army had a secure rear and that internal dissension was reduced to the minimum. Thus it was dangerous at this point to emphasise the radical aspects of the Zapatista programme. For the time being it was felt safer to promote unity among the civilians in the rear, rather than put any stress on potentially divisive issues. This is a consideration that will be seen again when I come on to deal with Maoist strategies during the period of military and political consolidation in the base areas.[11] But it is worth noting at this stage that, though the concept 'support of the people' sounds quite straightforward, it can in fact involve a guerrilla leader in quite complex decisions about the relative merits of a narrow-based radicalism or broad-based class unity.

But whatever Zapata's policy at a particular moment he was always aware of the absolute necessity of extensive popular support. During the period of peace in Morelos, in 1915, the work of harmonising the military and the civilian population went on. Under Zapata's guidance, and because of strong pressures from the inhabitants themselves:

'The Liberating Army of the Centre and the South was a "people's army" ... The army and the village leaders worked out in practice a federal chain of command. The army chief passed his orders down to the village chiefs, or their deputies, who campaigned with him, and they in turn passed the orders on to their respective followings. This mediation usually contained the tension between rival authorities.'[12]

In 1917 Zapata set up a system of political commissars, members of the Consultation Centre for Revolutionary Propaganda and Unification. These men were to tour the pueblos setting up revolutionary juntas, mediating between the guerrilla commanders and the civilians, giving public explanations of headquarters decrees and manifestos, and advising headquarters about future policy. In March he issued a decree which defined the responsibilities of the guerrillas and the civilians. The latter were to provide the soldiers with food and supplies, to help the wounded, and to act as guides and couriers. At the same time, however, they were allowed to elect their own governments and maintain their own courts and police. Soldiers had to refrain completely from intervening in civilian disputes, and had no rights over the land that was given back to the villages. Even in 1919, when Zapata was once again on the run in the mountains, his orders revealed his overriding concern with civilian-military relations. In March he wrote: 'When asking for food, you will do so with good words, and whatever you want ask for it in a good manner, and always showing your gratitude ... The better we behave the sooner we will triumph and have all the pueblos on our side.'[13]

Until the Government was able to mobilise enough forces for the campaign of 1918–19 their counter-insurgency methods were of a typical crudity. One of their basic tactics was wholesale deportation. In 1912 General Robles began a systematic resettlement campaign in which he forced the population to come to concentration camps built on the outskirts of the larger towns. He persuaded them to do this by simply burning down their pueblos. General Huerta went on to suggest that it might be advisable to deport between 15,000 and 20,000 labourers from Morelos. A little later Robles set this operation in motion and decreed that all inhabitants of pueblos, ranchos and the smaller hamlets had to 'reconcentrate' in the major towns. Suspected pueblos would be then razed to the ground. In 1916 Pablo González renewed this policy and ordered the concentration of all rural families in the nearest town, ready for deportation out of the state. In November he passed to outright terror. The summary death penalty was decreed for anyone 'who directly or indirectly lends support to Zapatismo ..., with no more requirements than identification.' Also liable for the death penalty was anyone caught without certified safe-conducts, anyone not resettled in the specified towns, and anyone who had given his pass to another person.

Cuba is well-known to anyone with even a passing knowledge of guerrilla warfare, because of the recent success and later notoriety of Fidel Castro and Ernesto Guevara. What is less well-known is that this island was the scene of a very determined guerrilla struggle at the end of the nineteenth century. There were, in fact, two distinct campaigns, one from 1868–78 and the other from 1895–98. The first campaign, often known as the First War of Liberation, began in the east of the island when many of the Creole planters there freed their slaves and then began military operations against the Spaniards. There were perhaps 20,000 rebels in the first two years, organised in small, mobile bands. Only one quarter of them had rifles, the rest being armed with machetes. They limited themselves to minor sabotage operations, cutting roads and railways. At first, indeed, the war was little more than formalised banditry, and the rebel forces included many escaped slaves who had turned to banditry, such as the famous chief 'Guillermón'. In late 1869 other leaders began to emerge, particularly Antonio Maceo and Máximo Gómez. They wanted to take the war beyond the localised stage and to launch an invasion of the west of the island. They began systematically to destroy the sugar plantations in the east but were unable to persuade the rebels to venture out of their base areas. In 1872 the Spaniards scored several minor successes and rebel numbers dwindled to 12,000 men at the most. In 1874 the invasion westward was at last undertaken, but by this time the insurgency had lost much of its momentum. Eventually the guerrillas had to pull back because of an acute shortage of ammunition. They tried again in January 1875, but the arrival of 25,000 Spanish reinforcements, bringing the occupation forces to over 60,000 men, and the increasing number of rebel desertions made their position untenable. Renewed Spanish offensives in 1878, under General Campos, rounded up most of the remaining guerrillas or drove them into exile.

In 1895 Gómez, Maceo and José Martí returned to the island. Once again they made their bases in the east and soon had a force of some 8,000 men. They operated in large mounted bands of several hundred men, and this time Gómez was able to extend the war westwards almost immediately. He took with him a Liberation Army of 500 infantry and 1,000 cavalry. These men were known as the Expeditionaries and were not recruited locally nor did they simply remain in one place to fight. As well as this mobile force of semi-regulars there were the local troops who remained in their own areas to carry out harassing operations. There was one division for each of the six provinces, and each division was broken down into bands known as brigades, regiments and troops (*fuerza*). By 1896 the rebels had almost reached Havana and General Campos resigned, to be replaced by General Weyler.

The latter began to organise much more extensive counter-insurgency operations. He cut down the number of static army posts in the countryside and organised each battalion as a mobile column, self-sufficient within its own 200-kilometre square area. These columns were encouraged to be as mobile as possible, remaining in the field and continually harassing the guerrillas. Instructions issued to the troops in December 1896 were particularly insistent upon the necessity for counter-insurgency troops to remain in the field:

'I observe that the columns operating in Havana and Matanzas provinces, instead of camping in places or mountains frequented by the enemy, go nightly to the towns or mills in their zone to sleep. This has grave consequences for the operations, since it makes it easier for the enemy to know the route which the columns will take the next day, and also their number and morale ... For these reasons, please arrange that all columns of both provinces, when setting out for operations, take with them three days worth of rations and four of biscuits; with these, and with the cattle that abound in the provinces, it is easy to sustain the forces for six days in operations, camping on the mountains and at crossroads, being able from the encampments to send picked troops swiftly for reconnaissance for four kilometres around, while the encampment is being prepared. In this way the enemy will be kept in a constant state of uneasiness ... My aim is that during my stay in Pinar del Río there should not remain a place or a mountain that will not have been crossed by the respective column, while all really suspicious places will have been camped in.'[14]

In addition, Weyler developed the *trocha* system. The *trocha* was a clearing some hundreds of yards wide that ran right across the island, dividing the eastern and the western provinces. The bush was cut down and barbed wire entanglements constructed. Forty yards behind the wire, blockhouses were built as quarters for the troops. The smallest of these, a simple mud and planks hut for five men, were every 150 yards, a larger type every quarter of a mile, and the largest every half mile. As well as this the whole island was covered with networks of loop-holed, bullet-proof blockhouses, commanding every eminence and valley. Sometimes the blockhouses were grouped in circles and sometimes in zig-zags or straight lines. Finally, Weyler resorted to the old expedient of resettlement. The whole of the population in 'military areas' – and the whole of Cuba was designated a military area at this time – were to be concentrated in specific and well-defined outposts, each served by its own special zone of cultivation. These measures soon began to take effect. Maceo's campaign of spring 1896, in Havana province, had been very successful, with many cane-fields burnt down, telegraphs cut, railway lines and bridges blown up. But then Maceo was killed and by the end of the year Pinar del Río, Havana and Matanzas provinces had been effectively subdued. By the summer of 1897, only Oriente province remained as a guerrilla stronghold, and the only significant leader left, Quintin Banderas, was almost surrounded by the Spanish troops. From then on the suppression of the insurgency would be only a matter of time.

The last notable guerrilla struggle to be dealt with in this section in fact took place in the twentieth century, in the inter-war period. However, as it does not form a part of the contemporary, post-Castro upsurge of guerrilla activity in Latin America it seems more appropriate to deal with it here. It took place in Nicaragua, between 1927 and 1933, under the leadership of Augusto César Sandino. He was a supporter of the liberal politician Juan Sacasa, who was deposed by the Americans in November 1926, and replaced by the conservative, Adolfo Díaz. Sandino began operations almost immediately, acting together with a liberal general, Moncada. The latter surrendered in the following year but Sandino continued to wage a guerrilla war. His successes obliged the Americans to send more and more troops into the country and Sandino's struggle took on a clear nationalist character. He himself had absolutely no interest in obtaining a post in any future government and was emphatic that: 'The day the gringos go, we arrange to lay down our arms.'

His original base area was in San Rafael del Norte, on Yacapuca mountain in the coffee country of Junetega province. When Moncada surrendered he moved to Yalí, from where he carried on his harassing operations. They were of the usual type, as is made clear by the report of a contemporary observer:

'Every tree, every thicket, every rock was a possible hiding place for a rifleman or a patriot spy. The invaders knew it and travelled only on known roads or in open fields, pistols and rifles ready to fire ... Even so, they were uneasy, for at any moment, without warning, a fusillade came from different points ... and when the North Americans reacted and counter-attacked, the tracks disappeared into the jungle, where it was even more dangerous. After killing their usual 'tenths' of the gringos, they retired in good order as silently as they had come.'[15]

Like most guerrilla groups, Sandino's men were dependent for their arms and other supplies on the enemy himself. In an interview the nationalist leader pointed out: 'If it weren't for the guns and munitions we've taken from United States convoys, we should be in a bad way. The more forces they send, the better we can fight.'[16]

In order to drive him from his base in Yalí, the Americans used aircraft to strafe and bomb his positions. This was one of the first times that this particular weapon had been used extensively in a counter-insurgency campaign and it proved quite successful. In the early 1930s Sandino was forced to shift his base back to the original hideout in San Rafael del Norte. Then, in 1933, the leader himself was captured and murdered. After this the patriot movement soon collapsed. Latin America had come to the end, though only briefly, of a cycle of guerrilla struggles that had gone on for a hundred years and more.

The Far East

In 1824–25, 1852 and 1885 the British fought three wars against the Burmese. The latter chose to fight more or less conventionally and the British were able to crush the resistance without much trouble. At the end of the Third Anglo-Burmese War, however, the British decided it was time to annex the upper regions of that country, between Yunnan and the Indian frontier. In the end they were successful, but not before they had struggled through a wearying series of guerrilla campaigns fought by the Kachin and Chin groups of tribes.

The fighting against the Kachins began in 1885 and Major-General White of the Burma Field Force left a typical description of colonial guerrilla warfare, revealing his contempt for this mode of combat, whilst at the same time showing how difficult it was for the small British forces to cope with it:

'These bands are freebooters, pillaging wherever they go, but usually reserving the refinement of cruelty for those who have taken ... part with us. Flying columns arrive too late to save the village. The villagers, having cause to realise that we are too far off to protect them, lose confidence in our power and throw in their lot with the insurgents. They make terms with the leaders and baffle the pursuit of those leaders by roundabout guidance or systematic silence. In a country, itself one vast military obstacle, the seizure of the leaders of rebellion ... thus becomes a source of greatest difficulty.'[17]

One is entitled to wonder whether the natives' motives were merely fear of the insurgents or whether they were not in fact based upon the same antipathy to the invaders that drove the guerrillas into the jungle.

The main Kachin tactic was to set up ambushes in small stockades which they constructed alongside the trails followed by the British. To one British officer they were 'a secret and treacherous foe ... armed with Sniders, jingals and dahs; elusive, murderous, lying in wait behind stockades, shooting and vanishing ...'[18] By late 1886 the British had not made much progress in crushing the revolt. But in October, the District Commissioner at Sagaing, Mr Colquhoun, tried to find inspiration in the lessons of history. He likened the insurgency to the rebellion in the Vendée, in 1793, and decided that the British might profitably adopt some of the tactics used by General Lazare Hoche during his occupation of the area. He circulated a description of these tactics and noted that they were 'equally applicable to Upper Burma'. He then outlined his own plans for containing and defeating the Kachins. He wanted:

> 'A system of inland posts fifteen to twenty miles apart, with constant patrols between them, so as to prevent raids of any strength upon the districts already pacified ..., these posts to gradually close in. The operations inside each converging line of posts are to be conducted by a mobile force under officers of marked energy ... to whom should be allowed great latitude of action. Behind the line of posts should come the district officer and his police and he should be able to disarm the whole district in several months ... Towards procuring the disarmament, fines should be inflicted ... which could be remitted later ... on good behaviour of villages. Support would then be given to good villages and arms issued ... to enable them to resist the attack of petty bands.'[19]

The war against the tribesmen went on almost without interruption until 1893, and there were also brief campaigns in 1896 and 1898, when dissident leaders returned from their sanctuaries in China, in Yunnan and Szechwan. By the end of the century, however, the British policy of stockade building, and the sending out of numerous punitive expeditions to impose fines or actually burn down villages and paddy fields, had broken the back of serious Kachin resistance.

Operations against the Chins began in 1888. At first the British simply tried to starve them into submission by blockading their supply routes from the plains. But the blockade was never sufficiently effective, and in November the standard policy of the punitive expedition was taken up. But the Chins proved to be as adept at guerrilla warfare as the neighbouring tribes and it was not until 1894 that resistance was finally crushed. Various British officers and administrators paid tribute to the Chins' tactical abilities. Of the operations in late 1888 one wrote: 'Whilst disputing every stage of our advance into the hills, the Chins showed considerable tactical ability by taking the offensive in the plains and attacking ... villages and our posts in the rear of the advancing column.' When they actually met a British column, another wrote: 'they fired at least a thousand yards, standing resolutely until actually charged, even trying to outflank us ... [They were] the most difficult enemy to see or hit I ever fought.'[20]

The British counter-insurgency operations fell into two distinct stages. For the most part they were concerned with trying to cow the whole population into submission. This involved a deliberate policy of sending out numerous punitive expeditions and attacking the very basis of the Chins' way of life – their homes and their crops. As Mr Carey, one of the British political officers, put it:

'In the plains disarmament can be effected without destroying villages and starving the people into submission, but in Chinland the enemy never sustains an attack, never holds a position, and never fights unless the physical features of the country give him every advantage. How, I ask, is such an enemy, in such a country, to be forced to surrender ... [his] arms ... without burning him out, driving him into the jungles, and starving him into submission?'[21]

Nobody could see a viable alternative to this basic strategy. In November 1892 General Palmer took charge of military operations and he immediately began building military posts at all the centres of cultivation. Unless the village in question agreed to surrender all guns in their possession, these garrisons were to destroy the crops actually in the fields as well as any stockpiles of harvested produce. As Palmer put it: 'Such an action may appear inhuman, but with a people whose tactics are so evasive that it is impossible to decide matters by general actions, and who ... are bound to get the better of us at their system of ambuscading and guerrilla warfare, no other course is likely to succeed.'[22] Eventually this ruthless policy paid its dividends. Gradually the villagers became more and more reluctant to support the guerrillas, and the bands shrank in size and effectiveness. Within a year they were reduced to a few marauding gangs, completely cut off from their main sources of supply and intelligence. Then British policy entered its second stage, and began to face the guerrillas themselves in overt military confrontation. As one commander wrote:

'Finding that the rebels were not to be disposed of by a *coup de grâce*, two outposts were placed in strategical positions; these were stored with rations and ... the sepoys emerged from these posts in small parties carrying their blankets and rations themselves, to scour the mountains and to track down the rebels, in exactly the same way as game is hunted, following up and keeping on their tracks.'[23]

At about the same time as the British were trying to pacify the tribesmen of Upper Burma, the French were facing bitter resistance to their intrusions into Indochina. In 1861, within the space of five months, they had easily defeated the conventional Vietnamese armies, but for the next 20 years they had to deal with a sporadic series of insurrections, in 1862, 1867, 1872, 1873, 1874, 1875 and 1878. These outbreaks were short-lived mass uprisings rather than guerrilla campaigns, and it was not until 1882 that Vietnamese resistance can be said to have taken this latter form. This stage began with Tu Duc's struggle against the French in Tonking, in the north of Indochina. His main fighting troops were Chinese Black Flag bandits from Kuangshi, under the leadership of a skilled guerrilla chieftain, Liu Yang-fu. The insurgents received much support from the surrounding villages and regularly destroyed isolated French columns by luring them from their strongpoints into carefully prepared ambushes. Even when the Black Flags opted out of the struggle in 1885, Vietnamese irregulars kept going until 1898. One of the main leaders at this stage was De Tham in the mountains of Thai Nguyen province. But the resistance movement was largely unconnected, made up of autonomous warlords who had little to do with their neighbours, even 20 miles away. French policy against them combined military operations with a strategy of 'divide and rule'. Where possible they made treaties with individual leaders, allowing them to raise taxes and even maintain armies so long as they undertook not to attack the French.

There were also important guerrilla revolts in Annam, in the south of Indochina. Two of these took place in the mountainous northern hinterland and one in the flat delta region of the south. The rebellions in the north were led by Thon That Thuyet and Nguyen Van Tuong, from 1885–88, the so-called Scholars' Revolt, and by Phan Dinh Phung, from 1893–95. The second was a particularly well-organised affair. Phan Dinh Phung had fought in the Scholars' Revolt and on its collapse he spent the next five years secretly preparing his forces for a new war against the French. His men were trained, disciplined and dressed in the Western fashion, and he divided the territory he meant to control into twelve military districts, each held by between 100 and 500 armed men. The revolt in the delta region was led by Nguyen Thien Thuat, De Kieu and Doc Ngu. It lasted until 1892 and the tactics were dictated by the nature of the terrain. In the mountainous northern regions the guerrillas were able to establish inaccessible fortresses as bases for their harrying operations. In the delta, however, the land was very flat and intersected by numerous roads and canals. Consequently:

> 'The war in the delta was fought by small and constantly moving groups of 20 to 25 guerrillas. These groups usually attacked at night and only when they were certain to take the enemy by surprise. They wasted no ammunition and promptly retreated when they met a superior force. Retreat, to the despair of the pursuing French, always meant that the guerrillas disappeared, either hiding in rice fields, or resuming their original role of peaceful peasants.'[24]

During these years of warfare French counter-insurgency policy underwent a profound transformation and various astute soldiers, notably Colonels Galliéni, Servière, Vallière and Pennequin developed a new, sophisticated theory of 'colonial warfare'. In the early years, as one Frenchman noted in 1904: 'We had ... no idea of the importance and quality of these Vietnamese bands. Our first columns merely traversed the country without occupying it; they were putting, a little too indifferently, steel and fire into every village where they met the slightest trace of resistance.'[25] This simply put the population at large more resolutely on the side of the guerrillas and made detection of the latter almost impossible. As the French Official History put it, in 1922: 'A column is helpless against these brigands, who at the approach of our troops, disperse in the villages, where, thanks to the complicity of the population, and probably the indigenous officials, they cannot be found . . . Our troops are paralysed by an absolute lack of information.'[26]

So, in the 1890s, the French adopted new policies based upon the need to improve the social and economic position of the population at large, and thus win over their whole-hearted support and isolate the guerrilla bands within an unfriendly population. The rationale behind this policy was admirably summed up, in 1895, by General Duchemin, reporting on operations in Tonking:

'The pirate [guerrilla] is a plant which grows only on certain grounds . . . The most efficient method is to render the ground unsuitable to him . . . There are no pirates in completely organised countries. To pluck wild plants is not sufficient: one must plough the conquered soil, enclose it and then sow it with the good grain, which is the only way to make it unsuitable to the tares. The same happens on the land desolated by piracy: armed occupation, with or without armed combat, ploughs it: the establishment of a military belt encloses and isolates it; finally the reconstitution and equipment of the population, the installation of markets and cultures, the construction of roads, sow the good grain and make the conquered region unsuitable to the pirate, if it is not the latter himself who, transformed, co-operates in this evolutionary process.'[27]

Nevertheless, it should not be thought that policy changed overnight. Their troops, like any army involved in a guerrilla struggle, were also forced to have recourse to more traditional repressive methods. Even in 1897 a French administrator, Jean-Marie de Lanessan, laid it down in his *Principes de Colonisation* that the old principles of collective responsibility and pure terror were still helpful: 'Every village that has given refuge to a band of guerrillas or not reported their passage is declared responsible and guilty. Consequently, the chief of the village and two or three principal inhabitants are beheaded, and the village itself is set on fire and razed to the ground.'[28]

Yet another European nation that became involved in guerrilla wars in their colonies were the Dutch, who took 150 years or so effectively to stamp out resistance movements in Java. Guerrilla warfare began as early as 1686 when the ex-bandit Surapati carved out a kingdom for himself in the Balambangan on the far eastern end of the island, and fought on until 1708. It was also one of the modes of resistance adopted by certain leaders during the Second and Third Wars of Javanese Independence, in 1719–27 and 1749–56, when the majority of the Javanese nobility, led by Mangkubumi and Mas Said, fought against the Dutch and their quislings.

But the most important outbreak was between 1825–30 when Dipa Negara, the Sultan of Jogjakarta, led a widespread resistance movement. There had long been popular resentment of Dutch rule, both on religious grounds and because of the general hatred of the Chinese tax-farmers. But Dipa Negara also needed the support of the aristocracy, and this he got when the Dutch suddenly refused to allow the landlords to lease out their lands and workers to European and Chinese entrepreneurs. By the middle of August 1825 the resistance movement controlled many of the Javanese provinces and even threatened Jogjakarta itself. The guerrillas, whose most important leader was Sentot, the Sultan's nephew, fought a typical campaign. They avoided fighting pitched battles, kept their headquarters constantly on the move, and concentrated upon setting up ambushes, raiding food columns, and descending upon small Dutch outposts. An interesting organisational refinement was the division of the guerrillas into two types of troops. Most of them were members of the irregular militia and were armed with knives and sharpened bamboo staves. But there was also a small force of mobile regulars who were armed with the few firearms that the insurgents managed to capture or buy.

At first the Dutch commander, de Koch, devoted himself to sending out punitive columns and burning villages and crops. Later he offered an anmesty to any guerrillas who would give themselves up, but neither of these policies, nor the huge reward offered for Dipa Negara, brought the Dutch much advantage. De Koch then had the wit to change his tactics. Instead of trying to terrorise the villagers he initiated a reform programme, which abolished many tolls and customs dues and introduced a new land policy. Then, in 1828, having won over many of the ordinary villagers, he began military operations against the remaining insurgents. He divided his forces into three main commands, built a network of forts around the guerrillas' base area, and linked these with roads patrolled by fast-moving columns of troops. By 1830 the revolt was almost over, but it had cost the lives of 15,000 Dutch troops and auxiliaries, and an estimated 200,000 Javanese.

As will be seen in due course, China was the scene of the biggest and most successful guerrilla war ever fought. In the nineteenth century, however, the country saw few important such struggles. The most well-known revolts were all conducted by conventional troops, intent on fighting pitched battles and storming the big cities. Amongst these were the Opium Wars, 1839–60, the Taiping Rebellion, 1852–64, and the Boxer Rebellion of 1900. But banditry was always rife in China at this period, and during the Taiping Rebellion, a widespread revolt against the decaying Manchu dynasty, certain of these bandit groups became involved in the general hostilities.

The most famous of these were the Nien, a secret association of poor peasants, salt-smugglers and bandits inhabiting the sandy region between the Yangtse Basin and the Yellow River, in the administrative no-man's land of the Kiangsu, Honan, Shantung and Chihli border region. The word 'nien' means twist or roll and was used to denote the secret cells of the organisation which became openly subversive from 1853, when the Taiping rebels captured Nanking. Until 1855 the Nien consolidated their forces, setting up small guerrilla groups mounted on sturdy horses that existed in plentiful supply in the region. In many basic respects they are a fascinating precursor of the Chinese Communist guerrillas of the 1930s and 1940s. As one eminent French historian has observed:

'The fighting methods of the Nien armies were . . . much more in harmony with the peasant temperament than those of the Taipings, who quickly raised enormous armies of tens of thousands of men . . . [They] fought in small guerrilla units, very mobile thanks to their horses, but still remaining close to the village population. Their code of conduct . . . [forbade] looting or taking food from the poor people.'[29]

From 1855 the Nien began to co-operate militarily with the Taipings. In 1857 they joined the rebels in Anhui, and in 1862 it was feared that they might come to help raise the siege of Nanking. Even after the Taiping collapse in 1864 the Nien fought on, and their guerrillas campaigned over much of north China. In 1865 they fought and killed the Manchu's best general, the Mongolian, Seng-ko-lin-chin. Their bands were able to move upwards of 30 miles a day and 'whenever their enemies . . . came too close for comfort, they managed to wear them out by marching in circles and darting about this way and that like swarms of ants. As a rule they avoided battle with the troops sent against them.'[30] In June 1865 the Manchus sent another of their best generals, Tseng Kuo-fan, against them but it took him the best part of three years to wear them down. One of his reports indicates the difficulties he faced:

'The Nien-fei suddenly appear and as quickly disappear – a hundred *li* in the flash of an eye! The reports of the spies are very uncertain. Being without definite information, I have not been able to turn and go everywhere. On the contrary there is nothing to do but take the word of each leader, allowing him to be his own spy, have full control, go or stop at will, with plans adapted to the circumstances.'[31]

Luckily for the general the Nien became carried away by their own successes. In 1867 they began to organise regiments made up of horsemen and infantrymen with heavy pikes. They consolidated into two main armies and gave Tseng

Kuo-fan the chance to slowly surround and inexorably close in. By early 1868 the movement had been utterly crushed.

The last major guerrilla action in the Far East, in this period, took place in the Philippines between 1897 and 1903. The war was fought in two stages. The first was a brief campaign, in 1897, against the Spanish who at that time included the sprawling archipelago in their empire. It was organised by a secret nationalist organisation known as the Katipunan and began as an attempted insurrectionary takeover in August 1896. The attempt failed and the insurgents fell back on guerrilla operations, in Cavite province. The main leader to emerge in this period was Emiliano Aguinaldo, who scored some notable military successes against the Spaniards and their auxiliaries. But the movement was not strong enough to survive and in 1897 Aguinaldo went into voluntary exile, in return for Spanish promises to introduce several democratic reforms. Once he had left the Spanish quietly forgot their promises.

In 1898, however, Filipino resentment found fresh stimulus in the out-break of hostilities between Spain and the United States. After Dewey's American fleet had pulverised the Spanish Navy in Manila Bay, Filipino irregulars began to harass the occupying troops and drive them into the main cities. But when the American troops finally landed they refused to allow the insurgents to enter Manila itself, and soon made it clear that they had no intention of allowing the islanders independence, the aim of almost all the rebels. In the treaty signed with the Spanish the Americans simply bought the islands for $20 million. Certain of the nationalists, Aguinaldo included, decided that armed resistance was the only answer and, in January 1899, plans were laid for an insurrection. The nationalists were to pretend to be American sympathisers so as to be able to keep an eye on American defences, and study their outposts and head-quarters. In fact the Filipino leaders never had any chance to attempt the siezure of power at one fell swoop, for on February 4 American and Filipino soldiers started firing on one another at various points. The islanders were soon pushed back into the interior, and on May 12 a conference was held to lay plans for a protracted guerrilla campaign. The war went on until 1902 when Aguinaldo was captured and other prominent generals, such as Lukban and Malvar, decided to surrender.

For those three years, however, the war followed a classic pattern. The terrain was of considerable help to the insurgents. As General Arthur MacArthur wrote, whilst in command of the American forces: 'The density of the jungle, which prevented seeing any distance, made it impossible to keep the troops together ... impeded and at times completely interrupted their movement ... To intercept the insurgent retreat was almost impossible.'[32] Added to which the guerrillas had the whole-hearted co-operation of the population, as MacArthur again made clear: 'The practice of discarding uniforms enables the insurgents to appear and disappear within the American lines in the attitude of peaceful natives, absorbed in that dense mass of sympathetic people, speaking a dialect of which few men and no Americans have any knowledge.'[33] In June 1900 a pamphlet was published by the nationalist representatives in Madrid, and it gives an indication of their clear insight into the nature of a revolutionary guerrilla war:

> 'The guerrillas must seek out the sympathies of the people and defend them against bandits and thieves ... They must make up for their small numbers by their ceaseless activity ... By day, hide in the woods and in distant areas then, when least expected, fall upon the enemy and disappear at once to enjoy whatever spoils ... taken from the Yankees, but they shall be careful not to rob their countrymen ... The commander must never camp twice in the same place, always march at night, show himself only in places where he does not usually operate and fall suddenly on the enemy when least expected ... When the enemy attacks they shall retreat towards the base of operations ... Once the enemy tires ... they shall unite to fall upon them ... with all the advantage of position carefully chosen beforehand ... It is essential always to have a tactical plan, to thoroughly reconnoitre the ground to ... take advantage of the conditions and to know the strength of the enemy.'[34]

But the Filipinos simply did not have the experience or the material resources to hold off the Americans for ever, and certainly not to drive them off the islands. By the beginning of 1902, Aguinaldo was on the run, moving his base from place to place in the mountains. At the same time the Americans resorted to the standard resettlement, or *zona* technique by which the whole population of an area was concentrated in one camp and anyone found outside it was shot on sight. Certain American commanders were even more ruthless. General 'Jake' Smith, on Samar Island, told his men: 'I want no prisoners. I want you to kill and burn; the more you burn and kill the better it will please me.'[35] His troops did their best to make him a happy man, at least until his court-martial and forcible retirement.

Central Asia

One of the lesser known imperialist forays of the last century was that undertaken by the Russians in central Asia. Russian expansion southwards involved her army in one of the bloodiest guerrilla wars fought by any country during the nineteenth century. This was in the Caucasus where, between 1836 and 1859, the Tsar's troops faced the fanatical resistance of the Moslem inhabitants, under the leadership of Imam Shamyl, one of the most determined guerrilla leaders history has yet thrown up.

This particular conflict was known as the Murid War, after the name given to the fighting monks who formed the core of Shamyl's forces. The Murids were headed by 100 Naibs who supplied the top officers and the spiritual inspiration. Under these were 1,000 Mursfiids who were in charge of the rest of the Murids, who were divided into units of 10, 100 and 500 men. This élite force was supplemented, when necessary, by a levy of one man to each household or, occasionally, of every able-bodied male. Many of these men were mounted on horseback and often adopted the Magyar tactic of galloping up, their reins between their teeth, to rein in a short distance away and let loose a devastating volley. Then, according to the effectiveness of their firing, they would close in with their swords or gallop away as swiftly as they had come. Any Russian force that pursued them was as likely as not to be lured into an ambush. For ambushes were a basic Murid tactic and they made the fullest use of the thick forests that covered much of the Caucasus. As one Russian general described it:

> 'Fighting went on from beginning to end of each march: men fell, but no enemy was seen ... Our sharp-shooters, who went in pairs ... often lost sight of each other in the forest, and strayed from the main column. Then the Tchetchens would ... spring on the isolated men, and hack them to pieces before their comrades could come to their rescue.'[36]

Indeed, it was the physical features of the area that gave the Murids their greatest advantage. Even the climate, with its scorching summers and freezing winters, was to their advantage. Moreover, as well as thick forests, the Caucasus had numerous mountain ranges, and those of Daghestan offered an almost impenetrable base area for Shamyl's followers. This description of the disastrous Russian expedition of 1845 shows just how Shamyl capitalised upon the terrain of his homeland:

> '[He] knew that ... the Russians ... could penetrate the mountains, but could not maintain themselves there. He also knew that he had no earthly chance of beating such an army ... in the open ... His opportunity would come later ... when ... the invaders, worn with toil, weak with privation, uninspirited by successes in the field, would have to face the homeward march over the barren mountains ... or through the forests of Itchkeria. Then, indeed, he would let loose upon them his mobile hordes, break down the roads in front of them, seize every opportunity of cutting off front or rear guard, of throwing the centre with its wearying baggage train and lengthy line of wounded into confusion, and give the men no rest by day or night.'[37]

One of Shamyl's messages to the Tsar, for whom the Caucasus was an 'underdeveloped', bandit-ridden wilderness, gives a perfect summary of the advantages that terrain might have for a guerrilla force:

'You may say my roads are bad and my country impassable. It is well: that is the reason why the powerful white Tsar and all his armies who march on me ceaselessly can still do nothing against me ... My bad roads, my forests and mountains, make me stronger than many monarchs. I should anoint my trees with oil, and mix my mud with fragrant honey, and garland my rocks with laurel and bay, so much do they aid me in my battle for Caucasian freedom.'[38]

The nature of the terrain also shaped Russian counter-insurgency tactics and forced them to the same 'logical' conclusion that underlay the American defoliation programme in Vietnam. The Russians, too, attacked the terrain itself rather than the men of Shamyl's armies. Under Prince Bariatinsky, in charge of the Russian forces from the early 1850s, a huge programme of forest clearance was set in motion. As the trees were methodically cut down the soldiers behind stormed the villages that were uncovered and pushed those rebels that wished to fight on up into the mountains. Once the forests were completely cleared, Bariatinsky attacked the very mountains themselves. He built bridges across the great gorges so as to avoid the necessity of tortuous ascents and descents along winding trails. Finally, when the Murids were isolated in a few remaining strongholds, he used dynamite and long-range artillery to literally blow them to pieces. In 1859 Shamyl was cornered with the remnants of his force in one last fortress, and after a short siege he was prevailed upon to surrender.

Terrain also dominated the fighting in the other area of central Asia that I wish to mention. This was the North-West Frontier where hostilities were continuous from the beginning of British annexation in 1843 right up until their withdrawal in 1947. It would be absolutely impossible to present here a detailed record of the numerous skirmishes, raids and punitive expeditions that made up these 100 years of frontier warfare. All that can be attempted is a brief description of the tactics and counter-tactics of the Pathans, a collective name for some 130 tribes and sub-tribes, and the Imperial soldiery.

Terrain dictated these tactics. The whole area was covered with hills and mountains, and there were hardly any open spaces not within rifle-range of high ground. The hills were always steep, usually covered with a treacherous surface of loose stones or boulders. The lie of the land was irregular, and it was rarely possible to move from one valley or plain to another without having to pass through some narrow ravine or gorge. It was, in short, the perfect environment for a war of petty ambuscades. The Pathan was the perfect warrior to carry on such a mode of combat, to perpetuity if necessary:

'He could cover the most difficult hill-side at top speed and on his home ground knew every yard of the way. Carrying only a rifle, a knife, and perhaps fifty rounds of ammunition, he was virtually tireless, as fresh at the end of a long day as when it started. Brought up in the shadows of the family blood-feud, where his life . . . depended on a highly developed sense of caution and cunning, he was a natural tactician, with a keen eye for a fleeting chance. His idea of an even battle was when the odds were at five to one or better in his favour. He could be very patient, and generally had plenty of opportunity to reconnoitre the scene of action before he committed himself to battle.'[39]

At first the tribesmen were only armed with rather inefficient home-made flintlocks, and their main tactic was to use them for short-range covering fire to support a rush of swordsmen. But the techniques of their gunsmiths soon improved and also more and more European weapons fell into their hands, through capture and trade. Then long-range fire-power became the dominant component of Pathan warfare. This, obviously, made it even more difficult for British troops to ever get to grips with their opponents.

British tactics were methodical rather than inspired. The most important breakthrough was the use of piquets to guard the higher slopes of a defile and so prevent the Pathans from being able to fire down on a column that was passing through. The method was first used by General Pollock, upon the suggestion of Frederick Mackeson, whilst forcing the Khyber Pass in 1842. 'The Afridis still remember the occasion; it was only when Pollock adopted, as they say, their own tactics . . . that he became successful.'[40] But the British did not go much further towards adopting the Pathans' own tactics. They almost always travelled in bulky columns that were encumbered by long baggage trains whose protection forced the troops to remain together always and slowed them down considerably. Nor was much progress made in the realm of minor tactics. The British rarely set up ambushes of their own, and hardly ever engaged in night-fighting, even though the Pathans were notoriously off their guard at this time. There was no permanent School of Mountain Warfare, even though such an institution was set up from time to time at Abbotabad. Intelligence, too, was badly neglected. A Frontier Intelligence Corps was set up in 1906, but until 1933 there was no central bureau to handle the information that came in from half-a-dozen separate intelligence agencies.

The basic British expedient was to try and strike at the very resources of tribal life. A punitive column did not try to deter the Pathans so much by killing their warriors as by destroying their means of livelihood, much as the British and French were wont to do in Burma and Indochina. The Tirah Campaign of 1907–8 was typical in this respect. Having battled through to a particularly fertile and well-populated part of the Maidan Valley, the British 'practically laid it waste with fire and sword from end to end . . . unearthed and consumed the grain and fodder supply of the country, uprooted and ringed the walnut groves, prevented the autumn tillage of the soil, and . . . caused the inhabitants to live the lives of fugitives, upon the exposed . . . and bitterly cold hill-tops.'[41] From 1920 aircraft were used quite extensively to assist in this kind of operation. They were employed in two ways. Usually they established what was called an air blockade. After two days of heavy bombardment on an area, the planes would make less heavy but persistent raids over the villages and fields, by day and night, to make it almost impossible for the tribesman and his family to visit his house, grazing grounds or water supply. This relentless pressure would be kept up until the tribe in question made what were felt to be meaningful peace overtures. Sometimes aircraft were used to support the infantry, attacking carefully defined areas on their flanks, front and rear. Indeed, the British were probably the first to use aircraft as counter-insurgency weapons.

Africa

In June 1830 France landed an expeditionary force of 37,000 men in Algeria. In early July Algiers fell to the invaders. But the occupation of the coastal towns and the destruction of Ottoman power was but a very small step towards the effective occupation of Algeria as a whole. From the beginning the French came up against the resistance of the tribes of the interior, both the nomads of the plateaux and the Berber peasants of the coastal mountain massifs. In 1832 the Arabs chose as their leader Abd-el Kader, who organised a bitter guerrilla resistance which lasted until his capture in 1847. Abd-el Kader did fight some more or less conventional engagements with his hordes of fast-moving Arab cavalry, as at Macta in 1834 and Tenia in 1840, but his strategy was basically of a guerrilla nature, particularly after his defeat in the latter battle. His main opponent, from 1840, was Marshal Bugeaud who was quick to see that only a guerrilla war could be effective against the large French forces in the country, 78,000 men after 1841. Referring to the Emir's attempt to keep a regular army in being, Bugeaud said: 'This is not his strength. I will go further; it is even a source of weakness, because it is just this that will enable us to catch him one day. Do you know where his strength lies? It lies in his elusiveness, in the vast distances to be traversed, in the heat of the African sun, in the lack of water, in the nomadism . . . of the Arab.'[42] But the Emir was no fool. He too came to realise that his only chance lay in guerrilla operations rather than in any attempt to put concentrated masses in the field. As he himself said of his instructions to the tribal leaders: 'To do the maximum amount of damage to the enemy, without receiving any yourself, that was advice I gave them.' He went on to make an analogy that is strikingly reminiscent of a later, more famous metaphor of Mao Tse-tung: 'When you stand on the shore, and watch the fish swimming about freely in the sea, it seems as if you had only to stretch out your hand to grasp them; yet it needs all the skill and the nets of the fisherman to master them. So it is with the Arabs.'

Finally, in a letter to Louis-Philippe, written in 1838, Abd-el Kader made clear what his basic strategy was to be: 'It will be a partisan war to the death. I am not so foolish as to imagine that I can openly make headway against your troops; but I can harass them ceaselessly. I shall lose ground, no doubt; but then I shall have on my side a knowledge of the country, the frugality and hardiness of my troops.'[43] So it was. The Emir set up a three-line defence: around Algiers; along a line between Themcen and Médéa; and another between Sebdou and Biskra. In these areas the Arabs, sustaining themselves from huge granaries buried underground, ceaselessly harried the French, hanging on their flanks, cutting communications, seizing their baggage and transports, making unexpected attacks, and luring the enemy into ambushes by feigned retreats.

French counter-insurgency methods achieved nothing until the arrival of Bugeaud in 1840. Even in 1836 he was putting forward his basic ideas to the administrators in Algiers. In a memorandum on the methods to be used to finish the war he asked for an increase in the number of troops in Algeria, insisted that all such troops should be volunteers, that they should carry all their supplies on pack mules, and that it was futile to build great numbers of fortified outposts, as these simply absorbed men to garrison and supply them. It was preferable that as many troops as possible should be used in active pursuit of the Arabs. Minor successes against the guerrillas 'can [only] become decisive by persevering with the system of active, mobile columns which cross the country from end to end and fight the enemy wherever he appears. Only thus can one subdue whole peoples.'[44] As soon as he took command in Algiers he immediately began putting this policy into effect. His main emphasis was upon mobility. The troops' equipment was lightened and simplified as much as possible. Supplies were put on the backs of mules or camels, instead of being carried in wagons. The soldiers were ordered where possible to find their supplies on the spot, and columns were allowed to take only four days provisions with them, even when it was envisaged that they would be in the field for 20 days or more. Garrisons were built only in those areas that had been completely subjugated. There a network of blockhouses would be built, commanding the roads, and these would be used as bases for further penetrations by the light columns.

Bugeaud faced his toughest opposition in the coastal mountains which continued to resist even after the pacification of much of the interior. In 1846 Bugeaud wrote a small treatise concerned exclusively with the strategy and tactics of mountain warfare. In the Kabyles, he noted, the Berbers 'do not retreat great distances like the Arabs and, whilst they rarely make frontal attacks, they throw themselves upon . . . the flanks and rear of our troops when they are bottled up in the narrow paths which makes it difficult for the head [of a column] to come to the assistance of the rearguard.' Thus it is the nature of the terrain that must dictate the tactics of the invader, not the defenders themselves. For, with 'the Kabyle warriors ... like all bands without organisation or discipline, numbers do not add much to their effectiveness ... They only act intelligently when one is retiring before them, because then each man can act according to his ... warlike instincts; he can pursue one from rock to rock, from ambush to ambush.' Given all this the most important things for a commander to remember are that he must attack in force, to over-awe the Berbers, and that his force must always be split into three or four separate columns for mutual protection. Furthermore, it is futile for these columns merely to 'cross the mountains and defeat the mountain tribesmen once or twice'. Rather:

> 'To conquer them one must attack their livelihood. One cannot do this by simply rushing through; one must bear down upon the territory of each tribe; one must ... destroy the villages, cut down the fruit trees, burn or dig up the harvests, empty the granaries, scour the ravines, rocks and grottos to seize their women, children, old men, cattle and possessions ... If one contents oneself with following one or two roads, one will only see the warriors. One will have more or less the advantage in combat, but will not strike at either the population as a whole or their wealth, and the results will be almost nil.'[45]

In most other parts of Africa, during the nineteenth and early twentieth centuries, there was little concerted guerrilla resistance to European penetration. There was certainly extensive and bitter opposition to the activities of the imperialist powers, but it usually took the form of traditional battles in which the Africans took too little account of the devastating fire-power of the small expeditionary forces. Putting their faith in vast numerical superiority, the Africans would charge the enemy square or *laager*, only to be mown down by the Maxims and repeating rifles. This was the fate, for example, of the Zulus in 1879, of the Ndebele in 1893, of the Dervishes in 1898, of the Ngoni in what is now Zambia in 1898 and of numerous other tribes and peoples. To a large extent this mode of combat was a logical consequence of these tribes' social and political organisation. Authority was centralised and the warriors were accustomed to unite under one dominant war chief. Even when they had discovered that European firepower rendered their traditional tactics suicidal, they found it difficult to establish the decentralised command structures that are basic to an effective guerrilla organisation.

Not all tribes, however, were organised in this way, and among certain others one did see resistance movements that revealed at least some of the characteristics of a guerrilla strategy, though it was hardly ever used as a self-conscious tactic. In these so-called *segmentary* societies each village or federation of hamlets had its own war-leader. Thus the tribe as a whole rarely ever came together in one body, and could not be annihilated at one fell swoop by the invaders. By the same token, the Europeans found that they had to deal with each village separately and thus it could take months and even years of small-scale operations to convince such tribesmen that further resistance was useless. Examples of this type of struggle were found amongst the Tiv in Nigeria, the Baoule of the southern Ivory Coast, and the Balante of Guiné who resisted Portuguese encroachments right into the 1920s. Such tribes could be particularly troublesome in areas where the terrain was bad. The Baoule, for example, made great use of the dense forests of the Ivory Coast, to which they would retreat to avoid heavy Portuguese pressure. Indeed, terrain itself could give any resistance movement some guerrilla features. Such was the case with the Ashantis, in the Gold Coast, who fought against the British in 1822, 1874 and 1900. Their basic strategy was to engage in sieges or pitched battles, where superior fire-power inevitably won the day. But during the periodic British marches through the thick forests of the region the Ashantis proved they were quite capable of taking advantage of the physical features. Of the 1874 campaign, one British officer wrote:

> 'The peculiarities of Ashanti warfare were now strongly developed. We were in the midst of a semi-circle of hostile fire, and we hardly ever caught sight of a man. As [we] advanced into the ravine ... [the troops] were almost immediately lost sight of in the bush ... Another difficulty developed when a company was sent to support another in action; it saw nothing but bush in its front, and speedily came under heavy fire of slugs from the enemy.'[46]

Of the wars that can fairly be classed as guerrilla struggles, the following deserve some mention. The French, for example, found themselves involved in bitter war with the Malinke, in western Sudan, between 1882–98. Their leader was Samori Touré, who had carved out a veritable empire for himself in this part of Africa. He had built up a professional army of infantrymen, known as *sofa*, taken from amongst the various captive peoples. When necessary this force was supplemented by a militia made up of 1 in every 10 able-bodied males. By 1883, however, Samori had realised the effectiveness of French firepower, and began to adopt cautious guerrilla tactics. He divided his men into mobile companies of 150 to 200 warriors and where possible equipped them with modern firearms. He even obtained the services of several European instructors and his companies became very adept at disciplined volley-firing. However, they were trained to limit themselves to short, sharp raids on the enemy columns and to avoid any prolonged fights. But Samori's tactics were essentially defensive. He built many earthworks overlooking the roads, rivers, passes, and forest corridors and hoped thereby to keep the French out of his territory. From 1892 he tried to avoid any contact with the French at all, hoping, rather naively, that he might thus persuade them to give up and leave him in peace. The French preferred to break his power by military action, lest other tribes become convinced that they could ignore the colonial nation with impunity.

The French also faced stubborn guerrilla resistance from the Sarrakole in Senegal and Gambia, between 1886–87. Here the leader was Mahmadou Lamine, at the head of a large army made up if necessary of every fit adult male. Even so Lamine tried to limit their operations to small-scale surprise attacks from hitherto unexplored base areas in Diafounou and Guidimaka. But the French carried the war into those areas and eventually their tightening circle forced Lamine to risk a last pitched battle at Toubakouta, in December 1887. Lamine was killed and the resistance movement soon collapsed.

In northern Sierra Leone, the British found a redoubtable guerrilla opponent in Bai Bureh, the leader of the Temne. Between January and November 1898, they were very hard-pressed by the activities of this tribe and its warrior aristocracy. Like Samori, Bai Bureh relied on the construction of stockades, though his were nearly always constructed at the entrance to a village. He had an exceptionally good spy system and when he received intelligence of the approach of a British column, an ambush would be laid around the approaches to the stockade. Should the column manage to fight its way through, a pathway was always left at the rear of the stockade so that survivors could effect their retreat. They would fall back to a different stockade and, when the way was clear, return to rebuild the old one. The stockades also served as bases for repeated attacks on the British lines of communication, running between Port Loko and Karene. As a Frontier Police officer wrote of Bai Bureh and his men: 'Savages they might be, but even in their fighting they displayed such admirable qualities as are not always to be found in the troops of the "civilised" nations. They loved their chief and remained loyal to him to the very last, whilst they understand bush-fighting as well as you and I do our very alphabet.'[47]

But the most well-known guerrilla war in Africa in this period was that conducted by one group of whites against another. This was during the latter stages of the Boer War, from November 1900, when the South African rebels had been beaten in terms of the conventional war and so decided to prolong the conflict by resorting to irregular tactics. The last regular action was fought at Rhenoster Kop in November 1900, and it marked the end of the era of open warfare that had characterised the campaigns in Natal. From now on, right up to the end of the war in May 1902, the centres of operation were to be the Orange Free State and Transvaal, vast areas of mountain and *veld* to the west and north of Natal. Under bold leaders like Louis Botha and C. de Wet, the Boers succeeded in bringing the British commanders, and the government at home, to the very brink of despair and defeat.

The Boers had many advantages as guerrilla troops. One of the most important was the *cultural* factor. As one writer has put it: '... their military philosophy was unique. It is best expressed in a single sentence which, with slight variations, was heard from many prisoners' lips: "You English fight to die: we Boers fight to live." With the future and security of the homestead depending on the safe return of its males, the Boers saw no virtue in dying for their country ... War was a business ... to be carried through to victory at the lowest possible cost ... There was no ignominy in flight.'[48] Even during the positional campaigns, at such battles as Belmont, Magersfontein and Spion Kop, the Boers had been content to hold off the British for a while from their entrenched positions and then melt away when the pressure became too strong. Such a philosophy, quite different from the usual European breast-beating about 'honour' and 'dying to the last man', was obviously a vital prerequisite for a mode of warfare based upon the swift surprise attack and the equally swift retreat.

The Boers also had innate advantages stemming from their mode of social and political organisation. Though they had elected a central government to lead the revolt, their society had much in common with the segmentary African societies mentioned above. The Boer was very individualistic, quite happy to be left alone with his family and servants on his isolated farm. His military organisation reflected this individualism. Each electoral district, of which there were 40 in the Free State and Transvaal, produced a commando out of all the adult males between the ages of 16 and 60. Even after he was called up no Boer could be made to do anything against his will, and was free to go home whenever he chose. He voted for his officers and by his vote they could also be dismissed. A *kriegsraad*, or war council of all members of the commando, was held before any significant tactical decision was taken. Though these pious, Bible-carrying stalwarts would turn in their grave for being so maligned, one could even say that their commandos had more in common with the Anarchist units of the Spanish Civil War than with any other recent type of European military formation. Be that as it may, this fierce sense of independence was of the greatest help in allowing the growth of initiative and tactical flexibility at all levels, a basic prerequisite of effective guerrilla operations.

Finally, the Boers were supremely mobile, being mounted on small but sturdy ponies with great powers of endurance. Though a commando preferred to travel with some kind of supply train, it was always ready to abandon this rather than risk capture or destruction. The Boers would then wait until they were able to capture more British supplies, obtain them from local farms, or if need be live by their own ingenuity:

'Though the commandos and ... their families trekking in constant flight could hope for luxuries only by captures from the British, they had enough meat, and also mealies which they ground in portable mills. They made ersatz coffee from dried peaches, sweet potatoes, tree roots and other ingredients; they found salt in natural deposits; they traded with the natives. For clothing, women revived the art of wool-spinning on wheels adapted from old sewing machines and fruit-peelers; sheepskins were tanned into jackets; leather was used until all tanning apparatus had gone; and uniforms were even stripped from captured soldiers.'[49]

When the Boers first organised themselves for guerrilla warfare proper, the British were totally unequipped to cope with the small, fast-moving columns. Though they had 210,000 men to the Boers' 60,000, and only a quarter of the latter were ever in the field at one time, they were lamentably short of cavalry. The standard counter-insurgency tactic in the early months was to send out an infantry column to clear the area of rebels. The *Times Official History* admirably summed up the futility of such operations:

'Each was composed mainly of infantry, with guns, howitzers, field hospital and bearer companies, engineers, and ... cumbrous trains of wagons drawn by oxen [and] generally overloaded ... These columns marched solemnly about the country at an average pace of ten to fifteen miles a day ... The word had gone out that they were not to be opposed but that after their departure, the towns and districts through which they had passed were immediately to be reoccupied. Accurately informed of the British movements by their scouts ... the burghers ran few risks of capture, and even on rare occasions when they were surprised, simply scattered and galloped away until they were out of sight.'[50]

It was not until the arrival of Kitchener, in December 1900, that systematic efforts were made to improve British techniques. These took various forms. Firstly, a request was made for more men, particularly cavalry. In this respect it is interesting to note that the British were now at least aware of the type of war they were fighting. The Secretary of War, Mr Brodrick, when asking Parliament for more money, took great pains to emphasise how many men Napoleon had needed to counter the Spanish guerrillas, as well as the numbers needed by the Spanish in Cuba and the Americans in the Philippines. By May 1901 one third of Kitchener's force of 240,000 men was mounted, whilst total Boer effectives were now reduced to 45,000. Kitchener then began to form special mobile columns to operate as individual raiding parties, almost totally independent of central control. These were used particularly extensively in the Free State, where commanders like Major Remington made great reputations for themselves. Later use was made of night raids. These had been initiated by Colonel G. E. Benson who began to make long marches at night to bring himself within striking distance of a Boer *laager*, which he could attack as dawn rose. Though two thirds and more of the Boers generally escaped, this tactic greatly increased their sense of insecurity. Benson's most successful raids took place in August and September 1901, and by December General Bruce Hamilton was put in charge of organising a much more extensive series of such attacks.

But the British never completely abandoned the old tactics. Even after Kitchener's arrival many large-scale drives were organised, intended to clear the Boers out of vast areas of the Free State and Transvaal. These drives were made up of several columns which were meant in theory to envelop the enemy by their co-ordinated actions. Not only this: '[They were also] to clear the country systematically of supplies, horses, cattle, crops, transport vehicles, and non-combatant families ... Supplies, wagons and standing crops, if they could not be used, were to be burnt. Bakeries and mills were to be destroyed.'[51] Though the British were most successful in laying waste the areas they traversed, they rarely made any significant captures, nor even saw their enemy except from a distance. The Boers were always able to escape through the gaps between the various columns. At first Kitchener tried to solve this problem by attaching a very mobile unit to each column so that it might plug the gaps. As he said: 'The rate of captures can only be maintained by the more extended action of extremely mobile troops freed of all encumbrances, whilst the remainder of the column clears the country and escorts transport.'[52] But the Boer commandos continued to extricate themselves from the ponderous clutches of the columns, mobile or otherwise. Finally Kitchener was driven to carry the concept of the drive to its logical conclusion. He began a system of what were known as 'new-model drives'. They were planned down to the very last detail, with a precise time allotted for every possible contingency. But their main feature was that no gaps at all were to be left in the slowly advancing line. In the first of the drives, in February 1902, 9,000 men were drawn up in a continuous cordon 54 miles long – one man to every 12 yards. Some commandos did manage to cut their way through, but the rest, as Edgar Wallace saw: '... were shot like game ... [or] fell back, stunned and bewildered, into the interior of the trap, their horses foundered, their bandoleers empty, their bodies worn out, to await capture.'[53]

There were two other important British tactics. One was the block-house system. At first these were used only to protect the railway lines. But gradually whole areas of the Transvaal and the Free State were separated by lines of iron block-houses, yards apart, in which parties of 10 soldiers kept in contact with one another by telephone and sent out regular patrols to prevent the Boers from moving one area to another. It was between these lines of block-houses that the new-model drives were usually carried out. The second tactic was the old favourite, the resettlement of the population of affected areas. In a memorandum to his officers, in December 1900, Kitchener pointed out the desirability of such a policy:

'The General Commander-in-Chief is desirous that all possible means shall be taken to stop the present guerrilla warfare. Of the various measures suggested for the accomplishment of this object, one which has been strongly recommended ... is the removal of all men, women, children and natives from the Districts which the enemy's bands persistently occupy. This course ...[is] the most effective method of limiting the endurance of the guerrillas, as the men and women left on farms, if disloyal, willingly supply Burghers, if loyal, dare not refuse to do so.'[54]

It was some months before this policy was put into effect, but by May of the following year there were some 98,000 persons in the specially constructed concentration camps, whilst by October this figure had reached its peak, 161,000. By December all the accessible *laagers* had been destroyed and their occupants deported. But the measure aroused considerable opposition abroad, as well as in England itself, because of the appalling conditions in which the prisoners lived. In October, for example, the average death rate had risen to 344 per 1,000, although in some camps the figure was twice as high. More importantly, from the British point of view, the policy had exactly the opposite of its intended effect. For the Boers the deportation of their families at least meant that they would no longer have to worry about their welfare, and make periodic returns to the farm. Now they could spend all their time in the field. And insofar as they disapproved of British policy as being somewhat barbaric, this merely strengthened their resolve to fight to the bitter end.

And yet, eventually, the combination of all these counter-insurgency techniques succeeded in wearing the Boers down. By early 1902 they had no more than 22,000 fighting men. Though they could ensure that it would take many months, even years, for the British to destroy them, it was becoming clear that the British were actually prepared to pay this price, and pursue Kitchener's slow but methodical policy of attrition. On April 12 the Boer leaders presented a set of peace proposals to Kitchener, and in May, two years and eight months after the war began, the final treaty was signed.

1. J. Lynch, *The Spanish-American Revolution 1808–26*, Weidenfeld & Nicholson, 1973, p118
2. R. O'Connor, *The Cactus Throne*, Allen & Unwin, 1971, pp 132–3
3. *ibid*, pp 190–1
4. J. F. Elton, *With the French in Mexico*, Chapman & Hall, 1867, p91
5. O'Connor, *op cit*, pp 195–6
6. N. Reed, *The Caste War of Yucatan*, Stanford University Press, Stanford, 1964, p60
7. *ibid*, p99
8. *ibid*, p226
9. J. Womack Jr, *Zapata and the Mexican Revolution*, Penguin Books, 1972, p243
10. *ibid*, p250
11. See pp 160–5

12. Womack, *op cit*, pp 313–14
13. *ibid*, p433
14. H. Thomas, *Cuba or the Pursuit of Freedom*, Eyre & Spottiswoode, 1971, p344
15. C. Beals, *Great Guerrilla Warriors*. Prentice-Hall, Englewood Cliffs, 1970, p95
16. *ibid*, p88
17. D. Woodman, *The Making of Burma*, The Cresset Press, 1966, p337
18. I. Colvin, *The Life of General Dyer*, William Blackwood, 1929, p12
19. Woodman, *op cit*, p338
20. *ibid*, p384
21. *ibid*, p410
22. *ibid*, p411
23. *ibid*, p416
24. J. Buttinger, *Vietnam: a Dragon Embattled*, Praeger, New York, 1967, p134
25. *ibid*, p135
26. *ibid*, p136
27. J. Gottman, Bugeaud, Galliéni, Lyautey: 'The Development of French Colonial Warfare', in E. M. Earle (ed), *Makers of Modern Strategy*, Princeton University Press, Princeton, 1941, p242
28. Buttinger, *op cit*, p135
29. J. Chesneaux (trans C. A. Curwen), *Peasant Revolts in China 1840–1949*, Thames & Hudson, 1973, pp 33–44
30. W. J. Hail, *Tseng Kuo-fan and the Taiping Rebellion*. Yale University Press, New Haven, 1927, p297
31. *ibid*, p300
32. Beals, *op cit*, p28
33. *ibid*, p30
34. *ibid*, pp 31–32
35. T. A. Agoncillo, *A Short History of the Philippines*, Mentor Books, New York, 1969, p143
36. L. Blanch, *The Sabres of Paradise*, John Murray, 1960, p91
37. *ibid*, p233
38. *ibid*, p129
39. Maj-Gen J. G. Elliott, *The Frontier 1839–1947*, Cassell, 1968, p110
40. O. Caroe, *The Pathans 550BC–AD1957*, Macmillan, 1958, p321
41. Elliott, *op cit*, p204
42. W. Blunt, *Desert Hawk*, Methuen, 1947, p160
43. *ibid*, pp 142 and 149
44. Gen P. Azan (ed), *Par l'épée et par la charrue: écrits et discours de Bugeaud*, Presses Universitaires Françaises, Paris, 1948, p16
45. *ibid*, pp 110–16
46. M. Crowder (ed), *West African Resistance*, Hutchinson, 1971, p40
47. *ibid*, p244
48. W. B. Pemberton, *Battles of the Boer War*, Pan Books, 1969, p19
49. R. Kruger, *Goodbye Dolly Gray*, Four Square Books, 1964, p419
50. E. Childers, *The Times History of the War in South Africa*, Sampson Low, 1907, Vol 5, p5
51. *ibid*, p162
52. *ibid*, p323
53. Kruger, *op cit*, p467
54. Childers, *op cit*, p53

CHAPTER 6

The World Wars

Africa

The story of guerrilla resistance in the first 40 years of this century is once again largely concerned with Africa, particularly amongst the Arabs and Berbers who fought a dogged if somewhat desperate war against their various overlords, notably the French, Italians and Turks. One of the most persistent centres of rebellion in the years before World War I was Morocco, control over which was divided between the French and Spanish. Up until the 1920s the bulk of the actual fighting was done by the French, and they found another opportunity to put their theories about colonial warfare and administration into practice. The two most important proponents of these theories in North Africa were Marshal Lyautey and Professor Gautier of the University of Algiers. For both of them, as for the French commanders in Indochina, effective counter-insurgency was not just a military problem, not even predominantly so, but more one of effective administration. Gautier put the problem well in 1910:

'All our recent conquests ... would seem to point to the uselessness of battles in wild countries ... Needless to say, we are not naive enough to believe force useless, but the question is to know how to use it. In a European war victory is the goal, because you have to crush an organisation, a military machine. It has no sense in an anarchic country where, as nothing exists, there is nothing to destroy and where the difficulty is, on the contrary, to create.'[1]

Lyautey paid close attention to this definition of counter-insurgency throughout his long service in North Africa. In 1903 he took charge of the sub-division of Ain-Sefra where he remained until 1906. He was then moved to the division of Oran in western Algeria, and in 1912, after a brief period of service at home, he became the Resident-General and Commander-in-Chief of the whole of Morocco. The basic features of his colonial policy were clearly set down as early as 1900 in an article he wrote entitled *The Colonial Role of the Army*. In it he made use of extensive quotations from his superior, Galliéni, and one of these gives a succinct summary of French aims:

'The best means for achieving pacification in our new colony is provided by combined application of force and politics. It must be remembered that, in the course of our colonial struggles, we should turn to destruction only as a last resort, and only as a preliminary to better reconstruction. We must always treat the country and its inhabitants with consideration, since the former is destined to receive our future colonial enterprises and the latter will be our main agents and collaborators in the development of our enterprises. Every time that the necessities of war force one of our colonial officers to take action against a village or inhabited centre, his first concern, once submission of the inhabitants has been achieved, should be reconstruction of the village, creation of a market, and establishment of a school. It is by combined use of politics and force that pacification of a country and its future organisation will be achieved. *Political action is by far the most important*. It derives its greater power from the organisation of the country and its inhabitants.'[2]

This passage, and that from General Duchemin's report on Indochina, quoted in the previous chapter, are absolutely fundamental in terms of the development of guerrilla warfare. Here, for the first time, one finds the realisation that this type of conflict involves the social and economic interests of the insurgents, and cannot be dismissed as a purely military problem. It is this realisation that has given guerrilla warfare in this century its distinctive characteristics. Mao Tse-tung's concern for the well-being of the peasants in the Red base areas, and the American rhetoric about the necessity to win over the 'hearts and minds' of the peasantry in South Vietnam are both further instances of this crucial notion that guerrilla warfare is as much a political as a military struggle.

Lyautey's military theories were a natural consequence of this emphasis upon constructive political action. He wanted to make French establishments in a disputed area centres of attraction rather than of repulsion. They should offer protection to the natives and encourage trade and attract caravans. To do this it was necessary to extend the French-controlled areas gradually, always consolidating a base before advancing further. In 1903 Lyautey sent a letter to Galliéni explaining how such considerations affected his long-term strategy:

'In fact, the final establishment of the system of protection that I project will be accomplished very gradually ... It will advance not by columns, nor by mighty blows, but as a patch of oil [*tache d'huile*] spreads, through a step by step progression, playing alternately on all the local elements, utilising the divisions and rivalries between tribes and between their chiefs.'[3]

Two new strategical principles were evolved by Lyautey as a basis for French operations. Firstly: 'In the use of armed forces, avoid as far as possible the column, and replace it by progressive occupation.' Secondly: 'Military occupation consists less in military operations than in an organisation on the march.'[4]

Nevertheless, direct military confrontation was inevitable on certain occasions, and Lyautey also worked out a system of tactics for the assaults on mountainous areas that were sometimes necessary. First one section or massif was encircled and isolated by a continuous line of troops. The front would be established in the lowlands and gradually pushed forward into the mouths of valleys and depressions, so that it slowly climbed higher and higher. When the mountain itself was tightly contained on three, or at least two sides, two strong columns were sent in a pincer movement to converge on the main passes separating this massif from the next. Then the grip on the massif was slowly tightened as the troops continued to penetrate the gaps in the terrain and climb still higher. Eventually, when the tribesmen were sufficiently tired and demoralised, cut off from all supplies, the final assault would be launched, usually resulting in a swift surrender.

In fact the most formidable resistance to European rule was not mounted against the French, but against the Spanish, who held part of northern Morocco. In their zone of control was the mountainous Rif in which, between 1921 and 1926, was fought a bitter war which almost permitted the establishment of a separate Rif Republic. The leader of the Berber tribesmen, notably the Beni Wariaghel, who inhabit this part of Morocco, was Abd-el Krim. By the sheer force of his personality and the clever manipulation of tribal customs regarding alliances, Abd-el Krim managed to weld the various tribes together into an unprecedentedly united fighting force. The war began with a reckless push into the Rif which was expected to cover Spanish arms with overdue glory. In May, June and July 1921 the Berbers harassed the Spanish column and then took the offensive. A mere 500 Rifis seized various strongpoints from a Spanish army of 14,000 men. They then decided to descend the mountains and tackle the Spaniards in the valley below. A pitched battle was fought outside Anual during which the Berbers dug themselves in trenches and foxholes and mowed down the hapless Spanish infantry as they charged forward. It was, as Abd-el Krim's brother said, 'an Omdurman in reverse.' Then, as the Spanish retreated towards Monte Acruit, to the east, they were ceaselessly harassed by ever-increasing numbers of tribesmen. On August 2 the Spanish surrendered. In the intervening months they had lost 18,000 men, whilst the Rifis had captured 19,504 rifles, 392 machine-guns, 129 cannon, and 1,100 prisoners. Abd-el Krim later ransomed these prisoners and with the money he received bought more rifles and machine guns, as well as an airplane and a field-telephone system.

After the annihilation of the Spanish army Abd-el Krim set about the creation of a Rif state, whose independence was announced in January 1923. As part of that state he established a regular army. All able-bodied men between the ages of 16 and 60 were liable for service, but they were called up in batches of 5,000 whilst the remainder stayed at home to tend the crops. Officers were known as *Cairds* and were paid by the state, receiving 250 *duros* a month as opposed to the ordinary soldiers' 60. In times of crisis this regular army was supplemented by a levy of the tribesmen of the particular locality, bringing the total numbers to about 25,000 men. The mobilisation of these tribesmen might be general or partial. As a French observer reported:

> 'When mobilisation is general ... all the effective forces are brought together or dispersed following ... orders ... Each man arrives with his rifle, his cartridges, and several ration loaves, which he puts in the haversack of his jillaba. When mobilisation is only partial ... individual or collective relief forces [are orga-nised]. The relief unit, or the one relieved, does not move in a group – each man knows his post and goes there at a given date.'[5]

No more large battles were fought between 1922 and 1924, though by the end of the former year the Spanish had 200,000 troops in the country. Abd-el Krim concentrated upon harassing them with guerrilla warfare, making the most of the mountainous terrain and the Berbers' mobility, marksmanship and ability to conceal themselves. Moreover, he was well aware that the temperament of his tribesmen was not commensurate with excessive regularisation or herding into large units. On the contrary: 'Each Rifi soldier must be treated as an individual, he told his commanders; they must explain to their men what was afoot, put them in the picture, so that every man understood the overall strategy.'[6] But even these tactics proved too much for the Spanish. As Primo de Rivera, the Spanish dictator, told a reporter in 1924:

> 'Spanish troops are holding a number of isolated posts, some of which are dominated by mountains infested by well-armed rebels who, moving swiftly about a terrain where it is very difficult for regular troops to follow, can inflict casualties out of proportion to their numbers by employing guerrilla methods. The Spanish outposts have to be supplied with stores, even with water, from the base. Sometimes the rebels cut the Spanish lines of communication, and the convoys, when thus faced with enemy concentrations, are obliged to fight their way through.'[7]

So Rivera decided to withdraw all his forces from the interior and concentrate them in the coastal towns. Abd-el Krim saw that this withdrawal presented him with the opportunity for a knockout blow. So, in the west and the east, as the Spanish attempted to fall back on Ceuta and Melilla respectively, he harried their forces mercilessly, inflicting huge casualties. In the retreat from Shauen, in the west, the Spanish lost over 17,000 soldiers, dead or missing. As Rivera frankly admitted: 'Abd-el Krim has defeated us.'

He might have gone on to become the undisputed leader of a peaceful, independent Rif state, had it not been for the unfortunate demands of his alliance system. The Rif frontier with French Morocco, to the south, had long been a subject of some dispute, and this became more acrimonious as Abd-el Krim's power grew. Eventually, in April 1925, the French sent troops into the region inhabited by the Beni Zerual. They called for assistance from Krim according to the terms of their alliance with him. The latter, even though he knew that he could not hope to hold out for long against the combined forces of the French and the Spanish, immediately dispatched a force of 3,000 regulars. From then on his defeat was only a matter of time. In the end, vastly superior numbers must wear down even the most determined guerrillas. Peace talks were held, but Krim refused to settle for anything less than complete independence. In May the French and Spanish forces linked up and surrounded the Berber remnants. On May 24 Krim surrendered.

The story of Moroccan resistance has taken us well into the twentieth century, but it is now necessary to go back in time and discuss the two guerrilla campaigns that formed an integral part of World War I. Both were fought in Africa. Of the two, probably the lesser known is that waged by the Germans in East Africa, under the brilliant leadership of General Paul von Lettow-Vorbeck. His campaign was in no sense a war of national liberation or a civil war, as have been the bulk of the guerrilla struggles described thus far, but rather a calculated attempt to pin down as many Allied troops as possible and thus keep them away from more vital theatres of the war. When war broke out, Lettow-Vorbeck had under his command 260 German officers and 2,500 native troops, or Askaris, based in German East Africa, what is now Tanzania. These troops were organised into 14 companies, each about 200 strong, which were self-contained tactical units with their own supply and transport sections. By the end of 1915 there were 60 such companies, giving a total strength of 3,000 Europeans and 11,500 Askaris. This was the maximum strength ever attained by the German forces, whilst the Allies at this time had some 27,350 fighting men on this front, and later their numbers were increased still further. Yet Lettow-Vorbeck continually managed to avoid meeting the Allies in a decisive battle. Even at the end of the war he still had an intact fighting force that could have kept up the struggle for some months more. During the four years of fighting Allied casualties were 9,100 killed, 7,750 wounded and 929 missing. The German commander had undoubtedly succeeded in making his 'sideshow' a more than trifling annoyance to the Allies. In this respect it is worth noting that the British were forced to maintain in East Africa an army equivalent in size to that which had been needed to suppress the Boers.

Lettow-Vorbeck began operations by making raids against the vital Uganda railway. To counter this threat the British established a fortified line along the railway, and also decided upon a landing in German East Africa, at Tanga, to hit the Germans in the flank. The landing, made with inexperienced Indian troops, was a total fiasco, involving great losses of men, equipment and reputation. The British then concentrated upon simply trying to protect the railway. One of their advanced posts for this purpose was at Yasini, which Lettow-Vorbeck feared might be the jumping-off point for another attack on Tanga. In January 1915 he attacked Yasini with nine of his companies and the British garrison soon surrendered. But the British had control of the sea and this kind of tactic did not have much potential for a small force that could not expect any reinforcements from other theatres. As Lettow-Vorbeck wrote in his memoirs:

'Although the attack carried out at Yasini . . . had been completely successful, it showed that such heavy losses as we had suffered could only be borne in exceptional cases. We had to economise our forces in order to last out a long war . . . The expenditure of 200,000 rounds also proved that with the means at my disposal, I could at the most fight three more actions of this nature. The need to strike great blows only quite exceptionally, and to restrict myself primarily to guerrilla warfare, was evidently imperative.'[8]

He never deviated from this course of action. Throughout 1915 he broke his companies down into small patrols of about 10 men who carried all their supplies and were completely self-sufficient. These patrols made continual raids on British outposts and on the stretch of railway between Simba and Samburu. Lettow-Vorbeck also set about making his base as self-sufficient as possible. Farmers were encouraged to increase food production, planters used their rubber trees to produce their own tyres, the women of the colony produced cotton cloth and invented their own khaki dye, boot factories were established, and the Germans even evolved a method of producing their own motor fuel.

In early 1916 General Jan Smuts was put in command of the Allied effort in East Africa and substantial reinforcements were sent in. Smuts resolved to dispense with the containment tactics and to launch a multi-pronged offensive into German East Africa itself. The offensive began in March 1916, and by the end of 1917 the Allies were in control of the whole of the German colony. Unfortunately they had never in all those months managed to trap Lettow-Vorbeck's main force. Whenever they reached a particular town or spot where the Germans were known to have been resting or regrouping, it was found that Lettow-Vorbeck had managed to slip away some hours before. This was the case throughout the whole drive through German East Africa – at Taveta, Kahe, Morogoro, Kisaki, and the Rufiji river. But the German commander was being made to suffer under the persistent pressure. Food was a particularly acute problem. In 1917 he was forced to spend a lot of time in planning the location of secret maize plantations. They had to be in areas which would be far enough away from the fighting to allow the crop time to ripen and yet not so far that the harvest could not be brought up to his troops. On November 25, 1917, he decided that he could remain no longer in the German colony. With 2,000 of his picked troops he crossed over into Portuguese East Africa. From this time on he resolved to live off the land and was obliged to split his force into several independent formations, small enough to be able to supply themselves. However, this necessity had certain inherent advantages for a commander prepared to make the most of guerrilla forces. As he himself wrote:

'If we succeeded ... in maintaining the force in the new territory, the increased independence and mobility used with determination against the less mobile enemy, would give us a local superiority in spite of the great numerical superiority of the enemy. The enemy would be compelled to keep an enormous amount of men and material continuously on the move and to exhaust his strength to a greater extent proportionately than ourselves.'[9]

He succeeded in forcing the Allies to do just this, and when he finally surrendered on November 25, 1918, it was because of his country's collapse rather than his own imminent defeat. Lettow-Vorbeck was undoubtedly a brilliant commander, able to make the most of very limited resources, but the East African campaign is yet another clear indication of the paramount importance of terrain for the waging of an effective guerrilla struggle. The following remarks by a British officer who fought in this theatre show just how the dense bush facilitated the Germans' attempt to limit the fighting to petty ambushes and swift retreats:

'Truly the enemy chooses his positions well, and it is the country, not he, well though he fights, that robs us again and again of decisive battle. Their positions are ... chosen where they and their movements cannot be seen, and thus their strength, at the many points of battle, may be either a handful of men or a dozen companies. Moreover, under cover of the bush, their lines are flexible to any change, while always, in the rear, they have sure and swift lines of retreat by which they can escape in the bush, in a dozen directions, to meet again at a given point, when their flight is over.'[10]

A much more famous guerrilla war, indeed to some people the most well-known of all, was that led by T. E. Lawrence against the Turks, in Arabia. Early in World War I the Sherif of Mecca had refused to join the Turks in proclaiming a Moslem *jihad*, or holy war, against the infidels. In June 1916 he went further and raised a revolt in the Hejaz against Turkish rule. Up to this time the large British garrison in Egypt had remained inactive, but the diversionary activities of the Arabs persuaded the British to try and advance towards El Arish and regain command of the Sinai Desert. El Arish was reached at Christmas and the British commander, Sir Archibald Murray, was then persuaded to make for Gaza and Beersheba, guarding the approaches to Palestine. Unfortunately his two attacks on the first city, in March and April 1917, were costly failures. But the British efforts were saved from collapse by the masterly manoeuvrings of the Arab insurgents, following the advice of a handful of British advisers, notably Lawrence. In May, Lawrence persuaded Feisel to make a sudden flank move up to Wejh, and from this base they consistently harassed the Hejaz railway which ran through the area as far south as Medina. In May 1917 Lawrence led an Arab expeditionary force into Syria. After sowing new seeds of revolt there, they fell upon Aqaba, the Turkish base on the northern arm of the Red Sea. Its capture removed all danger to the British communications in the Sinai and made the Arabs a menacing presence on the flank of the Turks. By this time, for example, more Turks were employed in guarding the Hejaz railway and the territory south of it, than were facing the British in Palestine.

In his *Seven Pillars of Wisdom* Lawrence has left an account of the calculated way in which he came to realise that only guerrilla methods could make the most of the Arabs' opposition to the Turks. According to him the whole strategy of the Revolt was revealed whilst he was recuperating from a particularly heavy fever. Up to this point he had acted instinctively, and now he used his 10 days of inactivity to look for 'the equation between my book-reading and my movements'. He began by realising that the British obsession with capturing Medina, at the end of the railway, was in fact a pointless ambition, rooted in the desire of the classical military strategists, Jomini, Clausewitz, Foch, to have some specific target at which to aim, be it the enemy army or a large town. But whilst this positional conception of warfare might make sense on the battlefields of Europe, it was quite irrelevant to the realities of the Arabian situation. Certainly the capture of Wejh had been important, because even a guerrilla movement needs some sort of fixed base, but since then 'we were blockading the railway and they only defending it. The garrison of Medina, reduced to an inoffensive size, was sitting in trenches destroying their own power of movement by eating the transport they could no longer feed. We had taken away their power to harm us, and yet wanted to take away their town ... What on earth did we want it for?'

Lawrence then went on to assess the advantages and shortcomings of his own troops. The most obvious of the latter, at least to a Foch or any other strategist who preached the logic of attrition, was that:

'The Arabs would not endure casualties ... Their aim was geographical, to extrude the Turk from all Arabic-speaking lands in Asia ... In pursuit of the ideal conditions we might kill Turks ... but the killing was a pure luxury ... In the last resort, we should be compelled to the desperate course of blood ... but as cheaply as could be for ourselves, since the Arab fought for freedom, and that was a pleasure only to be tasted by a man alive. Posterity was a chilly thing to work for, no matter how much a man happened to love his own, or other people's already produced children.'

Therefore 'we could not afford casualties'. But the Arab irregulars had certain great tactical advantages. 'The active rebels had the virtues of secrecy and self-control, and the qualities of speed, endurance and independence of arteries of supply.' They also had the support of the whole people. Though 'only two in the hundred were active ... the rest [were] quietly sympathetic to the point of not betraying the movements of the minority.' This popular support also afforded the insurgents 'perfect intelligence so that we could plan in certainty ... When we knew all about the enemy we should be comfortable. We must take more pains in the service of news than any regular staff.' Finally, the very mobility of the Arabs and the impermanence of their settlements meant that 'we had nothing material to lose' and never needed to be forced to defend any spot to the death. To the Turks, on the other hand, cut off in the middle of the desert, 'things were scarce and precious, men less esteemed than equipment ... The death of a Turkish bridge or rail, machine or gun or charge of high explosive, was more profitable to us than the death of a Turk.'

From this combination of factors Lawrence arrived at his definition of the type of war the Arabs must fight:

'Our war should be a war of detachment. We were to contain the enemy by the silent threat of a vast unknown desert, not disclosing ourselves till we attacked. The attack might be nominal, directed not against him, but against his stuff; so it would not seek either his strength or his weakness, but his most accessible material. In railway-cutting it would be usually an empty stretch of rail; and the more empty, the greater the tactical success. We might turn our average into a rule ... and develop a habit of never engaging the enemy.'

Lawrence's indubitable literary talents make the following passage possibly one of the most elegant, and succinct, definitions of guerrilla warfare yet written:

'... [taking] practical account of the area we wished to deliver ... I began idly to calculate how many square miles: sixty: eighty: one hundred: perhaps one hundred and forty thousand square miles. And how would the Turk defend all that? No doubt by a trench line across the bottom, if we came like an army with banners; but suppose we were (as we might be) an influence, an idea, a thing intangible, invulnerable, without front or back, drifting about like a gas? Armies were like plants, immobile, firm-rooted, nourished through long stems to the head. We might be a vapour, blowing where we listed. Our kingdoms lay in each man's mind; and as we wanted nothing material to live on, so we might offer nothing material to the killing. It seemed a regular soldier might be helpless without a target, owning only what he sat on, and subjugating only what, by order, he could poke his rifle at.'[11]

The last guerrilla war of any importance during this period of African history also involved the Arabs. This time, however, their opponents were the Italians, who had long felt that their central position in the Mediterranean should entitle them to some share in the carving up of North Africa. The Italian attempt to replace the Turks in Tripolitania and Cyrenaica, the west and east of Libya respectively, began with an invasion from the sea in 1911. Much to the surprise of the Italians, the Libyans generally fought with the Turks rather than flocking to the banners of their 'liberators'. Peace was signed with the Turks in October 1912, but the Libyans continued to fight on. At first, the Libyan irregulars, armed with old single-shot Greek rifles, attempted to drive the Italians off with old-style, free-for-all cavalry charges, but they soon learnt the futility of such tactics in the face of European firepower, however indifferently deployed. Even so, some were a little too slow in learning the lesson, and after the battle of Asabaa, in 1913, the Italians secured the submission of most of the Tripolitanian tribes. In Cyrenaica, however, under the leadership of the Senussi, a powerful Moslem revivalist movement, the tribes fought on. They adopted guerrilla tactics and confronted the Italians in the mountainous Gebel Akhdar, in the north of Cyrenaica. But they were slowly pushed out of the mountains and retreated into the southern desert wastes of Fezzan. Here the Italians had to cope with the same kind of problems that had faced the Turks in Arabia, and a series of raids on supply columns and garrisons gradually forced them back into northern Tripolitania. In April 1915 the Italians counter-attacked but a column of 4,000 of their troops was ambushed and wiped out almost to a man. With the arms captured the Libyans were able to throw their enemy right back to the coast. In 1917 increasing British interest in this area forced them to try and bring the Italians and Libyans to some kind of agreement and these initiatives, coupled with increasing political chaos in Italy itself after 1918, ushered in a brief period of uneasy peace. The Libyans in Tripolitania and Cyrenaica were granted their own parliament, governing councils, and Italian citizenship for all. But the accession of the Fascists to power in 1922 ended this brief armed truce, and the Italians took on the task of subjugating Libya once and for all. Thus began the Libyan War of 1922–32, one of the bloodiest of North Africa's many guerrilla struggles.

The war was fought in Cyrenaica, mainly in the mountainous strongholds of the Gebel Akhdar, and was led once again by the Senussi. At the beginning of the war the Senussi could muster perhaps 2,000 more or less regular fighting men. But straight away the Italians embarked upon a policy of massive retaliation. They launched numerous attacks with columns of armoured cars and motorised infantry upon the encampments of the Arab nomads. Between April and September 1923 some 800 nomads were killed. The Italians also slaughtered over 12,000 sheep and it was the basis of their policy of reprisals to kill the flocks of any nomads who failed to surrender. The nomads were forced to retreat into the Gebel, a limestone tableland covered with woods and tangled brush, and pitted with caves and ravines, ideal terrain for a guerrilla struggle.

The leader of the bands in this area was the Senussi *shaikh*, Omar Mukhtar, who had already fought against the Italians between 1911–16. Mukhtar never had more than 1,000 guerrillas in action at any one time, but his close links with the surrounding population, made stronger by years of Senussi propaganda and organisation, ensured a steady flow of recruits and information. The Italians nominally divided the Libyans into 'rebels' and 'non-combatants', or *sottomessi*. In fact, many of these *sottomessi*, and even the Libyans actually in Italian service, were secret supporters of the overt rebels. The *sottomessi* gave their support by gifts of arms, clothes, foodstuffs and horses. They also provided shelter for any guerrillas on the run. Some of the supposed *sottomessi* were in fact part-time guerrillas, working as shepherds during the day and riding with a guerrilla band by night. The Senussi's agents in the various camps were in charge of organising liaison between the guerrillas and the nomads, and in most of them they even managed to levy a regular tax, on top of the normal religious contributions. This money found its way to Egypt where it was used to buy arms and additional supplies of all kinds.

For their other arms the guerrillas relied upon what they could capture from the Italians. This problem was often simplified by the Libyan auxiliaries who during skirmishes would 'lose' their rifles and leave large amounts of live ammunition on the ground for the guerrillas to pick up later. Omar Mukhtar's men were divided into small mobile bands, *adwar*, of 100 to 300 men. But for actual operations they generally split up into smaller groups, so that they could easily hide their arms and disperse to the camps if too hard-pressed. Each band was manned and supplied by the tribe after which it was named. Mukhtar used his religious authority to keep the peace between these traditionally rival groups, and was also in charge of the planning and co-ordination of operations, the collection of taxes, and the purchases in Egypt. He was also the personal leader of one of the guerrilla bands.

From 1928–30 the Italians concentrated upon mopping up resistance in other parts of Libya. Progressively they pacified the desert regions of Tripolitania, Sirtica and Fezzan. The first area was secured by planting numerous garrisons, disarming the tribesmen, and blocking and poisoning wells to prevent the insurgents from joining their allies further to the south. In these years there were also some attacks on Omar Mukhtar's forces. The Italians managed to keep his bands continually on the move and wearied them considerably. But they were never able to pin them down and bring them to battle. In January 1930, however, the vice-governorship of Cyrenaica was given to Rodolfo Graziani, who had been in charge of operations in southern Tripolitania and Fezzan. Within 18 months he had succeeded in breaking the back of the Cyrenaican revolt.

He began by simplifying the military command system and uniting the three commands in the Gebel Akhdar zone under one leader. He then concentrated upon making his troops as mobile as possible, hoping to nullify the guerrillas' one great advantage and to seize the initiative from them. He sent out scores of small, fast-moving patrols which were to penetrate right into guerrilla territory and harry the *adwar* wherever possible. He also disbanded most of the units of Libyan auxiliaries and replaced them with Eritreans, tough fighters and, as Christians, implacable foes of the Muslim rebels. For Graziani the aim of these mobile patrols should be 'to dominate the territory by continual movement ... We must always be on the move, even in empty country, to create the continual impression that we are masters of the country.'[12]

Graziani also directed much attention to the *sottomessi*, realising that it was on their support that the future of the rebellion ultimately depended. In the spring of 1930 he had them completely disarmed. It was then made a capital offence to have any contact whatsoever with the guerrillas, and a special air-borne military tribunal was created to give speedy judgment in cases of this nature. Graziani also fell back on the well-tried devices of the removal and resettlement of the population. Almost the entire nomad population of northern Cyrenaica, along with their herds and flocks, were forcibly removed from the war zone and resettled in isolated concentration camps. By July 1930 almost all of them were living in 12,000 government tents, organised in various camps, one kilometre square, surrounded by barbed wire and dominated by machine-gun posts. Graziani also had much recourse to straightforward terror tactics. Executions were frequent, by hanging or shooting in the back. One observer noted: 'During the time I was in Cyrenaica, thirty executions took place daily, which means that about twelve thousand Arabs were executed yearly ... The land swam in blood.'[13]

But these policies had the desired effect. The stranglehold on the Gebel was slowly tightened and the bands began to lose more and more men, with little chance of replacements. In late 1930 Omar Mukhtar was forced to shift his base eastwards, into Marmarica. Then, in September of the following year, he returned to the Gebel where he was caught in an ambush. After a summary court-martial he was hung, and the insurgency, already at its last gasp, soon collapsed.

Ireland

On Easter Monday 1916, 150 Irish nationalists paraded through the streets of Dublin and then seized the General Post Office, the Four Courts and other buildings in the centre of the city. There was also an attack on Dublin Castle, but this proved abortive. It had been hoped that this insurrection would be the centre of an uprising throughout the whole of Ireland, based upon the men of the Irish Volunteers, a secret army formed in November 1913. In fact, certain leaders of the Volunteers, notably Eoin MacNeill, were opposed to the whole idea and the rising was confined to Dublin, except for minor outbreaks in Galway and Wexford. The rebels held out against the British troops for six days, but the end was inevitable. Artillery pounded the barricaded buildings to rubble and the survivors were forced to surrender. The prisoners were speedily court-martialled and 14 of them were shot by British firing-squads.

The legality of the British reprisals is unquestioned. Their justice is not at issue here. But it does seem an undeniable fact that their severity had a profound effect upon many Irishmen who were otherwise unsympathetic to the demands of the radical nationalists. An indication of the swing in public opinion is offered by the elections of 1908 and 1918. In the first, the nationalist party Sinn Féin, contesting seats for the first time, did very badly and none of their candidates were successful. In the 1918 elections, however, they won a resounding victory and completely demolished the hitherto impregnable position of their rivals, the Irish Parliamentary Party. Of course, outrage over the executions was not the only reason for Sinn Féin successes. Many Irishmen were also very disturbed by the threat of national conscription, which was very much in the air in this year. But whatever the exact reasons, the essential point remains that by the end of World War I the nationalists were operating within a much more sympathetic environment than had ever existed before. Moreover, the internment of hundreds of nationalists in Frongoch camp gave them an unparalleled opportunity to discuss just what had been wrong with Irish tactics at Easter, and to plan more effective action for the future. In this period Michael Collins emerged as one of the main leaders of the nationalist movement, and he concentrated upon organising the Irish Republican Brotherhood, a nineteenth century secret society, also known as the Fenians, which had been given a new lease of life in 1913. The IRB extended its influence within the Irish Volunteers. In 1916 this organisation had had about 16,000 members, whilst in October 1918 it had soared to 100,000. Most of these were unarmed and the number fell off again after the war. Even so there was clearly a substantial amount of grass-roots support for any group thinking in terms of armed action against the British.

The IRB was most definitely thinking along these lines. But the experience of 1916 had taught them that urban insurrection was not the answer. They decided instead to take to the countryside and organise guerrilla warfare. As Collins wrote later: 'On the Irish side [the conflict] took the form of disarming the attackers. We took their arms and attacked their strongholds. We organised our army and met the armed patrols and military expeditions which were sent against us in the only possible way. We met them by an organised and bold guerrilla warfare.'[14]

The guerrilla campaign fell into two main stages. It began on January 25, 1919, with an attack on an explosives consignment guarded by armed men of the Royal Irish Constabulary, at Soloheadbeg. Attacks on groups of policemen and isolated police barracks were the principal activities of this first period, the main aim being to capture arms. In March and July barracks in Cork were attacked, in July and August the prime targets were in County Clare. By Easter of the following year the RIC had abandoned some 300 of its outlying outposts and was concentrated in the larger towns. These abandoned posts were blown up or burnt down by the IRA insurgents. The British began reinforcing their units in Ireland. In March 1920 the notorious Black and Tans began to arrive, British replacements for the badly demoralised RIC. In April 7,000 extra troops were shipped across bringing the total number to 35,000. In July the first 500 members of the Auxiliary Division of the RIC arrived, all British ex-officers, concerned only with the more repressive functions of police activity.

By now the IRA was reasonably well-armed and much more experienced, and the RIC had been driven out of the more remote rural areas. From September 1920 it began to change its tactics and the ambush became the prime offensive technique. These ambushes were undertaken by flying columns, small units of 30 or 40 men attached to the brigade of a particular area. These were standing units, as opposed to the usual part-time companies and battalions that made up a brigade, and their creation marked a new stage in the development of mobile guerrilla warfare. The first official one was formed in Dublin itself, and at the end of 1920 all brigades were ordered to form such a unit. In fact, according to one writer, an unofficial flying column was operating in East Limerick in May 1920, when it was known as an active service unit. It fulfilled much the same kind of function as the flying columns that followed it: 'What we had in mind was an efficient, disciplined, compact and swift-moving body of men, which would strike at the enemy where and whenever a suitable opportunity arose.'[15] By far the most important flying column was the one in West Cork which had a complement of 110 full-time fighters. It was commanded by Tom Barry, and his description of its main tasks is a fine summary of the nature of guerrilla warfare:

'... it was accepted in West Cork that the paramount objective of any Flying Column ... should be, not to fight, but to continue to exist. The very existence of such a column of armed men, even if it never struck a blow, was a continuous challenge to the enemy and forced him to maintain large garrisons to meet the threatened onslaughts on his military forces, and for the security of his civil administration ... But the Flying Column would attack whenever there were good grounds for believing that it would inflict more casualties on an enemy force than those it would itself suffer. It would choose its own battleground, and when possible, would refuse battle if the circumstances were unfavourable. It would seek out the enemy and fight, but would not always accept an enemy challenge ... The mission of the Flying Column was continually to harass, kill, capture and destroy the enemy forces; to keep in check his attempts to rebuild his badly shaken civil administration; to guard and protect the building of our own state institutions and the people who were establishing and using them.'[16]

The Irish struggle ended with the Truce of March 1921, when the British realised that its repression would involve an unacceptably vicious campaign of terror and bloodshed. There are, however, two other features of it that are of considerable interest within the terms of this book. The first of these concerns the activities of Michael Collins who, although a prominent organiser of the whole Irish effort, was not a guerrilla leader as such. His own function is best explained in his book *The Path to Freedom*:

'If we were to stand up against the powerful military organisation arrayed against us something more was necessary than a guerrilla war ... England could always reinforce her army. She could replace every soldier that she lost. But there were others indispensable for her purposes who were not so easily replaced. To paralyse the British machine it was necessary to strike at individuals. Without her spies England was helpless. It was only by means of their accumulated and accumulating knowledge that the British machine could operate ... [So] we struck at individuals, and by so doing we cut their lines of communication and we shook their morale.'[17]

In other words, Collins realised the prime importance of counter-intelligence in guerrilla warfare. Operating in Dublin, he and his squad of trained killers waged a ruthless war against Irish informers and British intelligence officers. On November 21, 1920, 'Bloody Sunday', he engineered his greatest coup of all when he simultaneously liquidated eleven such officers.

The second feature concerns the role of Sinn Féin in the Anglo-Irish War. From 1916 it was dominated by Arthur Griffith, and throughout the war he devoted his energies to making it a party of national solidarity rather than a representative of one or other sectional interest. His task was greatly facilitated by the execution of James Connolly, a brilliant Marxist thinker who might well have been able to link the independence movement with working-class militancy. Under Griffith, however, the party attracted many middle-class adherents and so created a firm base upon which to build the nationalist struggle and the new nation which it was hoped would emerge. From the beginning of Griffith's leadership 'Sinn Féin was determined not to confuse the political struggle by becoming involved directly in any clash of social interests that might divide the growing numbers of mixed supporters it had gathered to itself.'[18] It is interesting to note that after Sinn Féin had set up its own underground Parliament, the Dáil Eireann, in January 1919, one of its few effective pieces of civil machinery was the Courts of Justice, the Dáil, which suppressed the British police and were 'arbitration tribunals which averted the deadly danger of class struggle in the Sinn Féin ranks.'[19] Here one sees an example of the real importance of *nationalism* for a guerrilla movement. By stressing the demands of the common national interest at the expense of any emphasis upon class divisions within Irish society, which were in all truth real enough, the Sinn Féin leadership was able to minimise the possibility of internal divisions, and present a united front to the English enemy. Only then could the whole resources of the Irish people be committed to the military struggle, instead of being expended in ultimately futile internecine strife. It will be seen in the next chapter how, even in a civil war, this kind of class unity, at least in certain key areas, is vital to the success of the guerrillas.

Europe and the Nazis

After the German conquest of mainland Europe, including western parts of Russia, in 1940 and 1941, resistance movements sprang up in many of the occupied countries. In Holland, Belgium and Norway this resistance was limited to the publication of underground newspapers etc, and the carrying out of isolated acts of sabotage. But in other countries, notably Albania, Bulgaria, Czechoslovakia, France, Greece, Italy, Poland, Russia and Yugoslavia, the emphasis was more upon the creation of secret armies and, at one stage or another, the waging of guerrilla warfare.

By far the most bitter guerrilla struggle in Europe during World War II took place in Yugoslavia, between 1941 and 1944. On April 6, 1941, German troops entered Yugoslavia and within a few days had overwhelmed its regular army. Two resistance movements sprang up in the first months. The first was the Četnik bands led by a regular officer, Colonel Draža Mihailović. The second, which followed a little later, after Hitler's invasion of Russia, was the Communist Partisan movement under Tito (Josip Broz). Initially, both were based in Serbia, in the same inaccessible mountain and forest regions that had served as bases for the resistance to the Turks. The Četnik movement remained based upon Serbia throughout the whole war, though sympathetic groups sprang up in other parts of the country. The Partisans, on the other hand, were driven out of Serbia during November and December, in the so-called First

Enemy Offensive, and they retreated to a new base in the wild, mountainous regions of eastern Bosnia.

But for the next two years the Partisans were ceaselessly harried by the Germans and Italians and were forced to move their base area from region to region. In January 1942 the Fascists began their Second Offensive and Tito was forced to move southwards, below the Sarajevo-Vissegrad railway, and set up a new headquarters in the little east Bosnian town of Foča. At about this time there was also a massive national insurrection in Montenegro, and Partisan and Četnik bands succeeded in liberating extensive areas of the countryside. Between March and June the enemy launched their Third Offensive, mainly against the Montenegrin Partisans, and Tito withdrew them and his own main forces into the highlands of eastern Bosnia, in the Šutjeska Valley. But it proved impossible to feed a large guerrilla force in these barren mountains and on June 22 Tito decided to move his whole force to western Bosnia, establishing his headquarters at Glamoč and later Bosanski Petrovac. The Partisan movement also began to make headway in other parts of Yugoslavia, in Dalmatia, Slovenia and Slavonia. The main effort in Bosnia also snowballed and on November 5 Partisan forces captured Bihać in eastern Bosnia, and were now in control of almost the whole of the province.

On January 20, 1943, however, the Germans and Italians launched their Fourth Offensive, throwing in 90,000 men with aircraft, tanks and artillery against 25,000 guerrillas. They penetrated deep into Partisan territory and soon threatened to encircle them completely. Tito decided upon a counter-offensive towards the Neretva River, in the direction of Herzegovina and Montenegro. This was launched early in February but petered out late in the month, forcing the Partisans once more on to the defensive in the Rama and middle Neretva valleys. Tito decided upon another desperate attempt to break out. He would attack towards Bugojno in the north, leading the enemy to believe that that was the direction he intended to take, and then swing back into the Neretva valley and force a passage over the river. To make his feint more plausible he had every bridge across the river blown up. The desperate ploy worked. The attack northwards began on March 3 and between the 7th and the 14th the Partisans managed to extricate the bulk of their forces, crawling along a narrow 'bridge' built upon the wreckage of one of those already demolished. By May they were once again established in parts of eastern Bosnia and Montenegro.

In the middle of May the Germans launched their Fifth Offensive, known as Operation Schwarz. 50,000 Germans were employed as well as 50,000 Italians, Bulgarians and Croat Fascists, all this against a mere 20,000 Partisans. The Germans also developed more sophisticated tactics. Instead of frontal assaults based on a few major lines of communication they tried to baffle the guerrillas by rapidly shifting their mechanised and armoured formations from place to place. They also sent small, specially trained units of mobile shock troops ahead of the main forces to follow devious routes and try to take their opponents unawares. The Germans also waged all out war on the civilian population in the base area. Their instructions read: 'Every Partisan found is to be shot. If the local inhabitants are hostile to the German troops, treat them with the greatest possible brutality and severity. If they are friendly, harness them in the struggle against the Partisans. Destroy anything that could be of the slightest use to the Partisans. Foul all water supplies.'[20]

But once again Tito managed to slip away with his main striking force still intact, though much reduced. This time they broke through the encirclement by moving westwards over the Šutjeska mountains. From then on, although the forthcoming struggle was to be very bitter, the basic issue was no longer in doubt. Recruits flocked to the Partisans and after the Italian surrender in July 1943 large areas in Dalmatia, Montenegro, Slovenia and Primorje fell into Partisan hands, as well as the equipment of at least six Italian divisions. In early 1944 the Germans launched another offensive to clear the territory between Belgrade, the Danube and the Greater Morava Valley. But by this time the Russians were pressing in from the east and the Germans were beginning their evacuation of Greece and the Balkans, ready for a last-ditch stand in the heart of Europe. In spring 1944 Tito dispatched Partisan forces into Serbia, under Koča Popović, and began a drive out of east Bosnia and Montenegro, under Peko Dapčević. On September 29 the Red Army entered Yugoslavia, from Romania, and on October 20 Belgrade was liberated. Six months of heavy regular fighting side by side with the Russians lay ahead but there was now no doubt that the Germans would be driven out sooner or later.

Even from such a brief survey of the Yugoslav war of national liberation it should be clear that the Communists in that country had very soon succeeded in building up a military force that was capable of offering very determined resistance to the best regular troops that the Germans could throw against them. In a *strategic* sense the Yugoslavs followed the old guerrilla principle of always retreating before a superior force rather than risk annihilation. But within this broad strategy the Partisans were quite capable of most impressive *tactical* offensives. This had been Tito's aim from the very beginning. At first the Partisan units had been merely scattered bands based around a particular village and engaged in small-scale raids, ambushes and acts of sabotage. But such an approach was not judged adequate, for various reasons.

Firstly, for military reasons; as Tito wrote later: 'Militarily and tactically our tactics were: to prevent what had started as a partisan war from turning into a war for the defence of towns and villages: to overcome the tendency of villagers to stay in or near the villages and gradually to accustom them to the idea of fighting wherever they were needed.'[21] During the war itself he wrote:

'It became crystal clear that we could not carry out large-scale operations with combined Partisan detachments and battalions, and that we had to undertake the creation of larger, purely military, formations. This was necessary for the following reasons: it was very difficult to conduct a frontal warfare with scattered Partisan detachments; these were semi-military formations ill-adapted for fighting outside their areas, because many partisan fighters still felt that they were fighting only to defend their own villages; the Partisan fighters were in constant contact with the members of their families, often slept at home and so on, which sometimes had very adverse effects, especially when they were killed fighting in front of their families. All this compelled us to begin the organisation of purely military formations.'[22]

Tito, then, was not intending to fight a petty guerrilla war of the type so often noted in the previous chapters. He wanted to go beyond this stage and create regularised mobile formations that would be capable, *on occasion*, of meeting the Germans in brief pitched battles, or in cases of absolute desperation, of conducting suicidal holding operations. There was an example of the latter case during the Fifth Offensive, when Djilas' Third Division was almost completely wiped out whilst guarding the rear of Tito's retreating units.

This process of regularisation began as early as December 1941, when the First Proletarian Brigade was formed, a second one being formed in March of the following year. In late spring of the same year the Third, Fourth and Fifth Brigades were created, giving Tito a mobile élite force of about 5,000 men. By September there were 28 such formations, and in the following month the Yugoslav leadership decided to set up divisions and corps. The first two were formed that month and by the end of the year there were eight in existence. Each division was quite self-contained with its own party section, responsible to the regional Party Committee, and its own hospital, supply and finance organisation as well as a military court, police section and postal service. But let us be quite clear that, although these formations represented a great step forward from the guerrillas of Napoleonic Spain, Imperial Mexico, or Ottoman Serbia, for example, they were not regular units as such. At the strategic level, as has already been noted, they were still forced to retreat before the great German offensives. The following quotations help to give some idea of exactly what this type of *mobile warfare*, half-way between guerrilla operations proper and full-scale positional warfare, consisted of. The first is by Tito himself, and is a part of his instructions to the Partisan divisions prior to their counter-attack during the Fourth Offensive:

'We must avoid fixed fronts. We must not let the enemy force us by clever tactics on the defensive. On the contrary, the spirit of our troops must be offensive, not only in the attack, but in defence as well. During an enemy offensive the offensive spirit must find expression in vigorous and audacious guerrilla tactics, in operations behind the enemy's lines, in the destruction of his communications, in attacks on his supply centres, and on bases which are temporarily weakened. We must be no more afraid of being surrounded now than we were when we had few troops. We must make up for the loss of one area by the conquest of a larger and more important one.'[23]

The second quotation is from one of the German commanders who had to face the Partisans in the field, General Liters, writing in May 1943:

'A characteristic [tactic] was the mass-attacks with forces concentrated in one spot, carried out in atmospheric conditions favourable to the enemy (when air operations were not possible), and where our artillery was unable to make itself felt. The Communists always succeeded in making up for their lack of heavy weapons and, taking advantage of the dark, the mist or the rain, managed to get within a short distance of our troops and fight hand-to-hand. On such occasions they showed themselves to be good fighters, perfectly aware of the difficulties of a mountainous terrain ... By first-class infantry tactics (with the aid of the population etc), by a shrewd utilisation of the terrain, and by camouflage ... they always succeeded in setting traps for our troops.'[24]

But the reasons for this regularisation were far from being merely military. It had very important political implications. One of these was the question of nationalism. Yugoslavia was a very new state, having been created in the aftermath of World War I, and there were many internal rivalries between, for example, the Serbs and other groups, and between the various religious groups, Catholic, Muslim and Orthodox. As long as the Partisans fought in local guerrilla bands these rivalries were likely to remain. Only if the individual fighters could be taken far from home, within a homogeneous regular unit, would it be possible to overcome these traditional animosities and create a unified national base for the anti-Fascist struggle. In this respect the Partisans compare well with the Četniks who were nearly all Serbs and never threw off their belief in the necessity for Serbian supremacy in any Yugoslav state. As one writer has noted:

'... by a rough calculation, two fifths of Tito's forces by the end of 1943 represented Slavic elements simply not to be found in Mihajlović's command: Croatians, Slovenians, Bosnians. This ethnic distribution is also reflected in the composition of the Partisan Anti-Fascist Council of Liberation (AVNOJ) at its foundation in November 1942. Of AVNOJ's 70 members, 35 were Serbs, 17 Montenegrins, 13 Croats, 4 Muslims, and 1 was a Jew.'[25]

Regularisation also meant that political control of the guerrilla movement would be easier. On the one hand, this would simplify the Communists' task when the war was over and they began to think in terms of actually taking power. Yet it was not simply a cynical act of political opportunism. Regularisation inevitably meant centralisation and the creation of stable command structures which in turn make the task of co-ordinating operations much more straightforward. Regularisation offered the most effective means of controlling a disparate military effort that threatened to break down into apolitical, parochial fragments.

The Partisan leadership countered this tendency in three main ways. The formation of large military units I have already discussed. The second method was the appointment of commissars and the organisation of party cells in each unit. This process was complete by 1943 and gave the Yugoslav guerrillas an unusual degree of central direction and cohesiveness. A letter from Tito, of January 1943, to the Macedonian Partisans shows the extent of Party control over the guerrilla units. It is worth quoting at some length as it offers fascinating parallels with the other great Communist guerrilla struggle, that of Mao Tse-tung against the Nationalists and the Japanese:

'The party organisation in the army has been so established that all party members in one company form a single cell ... The secretaries of all company cells in a battalion or detachment comprise the party committee ... The secretary of the party committee ... maintains ties with party forums in the field, with the municipal committee and the district committee, both for the purposes of party work in the army and party work in the field ...

'The political commissar is the party delegate in the Army. Political work and activities among all the partisans in the unit are his responsibility (this includes political, as well as cultural-educational and allied activities), as are concern for the health and well-being of the men (health and nutrition ...), general supervision of HQ work ... [and] the fighting efficiency, the morale, the political level and the cohesion of his unit ...

'Care must be taken to prevent the "army line" ... from overriding the party line, that is, party members in positions of military or political leadership must not attend exclusively to their official duties to the neglect of their party responsibilities ... This would detract from the political significance of the goal we are fighting for and the party would lose its leading role and its influence in the units.'[26]

The third centralising influence was the insistence by Tito on the setting up of 'liberated areas' wherever the guerrillas were in sufficient strength. These areas were not simply secure bases for military operations but were miniature states controlled by the administrative machinery of AVNOJ. In this way the Communists both created a uniform administration in all the areas they controlled and also, particularly towards the end of the war, gradually built up the framework of a future national administration. To cite Tito again, from an article written in 1946:

> '. . . at the very beginning of the struggle . . . we had to shed the previous form of government both in the villages and in the towns, and start creating new organs of power which we called people's liberation committees . . . These were the nuclei of the new state . . . There was nothing casual and spontaneous about it; it was thoroughly prepared, deliberated and organised.'[27]

This was a type of guerrilla warfare radically in advance of anything yet encountered in these pages, with the partial exception of Zapata's efforts in Morelos. Tito was not simply endeavouring to fight a defensive military struggle against a foreign invader. He was rather using that struggle as the catalyst from which would emerge a new type of state, founded upon new ideals of social justice. Given this ambition, Tito saw that he must advance beyond the old parochial, defensive concept of guerrilla warfare and create an army that put people beyond the pale of the old forms of social and political organisation and committed them to fight for a new form of state. In this respect it was in his interests to make the war as destructive as possible. People were not simply to defend the old, but to go on and fight for something quite new. It is this visionary aspect of the Partisan efforts that distinguishes them from the Četniks. The latter recruited their members from amongst the wealthier elements of Serbian society, those with something material to lose. Therefore, as the war progressed, they became more and more dilatory about engaging the Germans because of their fear of retaliations. As a British liaison officer reported:

> 'Mihajlović and the Montenegrin leaders are essentially opportunists and will not risk their at present comparatively secure positions for the sake of what they would call "adventures" . . . In Serbia, Mihajlović's groups . . . are . . . little more than symbols of resistance . . . The poor sabotage results obtained hitherto are due to lack of willingness . . . and to lack of energy . . . [They will] reply that half a million Serbs have already been killed . . . and that they cannot risk reprisals.'[28]

Value judgments as to the relative merits of Tito's and Mihajlović's strategies would be impertinent. Nevertheless, as one writer has shown so well, the Partisan mode of all-out resistance led to the creation of an army whose dedication and fighting efficiency is almost without parallel in the history of guerrilla warfare:

> 'The deepest impression of Partisan military formations . . . was that each unit

was a closed society, and a human refuge from the destruction of their villages and the slaughter of their kin ... They were fighting to return to their homes, which would be reconstructed in a new and better world than they had known. In the mass, they represented the under-privileged and the neglected of a former society ... This was the basic strength of the movement: the mobilisation of the youth, the women, and the aged, and the creation of a new kinship and a special indefinable morale.'[29]

No other guerrilla struggle in Europe during World War II ever approached the intensity of that in Yugoslavia. In other countries the resistance movements never really got off the ground until the Allied Armies, Russian, American or British began to intervene. This was the case, for example, in Bulgaria and Czechoslovakia.

In Bulgaria the Communist Party decided upon armed resistance in June 1941. In October a few scattered small bands appeared but they had few arms as the government itself was in alliance with the Nazis. These bands conducted perhaps 200 minor sabotage operations up to the end of 1942. In March and April 1943 the Communists divided the country into 12 zones under the command of Party district committees and the Central Committee itself. The leaders were now trying to turn guerrilla warfare into a full-scale national insurrection, and in 1943 there were a reputed 1,685 guerrilla actions. By spring of 1944, 39 new guerrilla detachments or divisions had been created, as well as 26 new armed bands of varying sizes. From the spring of this year guerrilla activity increased. In June there were 350 actions, in July 510, and 540 in August. The army of liberation proper grew to some 18,000 men, whilst there were a further 12,000 in the parochial village combat groups. On August 26 the call went out for a full-scale national insurrection, but this was not actually attempted until September 9, four days after the Russians had declared war on Bulgaria. With the help of the Red Army the old regime was swiftly overthrown.

In Czechoslovakia resistance began in early 1942, the first engagement between partisans and the militia of the pro-German Slovak state taking place in April. The Communist Party was particularly prominent in encouraging the formation of partisan bands, to be known as Janošík groups, after an early Czech patriot. A newspaper, produced in Russia, contained this appeal to the Slovaks: 'Our native Slovak mountains ... call to you with open arms! Form detachments of lads in the mountains! ... Janošík's lads fought with axe and pistol, you with rifles, machine-guns and dynamite ... The conscious Slovak peasants will feed and aid you.'[30] Recruitment was slow at first, but in mid-1943 the movement began to gather momentum. The Communist Party set up National Revolutionary Committees in various areas, and in September it joined with various exile groups in founding a National Slovak Council. By this time the Russian advance into Europe was well under way. The Carpathians lay in the middle of the twin prongs of the Russian advance, into Germany and into Romania and Hungary, and they became the centre of operations against German communications. This activity reached a peak in mid-1944 and in August certain leaders felt that the time had come for a national insurrection. Some 15,000 guerrillas rose up and took over the whole of central Slovakia, the main defensive base being in the triangle Zvolen, Banska Bystrika, Brezno. The insurgents were joined by mutinying units of the regular army and a joint army-partisan high command was set up. But the influence of the army leaders proved pernicious. The guerrillas were precipitately regularised into sections, companies, battalions, etc, and, even worse, they committed themselves to a static defence of the base area. A German offensive of October 1944 completely overran the base and the surviving guerrillas resolved to return to their original tactics:

> 'Then the national liberation movement entered a new phase ... The insurgents adapted themselves to the new situation by adopting new tactics which were a combination of the defence of viable bases and movement and attacks ... against small German units and military installations ... [It was] a vast series of independent operations by small detachments ... When the enemy was numerically superior, the guerrillas fell back, abandoning their base to move on elsewhere.'[31]

The movement retained this defensive character until the arrival of the Red Army in February 1945, when it again assumed the dimensions of a national insurrection, this time successful.

In France too the resistance movement was mainly limited to sabotage and sullen non-co-operation until the arrival of the Allied armies, in June 1944. The main resistance movements were *Libération*, which was mainly concerned with promoting a general strike, though it formed a paramilitary section in spring 1942; *Combat*, which wanted a national military insurrection at some future date, to which end it formed numerous thirty-strong cadre shock units; and the *Front National* which was mainly a Communist group whose guerrilla formations were known as the *Francs-tireurs Partisans* (F-TP).

The underground movement as a whole was known as the *Maquis* (literally 'dense undergrowth'). It gained many new recruits in 1943 after the passing of a decree on February 16 calling for French workers to go and work in German industry. Some 100,000 Frenchmen fled to the countryside to avoid this obligation, though far from all of them actually joined the armed resistance. In January 1944, for example, there were only 30,000 *maquisards* proper. One of the main problems was the availability of arms. Thus, whilst there were three large bands of guerrillas in Mont Mouchet, in spring 1943, their 9,000 members could only muster between them 60 muskets, 2 rusty sub-machine guns, 45 revolvers and 4 Lebel rifles. Other important guerrilla groups were to be found in areas of particularly favourable terrain, such as the 1,000 men around Vercors, the 600 around Glières, and the 1,000 or so in the Montagne Noire. But these units were no match on their own for the German army. The Glières group was annihilated in a German offensive of February and March 1944. Shortly after D-Day the Maquis leaders attempted to establish a defensive redoubt in the Massif Central, based upon Vercors, and several thousand guerrillas were concentrated there. They were totally crushed and over 1,000 of them lost their lives.

Nevertheless, from D-Day, where the Germans were obliged to concentrate upon dealing with regular Allied units, the guerrillas, or Forces Françaises de l'Intérieur (FFI) as they were known from January 1944, scored some notable successes in both the north and south of France. General Eisenhower, perhaps with more diplomacy than military objectivity, estimated that the guerrillas were worth the equivalent of 15 divisions and that they had hastened the end of the war by two months. Their activities reached a peak in August 1944:

'The guerrilla war and the sabotage of German communications had by now spread over the whole of France. The railways between the German border and Normandy were practically out of action. German troop movements were often hopelessly slowed down ... Their own forces were liberating numerous towns, and whole provinces such as almost the entire Alpine part of France ... Similarly practically the whole of the Massif Central and the south-west of France were liberated by the FFI. It was thanks to the FFI that the German garrison of Limoges surrendered. Thanks largely to the constant harassing tactics of the FFI, only a quarter of the German forces in the south-east that had been ordered to pull out got as far as Dijon. Altogether in the south-east, the FFI captured 40,000 prisoners.'[32]

The resistance movement in Italy began to get underway after the fall of Mussolini in July 1943. A new government was set up under Badoglio, but the Committee of National Liberation, embracing all anti-Fascist parties, at first refused to join him. Then in March 1944 the Russians recognised Victor Emmanuel as the legitimate ruler of Italy and the Communists hastened to join the new government. Not wishing to appear to be further left than the Communists, other political parties soon followed suit. But even before this, from September 1943, armed bands were springing up, mainly in the mountainous areas of northern Italy. The chief bands were set up by the Communists (the Garibaldi Brigades), the Socialists (the Matteotti Brigades), and the Action Party (the Liberty and Justice Brigades). In December 1943 there were 9,000 guerrillas, in March of the following year 25,000, in June

80,000, and in May 1945 250,000. The Communists produced probably two-thirds of the total figures, and like their counterparts in other countries the Garibaldi Brigades were well organised and disciplined, each unit having its own commissar and, usually, party cell. By the middle of 1944 a typical partisan formation was on a semi-regular footing, organised into nuclei of five or six men, squads, detachments, battalions, brigades (of approximately 450 men), and divisions of two or three brigades. In April 1944 the guerrillas were involved in 1,942 actions, in May 2,035, and in June 2,200.

In the summer of 1944, the guerrillas, emboldened by their rapid growth and military success, set up liberated areas in various northern regions. As in Yugoslavia they set up their own administration in these areas and introduced free elections, taxation and price controls. Examples of such liberated areas were to be found in the Modenian Appenines, Coni province and the Ossola Valley. But in many cases such action was premature and, as in Slovakia and France, the Germans launched determined offensives against them, overwhelming them with brutality and simple military efficiency. In Boves, Cumiana, Fondo Toce, Santa Anna de Versilia and Marzabotto, for example, populations were massacred and whole villages burnt to the ground. Altogether some 72,000 guerrillas and civilians lost their lives in these counter-offensives. Only slowly did the Italians come to realise that they were not yet capable of abandoning guerrilla warfare for defensive positional combat:

> '[The Germans] introduced new raking techniques . . . In south-west Piedmont . . . they employed an entire division for the combings and blocked off whole valleys with the goal of either destroying or dispersing the . . . partisans. Several motorised columns would advance from the valley floor in an encircling fashion toward a cul-de-sac . . . [The guerrillas] learned the hard way to give up the outmoded transversal defence tactics and adopted . . . a multiple defence system in depth along only one side of the valley and based fairly high up it, using also numerous and complex road-blocks . . . Increasing flexibility became the rule. Some units dispatched "flying squads" down on to the plains on swift assault missions against . . . the enemy's communication and supply lines. But the most common tactic in the face of overwhelming power was to fall back to higher elevations to regroup.'[33]

So the guerrillas survived their premature moves and went on to be of great service to the Allies as they pushed their way through Italy. Just before the disbandment of the guerrilla formations in May 1945, Colonel Hewitt of Special Force Number One, in charge of liaison with the guerrillas, wrote:

> 'The partisans took in all 40,000 German and Fascist prisoners. Large quantities of arms and equipment were destroyed or captured. The Allies were able to

advance freely, the partisans taking charge of the elimination of the enemy that stood in their way. Bridges, roads, telegraph and telephone wires, most important for a rapid advance, were saved from destruction. In all, more than a hundred urban centres were liberated by the partisans prior to our arrival. The contribution of the partisans to the Allied victory in Italy was very considerable and far surpassed the most optimistic forecasts ... Without the victories of the partisans, Allied victory in Italy would not have been so rapid, decisive and bloodless.'[34]

The last guerrilla activity of importance in World War II was that in Russia after the German invasion in 1941. Here the general pattern of guerrillas acting as auxiliaries to the regular forces was even more marked. The Soviet partisans were never regarded as being able to take on the invaders on equal terms, but were simply to harass them in their rear areas and restrict their freedom of action against the advancing Red Army. Moreover, the guerrillas were not so much a spontaneous resistance movement as a tightly controlled component of the total military effort. According to certain writers, the Russians had been preparing for partisan operations even before the German invasion, and had already selected the officers and laid up secret supply dumps. Certainly partisan warfare began almost immediately. On July 18, 1941, the Central Committee of the CPSU issued a decree on the Organisation of the Struggle in the Enemy Rear. During the Battle of Moscow in winter 1941–42, 10,000 guerrillas took part in operations against the German rear, though these had been sent in by the High Command rather than being the result of a spontaneous popular upsurge.

On May 30, 1942, the Central Committee created a Central Staff of the Partisan Movement directed by Lieutenant-General Ponomarenko, and a little later regional staffs were set up in the key areas of Belorussia and the Ukraine. These were responsible for the co-ordination of the guerrilla activities with the operations of the Red Army. The next lower echelon was the Operation Group which was situated behind enemy lines and dictated the actual operations in each region. The basic guerrilla unit was the brigade which was divided into various *otriadi*, or bands, of 30 to 100 men. Wherever possible, centralisation was the key-note. Strict discipline was maintained in the bands themselves by NKVD commissars, or *politruki*. But these were not simply the Party inquisitors of popular myth. Their function was not merely to punish back-sliders or political opponents, but also had a more positive aspect. They were to ensure that: 'The guiding principles of partisan activity must be fulfilment of combat assignments hand in hand with political education work among the population: the partisan must enhance his ideological and political level, maintain close contact with the population and help them in every way.'[35]

Nevertheless, though the extent of the guerrilla activity in occupied Russia indicates a genuine outburst of national feeling, the Soviet leaders were clearly most anxious about the implications of any kind of real popular movement. After the war one Russian writer noted the official reaction to democratic tendencies within the partisan formations:

'In some detachments, mainly those organised after occupation had set in, there arose the practice of electing officers, a practice long since condemned by the party. The Regional Committee condemned this practice and re-required that all the detachments ... be connected with regional headquarters and co-ordinate their actions with it. Simultaneously the Regional Committee worked to strengthen one-man leadership and the authority of the commander. The commander's word was law. The Regional Committee promptly nipped any attempts to hold meetings to discuss decisions taken or the orders of the commander.'[36]

Moreover, the Soviet leaders tried to ensure that the guerrillas, whose discipline was inevitably looser than that of the Red Army, no matter what the precautions of the Party, did not mingle with the regular soldiers. 'Rather, the guerrilla forces had a chain of command all of their own ... Merging of partisan units with the advancing Red Army was prohibited; in fact, the partisans were directed to avoid all contact with regular troops for reasons of policy and discipline. When the battle line moved beyond them, the guerrillas were ordered to reinfiltrate through the German lines immediately and operate as before.'[37]

The guerrilla campaign was of incalculable assistance to the efforts of the Red Army. In 1942 the guerrillas were strong enough to start setting up *partizanskie kraya*, or partisan regions, which were completely free of Germans. Particularly large regions were to be found in Orel province (54 detachments of 18,000 partisans) and Smolensk province (72 detachments of 22,000 partisans). By December 1943 there were 360,000 partisans throughout Belorussia and 220,000 in the Ukraine. Their achievements were no less impressive. By November 1944 the Ukrainians are said to have destroyed or damaged 527 tanks, 64 aircraft, 2,331 trains, 2,230 locomotives, 2,421 wagons. In 1943 they were knocking out an average of 200 locomotives per month. On the night of July 20–21 they simultaneously blew up 5,800 rails in the Briansk, Orel and Gomel regions to coincide with a Red Army offensive there. Even in 1942 the Germans had deployed 15 field divisions, 10 SS and SD divisions and 5 Hungarian divisions in anti-guerrilla operations, at a time when the total German force in North Africa was a mere 12 divisions.

As in other countries, German counter-insurgency measures relied largely upon terror, though its sheer extent in Russia almost beggars description. The

tenor of the Nazi response was set in September 1941 in the notorious Keitel
Befehl:

> 'Insurrectional movements have arisen in German occupied territory ... We
> must undertake without delay the most rigorous measures to affirm the
> authority of the occupying power and to avoid an extension of these attacks. We
> must never lose sight of the fact that, in occupied countries, a human life is
> worth less than nothing and that intimidation is only possible through extra-
> ordinarily harsh measures. When taking reprisals for the death of a German
> soldier, the execution of 50 to 100 Communists is essential ... The method of
> execution should reinforce yet more the impact of the punishment.'[38]

This decree was obeyed to the letter. To give just one example, after the
Germans had pushed a partisan band out of the Osveia district in northern
Belorussia, the Germans proceeded to burn down 158 villages in the region,
deport all remaining able-bodied men as slaves, and murder all the women,
children and old people.

Militarily the Germans made little headway against the guerrillas. It was not
until autumn 1944, by which time it was far too late, that the OKW began to
formulate a general policy on counter-insurgency. This was set down in a
manual entitled *On Fighting Bands*. It cited the need for small groups of highly
trained soldiers who would adopt the guerrillas' own tactics and relentlessly
pursue them in their own environment. These groups were known as *Jagd-
kommandos* and their basic tactic was denoted by the hunting term '*kesseltreiben*'.
A *Kessel* is literally a kettle or cauldron and has the same military connotation as
'pocket' in English. *Treiben* means to beat, referring both to the scaring of game
into a trap and the final struggle that follows. As the manual said:

> 'The fighting of bands is no second-rate fight. It requires soldiers who are
> particularly agile, cunning, fighting like hunters, hardened and frugal. Only
> continual vigilance protects troops from serious casualties ... A hunting section
> should not be smaller than a platoon nor stronger than a company. Fights with
> superior forces should be avoided ... Hunting is an intensified, indefatigable
> kind of pursuit, its aim is outrunning, bringing to a stand and crushing or
> capturing the prey.'[39]

It is interesting to assess how successful the Germans would have been had
they ever had the chance of mounting such operations on a large scale. But this
does bring one to what is probably the basic point about all the guerrilla
activity in Europe during World War II. Had the Germans only had to face
guerrilla opponents, rather than guerrillas acting in conjunction with large
regular armies, it seems most likely that they would have eventually been able

to suppress all such movements, even in Yugoslavia, or at least contain them as a minor irritant. More than this, in most countries, such as France and Italy, the guerrilla bands would never have got off the ground without the intervention of the Allied expeditionary forces.

1. E. M. Earle (ed), *Makers of Modern Strategy*, Princeton University Press, Princeton, 1941, p249
2. *ibid*, p243
3. *ibid*, p248
4. *ibid*, pp 241 and 242
5. R. Furneaux, *Abdel Krim*, Secker & Warburg, London, 1967, p157
6. *ibid*, p117
7. *ibid*, p98
8. Maj J. R. Sibley, *Tanganyikan Guerrilla*, Pan/Ballantine, London, 1973, p41
9. *ibid*, p135
10. Capt A. Buchanan, *Three Years of War in East Africa*, John Murray, London, 1919, pp 138–39
11. T. E. Lawrence, *Seven Pillars of Wisdom*, Penguin Books, 1973, pp 193–202
12. J. Wright, *Libya*, Ernest Benn, 1969, p164
13. *ibid*, p167
14. M. Collins, *The Path to Freedom*, Mercier Press, Cork, 1968, p69
15. Col J. M. MacCarthey, *Limerick's Fighting Story*, Anvil Books, Dublin, nd, p87
16. T. Barry, *Guerrilla Days in Ireland*, Anvil Books, Dublin, 1969, pp 26–27
17. Collins, *op cit*, pp 69–70
18. P. Lynch, 'The Social Revolution that Never Was', in D. Williams (ed), *The Irish Struggle 1916–26*, Routledge & Kegan Paul, 1966, p45
19. D. Ryan, 'Sinn Fein Policy and Practice', in *ibid*, p35
20. F. Maclean, *The Battle of Neretva*, Panther Books, 1970, p36
21. Maclean, *Disputed Barricade*, Jonathan Cape, 1957, p236
22. F. W. D. Deakin, *The Embattled Mountain*, Oxford University Press, 1971, pp 100–101
23. Maclean, *Neretva, op cit*, p73
24. First International Conference on the History of Resistance Movements, *European Resistance Movements 1939–45*, Pergammon Press, Oxford, 1960, p332
25. R. V. Burks, *The Dynamics of Communism in Eastern Europe*, Princeton University Press, 1961, p123
26. W. Pomeroy (ed), *Marxism and Guerrilla Warfare*, Lawrence & Wishart, 1969, pp 151–53
27. *ibid*, p150
28. Deakin, *op cit*, p153
29. *ibid*, pp 106–107
30. J. Solc, 'Le mouvement slovaque des partisanes', *Revue d'Histoire de la Deuxième Guerre Mondiale*, No 52, 1963, p62
31. *ibid*, p75
32. A. Werth, *France 1940–55*, Robert Hale, 1956, p167
33. C. F. Delzell, *Mussolini's Enemies*, Princeton University Press, 1961, p377
34. *European Resistance Movements, op cit*, pp 92–93
35. Pomeroy, *op cit*, p134
36. *ibid*, p132
37. F. M. Osanka (ed), *Modern Guerrilla Warfare*, Free Press, Glencoe, 1962, p83
38. M. Adler-Bresse, 'Témoignages allemands sur la guerre des partisans', *Revue d'Histoire de la Deuxième Guerre Mondiale*, No 53, 1962, p57
39. Osanka, *op cit*, pp 98–99

CHAPTER 7

The Birth of People's War:
The Chinese Revolution 1926–49

I have chosen to deal with the Chinese Civil War in a short chapter of its own because it was in this war, probably the most successful guerrilla struggle in history, that the themes dealt with in isolation in previous chapters were brought together in a systematic effort to turn the guerrilla mode into an effective revolutionary and military method. Thus, rather than attempt a simple chronological survey of the progress of the war, I will deal with it under various theoretical sub-headings to show how Mao Tse-tung dealt with the various problems inherent in transforming defensive guerrilla warfare into a means of seizing power. Each of these sub-headings is already familiar to us in the context of other guerrilla wars, but it was only during the Chinese Civil War that they were all dealt with in such a thorough and coherent way. It would be rash to assume that any would-be guerrilla leader need only follow the dictates of Mao Tse-tung to ensure victory – objective circumstances differ too greatly from place to place – but it is still true to say that the theoretical bases of the Chinese struggle were a response to fundamental problems inherent in all guerrilla struggles. The exact solution of the problems discussed in this chapter might vary from place to place, but any guerrilla force will have to confront them in some form or other. These problems concern the notion of 'protracted war'; 'base areas'; 'guerrilla tactics'; 'Class unity' and 'popular support'; 'regularisation' and 'political control'.

Protracted War

China was almost entirely a rural society, and any thorough revolution would have to initiate measures to satisfy the discontent of the increasingly impoverished peasantry. But in China, the incumbent regime, though corrupt and incompetent, was far from disintegrating. The revolutionaries could not realistically hope to seize power in a swift *coup d'état* but rather had to wait until they had a large military and political *apparat* of their own, equal to the task of meeting the sizable incumbent forces in open conflict. It would take many

years to build up such an *apparat* and a realistic appraisal of the situation
demanded that the Communists be prepared for a long struggle which would
give them that time. Only then could the Chinese Communists hope to
overthrow the Kuomintang state. A few Communist leaders, notably Mao Tse-
tung, realised this at an early stage, but it was many years before they were in a
position to put such theories into practice. Until 1934 and the beginning of the
Long March the revolutionary and military history of China was bedevilled by
many misconceptions and opportunistic theories that precluded the possibility
of bringing about an effective social revolution.

Before 1934 and the triumph of Maoism Communist policy was based upon
two successive doctrinaire assumptions. At first they held that the socialist
revolution could only come about after the emergence of a progressive,
nationalist bourgeoisie. Once China had gone through a nationalist revolution
that would permit the full emergence of this bourgeoisie, this class would then
be free to set about the creation of a national industrial base that would in turn
guarantee the growth of a large working class. Then, according to Marxist
orthodoxy, the eventual triumph of the socialist revolution would be inevitable. To this end, in June 1923, the Party formally announced that it was
prepared to ally with the Kuomintang (KMT), the foremost nationalist party
within China, and to accord the latter the leading role within the alliance. But
CCP policy was based upon a rather unrealistic assessment of the historical
process. Whilst there was some validity in adhering to the Marxist dictum that
the bourgeois revolution must precede the proletarian, it was utopian to expect
the KMT to look with favour upon an ally whose ultimate aim was the
destruction of the very society for which the Nationalists were fighting. From
the very beginning many within the KMT were intensely suspicious of their
new allies. From 1925–27 the KMT undertook a series of anti-Communist
measures, culminating in a purge of leading cadres in Shanghai, Canton and
other big cities. For a time the CCP tried to ally with a 'leftist' faction within
the KMT, based in Wuhan, but by July 1927 the Wuhan government also
tired of their Communist allies and they were expelled from its party.

But the CCP could still not bring itself to break its links with Marxist or
Soviet orthodoxy. If there was no hope of a progressive bourgeois revolution
then clearly the Communists would have to count upon the proletariat alone.
After their disillusionment with the KMT they began to put the alliance with
the Chinese working class at the very centre of their programme. At an
Emergency Conference in August 1927 it was decided 'that the leadership of
the Chinese Revolution had passed to the proletariat.'[1]

But even though it was growing very fast, the working class in China was
still very small in relation to the population as a whole. Moreover, whatever
organisational bases the Communists had been able to establish amongst the
workers had been severely disrupted by the anti-Communist offensives of the

KMT. So the Communists found themselves compelled to seek other allies to supplement their dwindling forces in the cities. The only possible choice was the peasantry. In forming such an alliance the CCP was taking the first steps along the road to the Maoist conception of the Chinese Revolution. But it is most important to bear in mind that at this time the peasantry was only regarded as the cannon-fodder of the revolution. Revolutionary power was still envisaged in terms of the dictatorship of the proletariat, and the key revolutionary acts were still to take place in the cities. Peasant unrest was merely to create a climate of uncertainty and chronic instability in which the cities could find the inspiration and the freedom of manoeuvre to act. As one historian has written: 'Although for the moment it was realised that the peasantry in the countryside was more active than the working class in the cities, this was regarded as an unnatural state of affairs . . . to be remedied as soon as possible. "Proletarian hegemony" remained an unquestioned dogma.'[2]

This dogma pushed the Party inevitably in one strategic direction. Whilst the rural unrest was not a self-sufficient phenomenon, it could be utilised to aid the urban masses. And the aid must come swiftly if the Communist bases in the cities were not to be entirely lost. Thus there followed, over the next eight or nine years, a consistent policy of trying to use the peasantry to storm the cities and take power at one fell swoop. Sometimes not even the peasantry as such was used. On August 1 1927 a Front Committee formed the previous month in Nanchang attempted to take over that city with certain military units commanded by Communist sympathisers. On the 5th the approach of loyal nationalist units forced them to abandon the city completely. A little over a month later the CCP once again tried to ensure themselves a permanent urban base in a series of attacks known as the Autumn Harvest Uprising. The prime targets were a series of cities in Hupei province. Once again the attempt proved abortive. Mao Tse-tung, who had been ordered to form a military force for the purpose, pulled his men out of the campaign in defiance of Party orders, before they were all uselessly squandered. He took them into the mountainous Ching Kang Shan region where he set up the first Communist rural base in Central China.

The Communists also decided to take action in Canton to coincide with the hoped for Autumn Harvest successes. Despite the miserable failure they did not go back on this decision. Even though they could only muster 2,000 poorly armed militia against a possible opposition of 50,000 Nationalist troops, the local Provincial Committee approved a plan for an insurrection on December 7. It began on the 11th in the early morning. The rebels set up a local Soviet government and announced several sweeping revolutionary measures. By the 13th, however, government forces had recaptured the city, and between 5,000 and 8,000 rebels are said to have perished in the brutal repression that followed.

At about this time Mao Tse-tung moved his forces from the Ching Kang Shan to a new base in the Kiangsi-Fukien border region. There Communist influence expanded among the peasantry and the Red Army grew accordingly. But despite the previous mistakes, the Communist leadership, now dominated by Li Li-san, was incapable of regarding this as anything but proof of the imminence of large-scale Communist victories and the vulnerability of the towns and cities. The so-called Li Li-san line was formulated, complete with the old urban fixation and stress upon short-term insurrectionary activity. In March 1930 he wrote: 'The villages are the limbs of the ruling class. The cities are their brains and hearts. If we cut out their brains and hearts they cannot escape death; but if we cut off their appendages it will not necessarily kill them.'[3] In June he was even more specific: 'The great struggle of the prole-tariat is the decisive force in the winning of preliminary successes in one or more provinces. Without an upsurge of strikes of the working class, without armed insurrections in key cities, there can be no successes in one or more provinces.'[4] So the Central Committee in Shanghai decided that the time was once again ripe for armed assaults on the cities. The offensive began in late July. Failure was total, and once again Mao took it upon himself to disobey Party orders and avoid what he knew would be a futile attack on Nanchang. The Party reacted strongly to this fiasco. Li Li-san was bitterly attacked and power devolved upon a new group of Moscow-trained men, led by Mif, the Comintern delegate.

But even at this stage the CCP retained some kind of urban fixation and overriding optimism about the possibility of precipitate successes throughout China. In early 1933 the Central Committee was forced to quit Shanghai and move to Juichin, the capital of the Kiangsi-Fukien base area, or Chinese Soviet Republic as it was now called. But it took massive defeat in the Nationalist Fifth Encirclement Campaign finally to bury their obsession with urban cen-tres. From the time of the Second Encirclement Campaign in May 1931, and the attendant Communist successes, the Central Committee was constantly urging that the time for cautious guerrilla warfare was past and that the Red Army must adopt a forward offensive strategy based upon the seizure of the towns. Indeed this policy had some initial successes, in early 1932. But such gains proved ephemeral in the absence of a sympathetic and organised base in the surrounding countryside. By 1934 the Kiangsi Soviet Republic had been reduced from 90 to 6 counties and the Nationalist grip was tightening with every day. In terms of real political power urban bases were mere mirages in a desert of apathy and oppression. The irrelevance of the Central Committee's line had now become all too apparent and Mao Tse-tung was at last given the chance for an unhindered application of his own strategies and tactics to the revolutionary struggle.

The starting point for his theories was the realisation that the agricultural crisis in China during the 1920s and 1930s and the gradual pauperisation of the rural masses was fundamental to an understanding of the Chinese Revolution. The population was expanding so that land *per capita* was steadily declining. There was also a steady decline in the total area under cultivation. Because land was in such short supply rents rose rapidly. Worse, many peasants could not afford to keep themselves in the period between sowing and harvesting and had to borrow money, at staggeringly high rates of interest, to tide them over. But this was not the end of the story. The Chinese peasant was also suffering the effects of the gradual commercialisation of agriculture, as middle-class elements in the cities invested in land itself and in the raising of commercial crops:

'The introduction of commercial crops and the commercialisation of land affected land prices, tenure conditions and rent charges. Prices for land doubled and tripled in some areas, and secure tenure was replaced by short-term contracts. At the same time rents increased outright or rose through the use of such mechanisms as advance collections or the payment of rent deposits to ensure rights of permanent tenure.'[5]

All this meant that the peasant had a continuous need for money to ensure that he was able to hang on to his patch of land. The middle classes were unable to make much investment in indigenous industrial development because of the low tariffs created by the 'unequal treaties', and because of the extent of Japanese investment at all levels in the economy. Therefore, in the majority of cases, 'it stayed in the village and became the usurious class, lending money to the peasantry. In that field it could get immediate profits, at so high a rate of interest as to make the whole system iniquitous. As a result its members often became landlords, in addition to lending money.'[6] On top of all this the China of this period was controlled by the warlords in particular areas. Each one issued his own paper money, always without an adequate metallic reserve, and so inflation was rampant. Further, the warlords depended totally on their armed forces for both internal repression and inter-provincial prestige and security. To pay for the upkeep of this soldiery it was necessary to extract revenue from the peasantry in the shape of taxes. The taxes were heavy enough, but in many cases the demands of the military budget forced the warlords to collect them 2, 5, 7, or in one case, 31 years in advance.

Under these circumstances it is hardly surprising that rural China was in an almost continuous state of ferment. In 1925 and 1926 there had been a mushrooming of the organised peasant movement. In Hunan in November 1926 the peasant associations had just over one million members, whilst in 1927 some two million were involved in outright seizures of land.

At about this time Mao Tse-tung himself was in Hunan, and in March 1927 he presented a study of the peasant movement there. In it he stressed the importance of peasant militancy for the prospects of revolution in China. He criticised those within the CCP who still maintained a somewhat vacillating attitude towards the rural masses: 'All talk directed against the peasant movement must be speedily set right. All the wrong measures taken by the revolutionary authorities concerning the peasant movement must be speedily changed. Only thus can the future of the revolution be benefited.' But in one important respect this excursion into an analysis of the revolutionary potential of the Chinese peasantry differs from the later Maoist line. He goes on to say: 'In a very short time . . . several hundred million peasants will rise like a mighty storm, like a hurricane, a force so swift and violent that no power, however great, will be able to hold it back. They will smash all the trammels that bind them and rush forward along the road to liberation.'[7] The crucial words here are 'in a very short time'. Mao had still not developed the concept of protracted warfare that underpins his mature conception of the road to revolutionary power. But the failure of the Central Committee's attempt to storm the towns and effect a swift seizure of revolutionary power soon persuaded Mao that such a short-term perspective on the Chinese Revolution was doomed to disappointment. For one thing the revolutionaries were simply not strong enough to take on the Nationalist forces in this kind of engagement. More importantly, given that one had decided to rely upon the peasantry to supply one's revolutionary manpower, one had to take account of their particular characteristics. Peasants are parochial, traditionalist and fatalistic. They would not be prepared to fight for a revolution concentrated on distant urban centres or that defined its ideal society in terms of the liberation of the proletariat. They would only fight in a revolutionary army that stressed the importance of their own preoccupations about the importance of rural reform. Certainly the towns had to be taken *eventually*. But such seizures meant something only in the context of a militant, radicalised countryside, and thus the whole of the initial Communist effort had to be directed to the long and arduous task of arousing and training the rural masses. When Mao said that the countryside had to surround the towns he gave a clear indication of the siege-like nature of the operation. And sieges are not based upon swift assaults but a slow and painstaking process of erosion. Therefore there was absolutely no point in hoping for a revolutionary war in which victory could be swiftly achieved. By its very nature it was bound to be a protracted war:

> 'Because the reactionary forces are very strong, revolutionary forces grow only gradually and this fact determines the protracted nature of our war. Here impatience is harmful and advocacy of 'quick decision' incorrect. To wage a revolutionary war for ten years, as we have done, might be surprising in other countries, but for us it is like the opening sections in an . . . essay – the 'pre-

sentation, amplification and preliminary exposition of the theme' – and many exciting parts are yet to follow ... We should not expect successes overnight. The aspiration to 'wipe out the enemy before breakfast' is admirable, but it is bad to make concrete plans to do so ... Our revolutionary war will continue to be a protracted one until China's revolutionary forces have built up enough strength to breach the main positions of our internal and external enemies ... To proceed from this point in formulating our strategy of long-term warfare is one of the important principles guiding our strategy.'[8]

Base Areas

Of course the protracted nature of the struggle has been one of the distinguishing characteristics of a great many of the guerrilla wars dealt with in the preceding chapters. It is, in fact, an almost inevitable consequence of the standard guerrilla tactics of harassment and the avoidance of large-scale combats. But Mao Tse-tung's policy was more than simply a passive response to certain material immutables. Though he realised that for the time being the Chinese Communists must be compelled to fight a long-term, defensive struggle, he nevertheless felt that there could be certain dynamic elements within such a struggle that could eventually transform it from a purely defensive to an offensive war. Thus from the very beginning he was opposed to the kind of defensive tactics that typified so many earlier guerrilla wars. In January 1930 he wrote:

'in semi-colonial China the establishment and expansion of the Red Army, the guerrilla forces and the Red areas is the highest form of peasant struggle ... and undoubtedly the most important factor in accelerating the revolutionary high tide throughout the country ... The policy which merely calls for roving guerrilla actions cannot accomplish the task of accelerating this nation-wide, revolutionary high-tide ... [The correct policy is that of] establishing base areas; of systematically setting up political power; of deepening the agrarian revolution; of expanding the people's armed forces by a comprehensive process of building up first the township Red Guards, then the district Red Guards, then the county Red Guards, then the local Red Army troops, all the way up to the regular Red Army troops; of spreading political power by advancing in a series of waves...'[9]

In other words, though one has to accept that the war will be protracted, this does not mean that one is merely seeking an eternal tactical stalemate, and hoping that eventually the enemy will simply give up. Rather the protracted war is in itself a dynamic process whose very duration is the condition for the gradual emergence of an increasingly powerful Communist political and military structure.

The establishment of base areas is absolutely fundamental to this process. Only within such liberated areas could one begin the military and political education of the peasantry that alone could ensure that they transcended the stage of being mere roving guerrilla bands. Moreover, the objective conditions within China, according to Mao, favoured such a tactic. Though the counter-revolutionary forces were very strong, the political situation in China was unique in that power was not in the hands of a single central authority but of a diverse selection of warlords, each very jealous of his own prerogative within a limited area. The warlords were in a constant state of rivalry and sometimes of open war, such that they, let alone the central government, were never able to concentrate more than a fraction of their forces against any revolutionary group. Thus the Communists could create for themselves the room for manoeuvre to set up some kind of permanent revolutionary base. As Mao said in October 1928:

'The prolonged splits and wars within the White regime provide a condition for the emergence and persistence of one or more small Red areas under the leadership of the Communist Party amidst the encirclement of the White regime . . . Some comrades often have doubts about the survival of Red political power and become pessimistic . . . If we only realise that splits and wars will never cease within the White regime within China, we shall have no doubts about the emergence, survival and daily growth of Red political power.'[10]

He stated the point again in an article of the following month:

'China is the only country in the world today where one or more small areas under Red political control have emerged in the midst of a White regime which encircles them. We find on analysis that one reason for this phenomenon lies in the incessant splits and wars within China's comprador and landlord classes. So long as these splits and wars continue, it is possible for an armed independent regime of workers and peasants to survive and grow.'[11]

But because this was a strategy dictated by what Mao referred to as the 'objective conditions' within China, he was very aware that one must adopt tactics that meshed with these conditions. Thus:

'An independent regime must vary its strategy against the encircling ruling classes, adopting one strategy when the . . . regime is temporarily stable, and another when it is split up. In a period when the ruling classes are split up . . . our strategy can be comparatively adventurous and the area carved out by military operations can be comparatively large . . . In a period when the regime is comparatively stable . . . our strategy must be one of gradual advance.'[12]

This is what one might call Mao's political analysis of Chinese society, and out of it arose his fundamental concept of the possibility of maintaining, for a varying period of time, an independent, self-sufficient Red area within which to conduct political propaganda and initiate a series of socio-economic reforms. Further:

'Since the struggle . . . [in such terms] is exclusively military, both the Party and the masses have to be placed on a war-footing. How to deal with the enemy, how to fight, has become the central problem of our daily life. An independent regime must be an armed one. Wherever such an area is located, it will immediately be occupied by the enemy if armed forces are lacking or inadequate, or if wrong tactics are used in dealing with the enemy.'[13]

Guerrilla Tactics

The question of right and wrong tactics introduces Mao's sociological analysis of China's revolutionary potential. The tactics he chose were those of guerrilla warfare, designed to make the most of an army of badly trained, badly equipped and parochially minded peasants. Just like the overall strategy, the tactics themselves were chosen to fit in with objective conditions. And just as the independent regimes as a whole had to advance boldly or consolidate according to the strength of the opposing White regime, so did the individual guerrilla units have to mould their tactics according to the strength and purpose of the opposing units. This unity of the strategical and the tactical, the political and the sociological, was admirably summed up in an interview between Edgar Snow and Peng Teng-huai in 1937. Speaking of the reasons for the development of guerrilla warfare, Peng said: 'Although the strategic areas of China are all more or less dominated by the imperialists, this control is uneven and not unified. Between the imperialist spheres of influence there are wide gaps, and in these partisan warfare can quickly develop.' Speaking of the actual tactics of guerrilla warfare, he noted: 'Many a Red "short attack" has been carried out with only a few hundred men against an enemy of thousands. Surprise, speed . . . and the selection of the most vital and vulnerable spot in the enemy's "anatomy" are absolutely essential to the complete victory of this kind of attack.'[14] By organising in the 'wide gaps' between the White spheres of influence, the Communists were capitalising upon the weaknesses of their enemy. By attacking the 'vulnerable spots' in the enemy's formations, they were making the most of their own troops, deficient in both training and equipment. As Mao said on this latter point: 'Guerrilla warfare has qualities and objectives peculiar to itself. It is a weapon that a nation inferior in arms and military equipment may employ against a more powerful aggressor . . . Conditions of terrain, climate and society in general offer obstacles to his progress and may be used to advantage by those who oppose him.'[15]

Mao's views on guerrilla tactics are fairly well summarised in the following two quotations, the first written in 1930, the second in 1937:

'The tactics we have derived from the struggle of the past three years are indeed different from any other tactics, ancient or modern, Chinese or foreign. With our tactics the masses can be aroused for struggle on an ever-broadening scale, and no enemy, however powerful, can cope with us. Ours are guerrilla tactics. They consist mainly of the following points:

Divide our forces to arouse the masses, concentrate our forces to deal with the enemy.

The enemy advances, we retreat; the enemy camps, we harass; the enemy tires, we attack; the enemy retreats, we pursue.

To extend stable base areas, employ the policy of advancing in waves; when pursued by a powerful enemy, employ the policy of circling around.

Arouse the largest number of the masses in the shortest possible time and by the best possible methods.

These tactics are just like casting a net; at any moment we should be able to cast it or draw it in. We cast it wide to win over the masses and draw it in to deal with the enemy.'[16]

The second quotation, in particular, despite the above pretensions to uniqueness, has much in common with the teachings of Sun Tzu, mentioned at the end of Chapter One.

'In guerrilla warfare, select the tactic of seeming to come from the east and attacking from the west; avoid the solid, attack the hollow; attack; withdraw; deliver a lightning blow, seek a lightning decision. When guerrillas engage a stronger enemy, they withdraw when he advances; harass him when he stops; strike him when he is weary; pursue him when he withdraws. In guerrilla strategy, the enemy's rear, flanks, and other vulnerable spots are his vital points, and there he must be harassed, attacked, dispersed, exhausted and annihilated. Only in this way can guerrillas carry out their mission of independent guerrilla action and co-ordination with the effort of the regular armies.'[17]

Guerrilla warfare was not just a response to the material weaknesses of the Communist peasant armies. It also took account of the nature of peasant society as a whole and the extent of its potential for organised armed resistance. It is in this selection of a mode of warfare absolutely in harmony with the basic characteristics of peasant society that Mao's political acumen is exemplified.

Firstly, guerrilla warfare is suited to a peasant society for purely technical reasons. Almost by definition such a society will be dispersed, terrain will be very difficult in large sections of the country and communications will be very primitive if not non-existent. In such circumstances it will be very easy for the revolutionaries to appear as from nowhere and then to effect swift retreat. By the same token the incumbent forces will find it difficult to concentrate their forces or to pursue the enemy. As Peng Teng-huai said: 'Partisan warfare has developed because of the backwardness of the hinterland. Lack of communications, roads, railways and bridges makes it possible for the people to arm and organise.'[18]

The second basic reason for the affinity between a peasant society and the guerrilla mode was anthropological. Mao recognised that the peasant was only interested in the cultivation of his own plot of land, within his own village. In a document written in January 1934 he said: 'Only since we have distributed the land to the peasants ... has their labour enthusiasm blossomed forth and great successes in production been achieved ... [We work] within the framework of a small peasant economy ... Of course we cannot bring up the question of state or collective farming.'[19] But as the peasant's horizons hardly stretched beyond anything outside his own village, he was little interested in fighting for anything outside of it. Mao increasingly fought against this 'localism' and attempted to develop mobile regular forces prepared to undertake long-range operations. In this he eventually succeeded, as will be seen below. Nevertheless, from the very beginning he was forced to concede that a vast percentage of his forces would be of the local guerrilla type, unwilling to operate far from their own villages. In the Ching Kang Shan period the troops were divided into guerrillas, mobile within a *hsien* (district), and 'rebel detachments' attached to each village and mainly concerned with police work and local defence. In the Kiangsi period the armed forces consisted of fairly mobile guerrillas and of the so-called Red Guards. All citizens aged between 18 and 40 were required to serve in the latter, but in practice only certain units of young, able-bodied men ever undertook actual military operations. Roughly the same system applied in the Yenan period, after the conclusion of the Long March to a new base area in north China, although by this time the mobile troops had reached a higher level of regularisation. The local troops, 2,222,000 in 1945 as opposed to 910,000 regulars, were again divided into model units and others. Only the model units actually fought, whilst the remainder were responsible for transport, supplies, evacuation, security etc.

Certainly the creation of regulars might have been necessary for the actual seizure of power, a point I have stressed throughout this book. But because Mao was engaged in the slow erosion of Nationalist power, within the context of a protracted war strategy, he was able to build up such forces slowly and accommodate his principles to the realities of a peasant society. Indeed he had to accommodate them in this way. In China the Communists had no power base at all apart from the support of the peasantry. Therefore they were in no position to force the peasants to indulge in a mode of warfare at odds with their natural inclinations. Guerrilla warfare was the only possible way of mobilising the Chinese peasantry. As Mao said in December 1936:

> 'In defining our policy . . . we should not repudiate guerrillaism in general terms but should honestly admit the guerrilla character of the Red Army. It is no use being ashamed of this. On the contrary this guerrilla character is precisely our distinguishing feature, our strong point, and our means of defeating the enemy. We should be prepared to discard it, but we cannot do so today.'[20]

Popular Support and Class Unity

The existence of the massive KMT and warlord armies demanded that any revolution in China would have to be of a military nature. The essentially rural composition of Chinese society, and the military and anthropological consequences of that fact, dictated a resort to a guerrilla mode of warfare. Yet it would be quite wrong to regard the Maoist guerrilla doctrine purely as a military response to the Chinese situation. For him the military demands of guerrilla warfare were always inseparable from the political, and it would be quite wrong to regard his policies in any way as being militaristic. In China the struggle was on an economic level and as such was relevant to broad sections of the population. Certainly to win this struggle it was necessary to indulge in organised military activity, and such activity had to be an important consideration in the shaping of day-to-day policy. But this only implied a partial, temporary militarisation of the society, during which the basic aims of the struggle always transcended the demands of the military organism as such. To put it another way, Mao realised that the guerrillas must be the people in arms, fighting for their real economic and social interests, rather than just an autonomous armed organisation claiming to have the people's interests at heart. Only if the guerrillas at all times, and at all levels, actually showed that they were fighting for the people's real interests would they be able to gain the necessary popular support to sustain guerrilla warfare as a dynamic force that could eventually attempt the seizure of state power. Only genuine and widespread popular support could sustain a commitment to the horrors of protracted war, maintain and expand the base areas, and produce enough recruits actually willing to join the Red Army.

One of Mao's clearest expressions of the political role of the Red Army came in December 1929, in an article *On Correcting Mistaken Ideas in the Party*. In the first section he denounced what he described as 'the purely military viewpoint'. These remarks were basic to his policy throughout the Civil War:

> 'The purely military viewpoint manifests itself as follows: these comrades regard military affairs and politics as opposed to each other and refuse to recognise that

military affairs are only means of accomplishing political tasks ... They think that the task of the Red Army ... is merely to fight. They do not understand that the Chinese Red Army is an armed body for carrying out the political tasks of the revolution ... The Red Army should certainly not confine itself to fighting; besides fighting to destroy the enemy's military strength, it should shoulder such important tasks as doing propaganda work among the masses, arming them, helping to establish revolutionary political power ... The Red Army fights not merely for the sake of fighting, but in order to conduct propaganda work among the masses, organise them, arm them.'[21]

In other words, for Mao, the existence of the Red Army had always to be seen, from within and without, as a logical extension of the most basic social and economic aspirations of the mass of the people. It was to be a true people's army in that its existence was only functional to the pursuance of popular political objectives. This subordination to grass-roots political opinion expressed itself at the most basic levels. In 1928 the following eight rules were drawn up to govern the army's relations with the civilian population:

(1) Replace all doors when you leave a house. (2) Return and roll up the straw matting on which you sleep. (3) Be courteous and polite to the people and help them when you can. (4) Return all borrowed articles. (5) Replace all damaged articles. (6) Be honest in all transactions with the peasants. (7) Pay for all articles purchased. (8) Be sanitary.'[22]

Again and again this question of identifying the Red Army with the popular struggle was underlined by the Party leadership. In January 1934 Mao wrote:

'Our comrades should in no way neglect or underestimate the question of the immediate interests, the well-being, of the broad masses. For the revolutionary war is a war of the masses; it can be waged only by mobilising the masses and relying on them ... We must lead the peasants' struggle for land and distribute the land to them ... safeguard the interests of the workers ... develop trade with outside areas, and solve the problems facing the masses – food, shelter and clothing, fuel, rice, cooking-oil and salt, sickness and hygiene, and marriage.'[23]

In 1937 he wrote: 'Without a political goal, guerrilla warfare must fail, as it must if its political objectives do not coincide with the aspirations of the people and their sympathy, co-operation, and assistance cannot be gained.'[24] In May 1938 he wrote, after the Japanese invasion:

'Political mobilisation for the War of Resistance must be continuous. Our job is not to recite our political programme to the people, for nobody will listen to such recitations; we must link the political mobilisation for the war with ... the life of the soldiers and the people, and make it a continuous movement . . . [Of the] conditions indispensable to victory . . . political mobilisation is the most fundamental. The Anti-Japanese United National Front is a united front of the whole army and the whole people, it is certainly not a united front merely of the headquarters and members of a few political parties; our basic objective . . . is to mobilise the whole army and the whole people to participate in it.'[25]

There is no doubt that these policies were carried out and were extraordinarily successful. A Japanese Army report of 1941 said:

'The main anti-Communist forces today are the Japanese Army and the Nanking Government, and they certainly do not possess the confidence of the broad masses . . . Today [the Red Army] champions army-civilian integration everywhere, and is continuously organising local armies. As a consequence it is extraordinarily difficult to separate bandit from citizen in Communist destruction work.'[26]

In 1944 an official American observer noted: 'The Communist governments and armies are the first governments and armies in modern history to have positive and widespread popular support. They have this support because the governments and armies are genuinely of the people.'[27]

But, as was seen with Zapata's army in Mexico, the notion of gaining popular support can involve complex decisions about class alignment in order to present as united a front as possible to back up the military effort. Without some degree of class unity in the rear areas the guerrilla struggle, particularly in its later more regularised stages, would find it very hard to maintain the necessary cohesion and momentum. Certainly such a struggle needs some sort of revolutionary dynamic to gain the support of the broad masses, but it is very dangerous to base this upon over-radical policies or an alliance with only a relatively narrow stratum of the population. Mao Tse-tung saw this very clearly. I have so far discussed his analysis of Chinese society in terms of what I called the political, sociological and anthropological considerations. But the problem also had an economic dimension.

When examined in these terms the peasantry was far from being a unified whole. There were wide gulfs in peasant society, dividing the rich, middle and poor peasant, the landed and the landless. But as the guerrilla war widened in extent and intensity, Mao came to realise that the only way effectively to utilise the full potential of the peasant movement was to ensure that all sections of the rural population participated in it. In other words, though it might make some sense in terms of the vision of the future society to turn peasant against landlord, poor peasant against rich peasant, and to insist upon equal land distribution to all, in political and military terms such internal dissension merely sapped the strength of the revolutionary base. Mao swiftly came to the conclusion that the immediate task was of a military nature and everything else would have to be temporarily subordinated to that policy which came nearest to guaranteeing military success.

Thus there is discernible over the period of protracted military struggle, a gradual softening of Mao's line on the peasantry, and a steady attempt to include as broad a spectrum of rural society as possible into the revolutionary movement. His attitude to the rich peasants is a case in point. In 1926 he was fairly dogmatic about the counter-revolutionary role of the rich peasants who, 'usually combine . . . [their] interest with that of the small landlord.'[28] Consequently the rich peasants had to be destroyed as a class by confiscation of their land and redistribution to the other peasant classes. During the Ching Kang Shan period: 'At the level of the villages . . . [agrarian] reform was carried out to the letter. Confiscated lands were divided into three categories – good, middling and poor – and shared out as equally as possible . . . The landlords who escaped physical liquidation were excluded from the sharing out of the land, and rents were abolished.'[29] The rich peasants suffered heavily under such measures. Mao's link between them and the landlords became a self-fulfilling prophecy as they, and even broad sections of the middle peasantry, became totally alienated from the Communist movement and looked to the warlords to re-establish their property rights. But the Central Committee of the CCP was at this stage more aware than Mao of the dangers of such a policy. In 1929 they ordered him to stop confiscation of rich peasants' land, and the Land Law of Hsingkuo county of April 1929 did contain such a stipulation.

The fall of Li Li-san caused a dramatic change in Central Committee policy. It now demanded an all-out attack on the rich peasants and a constant effort to maintain the fervour of the masses against them. The old attitude was dubbed 'the rich peasant line' and Land Investigation movements were set in motion to seek out rich peasants and the proponents of leniency towards them. But Mao had by now begun to appreciate the benefits of a more tolerant attitude and he was opposed to this new onslaught. From 1932 or so he was in constant disagreement with the Central Committee on this point. Thus, although the government of the Soviet Districts of north-east Kiangsi agreed, in 1932, to confiscate the land of the rich peasants it refused to concede to an absolutely equal redistribution of that land. Because the rich peasants had the capital and the equipment to exploit whatever land they might receive, the government 'made a distinction which it was impossible to check: rich peasants would get land of the worst quality.'[30]

If the Central Committee was still to the left of Mao with regard to the rich peasants, there does seem to have been a consensus on the question of middle peasants. The Land Law passed by the First Soviet Congress in November 1931 was remarkably moderate in this respect:

'The First Congress considers that equal distribution of all the land is the most radical way of destroying all feudal relations of slavery connected with the land . . .; even so, local soviets . . . must explain all the aspects involved to the peasants. Not until the peasants at the base, and above all the mass of middle peasants, desire it and give it their direct support, can this land reform be applied.'[31]

Mao himself was fully in agreement with this flexible attitude. His policies towards the middle peasants became even more moderate after the opening of hostilities with Japan and the formation of the KMT-CCP United Front between 1935 and 1937. From this time on the task of the CCP was of an increasingly overt military nature, and all social and economic policies had to be assessed in terms of the basic priority of mobilising a genuinely national resistance to the Japanese:

'During the war the Communists did not contemplate the redistribution of land or any other class-orientated measures that would have radically altered the pattern of land ownership. Instead, the economic policies implemented by the Communist Party during the Sino-Japanese War were designed to create maximum unity . . . As Mao put it, "The agrarian policy is a dual policy of demanding that the landlords reduce rent and interest, stipulating that the peasants pay this reduced amount of rent and interest".'[32]

From 1932 this was for a long time the sole concern of the Communist agrarian policy. At about this time Mao bluntly stated: 'It must be explained to Party members and to the peasants that this is not the time for a thorough agrarian revolution . . . The landlords shall reduce rent and interest, for this serves to arouse the enthusiasm of the basic peasant masses for resistance to Japan, but the reductions should not be too great.'[33]

Right through until 1946 this remained the basic policy of the CCP. The Central Committee resolution of January 28 1942 summed it up admirably, describing the principles that underpinned it in these terms:

'The Party recognises that the peasants constitute the basic strength of the anti-Japanese war . . . They must be helped and their living conditions improved. Most landlords are anti-Japanese and some are even in favour of democratic reform. They must be allowed to keep their political rights and their interests must be protected. The capitalistic mode of production is a relatively progressive mode of production in present-day China. The rich peasants are the capitalists of the rural areas and are an indispensable force; their work must be encouraged. Legislation must provide for the reduction of land-rent and stipulate that rent be paid. The landlord must keep the right to dispose of his land in accordance with existing legal provisions.'[34]

The key sentence of this pronouncement is that which relates to the progressive economic role of the rich peasantry. One of the most important considerations for the survival of the base areas was the question of their economic viability. They had to be made self-sufficient, and this demanded that those with any capital or equipment extra to their personal needs be given the opportunity to make use of that surplus for the good of the community, and the armed forces. But they would only do that if they also saw some possibility of personal profit. Thus the richer elements within the soviets had to be given some considerable measure of economic freedom. From 1930, or so, as has been seen, Mao consistently advocated such a policy.

Regularisation and Political Control

In previous sections of this chapter I have pointed out that Mao was fully aware that, on the one hand, a peasant army must be made up largely of guerrilla troops and, on the other, that such an army must have the full support of the people. But we have already seen in the section above how he was prepared to modify his most radical political objectives in the light of the demands of the military situation. There still remain two further modifications to be noted.

The first concerns the exact role of pure guerrilla warfare. Thus, though the Communists had to 'honestly admit the guerrilla character of the Red Army', they should not be deceived into thinking that such an army could alone actually defeat the Japanese or the Nationalists:

'The concept that guerrilla warfare is an end in itself and that guerrilla activities can be divorced from those of the regular forces is incorrect. If we assume that guerrilla warfare does not progress from beginning to end beyond its elementary forms we have failed to recognise the fact that guerrilla hostilities can, under specific conditions, develop and assume orthodox characteristics. An opinion that admits the existence of guerrilla warfare, but isolates it, is one that does not properly estimate the potentialities of such war.'[35]

Thus, though guerrillas are the only type of troops that an insurgent people can put into the field in the first stages of their struggle, and though such troops will always form an important, and, in numerical terms, predominant component of the fighting forces, the revolutionaries must always be ready to develop a proportion of their forces beyond the guerrilla stage and prepare them to meet the enemy in open battle. For, in the last analysis, as Mao clearly recognised:

'The destruction of the enemy is the primary object of war ... Attack [is] the chief means of destroying the enemy ... while defence ... is secondary ... In actual warfare the chief role is played now by defence and now by attack . . . but if war is taken as a whole, attack remains primary. Measures of tactical defence are meaningless if they are divorced from their role of giving direct or indirect support to an offensive . . . The offensive is the only means of destroying the enemy and also the principal means of self-preservation . . .'[36]

To attain this object of destroying the enemy one must slowly build up regularised forces. Mao discussed the requirements of this process in some detail:

'To transform guerrilla units waging guerrilla warfare into regular forces waging mobile warfare, two conditions are necessary – an increase in numbers, and an improvement in quality. Apart from directly mobilising the people to join the forces, increased numbers can be attained by amalgamating small units, while better quality depends on steeling the fighters and improving their weapons in the course of the war . . .

'To raise the quality of the guerrilla units it is imperative to raise their political and organisational level and improve their equipment, military technique, tactics and discipline, so that they gradually pattern themselves on the regular forces and shed their guerrilla ways. Politically it is imperative to get both the commanders and the fighters to realise the necessity of raising the guerrilla units to the level of the regular forces, to encourage them to strive towards this end, and to guarantee its attainment by means of political work. Organisationally, it is imperative gradually to fulfil all the requirements of a regular formation in the following respects – military and political organs, staff and working methods, a regular supply system, a medical service etc. In the matter of equipment, it is imperative to acquire better and more varied weapons and increase the supply of the necessary communications equipment. In the matter of military technique and tactics, it is imperative to raise the guerrilla units to the level required of a regular formation. In the matter of discipline, it is imperative to raise the level so that uniform standards are observed, every order is executed without fail and all slackness is eliminated. To accomplish all these tasks requires a prolonged effort, and it cannot be done overnight; but that is the direction in which we must develop.'[37]

In 1947 Mao described the kind of war that such regular units would be capable of fighting. The following quotation is a succinct summary of his concept of 'mobile warfare', and shows that, though it demands troops trained to a much higher level than the ordinary guerrilla, it nevertheless retains many of the basic characteristics, particularly mobility and flexibility, of all types of guerrilla warfare. The following were the operational principles of the Red Army in the months immediately prior to the actual destruction of the Nationalists and the Communist seizure of power:

'Attack dispersed, isolated enemy forces . . .; attack concentrated, strong enemy forces later. Take medium and small cities and extensive rural areas first; take big cities later. Make wiping out the enemy's effective strength our main objective; do not make holding or seizing a place our main objective. Holding or seizing a place is the outcome of wiping out the enemy's effective strength . . . In every battle concentrate an absolutely superior force, encircle the enemy's forces completely, strive to wipe them out thoroughly and do not let any escape from the net. In special circumstances, use the method of dealing the enemy crushing blows, that is, concentrate all our strength to make a frontal attack and an attack on one or both his flanks, with the aim of wiping out one part and routing another so that our army can swiftly move its troops to smash other enemy forces.

'On the one hand be sure to fight no battle unprepared, fight no battle you are not sure of winning . . . On the other hand, give full play to our fine style of fighting – courage in battle, no fear of sacrifice, no fear of fatigue, and . . . fighting successive battles in a short time. Strive to draw the enemy into mobile warfare, but at the same time lay great stress upon learning the tactics of positional attack and of stepping up the building of the artillery and engineer corps in order to capture enemy fortified points and cities on a large scale. Resolutely attack and seize all fortified points and cities which are weakly defended. At opportune moments, attack and seize all fortified points and cities defended with moderate strength, provided circumstances permit. For the time being, leave alone all fortified points and cities which are strongly defended. Replenish our strength with all the arms and most of the soldiers captured from the enemy . . .'[38]

But, as is hinted at in the quotations above, this regularisation of the Red Army demanded a high level of organisation and centralisation. Here we come to the second major qualification of Mao's doctrine. Thus, while he stressed the need for the closest identification between the Party and the army, and the aspirations of the rural masses, he was always aware that one must avoid any romantic notions about the spontaneity of the masses or undue concessions to the anarchic instincts of the peasantry. Remarks of Mao quoted above, from May 1938, give a broad hint in this respect. Whilst much stress is placed upon the necessity of attuning to popular attitudes, perhaps the root notion is the demand that 'political *mobilisation* must be continuous'.[39] This presupposes two things. Firstly that there is a group of revolutionaries to do the mobilising, and secondly that their role is much more than one of passively responding to outputs from outside. This group is of course the Party. Thus, for Mao, although the Party had to be at all times responsive to peasant demands, if it was to survive, that survival was also of crucial importance to the peasantry. Without the leadership of the Party the revolutionary struggle might merely dissolve into a fruitless series of anarchic, unconnected peasant insurrections.

The Chinese Communists were forced to rely to a large extent upon guerrilla warfare because of their need to build their revolution from the bottom upwards. But even so guerrilla warfare had its limits. It is by definition a fragmented, decentralised mode of warfare, and Mao tried at all times to ensure the maximum subordination to Party control and discipline, both to make the guerrillas themselves more effective and to facilitate the transformation to regular warfare. Thus one of the 'mistaken ideas' that the Party warned against in 1929 was 'the ideology of roving rebel bands'. 'This ideology manifests itself as follows: some people want to increase our political influence only by means of roving guerrilla actions, but are unwilling to increase it by undertaking the arduous task of building up base areas and establishing the people's political power.'[40] For Mao any armed force divorced from central control could never be an effective revolutionary body. In 1936 he had the following to say about the harmful effects of guerrilla warfare:

'One [of its aspects] is irregularity, that is, decentralisation, lack of uniformity, absence of strict discipline ... As the Red Army reaches a higher stage we must gradually and consciously eliminate them so as to make the Red Army ... more regular in character ... Refusal to make progress in this respect and obstinate adherence to the old stage are impermissible and harmful.'[41]

As the army became more regularised Mao became increasingly emphatic about the need for strict Party control. In 1937 he spoke of the struggle against 'the tendency towards new warlordism in the Eighth Route Army. This tendency is manifest in certain individuals who ... have become unwilling to submit strictly to Communist Party leadership, have developed individualistic heroism.'[42] In November 1938 he made his famous remark to the effect that 'political power grows out of the barrel of a gun'. But the corollary to this is of much greater significance: 'Our principle is that the Party commands the gun; the gun shall never be allowed to command the Party.'[43] To ensure that the Party did exercise control, political officers were attached to all units, who were responsible for the education of the troops and were also the Party's direct representatives within the Army. They were mainly concerned with the formulation of local policy and the transmission of Party directives to lower levels. Beneath them were political departments at the divisional and regimental levels, and political instructors at the battalion and company levels. These were the men responsible for the actual implementation of policy and propaganda work among the rank-and-file.

This system had been abandoned after the alliance with the KMT against the Japanese, but it was very soon reintroduced after the emergence of 'warlordism'. Party control over the Army was intensified between 1942 and 1944 during the so-called Chen Feng Reform Movement. The movement was basically aimed at heightening discipline within the Party. It tried to stress the importance of democratic centralism and vigorously denounced 'extreme democratisation [stemming from] ... the erratic nature of the petty bourgeoisie (agricultural production and urban petty capital)'.[44] The movement also concerned itself with Army-Party relations, and a Politbureau resolution of 1942 demanded the full integration of the political staffs within and without the Army:

'In the future the Main Armed Forces must carry out the decisions and resolutions of Party committees at all levels of government. The Main Armed Forces must also carry out the resolutions of the lower-level Party committees and lower-level governmental units ... of the area where they are stationed ... In the guerrilla areas ... there must be unification of Party, governmental, military and mass structures ... When there are hostilities ... [those cadres] are to participate in the work of the Army and the guerrilla units; when there is a lull, they are to carry out their former tasks in Party, government or mass organisations ... Within the Army it should be thoroughly understood that without the integration of the Party, government, and mass organisations, the Army by itself would not be able to fight for a single day.'[45]

Such, then, were the basic features of the Chinese Civil War and the Maoist conception of the transition from guerrilla warfare to genuine people's war. It might be thought that for a book concerned with military history there has been a great deal of emphasis in this chapter upon political, social and economic factors. In fact, any successful guerrilla leader must pay at least as much attention to these factors as to the purely military. Anything more than mere banditry usually involves building up an army pretty much from scratch. Its leaders have after all to persuade people to fight, as it is rarely possible, especially in the early stages, to coerce them into doing so. This persuasion can only be effective if people are convinced that their participation in the struggle is a means towards satisfying at least some of their most basic aspirations. This inevitably brings the leaders face-to-face with a whole array of seemingly non-military issues which will, in fact, if properly tapped, be the well-spring of committed, cohesive and protracted popular military endeavour.

What distinguished Mao Tse-tung from so many other guerrilla leaders was the way in which he thoroughly and systematically pin-pointed these issues and subordinated purely military considerations to the fundamental long-term demands of the peasant masses amongst whom he had chosen to operate. Any political romantic can pick up a gun and vanish into the hinterland. What is truly difficult is to stay there and painstakingly establish a rapport with a suspicious population, gradually building up their political consciousness. This must then be translated into active logistic, intelligence and armed support that will in turn build up sufficient military momentum to eventually permit large-scale regular operations against the incumbent forces. Few guerrillas have realised what was involved in just starting such a steamroller: even fewer have been able to keep one running, for years if necessary, and ceaselessly change up and down the gear-box of appropriate, ideological, economic, coercive, organisational, patriotic, tactical and strategic options. Mao Tse-tung was one who did just this, and, whatever one's views on the ultimate balance-sheet of suffering under the KMT and the CCP, his military achievements by 1949 must be regarded as some of the most remarkable in recorded military history, and comparable to such watershed campaigns as those of Alexander the Great, Genghis Khan and Stalin/Zhukov.

1. J. Guillermaz, *A History of the Chinese Communist Party 1921–49*, Methuen, 1972, p83
2. S. Schram, *Mao Tse-tung*, Penguin Books, 1966, p140
3. Guillermaz, *op cit*, p175
4. Schram, *op cit*, p142
5. E. R. Wolf, *Peasant Wars of the Twentieth Century*, Faber & Faber, 1971, pp 130–1
6. S. Swarup, *A Study of the Chinese Communist Movement*, Clarendon Press, Oxford, 1966, p57
7. Mao Tse-tung, *Selected Works*, Vol 1, Peking, 1964, pp 23–24
8. Mao Tse-tung, *Selected Military Writings*, Peking, 1966, p143
9. *ibid*, p66
10. *ibid*, p13
11. *ibid*, p21
12. *loc cit*
13. *ibid*, pp 27–28
14. E. Snow, *Red Star Over China*, Garden City Publishing Company, New York, 1939, pp 274 and 277
15. Mao Tse-tung, Yu Chi Chan (Guerrilla Warfare), in *Guerrilla Warfare*, Cassell, 1965, p33
16. *Selected Military Writings*, p72
17. Yu Chi Chan, *op cit*, pp 34–35
18. Snow, *op cit*, p274
19. *Selected Works*, Vol 1, pp 143–44
20. *Selected Military Writings*, p39
21. *Selected Works*, Vol 1, p106
22. Snow, *op cit*, p158
23. *Selected Works*, Vol 1, p147
24. *Selected Military Writings*, p94
25. *ibid*, pp 229 and 261
26. C. Johnson, *Peasant Nationalism and Communist Power*, Stanford University Press, Stanford, 1962, pp 53–54
27. J. Chen, *Mao and the Chinese Revolution*, Oxford University Press, 1965, p254
28. Swarup, *op cit*, p123
29. Guillermaz, *op cit*, p170
30. Swarup, *op cit*, pp 129–30
31. Guillermaz, *op cit*, pp 211–12
32. Johnson, *op cit*, p12
33. J. L. S. Girling, *People's War*, Allen & Unwin, 1969, p94

34. Guillermaz, *op cit*, p339
35. Yu Chi Chan, *op cit*, p41
36. *Selected Military Works*, p230
37. *ibid*, pp 182–83
38. *ibid*, pp 332–33
39. See p162
40. *Selected Works*, Vol 1, p114
41. *Selected Military Writings*, p141
42. Guillermaz, *op cit*, p329
43. S. Schram, *The Political Thought of Mao Tse-tung*, Penguin Books, 1969, p290
44. B. Compton (ed), *Mao's China: Party Reform Documents 1942–44*, Washington University Press, Seattle, 1952, p240
45. *ibid*, pp 167, 171 and 175

CHAPTER 8

People's War and Cold War 1944–60

World War II was won largely through the integrated operations of conventional land, sea and air forces, but guerrilla forces, as we have seen, did have some part in bringing about this victory. They had been particularly effective in the Far East where Chinese Communist guerrillas helped KMT regular divisions tie down some 25 Japanese divisions for most of the war (as opposed to roughly 20 divisions in S.E. Asia, the East Indies, New Guinea and the Pacific Islands). The Chinese Communists had also done much to codify their military experience, offering potential revolutionaries a proven blueprint for sustained peasant military mobilisation.

By 1945 conditions were ripe for the dissemination of such a blueprint. International communism was in triumphalist mode after the Chinese and Yugoslav successes and the creeping imposition of Soviet hegemony over much of Eastern Europe. The war had also fundamentally altered perceptions of the old colonial powers after the early Japanese victories, albeit temporarily, had swept aside seemingly immutable power structures. Nor was United Nations rhetoric about self-determination and democratic rights without its effect in raising political expectations amongst indigenous intellectuals and activists. This was particularly the case where those expectations had been knowingly fostered and harnessed during the war itself, to stimulate popular resolve to undertake armed resistance against Axis and Japanese occupation forces. In several countries, therefore, at the end of the World War II, the time seemed ripe for mass political mobilisation and perhaps for gingerly testing that most basic axiom of people's war – that political power grows from the barrel of a gun.

Greece

Guerrilla resistance began in Greece in late 1942, directed against the Germans. Two main organisations supplied the necessary combatants, the Communist ELAS (the armed wing of the EAM, or National Liberation Front) and

EDES (The National Republican Greek League), under General Napoleon Zervas. The guerrillas began to undertake effective operations in November 1942, after the arrival of British advisers and liaison officers. One of their biggest, combined, successes was the blowing up of a key viaduct between Salonika and Athens along which passed supplies for North Africa. In the summer of 1943 the guerrillas launched numerous attacks on German communications to coincide with the Allied landings in Sicily, and to make it appear that the main Allied effort would be concentrated in Greece itself. But operations tailed off after this, and the German withdrawal from Greece in 1944 was hardly harassed at all. Both sides seemed to be more desirous of keeping their forces intact in the event of a confrontation over the political future of the country. Already in 1944 there had been clashes between ELAS and EDES guerrillas, as well as units under Colonel Dmitrios Psaros, a later supporter of EKKA (Social Liberation Movement). The Communists had completely destroyed this latter organisation by the end of 1944.

The Allied occupation of Greece brought no respite to these internecine struggles. On November 27, 1944, EAM decided to launch an armed struggle against the new British and Greek authorities. Even at this stage, however, the Communists were still hopeful of a political solution and actual armed confrontations were rare. In January 1945 a new prime-minister, General Nicholas Plastiras, was appointed and the Communists, taking this as a hopeful political sign, signed an armistice. But the forces of the extreme right, including a certain General Grivas, head of the 'X' Organisation, were not ready for any kind of compromise, and an extensive 'white terror' was carried on throughout 1945, despite the drawing up of the Varzika Agreement in February, which finalised the cease-fire. Between February and July 20,000 ex-guerrillas were arrested, over 500 murdered and nearly 3,000 condemned to death. Elections were planned for March of the following year, but the Communists, angry at the continued harassment of their supporters, refused to put forward candidates. The Royalists and rightists swept the board and the persecution of the Communists continued unabated. In February 1946 they decided to take to the hills and lauch an all-out guerrilla war.

Without a doubt the Civil War that followed, and lasted until October 1949, was one of the most inept Communist attempts to take power through a guerrilla struggle. Since their defeat, the Communist leadership under Zachariades has been roundly condemned by their followers, a sure sign of a more than average incompetence. The most striking mistake of all was the anti-rural bias of the KKE, even though they recognised that a guerrilla struggle must primarily be carried on in the countryside. Zachariades was a firm proponent of Marxist-Leninist orthodoxy, and for him the decisive struggle for power was to take place in the cities. The guerrilla war was only to be an auxiliary effort, designed to create a climate of uncertainty that would undermine popular trust in the government. There is a lot to be said for such a long-term strategy, but only as long as the emphasis upon the *ultimate* crucial role of the cities does not beget a downright anti-rural prejudice. In Zachariades' case, however, this is exactly what happened.

In October 1945, at the Seventh Party Congress, it was decided actually to dismantle the Communist structure in the countryside and order all its members to join the Agrarian Party. As Zizis Zographos, himself a Communist, has written: 'This disorganised the Party in the rural areas at a time when all its branches should have been strengthened in every way, and when, according to the instructions issued by the leadership, the armed struggle was to be started . . . in the countryside.'[1] On top of this the city organisations were not allowed to leave the cities and join the guerrillas. Even large military units whose composition was of a leftist orientation were forbidden to join the Democratic Army in the mountains. In spring 1947 Zachariades went so far as to forbid the expansion of the guerrilla movement on the basis of conscription, and he limited the number of guerrilla effectives to 10,000 men. One writer has explained these absurd policies by reference to the fact that 'the KKE leadership was increasingly suspicious of the guerrilla leaders, who were seen as an eventual threat to the monolithic structure of the party.'[2]

But the Party did not even follow its own line through to its logical conclusions and few precautions were taken to safeguard the Communist network in the cities. It remained in the open and was gradually smashed in a systematic policy of arrests, imprisonment and execution. Prior to the Civil War conscription to the Greek Army had been on a selective basis which left free the bulk of the leftists. But this was now abandoned and the Communists called up were separated from the other conscripts and interned in concentration camps at Makronissos and Youra. Zographos has underlined the fatal character of these mistakes. In the event of 'armed struggle . . . it is essential to take steps in advance to ensure underground party activities. This applies primarily to the urban centres which are under the direct control of the enemy and where practically the entire vanguard force of the revolution . . . is to be found. But these things were not done, with the result that the steps taken by the enemy to isolate the party and the Democratic Army did not meet with resolute resistance.'[3]

The war itself fell into three stages. The first was from February 1946 to summer 1947 when Communist activities, within the limits described above, were confined to an extensive build up. Attacks were limited to hit-and-run raids on isolated villages and small units of government troops. By the end of this stage the original 2,500 guerrillas had risen to 8,000. The second period began in August 1947 when General Markos Vafiades, the commander of the Democratic Army, felt he was strong enough to intensify guerrilla operations. Over the year he increased his effectives to 18,000 men, and in the next year to

25,000. This period began with a series of attacks on towns such as Florina, Konitsa, Kastoria, Grevena, and Alexandroupolis, the object being to capture a respectable seat of government for a rival Greek administration which could be recognised by the Communist bloc. All these attacks failed and Markos returned to more orthodox guerrilla tactics. These were of two main types. The first was a limited time defence of an important area. Two rings of resistance would be set up around the area, consisting of machine gun pill-boxes dug into the ground and covered with logs and earth. Outside the defence area saboteur squads would operate, mining roads and railways, destroying bridges and telephone wires, and ambushing supply columns. The second key tactic was the hit-and-run raid, when two or more of the roving guerrilla units would assemble at some distance from the objective:

'By a forced march of up to ten hours, and carefully avoiding observation, these units reached their objective and attacked, usually at night. Good intelligence had supplied the attackers with a plan of the town defences . . . The bulk of the guerrilla force would attack and enter the town while supporting detachments isolated [it] . . . by mining the approach roads and trails, blowing up bridges and rail lines in order to prevent the arrival of any . . . reinforcements.[4]

During this period the guerrillas also built up fairly secure base areas in the northern mountains, in Grammos and Vitsi. But they were prepared to leave these if necessary, and during the Greek offensives of 1948 they moved between one area and the other, defending them alternately. At particularly serious moments many of the guerrillas fled across the frontier and found sanctuary in Yugoslavia, Bulgaria and Albania. The proximity of these friendly Communist countries was also useful as a source of supplies and as a training ground for the new recruits. Within the base areas, and in other parts of the country, the guerrillas built up a strong support organisation to sustain the military operations. It was based upon the so-called YIAFKAs, or cells of sympathisers in most of the populated centres. These 'self-defence' personnel were in charge of gathering intelligence, collecting funds and supplies, and taking reprisals against government sympathisers. Within each guerrilla area there were also regional support units of 50 to 60 men who were charged with delivering supplies to the guerrillas, guarding this food, ammunition and clothing, and tending the sick and wounded. They were forbidden to leave their area, and during a government offensive the unit would disperse and remain hidden until the coast was clear again.

But in late 1948 and 1949 the situation began to change in the government's favour. The army was reorganised under General Papagos and purged of dubious elements. It was increased in size from 147,000 to 250,000 men, largely by the creation of 97 battalions of the new National Defence Corps.

Vast amounts of American aid were poured into Greece and counter-insurgency operations were co-ordinated by the Joint United States Military Advisory and Planning Group (JUSMAPG). The government took great pains to remove as many of the Communists' supporters as possible, and by the end of 1949, 700,000 peasants had been uprooted and resettled in the larger towns. This had particularly serious effects on YIAFKA's efficiency. On July 10 1949 Tito closed the border to the guerrillas, following his expulsion from the Cominform and the total breakdown of Russo-Yugoslav relations. The Democratic Army thus lost one of its main sources of supplies.

But the die was cast even before this decision of Tito. Markos had always realised that the only hope of the guerrillas was to fight in small independent mobile units and he had made the battalion of about 500 men his largest unit. But for reasons that are not quite clear, Zachariades made the fatal mistake of thinking the guerrillas were capable of fighting regular warfare, and he ordered the creation of larger formations. It is difficult to say whether he was carried away by the successes of Tito and Mao Tse-tung in this respect, or whether his suspicion of the rural guerrilla movement as a whole prompted him to hasten its destruction. In the face of Markos' protests, in 1948, brigades were established and then divisions. By early 1949 there were eight divisions, consisting of 42 battalions, 25 bi-companies and 18 independent companies. Then Markos was dismissed and Zachariades took personal command, calling for a simultaneous positional defence of the Grammos and Vitsi base areas. The guerrillas were simply not capable of standing up to the revitalised regular army in this type of warfare, and on October 16 1949 the Communists announced a cease-fire, or, in other words, that they had been defeated. Even had they opted for a protracted war it is unlikely that the Democratic Army could have succeeded in overthrowing the Greek government. But it is an undeniable fact that their precipitate regularisation hastened their ultimate defeat by many months, even years.

The Philippines

In the Philippines too the defeat of the guerrillas owed as much to the mistakes of the leadership as to the competence of the counter-insurgency forces. When the Japanese invaded the Philippines during World War II many of the natives chose to resist, and numerous guerrilla groups sprang up. One of these was the *Hukbo ng Bayan Laban sa Hapon*, the People's Army to Fight Against Japan. Led by Luis Taruc the Hukbalahaps, or Huks as they came to be known, were dominated by Communist cadres, and during 1944 they were involved in frequent clashes with other nationalist guerrilla organisations. Nevertheless, between their formation in March 1942 and the liberation of the islands, the Huks conducted many effective operations against the Japanese. With a fighting strength of 5,000 men, 10,000 lightly armed reserves and 35,000 other supporters they came to dominate central Luzon. They fought over 1,200 engagements and killed 25,000 Japanese and their collaborators.

The Huks had fought for some stake in the future government of the country, but after the liberation they met with little enthusiasm from the Americans or from the ex-collaborationists who occupied many of the key posts in the new administration. Many guerrilla fighters were awarded back pay by the United States Army, but not so the Huks. Taruc and Casto Alejandrino, another prominent Communist guerrilla, were arrested and held for seven months by the US Army Counter-Intelligence Corps. So the Huks returned to their villages in an embittered mood. But their resentment had deeper roots than this. Three quarters of all Filipinos depended directly upon the land for their livelihood, yet most of these lived in the most appalling conditions which were, moreover, gradually worsening. The introduction of cash crops like sugar meant that cultivation was for sale on outside markets rather than for the peasants' own consumption. It also meant that the land increasingly passed out of the hands of the peasants into those of large landlords. Between 1918 and 1938, for example, the number of farms worked by their owners fell from 1,520,000 to 805,000. Those farms that remained in the hands of the peasants got progressively smaller. As one of the Filipino generals who fought against the Huks wrote: 'Well over half the farmers in the rich rice lands are share-croppers, farming large estates, often held by absentee landlords. So keen is the competition for land ... even though [it involves] further subdividing rented lands already too small to be economical, that the average farm runs from four acres in some provinces to eight in others ... [There are] heavy demands on incomes barely enough for subsistence. The tendency is to borrow, often at ruinously high rates of interest, sometimes exceeding one hundred per cent per annum.'[5] Thus 1.3 per cent of the population owned all the large farms of more than 50 acres, whilst all those on the smaller rented plots had to pay at least 50 per cent of their crop in rent. In 1946 a law was introduced to reduce the maximum rent to 30 per cent but it was neither 'enforceable nor enforced.'[6]

Thus the Huks had a perfect base of discontented peasants upon which to build a viable guerrilla movement. They made great efforts to ensure that they retained the support of the people. A set of instructions, very reminiscent of Mao's rules for the conduct of guerrillas, was drawn up. It included the following stipulations:

'Clean the houses provided by the people ... Speak in a friendly tone ... Buy and sell things fairly ... Return the things we borrow ... Pay for the things we destroy ... Do not do, and even refuse to do, things which may harm the people ... Forcing the people to work for the army is forbidden ... Help the people in ploughing, transplanting, harvesting or in cutting wood whenever it does not hinder the actions of the army. Help the people organise, and support the organisations of the people.'[7]

To help this task of organisation the Huks set up their own government within the insurgent area and gave the peasants their own representative institutions. These were known as the Barrio United Defence Corps (BUDC), village councils of 5 to 12 members, all posts on which were elective by a secret ballot of all villagers over 18 years of age. But the BUDC was also specifically designed to aid the military effort. As one ex-Huk has written: 'The BUDCs had three main channels of activity: the most important, aid to the military struggle; second, the development of an economic program that would both supply the army and keep food products from the enemy; and third the putting down of new political perspectives for the people ...'[8] Thus the BUDCs were a source of mass reserves for the Huks, in the shape of the *Sandatahang Tanod ng Bayan* (STB), or people's home defence guard. These were part-time guerrillas who worked in the village for most of the time, but were available for local, small-scale operations. The BUDCs were also responsible for gathering intelligence and conveying it through a system of couriers or by long-distance visual communication. The barrio councils were also responsible for the administration of justice and for the production of food for the guerrillas. From 1948 the Huks also produced food in special secret production bases carved out of the forest, where two or three families were responsible for the planting and harvesting of rice, sweet potatoes and other vegetables. The Huks' military establishment had at its apex a more mobile force of full-time guerrillas. These were 'organised on the basis of squadrons, composed of approximately 100 men each. The squadron was subdivided into platoons and squads. On the ascending scale, two squadrons made a battalion, and two battalions a regiment.'[9] In practice, however, most operations were carried out at the squadron level and the Huks never had an equivalent of the mobile regular forces of Mao Tse-tung. As one of their adversaries has written: 'This element was only rudimentally developed by the Huk ... There were no "safe" areas where substantial forces could be maintained securely for extended periods. The relatively good roads in the cultivated areas made any large forces stationed there vulnerable to attack.'[10]

This makes it all the more surprising that the Communist leadership should have adopted the strategy it did. From 1945–50 the Huks pursued a conventional guerrilla strategy, building up the self-defence groups and the village organisations and relying on a long-term erosion of the government's authority. But by the beginning of 1950 the full-time guerrillas had reached a total of 19,000 men and the Central Committee became convinced both that the Philippine state was entering a period of acute economic and political crisis, and that the guerrillas had enough grass-roots support to build up their forces speedily for the overthrow of the government. In January 1950 the Politbureau decided that the guerrilla movement could hope to expand, within a few months, to a maximum armed strength of 173,000 men, as well as $2^1/_2$ million active supporters. To this end the Huks were to send successive waves of 'expansionist' units into the neighbouring provinces and prepare for large-scale armed action and an assault on Manila itself. Within two years it was expected that the Communists would have seized power. A Central Committee resolution of 1951 backed up this decision and called for, in Taruc's words: '. . . intensified training and the conversion of the Huk from a guerrilla force into a regular army. It even levied revolutionary taxes on the people in our mass bases, who were already impoverished and broken by ten years of continuous war.'[11]

But the call for mass insurrection was premature. The guerrillas were neither sufficiently well-equipped nor experienced to undertake regular operations. The people were wearied by the constant hostilities and the base areas did not offer them sufficient protection against government reprisals. Above all the incumbent forces were far from being as debilitated as the Huk leadership had supposed. In fact the latter's decision to resort to large-scale operations gave the government forces the very chance they had been waiting for. Taking advantage, like the Greeks, of massive American aid, they built up their army. Corrupt officers were dismissed, promising young men promoted, and the strength of the army increased from 10 to 26 battalions, each known as battalion combat teams (BCTs). These consisted of three rifle companies, a heavy weapons company, a reconnaissance company and a field artillery battery. These BCTs were self-sufficient and were quite capable of countering any strong Huk offensives.

The 'expansionist' stage of Huk operations soon ground to a halt. William Pomeroy, an American who fought with the guerrillas, has described the deteriorating situation in August 1951:

'There was a time when the forest was wholly ours, and we lived in it as within a fortress, issuing forth at will to spread panic among our foes . . . Now the forest is like a breached wall, through which the government troops pour at will. There is no place in the forest to which they cannot go, armed with their massive firepower, and we are the ones who step aside, take cover . . . We do not seek encounters now . . . Ammunition is hard to get and it is difficult to replace a gun that wears out . . . Ambushes, once a prime source of weapons, are hard to stage now, when the army troops move on the highways in large convoys heavily armed . . . Enemy raids go on continually along the forest edge, striking at our district committees . . . In the barrios the army or the civilian guards have permanent barracks now and are always among the people.'[12]

In mid-October the Huks faced the inevitable and decided to return to guerrilla tactics and adopt a policy of 'preservation and conservation of strength'. As Taruc described it: 'We had to avoid all encounters in which the enemy would take the initiative. When fighting could not be avoided, we resolved to put up a good defensive resistance to sustain morale – but to break contact as quickly as possible.'[13] But the government forces had by now gained immensely in self-confidence and had developed adequate tactics to counter this return to orthodox guerrilla operations. The basic one was the use of small, self-sufficient patrols, able to survive in the jungle for a week or 10 days, who would constantly harass the guerrillas' own forces, now broken down into units of 20 men or so. As Valeriano put it: 'Patrols proved to be by far the most effective weapon for applying force to the Huk.'[14] The patrols were of two basic types: 'flag patrols to demonstrate presence and intention of government to assist and protect its citizens', and combat patrols 'to determine if enemy are in an area or at a designated place; attacking and destroying the enemy with violence. Aggressive leadership and a desire to close with the enemy are essential to success.'[15]

By the end of 1954 it was estimated that eight Huks were being killed for every one government soldier. Huk losses were nearly 10,000 killed, 4,300 captured and nearly 16,000 surrendered. The government forces had also rounded up 43,000 firearms and 15 million rounds of ammunition. With the surrender of Taruc in May 1954 the insurgency was effectively over, at least as a real threat to the central government.

Malaya

The Malayan insurgency lasted officially from June 1948 to July 1960, the dates of the State of Emergency that was proclaimed. In actual fact the military threat had been contained and was irrevocably on the decline by the end of 1954. Once again it offers a prime example of Communist over-optimism about the potential of guerrilla warfare.

The guerrilla movement was born during World War II, when the British took 200 hand-picked Communists and led them behind the Japanese lines to harass the enemy. In May 1943 Force 136, headed by British officers from Southeast Asia Command, landed by submarine and made contact with the Malayan People's Anti-Japanese Army, now 3,000 strong. The British supplied them with food, clothing and weapons so that they could support the projected invasion of the peninsula. In fact the Japanese surrendered in August 1945 and the invasion proved unnecessary. But the guerrillas were now well supplied with arms and at the end of the war some 7,000 insurgents emerged from their jungle hideouts, and in some places tried to set up their own government. In September they were compelled to hand over power to the incoming British Military Administration but they retained many of the weapons they had received from the British or captured from the Japanese. They also formed an Old Comrades Association through which they were able to keep intact the organisation of the guerrilla companies.

From 1945 to 1948 the Malayan Communist Party concentrated its efforts on gaining political power by creating maximum economic and civil disruption in the large towns. In 1947, for example, the Pan-Malayan Federation of Trade Unions called over 300 strikes. But the British introduced stringent limitations on the rights of union representatives, and the MCP's grip on the city began to weaken. It then decided to concentrate its activities among the rural Chinese, a particularly underprivileged community of more than one million, most of them living as squatters on the fringe of the jungle. Half of them were small peasants and the other half workers in the rubber plantations. The People's Army units were reactivated and the organisation was renamed the Malayan Anti-British People's Army.

The guerrilla war began in June 1948 with a series of attacks on the rubber plantations in the state of Perak. The guerrillas operated in companies of about 100 men, each of which had its own camp in the jungle, with parade-grounds, barracks and classrooms. Some of the raids were carried out by smaller groups but occasionally the guerrillas would concentrate as many as 300 men for a particular operation. Moreover, this was seen as only the beginning. The MCP General-Secretary, Chin Peng, had little conception at this time of 'protracted warfare' and he envisaged a dramatic build-up of Communist strength and capabilities that was quite as over-optimistic as that of his Greek and Filipino counterparts:

'Basing himself in the jungle, he hoped first to "liberate" the rubber estates along its fringes; he knew he could rely on the squatters living there. Then he hoped to extend his control into the neighbouring villages until he had an area in which he could establish a people's republic and to which he could bring his guerrillas from the jungle to be trained and equipped for big battles in the open. The final stage would be to challenge and beat the British-Malayan Government Army in conventional warfare.'[16]

But, even at this supposedly advanced strategic stage, the guerrillas were handicapped by one major weakness. They had undertaken fairly large-scale military operations *before* they had established a liberated area over which they, rather than the government, had economic and political control. Certainly many of the Chinese squatters were sympathetic to the Communist cause, but they were still very vulnerable to government attacks, as the guerrillas were living in jungle camps rather than being a self-defence organisation within the villages themselves. On top of this many of the squatters were dependent on the plantations for their livelihood and attacks on them only succeeded in alienating many of these labourers. When a guerrilla group does not actually control the means of production those that are economically dependent upon it are bound to have an ambivalent attitude towards attacks on its owners, albeit 'colonialists' and 'imperialists'. The fact that the Communists had not established any liberated areas also meant the people had no safe havens to which to retreat and that they too would be continually inconvenienced by the guerrillas' attacks. This disruption of the life of the guerrillas' supporters became so acute that in October 1951 the MCP issued a directive 'which ordered all members to desist from the following practices: seizing identity and ration cards, burning ... villages, attacking post-offices, reservoirs and other public facilities, derailing civilian trains, burning religious buildings and Red Cross vehicles, and committing sabotage against the major industries, thereby causing workers to lose their jobs.'[17] Finally this lack of a secure base area forced the guerrillas to devote an inordinate percentage of their manpower to the tasks of maintaining liaison with the civilian population and, where necessary, intimidating and coercing them. Because they were not living within a Communist-controlled zone the civilians could never be completely relied upon to provide the insurgents with intelligence and supplies. In this respect Richard Clutterbuck has supplied some very interesting figures. In 1951 the fighting units of the Malaysian Races Liberation Army, as it was thereafter called, contained 5,500 men as opposed to 2,500 political and supply personnel. In 1957, when guerrilla numbers had shrunk considerably, the MRLA was forced to maintain a force of 1,800 ordinary party workers and let the fighting strength sink to a mere 200, or 10 per cent of the total number. In short, the MRLA tried to invert the classic Maoist scheme of things. For Mao the insurgency began with the creation of distant base areas, built around village self-defence groups. From them mobile guerrilla formations are created, which, eventually, are forged into regular units. But the base area remains fundamental at all stages. The Malayan Communists, however, tried to use isolated guerrilla detachments to create the base areas, but found that without the initial organised popular base these guerrilla units never had sufficient freedom of manoeuvre. Certainly, they had popular support, but the problems of not alienating that support and of effectively turning it to their advantage severely undermined their combat capabilities.

British counter-insurgency measures served to aggravate this gulf between the guerrillas and the people. The basic tactic was that old favourite, resettlement, undertaken under the terms of the Briggs Plan, adopted in 1950. This plan had four basic aims:

(1) To dominate the populated areas and to build up a feeling of complete security which would in time result in a steady and increasing flow of information from all sources.

(2) To break the Communist organisations within the populated areas.

(3) To isolate the guerrillas from the food and supply organisations in the populated areas.

(4) To destroy the guerrillas by forcing them to attack the security forces on their own ground.

By the end of 1953 over 500,000 squatters had been moved away from the edge of the jungle and relocated in 600 new communities established in more accessible areas. To ensure that the Communists would find it difficult to re-establish contact in these new villages, a system of identification cards was introduced. Every morning cordons would be set up at a village and everyone screened. Anyone who did not have a card was picked up and anyone whose presence could not be explained satisfactorily was thereafter a target for police surveillance. The system was further underpinned by making possession of the card a condition for receiving a food ration, space in a resettled village, and a grant to build on it. From 1952 a system of collective punishments was also introduced for any village that persistently withheld information about the activities of a guerrilla group in its immediate vicinity.

On the purely military front British methods underwent substantial improvements. At first the incumbent forces concentrated upon large-scale sweeps into the jungle and these always alerted the guerrilla force long before their encampment was located. After 1951 these measures became even more futile because the MRLA abandoned its company-sized bands and split them into platoons of 20 to 30 men. Gradually the British learnt the basic lesson that only small, mobile, self-sufficient patrols, capable of surviving in the jungle for days on end, can hope effectively to surprise a guerrilla unit. The history of the Green Howards in Malaya is a revealing indication of the improvement. Between September and December 1949, whilst engaged in battalion sweeps, they saw the guerrillas five times and managed to kill one of them, as opposed to 800 casualties inflicted by their adversaries. Between January and June 1950 they killed many guerrillas in attacking camps that had been located by sending out small patrols to track and listen, so-called 'ferret forces'. In 1951 they doubled their kill-rate and 70 per cent of these kills were due to ambushes and raids on camps. Clutterbuck has described a typical operation of this kind:

'The army patrols were active day and night. Of the battalion now attacking each MCP branch, four or five platoons usually lived in the fringes of the jungle, each for ten or twenty days at a time, listening and watching for movements or fresh tracks. Other platoons patrolled the rubber all day, checking passes and watching for anything unusual ... After ... curfew half-a-dozen ambush parties moved into position, sometimes on precise information ... [or] the troops simply ambushed trails they thought the guerrillas were most likely to use.'[18]

From then on the elimination of the guerrillas as an effective threat to the government in Malaya was only a matter of time. Chin Peng was still alive, with a small group of guerrillas on the Thai border, but his precipitate attempt to win a short-term, total victory in Malaya cost him much of the popular support so essential to an authentic people's war. Yet the Malayan Emergency does underline one of the most crucial general points about guerrilla war. Though the MRLA strategy was wrongly headed and never really had any chance of military victory as such, it involved the deployment of vast counter-insurgency forces and the expenditure of huge sums of money. Thus, in 1952, there were in Malaya 20 battalions of troops, a para-military Police Field Force of 3,000 men, 50,000 ordinary policemen and a part-time Home Guard of 200,000. Such numbers are an eloquent testimony to a government's military capacity. But they must be kept in the field for many months, even years, and this will bring into question the government's financial capacity and the effect of public opinion, inevitably soured by this kind of bloody yet seemingly indecisive conflict.

Algeria

These considerations were nowhere more relevant than in Algeria and France between 1954 and 1962. For though the French might fairly be considered to have won the military struggle, they simply did not have the ability to maintain a sufficiently large military presence in Algeria that would keep the still hostile Muslim population under control. A few statistics might help to show what the cost of continued military occupation would be. By 1960 the war was costing the French nation £250 million per year. In 1954 they had 70,000 troops in Algeria. In the following year the figure was 120,000. By 1956 they had increased this number to 400,000 front-line troops, adminis-trative personnel and Muslim auxiliaries. By 1960 the number was an incredible 800,000. When the war ended the French had lost 26,000 troops and 8,400 settlers. It had also provoked two right-wing mutinies amongst the French generals, one in 1958, which brought de Gaulle to power, and one in 1961, in defiance of the President's decision to pull out of Algeria. Finally, the shocking casualties amongst the Algerian population, an estimated 700,000 people, and the stories of French torture and other barbarities, had ensured France's total diplomatic isolation in regard to the war, which was also aggravated by the fact that the National Liberation Front (FLN) leadership were simple nationalists rather than Communists. In July 1961 de Gaulle opened talks with the members of the Algerian National Revolutionary Council, in March of the following year the fighting stopped under the terms of the Evian Accords, and in July Algeria was declared an independent nation.

As the massive numbers of French troops indicate, they had been faced with a very well organised guerrilla campaign. The nationalists had claimed to take the Yugoslav experience as their model, and from the beginning they decided to build up a semi-regular force. In this they were greatly aided by having a sanctuary, rather than a liberated area, in neighbouring Tunisia. Here they organised and trained their men with impunity, safe from French counter-attacks. The regulars received a fairly comprehensive three months training, by ex-NCOs of the French Army, something that neither the Filipino nor the Malayan organisations had been able to offer. In the East Base in Tunisia the Army of National Liberation (ALN) maintained a force that, after 1958, never fell below 15,000 men. At its peak the ALN could muster 30,000 effectives. By 1956 they were all wearing uniforms. Enlistment was voluntary and lasted for two years. Officers and men drew the same pay and were allowed five days leave each year. They were organised into groups (*faoudj*) of 11 men, sections (*ferqua*) of three groups, companies (*katiba*) of three sections, and battalions (*failek*) of 3 companies. Each unit had a political commissar and a military adviser ranking equally with the military commander, and all three took collective decisions. One writer has described a visit to a battalion head-quarters:

'Two companies . . . were gathered by 35 man sections, each behind its German MG42, LMG or Bren Gun. They were in the bulgy, wrinkled heavy olive drab of the regular ALN, with British water bottles, US cartridge belts and ban-doleers. Slung from their shoulders were Lee Enfields and Mausers (sent from Egypt) or, more rarely, a captured Garand or French MAS semi-automatic rifle.'[19]

But the Algerians were by no means able to meet the French in open battle. The light machine gun was the most powerful weapon they had in any quantity. On top of this there was a grievous lack of communications equip-ment, and thus they were not capable of staging large-scale co-ordinated operations. Usually incursions from the sanctuary were at company strength and this unit would break up into squads to lay small ambushes. As soon as the French put any good-sized force into the field against them the guerrillas would flee back across the border. The ALN was not the only military orga-nisation. The liberation movement had much popular support throughout the whole of Algeria, and there were at one stage 100,000 members of the Organisation Politico-Administrative (OPA) who provided local guerrilla support. As opposed to the regulars, or *mujahidin*, these irregulars, *mussabilin*, lived at home, within Algeria, and were responsible for sheltering and feeding the ALN troops, as well as providing intelligence and undertaking certain sabotage assignments.

In 1959 de Gaulle sent out General Challes to organise a concerted counter-insurgency campaign. His plan, like that of Briggs in Malaya, had four basic aims:

(1) To close the frontier.
(2) To destroy the large ALN battalions and fragment them.
(3) To uproot the political infrastructure.
(4) To install native, pro-French administrations in the villages.

Thus his plan had two distinct stages, the *destruction* of the military potential of the guerrillas, and the *construction* of a viable socio-economic base for further expansion. This dual strategy is a direct descendant of the ideas of earlier French military administrators like Galliéni and Lyautey. The following speech by General Allard, given to SHAPE in 1957, could very well have been written by one of these men. Of the two categories of action, destruction and reconstruction, he said:

'These two terms are inseparable. To destroy without building up would mean useless labour; to build without first destroying would be an illusion.
(1) Destruction. This means first of all to uncover, dismantle and suppress the rebel politico-administrative framework, the nerve centre of the rebellion ... It is more in the nature of a police action than of a military operation. It requires the co-operation of all legal forces under a single command ...

Destruction further means to chase and annihilate the armed enemy bands ... which do not form the rebellion's nerve centre but one of its means of action. The guerrillas are in the fist of the rebellion ... This mission to destroy the bands, essentially military in character, assumes the form of anti-guerrilla operations with all the difficulties this implies in a country that consists largely of rugged mountainous terrain, often thickly covered with forest ...
(2) Construction. Destruction will achieve nothing if we do not go beyond it. If the population were left to itself the rebel organisation would soon emerge again. After having destroyed we must construct. To construct ... means preparing the establishment of a new order ... It calls first for the re-establishment of personal contact with the people; we must protect and help them in every area ... Pacification also means organising the people, separating them into hierarchies, that is to say, substituting for the political and administrative organisation of the FLN new groupings, beginning at the lowest echelon of the future organisation of Algeria ... Finally, construction means to persuade the population by the use of education, the establishment of self-defence systems, and the setting up of native auxiliary combat forces (*harkas*) to collaborate in the fight against the rebellion.'[20]

By 1962 the French had gone a long way to achieving many of these aims. To isolate the main forces of the ALN, the so-called Morice Line was constructed on the border with Tunisia. This was 200 miles long and stretched from the coast to the desert in the south. It consisted of two rows of barbed wire and electrified fencing, with minefields between the rows. At intervals blockhouses were constructed, equipped with floodlights and radar. Aircraft flew overhead during the day, and mobile forces of tanks and armoured cars were used to strike at any unit that attempted to break through. The line had considerable effect, and in late 1958 certain authoritative rebel sources admitted that they had heard of no major breakthroughs since the previous March.

To further limit the extent of armed guerrilla incursions, at least north of the Sahara, a system known as *quadrillage* was adopted. The whole territory was divided up into a chequer-board of small areas, each with its own garrison of troops. Wherever possible this garrison was to be of troops on permanent assignment, so that they could be totally familiar with the surrounding population. In this way they could strike up good relations with this population and/or be more sensitive to any untoward developments in their area. In the words of one French officer: '*Quadrillage* attempted to put French troops – to the last man, to the last private – in direct contact with the Muslims, turning each into a kind of ambassador to the Muslim population.'[21] By 1962 300,000 troops were involved in this kind of static defence. They were also supported by numerous motorised and helicopter-borne units, as well as the élite *Réserve Générale* of 30,000 legionnaires, paratroopers and marines.

At first the mobile units, like the British in Malaya, concentrated upon large-scale operations that rarely succeeded in netting any guerrillas. These were of two types: *bruclage*, or encirclements, and *ratissage*, or sweeps on an extended front. But from 1957 the emphasis was placed on small-unit operations, particularly the *commandos de chasse*, groups of 60 to 80 men who were to go into the mountains and stay there, imitating the guerrillas' own tactics. General Salan said of these units:

'... moving always on foot and nearly always at night, carrying out surprise attacks on well-chosen targets, unexpectedly arriving in villages, attempting to gain maximum intelligence on FLN units, and arrest or eliminate rebel personnel, setting up intelligence networks, ambushing local rebel bands, if necessary splitting up into groups as small as four men ... perhaps calling on artillery and the airforce to engage sizable rebel concentrations, these units would create constant insecurity for the opponent while gradually giving the rural population a comforting feeling of security.'[22]

Finally, the French used the tactic of resettling the population of certain of the most notorious areas. 250,000 villagers from the Constantine region were moved to new villages, as were 300,000 in the Blida region, south of Algiers, and altogether some two million Algerians were forcibly removed from their old homes and established in 1,840 new villages. The French tried to make this a positive part of their construction programme. A *Section Administrative Spéciale* was created, made of soldiers and civilian experts in charge of the administration, schooling and political mobilisation of the resettled Muslims. After the new villages had been built, the SAS men were to conduct education and propaganda work to make them economically viable, and then, it was hoped, the villagers would take over their own administration and even be issued with arms to resist ALN visits. In fact many of the villages never got anywhere near this 'take-off' stage and they remained little more than miniature concentration camps. In 1959 the government was driven to announce that no new villages would be built and efforts would be concentrated upon the improvement of existing ones. But the Army simply ignored this directive. Thus, though the French made great strides in the military field, reducing the 100,000 OPA members to 15,000, they never succeeded in making the population at large into more than sullen onlookers, and thus never created the conditions for a viable French administration.

Cuba

In many ways the guerrilla war in Cuba, from December 1956 to December 1958, is something of a feeble imitation of other great guerrilla wars of this century. Yet, on the surface at least, it seemed to follow the same course as the Chinese and Vietnamese struggles, and it was eventually successful. A landing party of 81 men, cut to less than half this figure in the first days, succeeded, within an incredibly short space of time, in overthrowing the incumbent regime. Consequently the potentialities of such minuscule revolutionary groups have been grievously overrated by those hoping for social and political liberation throughout Latin America.

The basic story is easily told. The first landing took place on December 21 1956 and the survivors eventually succeeded in fighting their way to the inaccessible Sierra Maestra, in Oriente province at the eastern end of the island. In the first months the guerrillas concentrated upon attacking small garrisons to obtain arms. The biggest such raid took place on May 28 1957 when the guerrillas attacked the garrison at Ubero, manned by 70 of Batista's troops. By this time the guerrillas' own strength was 80 men. In October Ernesto Guevara was sent out with a small force to try and establish a permanent base area in the El Hombrito Valley. The attempt failed and Guevara's 20 men had to be rescued by the main column under Fidel Castro. However, the guerrillas continued to attract recruits and by December their force totalled 200 men, who were divided into two columns under Castro and Guevara. In April of the following year the guerrillas succeeded in setting up their first permanent base within the Sierra Maestra. In May Batista launched a 10,000-man offensive against this base, but his troops failed to trap the insurgents. Castro's response was to announce a new phase of 'total war' against the Batista regime, and the Rebel Army was split into several groups. Guevara went to Las Villas province, only 150 miles from Havana, with 120 men, and was soon joined by Camilo Cienfuegos with another 90 men. Raul Castro was sent to open a second front in northern Oriente province with a mere 40 men. Guevara launched an offensive in Las Villas and captured the provincial capital of Santa Clara, after isolating it with a systematic campaign of cutting all major road and rail links. The last 'battle' of any consequence was fought at Guisa, in November, when the guerrillas successfully evaded a Batista offensive by 5,000 troops. On New Year's Eve General Eulogio Camillo announced the military's decision that Batista must step down. The latter, with several of his ministers and generals, packed his bags and fled from the island. A general strike was announced, the Navy rebelled, the principal garrison at Camp Columbia surrendered, and Castro marched unopposed into Havana. By this time the guerrilla army was at the most 2,000 men strong.

Subsequent writings by the Cuban leaders have tried to emphasise the similarities between their experience and other guerrilla wars. Guevara emphasised the Maoist principle of a three-stage struggle. Thus, during the first six months 'our troops consisted primarily of a single guerrilla group, led by Fidel Castro, and it was characterised by constant mobility. We could call this the nomadic phase.' During the second stage:

'Little by little, as the peasants came to recognise the invincibility of the guerrillas and the long duration of the struggle, they began responding ... joining our army as fighters. From that moment on, not only did they join our ranks but they provided supportive action. After that the guerrilla army was strongly entrenched in the countryside ... This is what we call "dressing the guerrillas in palm leaves" ... This was a period of consolidation for our army ... It was characterised by deadlock: we were unable to attack the enemy's fortified and relatively easily defended positions, while they did not advance on us.'[23]

During the third stage:

'We then have the beehive effect. One of the leaders, an outstanding guerrilla fighter, jumps off to another region and repeats the chain of development of guerrilla warfare – subject, of course, to central command ... The final stage is reached with the inundation of the repressive army, which leads to the seizure of the great cities, the great decisive battles, and the total annihilation of the adversary.'[24]

In his book *Guerrilla Warfare*, which is mainly concerned with the minutiae of guerrilla tactics, Guevara pays further homage to the basic Maoist precepts. He underlines the point about the third stage and notes that: 'Guerrilla warfare is a phase that does not afford in itself opportunities to arrive at complete victory ... Triumph will always be the product of a regular army, even though its origins are in a guerrilla army.' He also stresses the absolute importance of the closest links with the surrounding population: '... intensive popular work must be undertaken to explain the motives of the revolution, its ends, and to spread the incontrovertible truth that victory of the enemy against the people is finally impossible. Whoever does not feel this undoubted truth can never be a guerrilla fighter.'[25]

But this conventional analysis of the Cuban struggle omitted one crucial point. Certainly Castro's men had popular support, certainly they managed to set up a durable base area, and certainly they advanced out of this area to progressively take over the rest of Cuba. But the very smallness of the forces with which they did all this points to one inescapable fact. It was not so much that the guerrillas were all-powerful as that Batista's army was so corrupt, badly led and demoralised that it fell apart almost of its own accord. All guerrilla struggles depend on some degree of popular discontent and alienation from the central authorities. But in Cuba this discontent affected very broad sections of the population, including the peasantry, the urban working class, the intelligentsia and large numbers of the middle-classes. Political control in Cuba had long depended upon a complex system of bribery and patronage. Such a system can only be effective as long as there is enough wealth to go round. 'But in the period following [Batista's] 1952 coup the Cuban economy was in a very difficult situation. There were few economic benefits to distribute and the proportion of coercion to bribery employed in the social control of large groups was decidedly higher than in his earlier period.'[26] And when a system based upon venality loses its ability to provide the pay-offs, it swiftly collapses. Legitimacy based upon money has notoriously few ideological underpinnings. When the money is no longer forthcoming, there is simply nothing left to fight for.

The actual tactics of the guerrillas reinforce this impression of the collapse of the incumbent army. They had two basic stratagems. One was the ambush. Guevara wrote of one of these:

'The battle proved that it was easy ... to attack enemy columns on the march. We realised the advantage of firing upon the head of the column and of trying to kill the leading men, immobilising the rest of them. We continued this practice until it became an established system, so efficient that the soldiers stopped coming to the Sierra Maestra and *even refused to be part of the advance guard*.'[27]

After the troops had refused to venture into rebel territory they simply sat tight in their blockhouses in the populated centres. These the guerrillas reduced by assaults.

> '[But] the tactic which the rebels called an assault was not an assault at all as we use the word. It meant the rebel commanders would infiltrate their troops by dark to positions as close to an objective as they could find concealment. They would then keep it under uninterrupted small arms fire 24 hours a day. But they would not advance nor would they use demolitions . . . In spite of the fact that small arms fire spattering concrete walls hardly sounds effective, these encirclements of the Batista *cuartels* were the decisive actions of the revolution.'[28]

No army that retained the least amount of central co-ordination or respect for authority could have been defeated by such tactics. In any other country in Latin America, or even in Cuba earlier in this century, Castro's force would have been eliminated with contemptuous ease. It is far from being my intention to denigrate the courage and resolve of the *Fidelistas*. Nevertheless, they should never have been a serious military threat, let alone a victorious revolutionary army. Consequently it would be very dangerous to extrapolate from the Cuban experience about the possibilities of guerrilla campaigns in other countries.

Nevertheless, this is just what certain writers have done. The staggering success of the small band of rebels has led some theorists to assume that the infiltration of small armed groups into a remote area is an inevitable prelude to a successful revolutionary mobilisation of the rural masses. Guevara himself laid the groundwork for such theories with certain distinctly un-Maoist pronouncements. In his *Guerrilla Warfare* one finds the bold assertion that: 'It is not necessary to wait until all conditions for making revolution exist; the insurrection can create them.' In another text, the latter phrase has been rendered as 'the insurrectionary nucleus can create them'.[29] This idea of the insurrectionary nucleus was picked up by Regis Debray and expanded into a whole new theory of guerrilla strategy, at least in the early stages. The central idea was that of the *foco*, the guerrilla force itself, that remains apart from the people and concentrates on offensive military activity:

> 'By restricting itself to the task of protecting civilians or passive self-defence, the guerrilla unit ceases to be a vanguard of the people as a whole and deprives itself of a national perspective. By going over to the counter-attack, on the other hand, it catalyses the people's energy and transforms the *foco* into a pole of attraction for the whole country.'[30]

Debray does admit that the guerrilla force will then be able to go on to create a liberated base area and so proceed to pass the various stages of the classic guerrilla campaign. But his emphasis upon the initial primacy of autonomous military action, not linked to organisations within the people at large, is fraught with dangers. A successful guerrilla force cannot *assume* that popular discontent will lead to mass support for armed operations. The popular base has to be there at *all* stages of the guerrilla struggle. Without it, and opposed by a merely average incumbent army, the guerrillas face constant pursuit, encirclement and annihilation. Guevara himself died, in Bolivia, whilst discovering the fallacies in his theory of 'nuclear' revolution.

1. W. Pomeroy (ed), *Marxism and Guerrilla Warfare*, Lawrence & Wishart, 1969, p163
2. C. Tsoucalas, *The Greek Tragedy*, Penguin Books, 1969, p103
3. Pomeroy, *op cit*, p164
4. Osanka, *op cit*, p225
5. N. D. Valeriano and C. T. R. Bohannan, *Counter-guerrilla Operations*, Pall Mall, 1962, pp 33–34
6. W. M. Ball, *Nationalism and Communism in East Asia*, Melbourne University Press, 1952, p92
7. Pomeroy, *op cit*, p231
8. *ibid*, p235
9. *ibid*, p229
10. Valeriano, *op cit*, p63
11. L. Taruc, *He Who Rides The Tiger*, Geoffrey Chapman, 1967, p95
12. W. Pomeroy, *The Forest*, International Publishers, New York, 1963, pp 165–66
13. Taruc, *op cit*, p101
14. Valeriano, *op cit*, p130
15. *ibid*, p245
16. R. Clutterbuck, *The Long, Long War*, Cassell, 1966, p44
17. Osanka, *op cit*, p305
18. Clutterbuck, *op cit*, p121
19. Osanka, *op cit*, p383
20. P. Paret, *French Revolutionary Warfare*, Pall Mall, 1964, pp 30–32
21. *ibid*, p36
22. *ibid*, p38
23. E. Guevara, *Reminiscences of the Cuban Revolutionary War*, Penguin Books, 1969, pp 185–86 and 188
24. J. Gerassi (ed), *Venceremos: the Speeches and Writings of Che Guevara*, Panther Books, pp 389–90
25. E. Guevara, *Guerrilla Warfare*, Monthly Review Press, New York, 1961, pp 20 and 22
26. J. Dunn, *Modern Revolutions*, Cambridge University Press, 1972, p219
27. Gerassi, *op cit*, p135
28. Osanka, *op cit*, p331
29. Guevara, *Guerrilla Warfare, op cit*, p15 and Gerassi, *op cit*, p375
30. R. Debray, *Revolution in the Revolution?*, Penguin Books, 1968, p45

CHAPTER 9

People's War and Regular War: Vietnam 1945–75

Guevara's Bolivian experience which concluded the previous chapter represents something of a sad aberration in the history of modern guerrilla warfare. Persistently deluded both by the ease of the Cuban victory and by the remarkably pervasive, if simple-minded, revolutionary optimism of contemporary youth culture, Guevara allowed himself to become little more than a political icon, ludicrously over-confident about the actual impact of his personal will and vision upon a whole nexus of class and state oppression. In the end, despite his enormous personal courage, Guevara came to occupy much the same position in the pantheon of people's war as that occupied by John Lennon and Yoko Ono in international diplomacy.

Another guerrilla struggle that became a basic theme of the bell-bottoms and beads politics of the 1960s and 1970s was the Vietnam War, especially once American forces became fully involved after 1965. But there the similarity with Guevara's adventurism ends. Though the anti-war movement in the United States became an important constraint on the Presidency, and though the Vietnamese Communists did much to orchestrate domestic US and international opposition to the war, its actual conduct was very much their own affair, run in large part according to orthodox Maoist tenets of political discipline and military gradualism and flexibility.

The French Phase 1945–54

Like several of the wars mentioned in the previous chapter, the war in Vietnam grew directly out of World War II, when the Communist insurgents who had fought the Japanese resolved that they had not struggled so hard and long simply to let their old colonial masters, the French, take up where they had been so rudely interrupted. British use of rearmed Japanese POWs to police parts of Indochina until the French returned did little to mollify the Vietnamese, and in December 1945 Communist Viet Minh guerrillas made an insurrectionary bid for power, launching human wave attacks against the main

French garrisons. These attacks were repulsed, with heavy casualties, and the Viet Minh battalions driven back into the jungle. There they began to slowly establish liberated areas and later to start transforming certain of their permanent guerrilla units into a mobile regular army. The French consistently tried to engage these latter troops in a decisive positional encounter, and to this end, in November 1953, they embarked upon a substantial build-up of forces in a forward position at Dien Bien Phu. General Vo Nguyen Giap, the Viet Minh military commander, used two of his regular 10,000-man divisions to bottle up this garrison, of 15,000 French troops, and sent a third to penetrate into Laos. By Christmas Vietnam was effectively cut into two halves. In March 1954, the battle began in earnest as superbly camouflaged Viet Minh artillery, 200 guns in all, and rocket launchers proceeded to pound the garrison flat. On 7 May, the French, totally outgunned and without hope of substantial airlifts of supplies or reinforcements, surrendered. This crushing defeat spelled the end of any hopes of remaining in Indochina, and at the Geneva Conference later that year the country was partitioned into a communist North Vietnam and a 'democratic' South Vietnam.

The war as a whole, against the French, had been organised along much the same lines as Mao's protracted struggle in China. The Viet Minh swiftly absorbed the lessons of their first failed positional assaults and themselves concentrated on pursuing a protracted strategy. As Giap wrote:

'All the conceptions born of impatience and aimed at obtaining speedy victory could only be gross errors. It was necessary to grasp firmly the strategy of long-term resistance, and to exalt the will to be self-supporting in order to maintain and gradually augment our forces, while nibbling at and progressively destroying those of the enemy; it was necessary to accumulate thousands of small victories to turn them into a greater success, thus gradually altering the balance of forces, in transforming our weakness into power and carrying off final victory.'

This protracted war was to be fought in three stages:

'The general law of a long revolutionary war is usually to go through three stages: defensive equilibrium and offensive ... [In the first stage] in the armed bases ... self-defence groups ['to fight in the last extremity only'] and armed self-defence groups ['to fight the enemy as soon as he arrives at the village'] were set up which swelled afterwards to local armed groups, or armed platoons freed or partially freed from production ...'

These groups then became capable of mobile guerrilla operations, which consisted of the:

'Concentration of troops to realise an overwhelming superiority over the enemy where he is sufficiently exposed in order to destroy his manpower; initiative, suppleness, rapidity, surprise, suddenness in attack and retreat. As long as the strategic balance of forces remains disadvantageous, resolutely to muster troops to obtain absolute superiority in combat in a given place, and at a given time. To exhaust little by little by small victories the enemy forces and at the same time to maintain and increase ours. In these concrete conditions it proves absolutely necessary not to lose sight of the main objective of the fighting, that is the destruction of the enemy manpower. Therefore losses must be avoided even at the cost of losing ground.'

Then the struggle gradually moves to the final stage:

'This guerrilla warfare developed progressively into a form of mobile war that daily increased in scale. While retaining certain characteristics of guerrilla warfare, it involved regular campaigns with greater attacks on fortified positions. Starting from small operations with the strength of a platoon or a company to annihilate a few men ... our army went over, later, to more important combats with a battalion or regiment to cut one or several enemy companies to pieces, finally coming to greater campaigns bringing into play many regiments, then many divisions to end at Dien Bien Phu.'

Yet at all times 'side by side with that main force there must always be numerous guerrilla troops and guerrilla activities'.

The establishment of liberated popular bases was also accorded the highest priority:

'Throughout the Resistance War, the safeguarding of resistance bases and the consolidation of the rear were considered by our Party as of the utmost importance ... Parallel with the fight against the enemy, in order to safeguard the resistance bases and consolidate the rear, our Party implemented positive lines of action in every aspect, did its utmost to mobilise, organise and educate the masses, to increase production, practice economy, and build local ... forces.'

In these early stages the struggle had a political rather than a military character:

'Underground operating cadres' teams, underground militarised teams, armed shock teams and local armed groups and platoons gradually appeared. The most appropriate principle for activities was *armed propaganda; political activities were more important than military activities, and fighting less important than propaganda* ... Once the political bases were consolidated and developed we

proceeded one step further to the consolidation and development of the semi-
armed and armed forces.'[1]

Then, as one base became relatively secure, the guerrillas could move forward
to the kind of 'beehive' growth described by Guevara. As Giap wrote in 1950:

'Since "popular bases" were indispensable to the development of the guerrilla
war, we dispersed the companies of each battalion, and we permitted them the
necessary liberty of action so that they could infiltrate different regions and
cement their friendly relations with the local populace. Since the companies
were relatively weak they had no difficulty in understanding the necessity for
firm popular bases ... When the guerrilla units acquired sufficient experience,
when the local militia became powerful enough, the dispersed elements of the
companies in different localities gradually regrouped themselves.'[2]

But at all times political activity was seen as a vital component of the guerrillas'
task. Only then could they guarantee the popular support without which the
movement was doomed. In Vietnam this political activity had inevitably to
concern itself with the problem of land which during the French occupation
had progressively passed out of the hands of the villagers and been absorbed
into the large holdings of European or rich Vietnamese landlords. To cite Giap
once more: '... in a backward colonial country such as ours where the peasants
make up the majority of the population, a people's war is essentially a *peasants'
war under the leadership of the working class*. Owing to this fact, a general
mobilisation of the whole people is neither more nor less than the mobilisation
of the rural masses. The problem of land is of decisive importance.' Thus:

'Since the moment our Party paid attention to the anti-feudal task, especially
since the mobilisation of the masses for rent reduction and land reform, not only
broad peasant masses in the rear were ideologically aroused but also our army –
the great majority being peasants and eager for land – also saw clearly and more
fully its own fighting objective that it not only fights for national independence,
but also to bring land to the peasants, and consequently its class consciousness
and fighting spirit were raised markedly.'[3]

Nevertheless, the Viet Minh were also aware of the need for unity in the rear
areas. Thus, like Mao Tse-tung, they did not carry out any radical programme
of land reform during the actual struggle against the French. The task of
maintaining productivity was too important for the French to risk alienating
the rich peasants and smaller landlords. 'The resistance ... [put] the struggle
against foreign invasion above any immediate implementation of class conflict.
The major emphasis economically was placed upon raising agricultural production, socially upon a reduction of rents and rates of interest paid.' There

was, however, some redistribution of land to give the peasantry the prospect of more gains when victory had been achieved. Between 1945 and 1953 15 per cent of the total cultivable land was redistributed. The percentage held by the middle peasantry rose from 30.4 per cent to 34.6, by poor peasants from 10.8 to 15.6 per cent, and by agricultural labourers from 0.0 to 2.1 per cent.

The American Phase 1961–75

The French phase of the Vietnam War, up to the creation of a separate North Vietnamese state, clearly developed pretty much according to the Maoist formula, with due emphasis upon popular aspirations and on the need to evolve from protracted, preliminary guerrilla operations to the eventual seizure of the strategic initiative in a full-scale regular offensive. This last phase would ideally be characterised by large-scale mobile operations but in the Vietnamese case their opponents' arrogance actually invited the Viet Minh to concentrate most of their regular or 'main' forces against a single, fixed *point d'appui* and to whittle this away through siege tactics, often involving costly frontal assaults.

It was not long before guerrilla operations were under way once more, in newly created South Vietnam, and this second phase of fighting was generally regarded as practically a rerun of the first, with the peasantry of the southern provinces renewing their fight against the corrupt and callous indigenous ruling élite. This view of the second phase of war as largely a South Vietnamese affair, at least as far as the Communists were concerned, persisted throughout the war and it is still possible to find descriptions of the fighting that offer another classic example of the combination of domestic political mobilisation with a gradual military escalation from local hit-and-run operations to the all-out tank-led drive on Saigon in 1975.

Nor, indeed, is such a representation of events completely misleading. Certainly, the struggle for South Vietnam was in large part waged by the South Vietnamese themselves, with the Communist Party there and affiliated organisations such as the National Liberation Front playing a prominent role. The political programme they espoused, moreover, had a genuinely popular appeal, being based around the single core demand of the peasantry that they be given their own plots of land. During the French phase of the war the Viet Minh had redistributed much land in the south, and when the new government's own much-trumpeted land reform programme turned out to be largely an attempt to hand the land back to its original owners, this immediately alienated a substantial proportion of the population. Many of these people soon began to give at least tacit support to local guerrilla groups and over the next few years the vast majority of full-time and part-time soldiers in South Vietnam, from the Viet Cong main force battalions to the regional militias and the village self-defence forces, were recruited within that country. It was these troops, moreover, that did much of the fighting and even large-scale US operations were often against Viet Cong battalions and regiments.

However, none of this should obscure the fact that in many other respects the post-Geneva insurgency was very different from the original models of people's war. For the guerrillas in the south now had the very close support of a separate sovereign state, North Vietnam, and could rely on generous logistical support – both indigenous northern production and imports passing through it – as well as military support from the superb North Vietnamese regular army, either as whole divisions or as cadres to leaven Viet Cong main force units. In the event, the Viet Cong only ever created three main force divisions of their own (all with a sizeable complement of North Vietnamese troops) and thus were spared much of the trouble and risk incurred in the transition from guerrilla bands to properly trained and equipped mobile main forces. The elimination of risk was especially welcome and meant that even if Viet Cong main forces were in danger of succumbing to sustained US pressure, then a battle-hardened regular reserve was always on hand. Thus neither serious blows by the enemy nor over-optimistic military plans of their own were ever likely to have the devastating effect they could have in China, Yugoslavia or Indochina, where the only eggs in the basket were those laid locally.

Of course, even North Vietnamese regulars were not invincible and their troops were in fact sorely tried on many occasions by relentless US probing and devastating firepower. But, operating as they often did in the northern provinces of South Vietnam, around the Demilitarised Zone (DMZ), these formations were able when necessary to pull back into North Vietnam, where they were safe from pursuit by US ground troops. This marks another difference between the two phases of the Vietnam War. The notion of secure base areas and sanctuaries is nothing new, of course, but what is important in this case is that North Vietnam was not just safe by virtue of difficult terrain or immense distance, but because it formed part of a powerful international alliance which, according to the perceived logic of the Cold War, and the precedent of Korea, would almost certainly intervene on North Vietnam's behalf should its newly drawn borders be violated.

Nor was North Vietnam the only no-go area for US ground operations. Sensitivity to the reactions of allies and potential enemies also deterred the Americans from striking at the important troop sanctuaries in Laos and Cambodia, those in Laos being especially useful for the supply, reinforcement and refitting of forces operating in the provinces around Saigon. Thus Communist forces throughout much of South Vietnam always knew that they could elude undue American pressure by withdrawing into one or other of the numerous cross-border base areas, where they simply waited for the particular US search and destroy mission to be wound down and then quietly slipped back into South Vietnam. In the interim the guerrillas could enjoy a welcome, albeit forced, period of rest and relaxation. US reluctance to employ large ground forces in Laos and Cambodia also allowed the burgeoning of indigenous Communist guerrilla movements, the Pathet Lao and the Khmer Rouge respectively, which further weakened the ability of the incumbent governments to deter Vietnamese incursions.

None of this should imply that the Americans were paragons of international morality, ever scrupulous about the sovereign rights of others. The case for their being in Vietnam at all, propping up a profoundly corrupt, anti-democratic regime, was at best dubious. Moreover, throughout the war, when they thought they could get away with it, the Americans were always ready to employ special forces and covert bombing operations against South Vietnam's neighbours. In 1970 and 1971, they went still further and sanctioned large-scale raids into Cambodia and then Laos, attempting to break up Communist base areas preparing for forthcoming offensives. In Laos another major objective was to interdict the Ho Chi Minh Trail, along which enormous quantities of military supplies were infiltrated into South Vietnam. But these were one-off operations, launched after it became generally known that the Americans had decided to pull out of Vietnam, and though large stockpiles of supplies and weapons were destroyed, postponing some major Communist operations for up to twelve months, the guerrillas and regulars simply dispersed to await the fairly prompt withdrawal of American and South Vietnamese forces.

Even the bombing of North Vietnam, Laos and Cambodia, dreadful as this mode of warfare must always be, was severely circumscribed by the fear of international ramifications. Thus, although it often had economic and logistic targets and was thus dubbed 'strategic' bombing, following shaky World War II usage, the bombing was strictly controlled from Washington. Here President Lyndon Johnson (and to a lesser degree Richard Nixon after him) and his advisers showed intense concern to limit the bombing targets to locations with clear military implications and to ensure that international observers, especially the USSR and China, understood that it was never the intention to so destabilise North Vietnamese society or government that the state itself might collapse (major objectives of the bomber offensives against Nazi Germany and Japan). Both 'area' ('terror') bombing, à la 'Bomber' Harris, and strikes against basic civic infrastructure targets, such as North Vietnam's fragile irrigation system, were ruled out and this, together with the ban on major ground penetrations, seems to have persuaded the Russians and the Chinese that there was no intention to overthrow the North Vietnamese state and that there would thus be no unacceptable loss of international 'face'.

It is this international dimension to US bombing operations that casts doubt on later USAF claims that aerial efforts such as LINEBACKER II in 1973, which undoubtedly succeeded in its prime mission of forcing the North

Vietnamese back to the negotiating table, clearly show that the war could have been won through sustained strategic bombing. In fact, especially given the remarkable resilience of the diffuse North Vietnamese economy and the stoicism of the people as a whole, only a bombing effort that seriously threatened the very existence of that society could have seriously dented its resolve. Yet it was just such a threat that was most likely to risk Soviet or Chinese intervention and put the superpowers on the path to nuclear confrontation. US bombing, therefore, had to kept within certain consensual limits, even though this also meant that unless it could achieve miracles of 'surgical' precision, and keep on achieving them in the sort of sustained offensive that alone can disrupt economic and logistic networks, then the enemy within South Vietnam would always have secure bases and sources of supply.

International agreements, tacit or otherwise, usually have their *quid pro quo* and Soviet and Chinese flexibility about 'acceptable' levels of force against Hanoi was balanced by a US acceptance that the Communist bloc as a whole was going to do what it could to prop up the North Vietnamese, and thus the Viet Cong, with financial and material aid. This they most certainly did: it has been estimated that the $600 million of damage caused by US bombing was offset by some $26 billion in foreign aid. Much of this was military and one of the greatest threats to American operations was the sophisticated air defence system, radar-controlled surface-to-air missiles and anti-aircraft guns, that was established in North Vietnam. Later in the war SAMs and AAA also accompanied North Vietnamese units southwards. Also of crucial military value were the endless columns of Soviet trucks that helped move supplies within North Vietnam and down the Ho Chi Minh Trail, and the prodigious number of small-unit but powerful infantry weapons, recoilless rifles, rocket-grenade launchers and the like, supplied by the Chinese (though usually copies of Soviet originals).

Clearly, then, the isolation of the insurgent force, usually the prime reason for resorting to laborious and piecemeal guerrilla tactics in the first place, was nowhere near as big a constraint in the second, American, phase of the Vietnam War. In most of the guerrilla struggles examined in earlier chapters this isolation, whether by reason of remoteness, terrain, inadequate communications, international apathy, coordinated international opposition, blockade, embargo or whatever, has been a major guerrilla weakness, allowing the incumbent forces to take their time relentlessly hemming in, blockading, starving, relocating, terrorising and killing the guerrillas and their supporters, driving them into ever remoter and more marginal fastnesses, until they succumb or cease to be a political threat. In Vietnam, a veritable showcase for flood-lit Cold War arm-wrestling, but where an arm pressed to the table might press a nuclear button, the Americans were never allowed the privacy of their own battlefield on which to pursue the counter-insurgency to its 'logical' military limits. To this extent, at least, President George Bush was right to claim later that the Americans had fought in Vietnam with one hand tied behind their backs. Though one might also recall Lieutenant William Calley at My Lai who offered a clear example of what soldiers with both hands free will do, sooner or later, in a bitter guerrilla war.

As regards the purely military side of the Vietnam War, it has become fashionable to claim that US counter-insurgency was very effective, so effective, in fact, that by 1968 the Viet Cong main forces were on the road to defeat. Certainly US forces put up a much better show than some accounts at the time, and since, have allowed. In the first three years or so of the war both sides' commanders, Generals Westmoreland and Giap alike, were intent on fighting a war of attrition, gaining victory by convincing the opponent that the game was simply not worth the body count. Thus both sides were fairly satisfied to fight purely positional battles – usually comprising American attacks on fortified villages, hills or tunnel complexes – that seemed to have more in common with the savage island-hopping battles of the war against Japan than with 'orthodox' hit-and-run guerrilla engagements. And in these battles, tremendous US firepower, as well as individual fortitude and courage and often adept small-unit tactics, did rack up impressive casualty ratios sometimes reminiscent of the suicidal Japanese blood-letting on Iwo Jima, Okinawa and the rest.

The Americans also achieved an impressive degree of tactical mobility, using air-mobile troops such as 1 Cavalry Division, constituted in this role in 1965, to relentlessly harass Viet Cong and North Vietnamese regulars and on occasion to drive whole regiments out of a province. Where air mobility was not constantly on tap the Americans also had some success in linking ground units to a network of mutually supporting Fire Support Bases which could massively supplement a unit's organic firepower and thus allow it to roam reasonably freely within an area of operations. This supporting firepower was massively supplemented by tactical air assets, both gunships and fighter-bombers, fixed-wing and rotary, and ground-air liaison techniques were developed to high levels of responsiveness and accuracy. On occasion these aircraft were assisted by huge B-52 bombers, utilising the latest navigational and bomb-aiming electronics, which provided particularly devastating fire support whenever the Communists made one of their not infrequent assaults on fortified base camps or cities, such as Khe Sanh and Hue in 1968 and An Loc in 1972.

Yet such a flattering description of American operations does require several qualifications. Thus, though there were many attritional fire-fights in which US troops forced the enemy to withdraw after inflicting heavy casualties, almost all of these were where the Communists had chosen to stand and fight.

In 1968, for example, a CIA analysis claimed that less than 1 per cent of all small-unit operations actually resulted in contact, let alone in a fire-fight, whilst the comparable figure for the Army of the Republic of Vietnam (ARVN) was 0.1 per cent. Equally revealing about who really held the tactical initiative in search and destroy operations was a US Department of Defense survey which concluded that the enemy, in 1967, commenced the firing in 88 per cent of all company-size fire-fights. This advantage the Communists enjoyed in being able to dictate pretty much where and when they were going to fight is vividly encapsulated in two quotations from very different US command levels. According to one of 4 Infantry Division's after-action reports, in 1967: 'The most difficult tactical problem found in fighting the (N)orth (V)ietnamese (A)rmy in large areas of difficult terrain is *finding the enemy*. That is, finding him without having tactical units shot up and pinned down by automatic weapons and snipers ... at close range.'[4] Even more succinct was a judgement by Henry Kissinger in a National Security Study of January 1969 where, after having waded through some 600 pages of evidence from concerned security agencies, he was forced to conclude that 'the enemy basically controls both sides' casualty rates.'[5]

This control, moreover, had not just local tactical but also vital strategic implications. For it meant that it was the Vietnamese who were winning the real battle of attrition. They might well be enduring unfavourable casualty ratios in many of the big fire-fights, but this was not affecting their actual strength on the ground. As Kissinger noted in the same paper: 'Under current rules of engagement, the enemy's manpower pool and infiltration capabilities can outlast Allied attrition efforts indefinitely.'[6] Most importantly of all, the casualty rates inflicted on American divisions, lower though they might be, were nevertheless proving sufficient to sap public support for the war, and this dissatisfaction was providing a crucial input into White House policy, an input that was eventually to lead to President Richard Nixon's decision to wind down the American commitment and to posture increasingly shamefacedly behind the fig-leaf of 'Vietnamisation'.

But there were also telling tactical caveats to the favourable kill ratios claimed by the Americans, which provided further proof that the initiative on the ground usually lay with the Communists. Most important of these was the simple fact that US troops were hardly ever able to effectively surround an enemy unit, even those they encountered in prolonged, close-range fire-fights. The theory was there, and looked good on paper, and so too was much of the requisite air-mobile hardware. But the execution was usually somewhat lacking and one finds very few examples of engagements in which a substantial proportion of the enemy did not manage to slip away, at a time pretty much of their own choosing. They ceded ground to the Americans, of course, but were in fact perfectly happy to allow them this 'victory', knowing full well that fairly soon the Americans would depart, allowing Communist units to move back into the region. Thus, despite the enormous technological effort during the war to maximise mobility and firepower, the enemy remained as elusive as any successful guerrilla must, even the main force NVA units mostly operating as will-o'-the-wisps, whose exact location, intentions and combat status were the subject of intense but usually vague speculation.

This sense of a war without a tangible enemy, a giant nut-cracker without a nut, is amply illustrated by the aerial interdiction campaign against the Ho Chi Minh Trail and by most other air operations against Communist ground forces. Again a massive technological effort was mobilised, particularly with regard to remote surveillance and ground radar navigation aids, but again the results, zealously processed though they were through state-of-the-art mainframes and some of the best military brains, could only be filed under 'Don't Know' or 'Wishful Thinking'. Enormous truck kill-rates were claimed, especially during Operation COMMANDO HUNT between 1968 and 1973. Yet hard evidence, notably thousands of charred chassis along the Trail, was never produced and the abiding impression of much of the bombing campaign is of the 'virtual' war described by one historian: '... effectiveness soon came to be expressed in terms of bombs dropped in desired target boxes, release efficiency and sorties completing missions – quantitative measures adopted because of the lack of hard facts from infrequent ground follow-ups, the difficulty of post-strike photographic reconnaissance, and dubious POW accounts.'[7] General Peckem and his minions, in Joseph Heller's *Catch-22*, would have felt perfectly at home.

But neither the lack of tactical follow-through nor the over-reliance on technological 'fixes' are in themselves sufficient to explain the American failure in Vietnam. In the last analysis, the basic guerrilla concept that does most to explain Communist victory is that of 'protracted war'. The Viet Cong and North Vietnamese always placed this Maoist precept at the very heart of their strategy, fully aware that successful peasant revolution was unlikely to be a short-term cataclysm but rather a gruelling and bloody balance-sheet of temporary reverses and small victories. On occasions, of course, the Communist leadership abandoned this perspective, notably during the Tet Offensive in 1968 and the Easter Offensive of 1972. Both were attempts to make quick, very substantial military and political gains, leading to regional and even possibly national government. But both, the first a series of urban insurrections involving almost all the best Viet Cong formations and political cadres and the second a conventional ground offensive against the ARVN, were disastrous failures. During Tet the Viet Cong political infrastructure was largely destroyed and in 1972 enormous numbers of Viet Cong and NVA élite troops were killed, with vast quantities of military equipment, including T-54 tanks, also being destroyed by wave upon wave of US bombers and gunships.

But the essential point about protracted war remains. In many military cultures even one such shattering defeat might have had a profound effect upon the will to fight on, provoking serious consideration of armistice, withdrawal or whatever. But not for the North Vietnamese or their co-belligerents. After Tet they simply tightened their belts, considerably reduced the scale of their operations and set about painstakingly rebuilding some sort of indigenous political infrastructure. The 1972 defeat could be expected to have had even more deleterious consequences, involving as it did so many NVA units, with whole regiments thought to have been written off in their staging areas. Yet by the end of the same year the North Vietnamese had all of 13 divisions and elements of another in the south, as well as two full Viet Cong divisions brought up to strength with NVA drafts.

But this is not to say that the Communists eschewed the very idea of peace talks. These had in fact been going on since 1968, and in 1973 a treaty was signed in Paris by which the Americans agreed to withdraw all their remaining ground forces from Vietnam in exchange for a cease-fire during which a Council of National Reconciliation would take unspecified steps to absorb South Vietnamese Communists into the political process and engineer free elections under international supervision. For the Communists, however, these protracted peace talks had been just one phase in the overall protracted war, themselves ushering in yet another phase during which political cadres and parochial military units ceaselessly jockeyed for territorial and representational advantage, endlessly striving for a gradual accretion of political power.

The Americans had no real response. Nixon had made grandiloquent promises to President Thieu of South Vietnam that any violations of the treaty or threats to the integrity of his country would be answered by massive use of American air-power against North Vietnam. In the event, however, Nixon was increasingly distracted by the Watergate scandal, devoting less and less attention to foreign affairs. But even had his eye been squarely on the ball he would have found air-power a totally inappropriate response to Communist tactics. For one thing it was virtually impossible to point to specific articles in the treaty of which the Communists were clearly in violation, even to the satisfaction of international opinion. As CIA agent Frank Snepp wrote: 'In sum ... the peace of Paris was no peace at all ... It imposed no limitation, or obligation, on either side that could not be nullified through the unanimity principle, and apart from the withdrawal of US forces, all major provisions were subject to reinterpretation and further debate.'[8] But even had it been possible to pin-point clear violations, the Communists were doing their utmost to ensure that nothing they did was so flagrant as to conceivably justify a bombing strike in response. Protracted wars have their different phases, according to the political situation and the balance of forces, and Giap was quite clear that by 1973/4 the war had become 'protracted and complex' and was for the moment a struggle between 'anti-nibbling forces and the nibblers'.[9]

American hawks had no response to such duck-like tactics, showing yet again their lack of an all-embracing military-political doctrine or firm commitment that was properly responsive to the endless fluctuations and long-term demands of protracted war. Thus they always refused, for example, to mobilise the reserves or the National Guard, relying on a selective draft to keep existing regular units up to strength rather than a full deployment of experienced military personnel. Moreover, no troops, other than general officers, were expected to do a tour of more than twelve months in Vietnam. This continual through-put of men, even though a formation as a whole might be in place for several years, seriously retarded the development of institutional competence and the proper absorption and dissemination of the operational and tactical requirements of this kind of war.

The central importance of the notion of protracted war in Vietnam brings us back to our discussion at the start of this section about the high international profile of the war, at least in the American phase, and of the Cold War implications of the existence of a separate North Vietnamese state. This was extremely pertinent to the notion of protracted war in that this state had its own regular army and this spared the guerrillas in the south the necessity to raise substantial, self-sufficient regular forces of their own. Even more importantly, it meant that the Communists, particularly in the north, could afford to make quite serious operational errors with the Viet Cong, knowing that high-quality mobile forces were already in existence as a separate strategic reserve. It seems fairly clear, for example, that had the premature Tet offensive or some equivalent been launched during the French phase of the war, then this would more than likely have fatally weakened the whole guerrilla campaign and the possibility of a transition to full-scale mobile warfare. But there again, of course, if there had been no NVA, then the Viet Cong, not the North Vietnamese Politburo, would have been making the decisions and doubtless showing themselves extremely loth to indulge in potentially suicidal military opportunism. Only those who do not have to take the ultimate risk can afford to be careless of the stern logic of protracted war.

1. V. N. Giap, *People's War, People's Army* (1961), Praeger, New York, 1967, pp 28, 101, 79, 48–49, 145, 79
2. G. K. Tanham, *Communist Revolutionary Warfare*, Methuen, London, 1962, p18
3. Giap, *op cit*, pp 27 and 117
4. S. Stanton, *The Rise and Fall of an American Army*, Spa Books, Stevenage, 1989, p164
5. J. C. Pratt (ed.), *Vietnam Voices*, Penguin, New York, 1984, p375

6. *loc cit*

7. J. T. Greenwood, 'B-52s: Strategic Bombers in a Tactical Role', in R.Bonds (ed.), *The Vietnam War*, Salamander Books, 1979, p208

8. Pratt (ed.), *op cit*, p559

9. *ibid*, p580

CHAPTER 10

From Guerrilla War to People's War: an Overview

All the events covered in the previous chapters lead to one ineluctable and predominant conclusion. Though guerrilla warfare is an excellent method for embarrassing the regular forces of an incumbent regime, in a civil war or a national liberation situation, it is *not* a reliable way of throwing out an invader or actually seizing state power for oneself. In the Chronology I have listed over 160 guerrilla wars, yet less than 20 of them could really be considered to have been ultimately successful. And even in these cases, the issue was rarely decided in terms of the military confrontation between the insurgents and the incumbents. The guerrillas were often aided by other factors which had nothing to do with their own military capacity.

One of the most common of these was that the guerrillas had the *direct or indirect aid of regular troops*. Such was the case with Marion and Sumter in the American War of Independence. Had it not been for the threat of Washington's Continental Army, the British would undoubtedly have been able to concentrate enough troops within the Carolinas to crush the rebels in the swamps. The struggles against Napoleon in Spain and Russia would never have been successful without the direct participation of the British and Russian regular armies. The guerrillas certainly shortened these wars but they could not have won them on their own. The same considerations applied during World War I. Lawrence's operations were only strategically viable given the presence of Allenby's army, and the smashing blows he was able to deal to the Turks. Even Lettow-Vorbeck would not have found as much room for manoeuvre had not the demands of other theatres of war severely limited the number of troops the Allies could spare for this particular campaign. Indeed, it is perhaps a little unfair to judge the German effort in East Africa in such terms of defeat and victory. Lettow-Vorbeck always realised his limitations and never hoped to do more than keep a substantial number of troops occupied, fully appreciating that the decisive encounters would take place in Europe itself. In World War II, too, guerrilla successes were a direct consequence of the activities of the regular armies. The Italian and French partisans could never have risen up

235

without the invasions by the Americans and the British. The Russian advance had a similar effect on the situation in Bulgaria and Slovakia. Even Tito, though his struggle was much more self-sufficient, would have been surrounded and annihilated had not the Nazis been forced to deploy the bulk of their forces against the Russians and the threat of a second front in France.

Many unsuccessful guerrilla wars, also, depended for their very existence upon the support of regular troops. The French guerrillas during the Hundred Years War could hardly have functioned at all if the English had not been so concerned with the threat from more substantial bodies of French soldiers. The Camisards could not have risen up to such effect had not French forces been embroiled in the War of Spanish Succession. The Vendéans profited greatly from the Prussian, Austrian and Spanish threat to the Republic. Garibaldi could only afford to operate because of the presence of the Piedmontese regulars. Quantrill's men could not have survived so long except in the context of a full-scale civil war. Russian intervention in Eastern Europe was often of crucial importance for the guerrillas there. Things might have gone very badly for the Greeks had not the Russians declared war on Turkey in 1828. In 1877–78 the Bulgarian *četi* gained a new and brief lease of life during the Russian invasion of that country. The Filipino struggle against the Spanish only became a real insurgency when the Americans decided to intervene. More recently, it would be difficult to overestimate the military value of the presence of North Vietnamese regular divisions in South Vietnam and other countries of South-east Asia.

Of course, such foreign assistance need not be merely military. Diplomatic aid has often been of great importance. The Maccabees, for example, were aided by the support of the Romans and the tacit threat this posed for the Syrian forces. The Turks always suffered from their diplomatic isolation within Europe, and the Greeks and Bulgarians, in particular, profited greatly from the intervention of other great European powers. The eventual French withdrawal from Algeria was to a large extent precipitated by the odium aroused by their methods in other Western countries, especially when it became manifestly obvious that the Algerian resistance was not Communist-inspired. Foreign financial aid and the provision of supplies and equipment can also be very important. Louis XIV aided the *kurucs* this way, as did the Russians the Montenegrins in 1711. IMRO was very dependent upon the Bulgarians in the early stages of the struggle, as were their rivals upon the Greeks. During World War II the Allies made available a certain quantity of munitions for guerrilla groups in Europe and Asia, and they infiltrated many advisers and liaison officers who were sometimes useful in speeding up the training of the guerrillas. Since World War II, the Algerians have received important foreign aid from the Tunisians, the North Vietnamese from the Chinese, and the South Vietnamese from their northern neighbours. One might also say that the American embargo on Batista's Cuba was a kind of negative, though very important, foreign aid. Friendly neighbours can also be very important if they can provide sanctuary for the guerrillas, as a base area or a last resort when hard-pressed. IMRO guerrillas were able to find sanctuary in Bulgaria; the Kachins in Burma were able to flee into China; the Greek Communists found refuge in Yugoslavia and Albania; the Algerians operated from bases within Tunisia; the Malayan Communists often retreated into southern Thailand; NLF fighters in South Vietnam could always be assured of refuge in North Vietnam if necessary; the Palestinian guerrillas could not possibly have operated without the co-operation of Syria and various Lebanese groups.

The notion of sanctuaries brings one on to another vital component of any viable guerrilla struggle – the *base area*. Unless the insurgents are to be no more than roving bandits it is essential for them to find a region, preferably in their own country, where they can be relatively safe from enemy pursuit and counter-attack. Obviously such regions are more likely to be found in large countries where there is a much greater variety of terrain. It has already been seen how guerrilla theorists such as Mao and Clausewitz stressed the importance of a large country. Nevertheless, it is the nature of the *terrain*, rather than the sheer area of the country, which is the ultimate determining factor. In difficult terrain, communications will be backward and it is this above all that ensures the relative security of the base area. Below is a list of the typical types of difficult terrain in which various guerrilla groups have been able to establish themselves for a time at least:

Woods, forests, jungles: the Volsci, Cassivellaunus, the Chatti, William Wallace, the Tories, the Normans in the Hundred Years' War, the Hungarians in the War of the Austrian Succession, the Vendéans, the Maya, the Murids, the Kachins, the Javanese, the Temne, Lettow-Vorbeck, the Vietnamese, the Filipinos, the Malayan Communists, anti-Portuguese guerrillas in Africa.
Mountains: Sertorius and Viriathus, the early Welsh nationalists, the Montenegrins, the Haitians, the Greeks, the Carlists, the Rifi, the Pathans, the Libyans under Omar Mukhtar, Tito's Partisans, Castro's guerrillas, the Kurds, EOKA.
Deserts: the Jews, Tacfarinas, Abd-el Kader, the Senussi, T. E. Lawrence, the Algerian FLN.
Marshes and Swamps: Hereward the Wake, the Tories, Francis Marion, the rebels in the Lower Vendée, the Seminoles. (The Mekong Delta should also be classified under this type of terrain.)

But difficult terrain in itself is not necessarily a decisive advantage. Indeed, in certain circumstances it can even be a hindrance. Tito made this point when discussing the Yugoslav positions during one of the German Encirclement Campaigns:

'It might be thought that difficulties of terrain and natural obstacles are always of great importance for our army in defensive battles. But this is not so. In Montenegro they proved a disadvantage to us and an advantage to the enemy. They restricted our manoeuvring power and very nearly prevented our main striking force ... from breaking out of the enemy's encirclement ... There are other factors to be borne in mind, which for ordinary armies who possess all that is needed for waging war, are of second or even third-rate importance, but for our army are vital. For example, the economic position of the population in the area of operations is of first-rate importance to our troops. Unlike the enemy we have no stores of food or food-producing factories in our rear.'[1]

In a remote area of difficult terrain, it is unlikely that the population would be able to produce the necessary surplus to feed a large force of guerrillas that has appeared from outside. And if the guerrillas are unable to provide themselves with the basic necessities of life, the inaccessibility of their base area is a matter of little consequence. The insurgent forces need only cordon off the area and wait for their opponents to starve to death, surrender or disperse. This tactic was a basic element of Bugeaud's mode of mountain warfare. The sparse resources of the base area were also a significant handicap to the Carlist guerrillas and were one of the main reasons for Zumalacárregui's insistence that they must strike hard at Madrid at the earliest opportunity.

But if even one grants the guerrillas that there is enough food in the area to sustain their forces, the inaccessibility of their base area is still only the beginning of the story. They also need the *support of the people at large*. A guerrilla struggle is waged by men who do not have the requisite numbers or equipment to face a regular army in open battle. Whatever force they hope to muster has to built up from scratch. Because the guerrillas are so few in number in the early stages they simply cannot afford to coerce people into joining their movement. The people would soon turn against them and military operations would never get off the ground. Therefore people have to be persuaded to support the guerrillas, to see that it is in their own interests to do so. Moreover, this support must not be merely passive. The *haiduks* and the Tories in Ireland were popular heroes because they generally fought against the people's enemies. But these groups kept apart from the people and were merely symbols of resistance rather than active and overt champions of the people's cause. They did not mix with the people in the day-to-day course of their struggle. They did not personally help the people to better their own position, and neither did they try to organise them to fight for their own rights. Thus they were always doomed to be a very small group of bandit-guerrillas who were, in the last analysis, predators upon the very system which so oppressed the people at large. Though they attacked the agents of that system, they never reached the stage, nor even really wished to, of threatening the system itself.

This question of popular support also introduces the problem of the social groups from which the guerrillas are drawn. It has been seen repeatedly how certain groups, such as escaped slaves, herdsmen, cowboys, the landless, the dispossessed, are more able to take up the life of the guerrilla. They have no roots in society, no sort of vested interest in the *status quo*, and thus are very able to pack up their few belongings and take to the hills. Yet by the same token, their alienation from the rest of society and their lack of class attachments forces them to remain on the margins of that society. They have little notion of the kind of social and economic grievances that motivate the bulk of the peasant population, and even less interest in acting in support of those grievances. They are mobile, as all guerrillas must be. Yet an authentic guerrilla army must be able to put down, as it were, social and political roots, to identify with the population as a whole and formulate a coherent programme based upon *their* grievances. The differing fortunes of the Zapatista and the Villista guerrillas offer a perfect example of the importance of such considerations.

Yet even when a guerrilla movement can fairly claim to represent the interests of a broad section of the population, and to have the whole-hearted support of that group, this in itself may not be enough for the creation of an effective insurgency. Again we must return to the problems of creating a viable base area. Such a region must not only be theoretically capable of producing a large enough surplus to feed a guerrilla army; the guerrillas must also be able to mobilise that section of the population in the best position to ensure that that surplus actually appears. This means the involvement of small landowners and rich peasants in the struggle. But the guerrillas' socio-economic programme will almost inevitably be based upon the antipathy of the small peasant and the landless labourer, the vast majority of the rural population, to these very groups. So the advantages of popular support in terms of sheer numbers have to be balanced against the need for the base area to be self-sufficient. For the guerrillas, no matter how radical their vision of the ultimate perfect society, cannot simply go ahead and liquidate or disappropriate the richer strata of rural society. In the early stages of the struggle they are simply not strong enough to do this. And even when they have gained some popular support, such a policy would create serious internal upheavals, which would prevent the guerrillas from devoting all their energies to the external enemy. In other words, *class unity* within the base area presents more advantages for the guerrillas than a blind devotion to radical policies. Zapata's policies in Morelos and Mao's policies in the various base areas in China are clear examples of the value of a very broad-based popular appeal. In the Vendée, too, though it could hardly be claimed that it was a matter of deliberate policy, one saw the advantages of complete class unity within a particular region. All strata of the peasantry, the clergy and the aristocracy rose up together to face the common enemy.

This notion of internal unity also brings up the importance of the difference between the two basic types of guerrilla wars. By and large they can be divided into civil wars and wars of national liberation. In the latter, when the enemy can easily be identified as a foreigner, it is obviously much easier to unite the whole population under the banner of national regeneration. An astute guerrilla leader can use *nationalism* to paint over many of the cracks in the social structure of a particular nation. Even when the guerrilla struggle makes an overt issue of the necessity for far-reaching social reforms, nationalism can be used to blunt the implications of such policies. It seems undeniable that both Mao and Tito were helped greatly by the fact that they were able, one for part of the war, the other for the whole of it, to claim justly that they were fighting against a foreign aggressor, the Japanese and the Germans respectively.

But even popular support, with or without the inspiration of nationalism or some kind of group solidarity, is not enough to guarantee a successful conclusion to a guerrilla campaign. The examples of the nomadic tribes of Europe and the segmentary societies of Africa show this clearly. Because of the atomised organisation of their societies, and the lack of any focal point for an aggressor to attack, or the defenders to feel the loss of, neither the Celts of medieval Wales nor the Tiv of Nigeria, for example, could be speedily subdued. Each separate community had to be reduced in its turn. And each community hated the invader and was prepared to fight to the bitter end. The examples of the Old Prussians, the Montenegrin *brastvos*, the Vlach shepherds, the Maya Indians, African tribes such as the Baoule and the Balante are all further proofs of the resilience of this type of social organisation and its adaptability to a guerrilla situation.

Yet almost all of them succumbed in the end. This was largely attributable to the fact that the very advantages conferred upon them by the structures of their societies had in them the seeds of eventual defeat. Though it usually takes a long time to overwhelm this type of society, its atomised structure makes it almost impossible for its members to co-ordinate their resistance in any way. Though each village or community is capable of organising its own resistance, and of fighting to the end of its own accord, its struggle has little connection with that of neighbouring communities. Certainly guerrilla warfare demands a certain degree of flexibility and the encouragement of local initiative. At the same time, however, unless the guerrillas are able, at some stage or other, to mount co-ordinated operations and from time to time concentrate their fighters to take advantage of a particularly advantageous balance of forces, then they will never be able to inflict significant military defeats on the enemy. They might still be able to maintain a dogged resistance, even over many years, but the result of the war will not be in doubt – only the time it takes.

To be able to co-ordinate operations, the guerrillas need a strong *military-*

political organisation. This is the dominant lesson of the Chinese, Yugoslav and Vietnamese experiences, three of the most successful guerrilla wars. Most peasant societies, not just the segmentary ones, are made up of a great number of small communities whose members have an outlook that is both parochial and short-term. They are unable to concern themselves much with the people who live outside their own district or community, and neither do they have much conception of the long-term demands of a war that will almost certainly drag on for years. Their lives are ruled by the annual demands of harvesting and sowing and they are scarcely capable of adapting themselves to a time-span that looks beyond these annual requirements. I have already cited the Maya as a particularly striking example of this phenomenon, but the same holds true for almost all peasant societies. Thus, the guerrillas' organisational structures must be used to break down this mode of thinking and persuade the peasants to act in conjunction with other communities, and in the name of a long-term strategy whose dénouement might be many years in the future. The guerrilla must be taught that a local defeat does not necessarily mean the end of the struggle, and that a local victory, or indeed any victory that falls short of the complete annihilation of the enemy, does not mean that he can now go home and peacefully tend his crops.

Such an organisation, best typified by the Communist and Popular Front parties in China, Yugoslavia, Malaya, the Philippines and Vietnam, is also vital in terms of other considerations that have already been discussed. The party can help ensure the maintenance of class unity in the base areas, and mediate between the rich and poor peasantry. Mao, for example, formulated a policy that, though it allowed the richer strata of the rural population a great degree of economic freedom, made sure that the poor peasantry were very well represented in the actual political organisations. One of the most important slogans of the Chinese Communists during the Civil War was that: 'The Party represents the farm labourer, depends upon the poor peasant, allies with the middle peasant.' The party is also important in that it can organise the education of the people and yet ensure that that education is presented in consistent political terms. In other words, the better the guerrillas' political organisation the more they can hammer home their propaganda and make sure that it reaches large sections of the population. In this way they can strengthen and extend their popular support by emphasising that the war is being fought on the people's behalf, and to their ultimate advantage. The party is also vital as an agent for upholding the primacy of such social and political considerations. It can act as a mediating influence between the purely military demands of the situation and the necessity not to alienate large sections of the population by measures such as compulsory recruitment or requisitioning. As Mao said, the party must control the gun, and not the other way round. If purely military demands become dominant then the original socio-political vision will very likely be lost. And without such a vision it is quite impossible to meet for long the demands of a protracted war.

Yet the military demands are there. And once again, only a strong, centralised organisation can meet them adequately. As I have tried to show throughout the book, even a guerrilla struggle must eventually face the fact that the object of war is the destruction of the enemy. Guerrilla tactics are necessary to hold him off until one can build a *regularised army of one's own*, but at some stage or other one must create such a force, and it must face the enemy in open battle. Only then can one actually go on to seize state power. Even if, like Zapata, the guerrilla leader does not even wish to seize power, he will still be unable to come to suitable terms with his opponent unless he can show that opponent that he is capable of at least holding his own in open warfare. The defensive guerrilla stage can rarely do more than guarantee a long defeat. All the most successful guerrilla leaders, Judas Maccabee, Zumalacárregui, Zapata, Mao, Tito, Giap, realised this basic point, and from the beginning they began to build up the kind of organisational machinery capable of handling the training, disciplining, equipping, and strategic and tactical direction of such an army. The consequences of failing to do this were apparent in the Vendée, where the rebels were unable adequately to co-ordinate their local initiatives precisely because of the divisions within the military and political leadership.

However, there are two essential qualifications to this point. Firstly, the regularisation must not be carried through too quickly. One must be sure that the guerrillas have had enough combat-experience, that enough competent officers have emerged, and that the troops are well enough equipped to face regulars in open battle. Regularisation can mean the placing of all one's eggs in one basket. If it is done prematurely and one's forces are defeated in a big battle, this will mean that large proportions of one's forces are destroyed at one fell swoop, and it will then be very difficult to salvage enough survivors, or enough popular support, to return to guerrilla methods. Rakoczi in Hungary, the Serbians between 1802–13, the Nien, the Slovakian, Italian and French partisans of World War II, the Greek Communists and the Huks all learnt the hard way of the dangers inherent in precipitate regularisation. The second qualification emerges from the first. Even when building up a regular force it is dangerous to abandon completely the use of ancillary, part-time, local guerrilla troops. Should the regulars be defeated some kind of secondary military organisation will be necessary to keep the struggle alive. Ideally, a guerrilla army should always be based upon a two or three-tier system in which the regulars are always backed up by a much larger number of local irregulars. Such troops can support the regulars in a particular area. They provide a massive pool of reserves for the regular forces. They can also help to give the villagers a sense of security when the regulars are not actually operating in their locality. Finally, and perhaps most importantly, the more people that are actually involved in the armed struggle, the more the guerrillas can maintain close links with the population at large. The importance of this notion of supporting the regulars with the armed people is demonstrated by the partial and complete successes of such diverse guerrilla armies as the Jews under Maccabee, Tacfarinas's forces, the Vendéans, the Murids, the Javanese, the Maya, the Rifi, the Cubans under Gómez, the Algerian FLN, the Partisans, the Chinese Red Army, and the Viet Minh and Viet Cong.

In conclusion, then, unless a guerrilla force directs all its efforts to maintaining close links with the people it can have little chance of eventual victory. Guerrilla warfare is the war of the whole people, and as such demands that the closest attention be paid to those matters which concern the people most. Anyone organising such a struggle must always realise that military considerations are secondary to political, social and economic policies. In the end the confrontation will be on the purely military level, but the guerrillas' capacity to be adequately equipped for that confrontation is a direct function of the duration and intensity of their political effort. Power may grow out of the barrel of a gun, but one must first persuade people to take up that gun, care for it, hump it around for years in the most desolate regions, and then to stand firm and pull the trigger. To do that needs much more than mere military expertise.

1. F. Maclean, *The Battle of Neretva*, Panther Books, 1970, p 128

CHAPTER 11

The Degeneration of People's War 1975–94

Since the American withdrawal from Vietnam there has been no discernible slackening in the frequency of armed insurgencies around the world, many of which can be clearly categorised as guerrilla wars. These have taken place place in, for example, Afghanistan, Angola, Bangladesh, Bolivia, Burma (several), Cambodia, Chad, Colombia, El Salvador, Ethiopia, Guatemala, India (several), Iraq, Kurdistan, Laos, Lebanon, Morocco, Mozambique, Namibia, Nicaragua, Northern Ireland, Peru, the Philippines, Rhodesia (Zimbabwe), Sri Lanka, Sudan, Timor, and Uganda. Clearly it would be impossible to deal adequately with all these insurgencies in one short chapter. Therefore, especially as my aim throughout this book has been to establish a general historical context in which this mode of warfare can be studied, I shall limit the discussion here to those wars which offer some insight into significant changes in guerrilla theory and practice since the hey-day of 'People's War' in the aftermath of World War II. The case studies chosen are: Aghanistan, Eritrea, Central America, Peru, Sri Lanka, Cambodia, Kurdistan, Palestine and Lebanon.

Afghanistan

In many ways the Cold War reflected just the same tensions and mutual suspicions that had dominated international relations for a hundred years before. Not the least of these was intense concern about the razor-backed ridges and defiles of Afghanistan, seen by both Russia and the West as a potential back door into their respective spheres of influence. Since 1973 and the overthrow of the Afghan monarchy, the Soviets had been able to exert considerable influence on that country's politics, via leftist elements in the army and in the secular National Revolutionary Party. But this very secularism and the reliance on Russian advisers alienated many traditional Afghans and fanned the flames of Islamic-inspired nationalism. Attempts by the government to develop a more non-aligned international posture did little to mollify the traditionalists whilst at the same time disturbing pro-Soviet elements in the newly formed People's Democratic Party of Afghanistan. These latter over-threw President Daoud in 1978 which in turn galvanised the traditionalists, tribally fragmented though they were, into a general revolt. In December 1979, the Soviets, heeding the plea for fraternal aid from the beleaguered government, launched a three-pronged invasion, deploying over 50,000 troops, including élite airborne units, as well as tanks and helicopter gunships.

This impressive *blitzkrieg*, which took most official Western military observers by surprise, was sufficient to bring a noticeable stiffening of resolve to the local incumbent forces, and they were able to tighten their grip on the capital Kabul and certain other major centres. But the presence of a Russian army of occupation obviously did little to calm the religious and monarchist opposition in the country at large, and, indeed, did much to give their inchoate, essentially parochial mistrust a xenophobic focus that temporarily diverted attention from traditional clan and tribal rivalries. However, these were never completely subsumed under any centralised resistance movement, even of a purely religious nature. Throughout the war with the Russians such 'parties' as Hezb-i-Islami, Jamiat-i-Islami, Hezb-i-Wahdat and Ittehad-i-Islami, built upon Tajik, Pashtun or Uzbek particularism and funded by jealous Saudi, Pakistani, US and Iranian patrons, established only a very loose military alli-ance, one that was incapable of developing the sort of organisational dynamic that would produce mobile main force units on a par with the Chinese Red Army, the Viet Minh or the Viet Cong. With the exception of the forces led by Commander Massoud of the Jamiat-i-Islami, who was a great believer in continual military training and the gradual accretion of large-unit competence, hardly any of the *mojahedin* ever took their armed resistance beyond the level of roving bands, striking at targets of opportunity when the mood suited.

Remarkably, however, this fairly subdued tempo of operations eventually forced the Russians, in 1988–89, to withdraw all their forces from the country. As an example of the humbling of a super-power, the weary exodus of the 'zinky boys' back to the Soviet Union seemed very much of a repeat of the French and American withdrawals from Vietnam. There were, indeed, other parallels with the Vietnam experience. Thus a vital asset of the Afghan rebels was the availability of foreign aid, both financial and military, and the pro-vision of sanctuaries outside Afghanistan, both for the guerrillas and for those millions of their relatives who became refugees. These sanctuaries were in Pakistan and it was through that country, too, that the endless columns of aid flowed from the guerrillas' US and Middle Eastern sponsors. In 1988, for example, US military aid was estimated at some $600 million.

Much of the aid comprised small arms and ammunition but after 1986 also included more substantial items like state-of-the-art radio equipment, 120mm rocket-launchers and mortars, and Stinger missiles. This latter was a man-portable surface-to-air missile that was launched along the operator's line-of-sight but which then acquired the target by means of a passive infra-red seeker. Stingers, supplemented by some similar UK Blowpipe systems, were enormously effective against both Russian fixed and rotary-wing aircraft, disrupting their air operations almost as effectively as had the much larger, sited SAMs deployed in Vietnam against the US Air Force. Fixed-wing aircraft, usually on bombing missions, were forced to fly at high altitudes and thus sacrifice accuracy whilst the helicopters had to fly very low, to frustrate the IR seeker, and thus presented good targets to even rudimentary AA gunnery. The Russians did develop counter-measures, such as IR flares and heat deflectors and had, in fact, gone a long way to de-stinging these weapons by 1989. But by then the political decision to withdraw had already been taken.

This decision, too, had parallels with US experience in Vietnam, most notably the attempt to off-load continued counter-insurgency operations on to the internal government. Given Nixon's subsequent distraction by Watergate and the gradual choking-off of funds to South Vietnam by Congress, it is difficult to assess just how committed he was to actively perpetuating that regime. The subsequent level of Soviet aid to Afghanistan, however, up to $300 million per month, does seem to indicate a real commitment to keeping the Najibullah regime in place. And it was only the collapse of the Soviet Union itself that ended this commitment and led to Najibullah's overthrow in 1992.

It is arguable, however, that there was at least one important dissimilarity between the two withdrawals and the attempts to Vietnamise and Afghanise the conflicts, in that the former was a somewhat desperate response to intolerable losses of men and matériel and levels of domestic and international opprobrium, whereas the latter was a much more considered pull-out after a limited police action. For what seems more and more striking about the war in Afghanistan is the relatively modest effort the Russians actually made to win it. Even at the end they had only 115,000 troops stationed there (as opposed to a peak US figure in Vietnam of 536,000), and this represented a much smaller proportion of their forces (in 1989, 4 motor rifle and airborne divisions out of a total 157) than did the US commitment in Vietnam (in 1968, 7 out of 15 active infantry, airborne and cavalry divisions). Moreover, whilst the Americans indubitably made a whole-hearted effort to win their war, with massive aerial, naval and logistic support and stopping short only of full mobilisation at home, the Russians seem to have conducted the war in a curiously lack-lustre, desultory fashion. Soviet battle deaths, for example, put at only some 15,000 at most, are fairly low compared to the high levels of casualties that their conventional military doctrine regarded as acceptable. (US military deaths in Vietnam were over 46,000.)

This lack-lustre approach was particularly evident at the tactical level where throughout the war the Russians relied mainly upon fairly indiscriminate aerial bombardment supplemented by moving slow and unwieldy mechanised columns against selected guerrilla areas. The fact that most guerrillas never had to leave their homes for more than a few days, to withdraw into remote base camps, indicates the complete failure of such methods to significantly disrupt guerrilla operations. Of course, such tactical ineptitude can be partly attributed to the usual disdain of regular soldiers for 'bandit' operations, as well as to the inflexibility of Soviet military orthodoxy and of their command structures. Yet the inflexibility was so complete, and was matched by such a total lack of interest in sustained political work or in wooing the 'hearts and minds' of anyone except a narrow urban élite, that one can only conclude there was never any meaningful commitment within either Politburo or General Staff to winning the war against the *mojahedin*. Rather, they seem to have used the war as something of a laboratory through which they rotated as many units and men, especially officers, as possible to give them some experience of the 'sharp end' and of command under pressure.

In this regard, it is interesting to note that the one counter-insurgency tool with which the Soviets did experiment, the helicopter, was a weapon that was also deemed to have a vital place on the conventional battlefield and was one that the Americans, in particular, had made a vital element of their front-line cutting edge. Certainly the Russians did not have too much success with the helicopter in a specifically anti-guerrilla role. They were used primarily to insert a blocking force to cut off the retreat of *mojahedin* as they fell back in the face of the same old ponderous mechanised columns, and only very rarely was a trap successfully sprung. Similarly, the only other significant counter-insurgency gambit, the insertion of airborne night-ambush squads against guerrilla convoys and suspected ambushes, seems to have been mainly regarded as a form of combat training for conventional airborne shock troops, and there seem to be no examples of the formation of specialised counter-insurgency units. As for the occasional tactic of firing Scud missiles against these same convoys and ambush points, it is difficult to believe that this was a serious tactical initiative and not just the monitoring of accuracy and lethality under combat conditions.

In short, then, appallingly and cynically though the Soviets behaved in Afghanistan, being largely responsible for 1 million deaths and the exodus of 5 million refugees, most of them in exile, it is misleading to equate their eventual withdrawal with that of the Americans from Vietnam. This is not to say that they fared any better militarily – indeed, their effort was largely lamentable whereas the Americans did at least fight the Viet Cong almost to a standstill – but rather that they came into Afghanistan only to shore up the incumbent regime, 'blood' some of their vast military manpower and test some vital new military technology. All this they succeeded in doing.

Reservations about the real scale of the Afghan war also apply to the insurgents' own efforts, and it seems fairly apparent that the war of the *mojahedin* was in no way comparable to full-scale people's wars such as those fought in China and Vietnam. Indeed, it did not really even qualify as a successful war of national liberation, for even after the Soviet withdrawal and the formation of a Mojahedin Alliance it proved impossible for the various factions to arrive at any real political consensus. President Najibullah held out without too much trouble until the USSR itself collapsed in 1992, and even after his replacement by ex-*mojahedin* President Rabbani, with Massoud as his Defence Minister, relationships between the various factions deteriorated yet further. An Islamabad Accord, hammered out in March 1993, did not usher in the promised unified cabinet and at the time of writing a viable political set-tlement seems as far away as ever. As one regional strong-man said of the endless bickering that followed the Accord: 'In a year they couldn't even design a national flag. What can we expect they will do for this country?' An anonymous citizen of Kabul, which has largely been destroyed by the factional in-fighting, was even more trenchant: 'The only way to solve Afghanistan's problem is to put all the leaders on a plane and shoot it down.'[1]

Eritrea

There has, however, been one guerrilla war post-Vietnam that most certainly does qualify as a successful war of national liberation. This was that waged by the Eritreans against the Ethiopian government, from 1964 to 1991, during the course of which they created extremely effective, and generally popular, military, governmental and administrative structures, the foundations of a potential nation-state. Admittedly, the Eritreans are racially different from the Ethiopians, with whom they were forcibly federated in 1952, but the fact remains that they are one of the few peoples ever to have succeeded in militarily reasserting their identity in the teeth of bitter opposition from a determined central government.

Armed resistance began in 1964, after Eritrea was totally integrated into the fully unitary state established two years earlier. But the real test of Eritrean resolve came after 1974 when a military coup deposed the Emperor and brought General Teferi and later Lieutenant-Colonel Mengistu (President from 1987) to power as head of the Provisional Military Administrative Council. Mengistu came to espouse a draconian neo-Marxism that seemed to consist largely of treating the whole population as potential subversives who, as tools of US and Israeli imperialism, had to be beaten, tortured and liquidated without respite. Eritreans, being racially different, were of course regarded as the most dangerous of all the enemies within.

Mengistu began to demonstrate his revolutionary zeal in 1976, with the launching of the 'Red Terror' (his term) to root out dissidents, but his gov-ernment became a real threat to Eritrea from 1978 when the Soviets switched allegiance in the Ethiopian–Somalia dispute over the Ogaden desert and began pouring aid into Ethiopia, much of it military hardware. This influx of arms and technicians was a serious threat to the Eritrean Liberation Front (ELF) which by 1977 had 40,000 men under arms, having decisively beaten over 80,000 government troops and taken control of every important town within Eritrea with the exception of Asmara. Powerful government counter-attacks now forced them out of every one of these towns and the guerrillas had once again to take refuge in the remoter and least hospitable parts of the region. But once the first shock of these positional reverses had worn off the ELF started to slowly and methodically expand its area of operations, and over the next ten years, helped by the capture of vast quantities of ineptly handled Russian artillery, tanks, transport and small arms, transformed its guerrilla bands into hard-hitting mobile forces which in 1984 took control of several towns and in 1987 and 1988 worsted sizeable government forces in very well-planned conventional battles. In 1990 they scored another remarkable victory when they smashed an Ethiopian government offensive in a surprise attack on its staging positions.

By 1986, indeed, the Eritrean army was pretty much a regular force in its own right and one, moreover, that was at the service of a functioning, effectively independent state, a point underlined by the fact that this state was also protected by a fully-manned 340-mile border entrenchment running right from the Red Sea to the Sudan frontier. Even more remarkable was the society behind this rampart. Reminiscent of nothing so much as Frank Herbert's novel *Dune*, the Eritreans spent most of the daylight hours virtually underground, living and working in well-camouflaged settlements to protect themselves from the Ethiopian air force. Moreover, by 1989:

> ... 28 years of continual conflict ... has created an extraordinary economy in Eritrea. It has an underground and virtually cashless society, but the EPLF [successor to the ELF] nevertheless has a Ministry of Commerce ... [which] works to supply a wide variety of goods ... While the EPLF is no longer Marxist, the pressures of survival have made possible an unlikely classless and cashless society. The thousands of non-military EPLF members labour in factories, build roads and drill wells under the control of the various ministries and commissions. Transport in EPLF buses is free, as is medical care. EPLF drivers use vouchers to buy petrol from the EPLF's own chain of camouflaged petrol stations.[2]

Nevertheless, impeccable examples though the Eritreans were of military regularisation, social regeneration and national solidarity, their successes cannot be entirely divorced from the wider political context. The broader Ethiopian context was of importance in that several other guerrilla groups, notably the Tigray Popular Liberation Front and the Ethiopian Popular Democratic Movement (later combined in the Ethiopian Popular Revolutionary Democratic Front, the EPRDF) were themselves tying down large numbers of government troops. The wider international context was also important, and just as in Afghanistan the unravelling of the USSR had the gravest consequences for Mengistu. In February 1991, in fact, the EPLF and the EPRDF unleashed a combined offensive against the dictator and by May he had fled the country. On assuming power themselves, the EPRDF, under a Tigrayan President, restored Eritrean independence, subject to a referendum thereon in that region. In May 1993 Eritrea once more declared its independence, the culmination of perhaps the most remarkable, and still little known, guerrilla struggles of recent years.

Central America

Amongst the most publicised guerrilla wars of these same years have been the insurgencies in Nicaragua, El Salvador and Guatemala, each having been accorded potentially cataclysmic geopolitical significance by Presidents Ronald Reagan and George Bush, the former especially seeming determined to crank up the Cold War from Brezhnev truculence to Monroe paranoia. In 1980, Reagan attempted to mobilise electoral opinion by suggesting that left-wing forces in Nicaragua were only two days' march from Texas.

Reagan, in fact, went on to win that election but on taking office had to come to terms with the unpalatable fact that those same Nicaraguan leftists were actually in power, having driven out the loathsome President Somoza in July 1979, after an eighteen-year guerrilla struggle. Somoza's downfall, indeed, had been welcomed by outgoing President Jimmy Carter whose administration had cut off all US aid in 1978. This, together with Somoza's extraordinary brutality in putting down ill-advised urban insurrections in 1978 and 1979 – the bombing of his capital in June 1979 assumed Nero-like proportions – hastened the collapse of his regime. Another important element in the success of the Sandinista guerrillas, named after the 1920s leader Augusto Sandino, was that throughout the arduous, roving guerrilla days right up until 1978 they had been able to get sanctuary and aid in neighbouring Costa Rica, to which country Somoza remained blindly hostile.

But not only was Reagan facing guerrillas in power, bolstered, it has to be admitted, by a certain amount of Soviet aid, but also the unpalatable domestic truth that there was absolutely no chance of mobilising support, Pentagon or civilian, for US military operations to overthrow the Sandinistas. Ever since the humiliation of Vietnam it had become a commonplace of the national security establishment that American forces should on no account be used in low-level, chronic guerrilla situations where the increasingly 'hi-tech' US arsenal could find almost no tactical 'purchase' and where the only tangible results would be US body bags with their precipitous political down-side. Nor was Reagan himself at all hostile to the notion of using the most advanced weaponry to try and limit actual casualties on the ground, and he proved a staunch supporter of such projects as 'smart' weapons, drones, robotics, 'stealth' bombers and 'Star Wars'.

But hugely expensive conventional and nuclear forces, built around such weaponry, were no answer to Reagan's nightmares about the Soviet bogeyman slipping through the Sandinista keyhole and so, determined to roll back the red tide in Central America but fearful of any Americans getting killed doing it, Reagan and his advisers evolved a new theory of counter-insurgency warfare, and one that was also to be applied in El Salvador and Guatemala, where leftist guerrillas seemed likely to overthrow incumbent regimes every jot as corrupt and repressive as Somoza's had been. The new theory, known as 'low-intensity warfare', had two basic strands. The first was the use of proxy forces, either to undertake one's own subversion of the existing 'hostile' regime through a sustained 'White' guerrilla offensive, or to help eradicate 'Red' guerrillas by providing aid and advisers for the incumbent military and security forces. Such aid and advisers were the available options in El Salvador and Guatemala, where the guerrillas had not actually taken power in 1980. The second element of low-intensity warfare, though only really applicable to the Nicaraguan situation in Central America, was the destabilisation of a regime through economic attrition, not just by imposing the burden of fighting a prolonged guerrilla war against US-sponsored forces, but also by denying aid and trade and encouraging other countries to apply similar sanctions. In both regards the Americans were implacably vindictive. In 1985, Secretary of State Schulz averred: 'Our commitment is indefinite. It's just going to go on. I think the message is that ... we have staying power.'[3]

In Nicaragua, moreover, American ruthlessness paid off. The anti-Sandinista guerrillas they spawned, known as the Contras, were armed and trained in Honduran border camps, also used as bases for destructive forays into Nicaragua. The American advisers seem to have laid little stress upon any need to win Nicaraguan hearts and minds. The Contras were on the whole a remarkably unsavoury bunch and about the only technique of 'unconventional' warfare that they mastered was the massacre – peasants, militia, local government officials, aid workers and journalists all being grist to their mill. Their tactics were quite deliberately terroristic, designed to cow the population rather than win them over to any Contra 'ideology', and it is instructive to note that by 1984, active though they had admittedly been for almost three years, they still occupied not one jot of Nicaraguan territory.

Gradually, confirmation of the barbaric nature of the Contras' campaign began to reach the world media. US Congress, which had funded the destabilising effort from 1983, cut off all funds to the Contras two years later. The World Court, also in 1985, ruled overwhelmingly that the US was guilty of terrorism against Nicaragua and estimated that it owed the government and people some $14 billion for damages caused in an illegal war. For a while the Nicaraguan people, too, held firm and at the 1984 elections the Sandinistas won two-thirds of the vote. But popular support inevitably dwindled as the policy of economic attrition bit deeper. Media coverage had a diminishing impact (one commentator remarked that the American public would do anything for Latin America except read about it) and operations against the Contras, even though most were successful, were a terrible drain, causing some 5,000 military casualties and absorbing over 50 per cent of the national budget. By 1990 the country had had enough, and in elections that year opposition parties won 60 per cent of the vote.

Low-intensity warfare was also applied successfully in El Salvador and Guatemala, though here the proxy forces were those of the respective governments. The clearest victory was in El Salvador. Left-wing guerrillas had operated there in the 1970s, but the most important insurgency was that mounted by the Farabundo Marti Front for National Liberation (FMLN) from 1980. A premature 'final offensive' and general strike in 1981 cost the guerrillas most of the substantial gains made in the preceding months, and thereafter, sustained US military aid, notably A-37 aircraft and helicopter gunships, combined with extensive depopulation of guerrilla base areas, kept the guerrillas constantly on the move. Though they kept up a certain tempo of harassing operations throughout the 1980s, the guerrillas began to admit as early as 1984 that power-sharing with the government and the initiation of reform from within was their only real hope of exerting political influence. A political party, the Democratic Convergence, was formed in 1987 and eventually reached agreement with the government on terms for sharing. In 1993 the FMLN took the remarkable step of disarming itself and preparing for elections. These were held in May 1994, with the former rebels winning 26 per cent of the vote and the government ARENA party around 50 per cent. In the interim over 80,000 Salvadorians had died and some 1.5 million had left the country.

The Guatemalan insurgency has had two major phases, the first in 1960–69, based in the Sierra de las Minas among the Ladino population, and the second from 1972, led by the Guerrilla Army of the Poor (EGP) and basing itself among the desperately underprivileged Indian population. By 1979 there were upwards of 8,000 guerrillas in the country as a whole and by 1981 these claimed to have staged over one thousand ambushes and minor raids. But Guatemalan counter-insurgency methods were of almost unparalleled savagery, based upon a deliberate campaign to eradicate the Indians and their way of life. 'The civilian population's losses, as estimated by UN sources, ranged as high as 150,000 dead: more than one million people were relocated and a quarter of a million refugees poured into Mexico alone . . . 'The revolutionaries had lost their social base.'[4]

US advisers had played a prominent part in framing this counter-insurgency policy, at least insofar as it involved wholesale resettlement, and they (together with the Israelis) also put their imprimatur upon Guatemalan measures against urban dissidents. Not the least of these measures was the employment of death squads, the Guatemalans being the first to attempt the systematic elimination of political opposition, armed or otherwise, by deploying gangs of 'non-attri-butable' hit-men. Between 1970 and 1975 some 15,000 Guatemalans van-ished, whilst in 1981 alone, according to one estimate, a further 14,000 people were disposed of. Eventually, even the US tired of this blood-letting and military aid was suspended. The guerrillas, meanwhile, had reached similar conclusions to the Salvadorians about negotiated settlement being the only realistic option. Peace talks were initiated, with US blessing, in 1990, but at the time of writing these have still not led to any firm agreement or even to an end of the fighting.

Peru

The other significant guerrilla war in Latin America has been that in Peru, especially the campaign conducted by the Sendero Luminoso, or Shining Path, led by Professor Abimael Guzman. It came to prominence in 1980 when it severely disrupted local elections and by 1991 its operations had cost the Peruvian economy an estimated $18 billion. Like the second Guatemalan insurgency, outlined above, that of Shining Path is based among Peru's Indian population, a group treated with a degree of callousness that is unusual even in Latin America. The prospect of widespread Indian revolt alarms the Peruvian government a great deal, as something like 50 per cent of the population are pure Amerindians. Equally alarming has been the fanatical dedication of the guerrillas themselves, inspired by Guzman's strange but extremely potent mish-mash of Inca nationalism, anarchic nihilism and Maoism. There are probably only something like 7–8,000 active guerrillas but these have been able to tie down the best part of 112,000 men in the armed forces and 84,000 in the paramilitary police. Shining Path has been regularly anathematised by the government for acts of terror against wavering or unwilling supporters and at least some of these accusations seem to be based on fact. But it is also undeniable that at least half of the depredations against civilians in the war, 6,000-plus between 1980 and 1985, for example, have been caused by gov-ernment forces.

One pronounced weakness of Shining Path has been the wish, common to almost all Latin American revolutionaries, to give their movement an urban dimension. To this end Guzman himself moved to Lima, and though he survived for a while flitting from one safe house to another, sometimes just minutes ahead of the security forces, he was eventually captured in late 1992. Other leaders were subsequently also arrested, as were the city-based organisers of another guerrilla group, Tupac Amaru, in March 1994. These are serious blows though it is still far from clear that they will suffice to bring about the collapse of the insurgencies, especially that of Shining Path. A so-called Red Sendero leadership still exists (as opposed to Black Sendero leaders in prison) whilst guerrilla finances are generated within their rural base areas, mainly from taxes on the widespread cultivation and trafficking of the coca plant. Moreover, the Indian problem is always there. As one Peruvian academic noted sadly:

> Extreme poverty is the root cause of the violence, fuelled by the racism of the whites of Lima and the cities against the Indians. The standard of living amongst the peasants is so low that 25 per cent of infants die in their first year. It is impossible for the rule of law to replace the upsurge of anarchy.[5]

Thus it will take more than the arrest of a guerrilla leader, no matter how charismatic, to resolve the burning Indian sense of grievance. One can only hope that the Peruvian government can resist recourse to the Guatemalan solution, unashamed genocide.

Sri Lanka

The word 'genocide' is unfortunately all too applicable to the guerrilla war in Sri Lanka, where the root of the conflict is explicit, and mutual, racial intolerance. The struggle is between the Sinhalese government and a Tamil minority (1 million out of 14 million) in the north of the island. Animosities flared in 1948, with the granting of independence, but only led to widespread violence in the early 1980s, as the Tamils spread dark rumours of forthcoming pogroms and the Sinhalese absurd stories about floods of Tamil immigrants from India, intent on swamping the indigenous population. This combination of the most twisted fantasies of 'the enemy within' and 'the alien hordes without' rabble-rousers has provoked a vicious confrontation that seems irresolvable.

The main Tamil guerrilla group are the LTTE, popularly known as the Tamil Tigers, and they present a remarkably cohesive, disciplined and effective force. Their tactics revolve around attacking government forces, mainly by small ambushes and laying landmines; stealing or destroying state property or buildings; and terrorising any Sinhalese who encroach in areas simplistically defined as the Tamil 'homeland'. All these spheres of activity often employ something of a guerrilla novelty, the use of speedboats, often based in India, to harass the coast, smuggle in arms or disrupt Sinhalese fishing boats. But the Tigers are not particularly friendly to other Tamil insurgent groups. In 1986 they largely eradicated the leadership of their main rivals, the Tamil Eelam Liberation Organisation (TELO), and in 1988 fought against the Eelam People's Revolutionary Liberation Front (EPRLF), a 'constitutional' counter-weight to the Tigers, created by the Indian peace-keeping forces that arrived in Sri Lanka in 1987 to try to resolve the Tamil problem.

The Indians failed in their mission, which increasingly consisted in trying to eradicate the Tigers, and what is more, prompted the emergence of a Sinhalese guerrilla group, the avowedly Maoist JVP who, by the end of 1988, were tying down 33,000 government troops as well as many Indian units. This insurgency was snuffed out by the capture of seven out of eight members of the JVP Politburo which the Indians, under intense Sri Lankan government pressure, presented as a convenient excuse for quitting the island in 1989–90. Whatever impact they had had on the level of violence was dissipated over the months that followed and at the time of writing this most pitiless of racial confrontations, with frequent civilian butchery on both sides, grinds on.

Cambodia

An equally intractable war in Asia has been that in Cambodia, where the Khmer Rouge present a permanent threat to whatever government is in power. In 1975, of course, the Khmer Rouge had actually seized power themselves, in the wake of America's general disengagement from S.E. Asia, and proceeded to enact a mutant Maoism that turned a revolutionary war of the 'have nots' into the hideous excesses of the 'know nothings', an anti-intellectual holocaust that combined totalitarian organisation with the basest instincts of the *jacquerie*. Prior to this, Khmer Rouge cooperation had been important in maintaining the important Viet Cong sanctuaries in Cambodia but no sooner were both Communist regimes actually in power than traditional rivalries flared. In 1978 the North Vietnamese invaded, installing their own puppet government, but were unable to eliminate the Khmer Rouge, who allied with other Cambodian nationalist groups, notably that led by Prince Sihanouk.

Given their previous experience, the counter-insurgency abilities of the North Vietnamese Army proved less than might have been expected and the war soon settled down into a rather ritualised affair, in some ways reminiscent of the 'limited' campaigning in Europe in the 17th and 18th centuries. Climate was a major factor and fighting only lasted from January to May, during the dry season, when surprisingly cumbersome North Vietnamese offensives, heralded by prolonged and fairly ineffective artillery bombardments, alerted the guerrillas to move back into their sanctuaries in Thailand. This they did fairly unscathed, only to return at the start of the rainy season and re-establish their Cambodian camps, defending these positionally against sporadic, small-scale Vietnamese operations. Offensives in 1985 and 1986 were more successful, achieving a greater level of surprise, picking off the camps one by one, and closely pursuing the survivors right back into Thailand. But they were still unable to eliminate the Khmer Rouge or, indeed, either of the other two main nationalist groups. In 1990, having lost something in the region of 25,000 casualties, the North Vietnamese bit the counter-insurgency bullet and withdrew.

The Khmer Rouge soon began to spread out from their bases along the mountainous Thai border and started the same creeping advance on Phnom Penh that had brought them to victory in 1975. This time, however, they were baulked by some energetic international diplomacy and in 1991, seeking to improve their appalling political image, the Khmer Rouge grudgingly agreed to the terms of the Paris Agreement, whereby all sides agreed to disarm and start preparations for democratic elections. A United Nations peace-keeping force was introduced to supervise this transitionary period. Khmer Rouge promises proved worthless, however, and they immediately reneged on this agreement and resumed military operations.

Government forces had some success with a counter-offensive in 1993, and in March 1994 they took Pailin, an important Communist base. But this has since been lost again and the future of the present government, democratically elected but now bereft of UN support, looks increasingly uncertain. The Khmer Rouge have proved themselves an extremely resilient force over the last thirty years or so and their military experience, their ferociously dedicated political cadres, as well as the financial benefits accruing from a lucrative trade in gems and timber obtained in their base areas, must make them almost impossible to eradicate. Even more depressing is the knowledge that the Khmer Rouge are now deliberately basing their tactics upon creating widespread economic disruption and social dislocation, a particularly favoured method being the indiscriminate sowing of thousands of cheap but deadly plastic mines, which not only maim and disfigure but so deter the peasants from working the paddy fields that they fall into disuse, with obvious and terrible consequences for the local economy.

Angola

The guerrilla war in Angola is another that grew out of a seemingly victorious one in the 1970s. From 1961 to 1975, when the Portuguese withdrew from their Angolan possessions, the MPLA in Angola, along with FRELIMO in Mozambique and the PAIGC in Guiné Bissau, had waged authentic peasant guerrilla wars, utilising many Maoist techniques and precepts, against the colonial power. None of these movements could claim total 'national' support, however, and in Angola in particular there was considerable opposition to the MPLA by UNITA, another resistance movement, led by Joseph Savimbi, and recruited largely from amongst the Ovimbundu people.

In 1976, MPLA had controlled at least 90 per cent of the country but Savimbi, himself Chinese-trained, was gradually able to carve out substantial guerrilla bases in the southern half of the country. These came under intense pressure in 1985, when a big MPLA offensive was conducted with the aid of some 13,000 Cuban troops. But such unabashed Communist interference, with the Cubans acting very much as Soviet proxy troops, dragged the conflict on to the world stage and prompted the US to resume aid to UNITA, having blocked it for the previous nine years, and to encourage large-scale South African intervention. The South Africans were especially active in 1988, with 9,000 soldiers, 500 armoured vehicles and 600 artillery pieces deployed alongside UNITA forces. By 1990, UNITA was able to field around 60,000 soldiers of its own and the ensuing military stalemate persuaded both sides to seek some sort of negotiated settlement. Thus, as in Cambodia, both sides agreed to demobilise and abide by the results of national elections, to be held in 1992.

But UNITA, to their evident surprise, did not win at these elections and they immediately set in reverse such demobilisation as had been completed. They were now bereft of South African support, as the MPLA was of Cuban, and though the fighting still rages at the time of writing, it seems unlikely that they will be able to topple the government. Angola has plentiful oil revenues, thanks to its off-shore fields, and has been able to build up a fairly lavishly equipped army and air force. But UNITA, too, is well-financed, mainly from diamond-smuggling out of the Cafunfo region, and has built up a well-equipped army of its own. It now controls up to 70 per cent of the country, though perhaps only 35 per cent of the population, and military operations seem to have degenerated into an endless series of Thirty Years War-type sieges, as each side drags up its powerful and plentiful artillery and leisurely blasts away at the cowering, war-weary populations of the major towns, usually crowded with refugees. Anyone straying out of the towns or trying to continue making a living from the land runs serious risk of disabling injury from the estimated 12 million mines that have have been scattered throughout the country.

Kurdistan

The Kurds have been fighting for their independence, or at least for clan autonomy within some sort of Kurdish homeland, for hundreds of years. Their last major disappointment was in 1923, when the independence promised in the never-ratified Treaty of Sèvres was reduced to a meaningless statement of intent in the signed and sealed Treaty of Lausanne. Their case has always been complicated by the fact that though they are a distinct people, they have never had a separate homeland nor firm frontiers defined by historical precedent. That they will ever have one in the future is rendered most unlikely by the fact that such a putative Kurdish state would have to be carved out of adjacent corners of Turkey, Iraq, Iran and Syria. It would be difficult to think of four regimes less likely to tolerate secessionists, no matter how troublesome, or more prepared to impose their central fiat by draconian military force.

Nevertheless, the Kurds have consistently refused to abandon their struggle, and in Turkey and Iraq in particular have organised guerrilla forces that have consistently troubled these governments by hit-and-run attacks on military outposts and patrols as well as on agents of the political authorities and those regarded as collaborators. The latest round of fighting in Iraq began in the early 1970s when the Kurdish Democratic Front (KDP), under Mustafa Barzani, allied with the Shah of Iran and fought against Iranian Kurds as well as against the Iraqi government. This revolt collapsed in 1975 when the Shah withdrew support and the Iraqis, in typically ruthless fashion, went on to destroy all Kurdish villages within 20 miles of the Turkish border, and thus with access to important sanctuaries there, and deported most of the inhabitants to the south. The KDP sided with the Iranians once again during the First Gulf War and started anti-Iraqi operations in 1984. Some 15,000 guerrillas operated in small hit-and-run squads of ten to a dozen men, leaving their villages to walk many miles overnight to their target, where the operation was planned in detail with local sympathisers. By 1986, it was said that the KDP was tying down 160,000 soldiers who might otherwise have been on the Iranian front.

The end of the First Gulf War, in 1988, did the Kurds no favours. Although the KDP and the Iranian Patriotic Union of Kurdistan (PUK) allied their forces in this same year, giving joint forces of up to 45,000 soldiers and 15,000 militia, operating over a 30,000 square mile theatre, the end of conventional hostilities meant that both incumbent governments could devote more attention to their own minorities. In Iraq, Saddam Hussein seized the opportunity with typical zeal and in 1988 launched massive conventional assaults against Kurdish base areas, addressing the problem of the villagers' hearts and minds by spraying them with mustard gas and, it now seems clear, nerve gas. Saddam also sowed thousands of mines in vast areas of arable land, the better to force the population at large to quit the guerrilla areas. Documents captured during the Second Gulf War have shown that Saddam was striving for the total destruction of the Kurds as a socio-economic entity and the Anfal campaign, as it was known, went a long way to achieving this aim, with 500,000 people being forcibly relocated, 250,000 driven into Turkey, and the male population of entire villages being executed out of hand. Thousands of guerrillas, fearful for their families under gas attack, surrendered, many to be tortured and executed, and by 1989 the PDK had been reduced to perhaps 5,000 guerrillas, relying mainly on selective assassination rather than military confrontation.

But the Second Gulf War, in 1991, and Saddam's comprehensive military defeat therein, seemed to offer the Kurds their best opportunity yet for a successful uprising and they dutifully sallied forth once more, dispensing with much of the caution and secrecy that usually characterised their operations. Saddam, however, was by no means as weakened militarily as might have been thought. He had committed only token units of his élite Republican Guard to the Kuwaiti front, knowing full well that they might be needed for internal repression. In 1992, therefore, he launched yet another series of concerted offensives against the Kurdish guerrillas, making full use of carefully hoarded tanks, artillery and helicopter gunships. His intention to wage another Anfal Campaign was, however, thwarted by the Allies who marked out a Kurdish safe haven which Iraqi aircraft were not allowed to penetrate. This has permitted the KDP to establish a provisional government at Arbil, and has presumably also allowed a welcome reorganisation and replenishment of their armed units. In classic Kurdish fashion, however, they have done little to further their cause long-term, being drawn into fighting with the PUK in May 1994. A truce is in force at the time of writing, but the establishment of zones of influence for each major Kurdish party, rather than an attempt to hammer out plans for joint power-sharing, still does not bode well for the establishment of any Kurdish homeland.

The Kurds in Turkey have, in the main, achieved a higher degree of integration within the nation as a whole than in other countries. Nevertheless, the south-east of the country is a predominantly Kurdish region and some Kurds claim that 19 of Turkey's 71 provinces are rightfully theirs. Moreover, this demand is being most vigorously pressed by a particularly disciplined and ruthless revolutionary organisation, the Kurdish Worker's Party (PKK), established in 1978. Of Marxist, even Maoist leanings, the PKK was outlawed in 1980 but has since embarked on a reasonably successful guerrilla campaign. It regularly ties down 150,000 troops on routine pacification duties whilst in the fairly regular sustained Turkish offensives up to 300,000 troops are used, backed up with artillery, helicopter gunships and fixed-wing aircraft. The Turks themselves have put the death toll between 1984 and 1993 at 4,500 guerrillas, 3,100 civilians and 2,300 security troops. Turkish sources tend not to mention that relocation and depopulation programmes have accounted for upwards of 800 villages being razed to the ground in the last four years alone. But this considerable counter-insurgency campaigning has so far done little more than add to the sum of human misery. At the time of writing the PKK guerrilla structure remains robustly intact, the guerrillas still able to live in Kurdish villages and come together at night for hit-and-run military operations, usually involving small arms and mortars. Some AA guns are also available, however, as are light artillery pieces, particularly useful for protecting withdrawals during major Turkish sweeps. But it will come as no surprise to learn that the PKK is quite willing to turn its weapons against fellow Kurds, as was the case in 1993 when they helped Saddam's troops maintain an economic blockade against the Iraqi Kurdish safe haven.

Palestine and Lebanon

The question of Palestinian independence has long been a source of political violence, through the British Mandate of 1920–48, the emergence of the Israeli state and the partition of Palestine between that country, Jordan and Egypt, the Arab–Israeli War of 1956, and the war of 1967 when Israel occupied the West Bank and the Gaza Strip. However, until the 1980s the Palestinian resistance movement was not a convincing example of guerrilla warfare: dominated by Yasser Arafat's Palestine Liberation Organisation (PLO), founded in 1964, it adopted purely terroristic tactics in its resorts to violence which, despite the enormous publicity they attracted, were neither a real part of the national liberation–people's war continuum nor, it seemed, had any real chance of persuading Israel or her sponsors to accede to Palestinian demands.

Palestinian operations, whether or not directly organised by the PLO, retained this terroristic aspect throughout the 1980s, as exemplified in incidents like the seizure of the Italian cruise-ship *Achille Lauro*, the hi-jacking of a TWA airliner in Beirut, of an Egyptian plane *en route* to Malta, attacks at Rome and Vienna airports, and the blowing up of Pan Am Flight 103 over Lockerbie, in Scotland. Even after Arafat's renunciation of terror, in December 1988, splinter groups like the Palestine Liberation Front were prepared to stage outrages such as the sea-borne attacks on Tel Aviv sun-bathers, in May 1990.

Even before these attacks, however, the PLO was also developing a more orthodox type of guerrilla force. In 1970, in fact, the PLO had been ejected from Jordan, as too great a political liability, and its fighters had moved into Lebanon, in and to the south of Beirut, and through a mixture of proselytising and bullying amongst the Shiite Muslims in south Lebanon they established a base for hit-and-run raids into Israel, most of them suicidally abortive. But PLO *braggadocio* upset the fragile balance between Lebanon's Christian and Muslim populations, and within these groups themselves, and in 1975 sparked off a civil war that has continued to this day. This drew in the official Lebanese army, the Maronite Christian militia, the PLO (split), the pro-Iranian Shiite Hezbollah, the more secular Shiite Amal militia, and the Sunni and Druze Muslim militias, not to mention Syrian troops from 1975 and Israeli troops in

1978 and between 1982 and 1985. A UN force arrived in 1978 and a Multinational Force came and went in 1983, but none of them has been able to make much impact upon the fighting or on the endless bickering and occasional assassination that constitutes the 'peace process'.

The PLO appeared to fare particularly badly during all this. Their raids into Israel, as has been noted, though a constant and expensive irritation, had absolutely no impact upon that country's resolve to remain on the West Bank. But they did provoke a large-scale Israeli raid into southern Lebanon, in 1978, and four years later a full-scale invasion that drove right into Beirut, forcing the PLO to withdraw into Tripoli. This exacerbated a split between pro-Arafat and pro-Syrian factions, and after savage fighting some 4,000 pro-Arafat fighters were evacuated by sea to Tunis, in December 1983. At one stage the Israelis, who had invaded to get rid of the PLO, blockaded Tripoli in the hope that the two factions would destroy each other.

But Israeli success was not as lasting as they might have hoped. For the Shiite Muslims in southern Lebanon proved just as fertile a recruiting ground for Iranian fundamentalism as they had for the PLO, and Hezbollah-inspired attacks on Israeli occupation forces became a much greater military threat than PLO incursions had ever been. Even the superb Israeli armed forces were forced to take their turn in admitting that determined guerrillas could impose unacceptable burdens, both in terms of military budget and public opinion. It was decided to withdraw, but politicians and commanders alike were determined that such a withdrawal must not again open up guerrilla bases on their very borders. They therefore took great pains to establish a secure buffer zone between Lebanon and Israel. This zone, 1–10 kilometres in depth, is heavily fortified but, even more importantly, is manned on the Lebanese side by an Israeli-trained force, the nominally-Christian South Lebanon Army. This 2,000-strong force is supplied with captured Soviet tanks and sophisticated radio equipment to call down Israeli artillery and helicopter strikes. The Israelis also use pilotless reconnaissance drones to alert their air forces of impending guerrilla attacks. The solidity of this buffer zone has somewhat baffled the Hezbollah, who often resort to futile artillery and rocket attacks across the border or even to despairing human wave assaults on heavily fortified positions; however, neither lack of success nor heavy casualties prevented the number of raids and attacks rising sharply from 170 in 1992 to 330 in 1993.

At the time of writing the prospects for the fundamentalist guerrillas trying to undermine Israel look bleak, and surely only renewed conventional, regional conflict can afford them any sort of room for manoeuvre. Remarkably, however, the PLO have come back from the dead, and they have achieved this by adopting a dual strategy that owed almost nothing to guerrilla warfare or terrorism. Its first strand was to strive for international respectability and admission to the diplomatic 'jet set' that discusses face-to-face or brokers the deals shaping international politics. Military isolation in Tunis was a crucial push in this direction, the attempted *rapprochement* with Jordan in 1985 the first faltering step, and the Madrid Conference of 1991 the great leap forward. In September 1993, after intense activity by Norwegian mediators, this diplomatic offensive bore fruit, in the shape of an agreement between Israel and the PLO for Palestinian autonomy in the Gaza Strip and Jericho and for on-going discussions about extending some measure of Palestinian self-rule throughout the West Bank.

That the Israelis should be persuaded to make such concessions was also the result of the second strand of revised PLO strategy, the *intifada*, a sustained campaign of strikes and civil disobedience (though considerably more robust than anything Mahatma Gandhi might have sanctioned) within Palestinian territories. This began in 1987, though to what extent the PLO initiated the campaign or were simply riding a tiger let loose by grass-roots activists or rival Palestinian groups like the Islamic Resistance Movement (Hamas), remains unclear. Whatever the truth of the matter, it was the PLO who were able to present themselves as the legitimate, newly respectable leader of the Palestinians and thus persuade enough Israelis to accept the new agreement as a realistic compromise with Palestinian 'moderates' rather than a capitulation to fundamentalist zealots.

In other words, it is quite possible that the only clear-cut guerrilla success dealt with in this chapter, other than that in Eritrea, will have been achieved by a group that had largely renounced the way of the gun some ten years earlier. However, elegant an ending though this would be to a survey of guerrilla history, knowledge of the real world leaves one fearful that Hamas and Islamic Jihad terrorists, Israeli settlers, *intifada* activists, the humiliatingly small size of these first fragments of a Palestinian state, the continuing melt-down in Lebanon, and the proliferation of Muslim fundamentalism, will all doom the area to yet more years of mutually destructive guerrilla attrition.

It will be apparent by now that my conclusions on the future of guerrilla warfare are somewhat different from the almost dewy-eyed positivism of my original conclusion (now presented as Chapter 10, and retained for reasons stated in the Preface). For it has to be admitted, that though guerrilla wars are still often expressions of popular resistance to deprivation and oppression, just as were the 'people's wars' that concluded my original survey, it cannot be claimed that any of the actual insurgencies have much in common with these historical models. Any progressive ideology tends at best to be a gloss and there is rarely much evidence of the integrated grass-roots social and political work that was a genuinely progressive feature of the Chinese and Vietnamese revolutions or of the anti-Portuguese phases of the Angolan and Mozambiquan insurgencies. A small but significant indicator of this degeneration into mere militarism is the fact that where the Chinese Civil War was seen as a revolution, attracting sympathetic westerners like Edgar Snow and Norman Bethune, Agnes Smedley and Jack Belden to become involved in the war politically, on behalf of the guerrillas and (as they saw it) the great mass of the Chinese peasantry, modern insurgencies only draw in the (heroic) aid workers for such organisations as *Médecins sans Frontières* or the Red Cross, whose concern can only be with short-term palliatives for the helpless victims caught in the middle.

There are various reasons for this abrupt disappearance of a social revolutionary dimension from modern guerrilla warfare. One is a simple matter of geography. The Cold War was obviously a major factor in post-war guerrilla struggles, as in Greece or Vietnam, for example, and a major reason such wars attained the levels of violence they did was that the guerrillas had Communist sponsors with common frontiers, who could provide sanctuary and sustained military and economic aid. This material replenishment was essential in allowing the guerrillas to build up their military forces more quickly than might otherwise have been possible, and thus bought them the time to conduct the long-term social and political work that alone could permit the transition from local military reputation to widespread political influence. But the last war in which this was the case was Vietnam (together with Cambodia/Laos) and thereafter the Communists, notably the Soviets, had to look far afield to find guerrilla movements they might usefully support. The search was fairly fruitless, for even if such a movement was identified, the fact that it was some distance from the USSR or a suitable client-state meant that it would be difficult to insert significant amounts of material aid, ports and airports almost certainly being in the hands of the incumbent forces. Post-Vietnam, therefore, the Soviets turned to propping up beleaguered regimes in power, such as Ethiopia, Angola, Afghanistan and, to a much lesser extent, Nicaragua, to which aid could be delivered with reasonable ease. But even though all these governments espoused some sort of socialist ideology, they also had regular, standing armed forces, and so Soviet aid consisted largely of conventional weaponry and conventional advisers and technicians. Inevitably such weapons as tanks, artillery, fixed and rotary-winged aircraft were employed without much regard for the population at large, or for hearts and minds, and thus the Communist aid that had once been such a vital factor in permitting the protracted warfare that gradually and simultaneously expanded military operations and political organisation now just became another element in the brutalisation of all kinds of internal war.

But this is not the only aspect of the changing Cold War that has had a significant impact upon guerrilla warfare. Again Vietnam seems to have been some kind of watershed. There, as we saw in Chapter 9, fears about massive Chinese intervention, and a possible escalation to nuclear confrontation with the USSR, were an important constraint on US leaders, who developed a clear idea of just what seemed 'permissible' militarily, according to Cold War 'rules'. But such considerations now seem to belong very much to the first phase of the Cold War and are very reminiscent of Truman and Eisenhower's preoccupations during the Korean conflict. By the 1980s, however, even before the accession of Gorbachev, the prospect of nuclear cataclysm seems to have been dismissed to the realms of strategic bogeyland and, despite Reagan's apparent predilection for eyeballing the 'evil empire', both sides in the Cold War proved remarkably tolerant of mutual meddling in insurgency situations. In Afghanistan and Angola, in particular, both the US and the USSR, through their proxy forces, made serious efforts to achieve military victory, though in neither case did the level of world tension rise significantly (even in Nicaragua Reagan concentrated on aiding the Contras rather than on provocative Cuban missile-type showdowns, though of course the Russians were now very wary about the type of aid they sent to this region).

But this escalation of mutual interference has had the most unfortunate consequences for the 'host' countries, as it tended to mean that both sides in an insurgency were much better and more quickly armed, and that quite intensive though stalemated military operations soon became the norm, with a consequent emphasis upon purely 'militarist' insurgency and counter-insurgency strategies with an almost total disregard for the long-term, socially constructive, organisational dynamic associated with authentic people's war.

The end of the Cold War has not helped at all. The demise of Communism, it could be argued, has had a totally negative ideological impact in that any kind of socialist, even progressive liberal theories, have been discredited, and substituted by an avaricious individualism that has no place for any notion of collective social progress. Thus Britain's National Criminal Intelligence Service estimates that as much as 40 per cent of Russia's gross domestic product is now controlled by organised crime. If such are the fruits of the end of the Cold War then the implications for guerrilla warfare, which is only really distinguishable from banditry, tribalism, warlordism or putative totalitarianism by some concept of the common good, some consensual equation of rights and obligations, are depressing indeed.

Such fears about the criminalisation of guerrilla warfare are abundantly supported by some of the case studies included in this chapter. In Angola, Bolivia and Cambodia, for example, we saw how the guerrillas largely financed themselves through, respectively, smuggled diamonds, smuggled cocaine, and smuggled gems and hardwood, all of which are moved from the insurgent bases via corrupt local authorities and criminal middlemen. The implications for a guerrilla movement are clear. On the one hand, such revenues can easily become an end in themselves, leading guerrilla leaders to become mere warlords, intent only on maintaining armed forces to protect their trafficking. On the other, even where some political ideology remains, it is unlikely that this can really flourish, as guerrilla finances are now totally independent of collective endeavour. In other words, guerrilla taxes of the local population, often dismissed as merely predatory, can in fact be socially reinforcing as they derive from work within the collective and might encourage its further social and economic development. Whereas guerrilla criminalisation, as described above, is probably even more pernicious than run-of-the-mill gangsterism. For the latter, based usually upon booze, gambling, prostitution and drugs is only parasitic upon society, depending on a reasonable standard of living within that society as a whole to generate the surplus, earned or stolen, to purchase the gangsters' wares. Guerrilla criminals, however, who export their illicit goods, need have no interest at all in the society around them beyond providing tolerable wages and the odd *divertissement* for their young gunmen.

But even without such focused criminalisation there are other reasons for the growing depoliticisation of guerrilla warfare, at least in terms of any meaningful social dynamic. Fundamental is a widespread rejection of imperialist cartography by which colonies, eventually to become independent countries, were marked out on the map in the most arbitrary manner, with little regard to local custom, affiliations or animosities. Thus the concept of 'imperialism' is still relevant to modern guerrilla warfare, not so much in the old anti-colonial sense, the impetus behind so many 19th and early 20th century guerrilla wars, but as an explanation for the disintegration of so many post-colonial, Soviet and even post-Hapsburg political entities into their clan, tribal or ethnic constituent parts. For reasons I would hesitate to deduce, localism, particularism, racism and xenophobia are the global order of the day and separatist movements are having a most baleful influence in countries as diverse as Bosnia, Rwanda, Afghanistan, Somalia, Italy, Canada, the Ukraine, Sudan, Kurdistan, Nigeria and Burma.

This fragmentation of international affairs has of course been increased by the collapse of Soviet hegemony in Eastern Europe and the USSR, as well as by the consequent neo-isolationism of the US, but an equally important consequence of the end of the Cold War has been the remarkable proliferation of small arms on to the world market, mainly from Soviet or Warsaw Pact sources. This has allowed a whole array of *ad hoc* guerrilla forces to arm themselves quickly and cheaply and thus be able to adopt a locally impressive military posture almost from the beginning, without having first to establish grass-roots political credentials that go much beyond those of a xenophobic protection-racket. Of course, it is not just the ending of the Cold War that has encouraged this trend. In Afghanistan, for example, the deluge of arms provided by the Cold War adversaries has been a major factor in permitting age-old, chronic, tribal rivalries to degenerate into a frenzy of violence that has already destroyed much of the country's modest infrastructure.

But Afghanistan was not just a cockpit for Cold War rivalries. The bigots of Muslim fundamentalism were also hard at work, as were the agents of the fearful oil sheikhs of the Gulf. This regional rivalry has also had grim consequences for other guerrilla struggles. In Kurdistan and the Lebanon (and more than likely Palestine in the future), copious financial and military assistance from Iran, Syria, Iraq, Saudi Arabia and Israel to support one or other of the main rival guerrilla factions has done much to turn these struggles into glorified vendettas, in which the homeless and the refugees are outnumbered only by the number of guns available.

A final major reason for the degeneration of guerrilla warfare back to modes of combat more reminiscent of flint-tipped spears than the iconic Kalashnikov of old, has been the unwillingness of the great powers to take concerted action to end or even effectively mediate in any of these wars. This is largely a result of the crumbling of bloc international politics, as first the easing of the Cold War and later the complete collapse of Soviet Communism made these powers less and less fearful about possible 'subversion' in one or other Third World state. What had once seemed to be the imminent collapse of a domino that might topple a whole region came to be seen as pretty much an irrelevancy in a world where blocs and even nation-states have a diminishing role in the supernational corporate free-for-all heralded by the latest round of GATT negotiations.

However, international politics are not quite dead, nor even completely without shame, and efforts have been made to hide behind the fig-leaf of the UN, with many pompous resolutions passed bidding it to go forth and pacify. Unfortunately, UN forces have neither the financial support, the requisite general staff with both the expertise and the authority to command a multi-national force, nor sufficient numbers of adequately trained and equipped troops to effectively orchestrate the programme of humanitarian relief, military logistics, tact, shows of local force, and above all infinite patience that is required in each and every one of the UN's numerous peace-keeping commitments. But neither do the great powers seem able to act of their own accord, either singly or in the context of a regional alliance. The greatest test of this has been in former Yugoslavia and the results have been abysmal. For the Serbs, in a masterly campaign combining bluster, evasion, deceit, piecemeal yet inexorable military 'nibbling', atrocities and effusive apologies, have now come well down the road to the Greater Serbia that would have seemed utterly unthinkable four or five years ago.

The Serbs seem to have grasped one of the fundamental truths about modern warfare, that the 'hi-tech' forces of the great powers are largely powerless in the internal war situation. For such forces are unable to apply either the requisite manpower or the long-term but fairly modest level of force that are required in such wars. Modern, hi-tech armies have only two levels of response: lightly armed rapid reaction, with its corollary of rapid withdrawal, or the fairly sedate concentration of overwhelming firepower, by land, sea and air. But neither of these options is particularly applicable in Yugoslavia, where there are no targets sufficiently important for an elaborate airborne or amphibious insertion, or for a barrage of precision-guided munitions.

Nowadays, unless targets offer a sufficiently large pay-off, such as the oil-fields of Kuwait and Saudi Arabia, it is simply too costly to expend either sophisticated weaponry or highly trained soldiery against them. Modern armies no longer deploy either cannon balls or cannon fodder. But neither do they meet enemies so ill-armed and tactically naive as to allow them to take easy and cheap advantage of their technological superiority, as tiny 19th century armies were able to do with that remarkable 'force multiplier', the machine gun. Thus modern armies are simply going to stop getting involved in guerrilla and Balkan-type wars, as they will not be prepared for protracted, labour extensive peace-keeping or for providing a relevant military response. Yet it is just such wars, in our increasingly parochial yet adversarial world, that are on the increase, and apparently getting more and more indecisive. It seems that such violent stalemates can only proliferate until whole areas of the globe are gradually devastated by chronic blood-letting and fanatical intolerance. According to the old Maoist axiom, guerrillas had to be fish swimming in the sea of the people. Today it seems much more likely that the people will drown in a sea of guerrillas.

1. Both quoted in *Financial Times*, 13 May 1993
2. J. Laffin, *The World in Conflict 1990*, Brasseys (UK), 1990, p85
3. S. Landau, *The Guerrilla Wars of Central America*, Weidenfeld & Nicholson, 1993, p63
4. *ibid*, p.84
5. J. Laffin, *The World in Conflict 1991*, Brasseys (UK), 1991, p172

Bibliography

This bibliography is not intended to be a listing of the many hundreds of books that I have consulted in the course of this study. The most useful of those will be found in the Notes. Rather it is intended as a preliminary guide to anyone interested in pursuing the subject further. Though I have been at pains to stress the socio-political context of guerrilla warfare, I have omitted to include in this bibliography those works dealing with revolutions as a whole. The last section of the bibliography in J. Dunn's *Modern Revolutions* (see below) lists the most important of such works. Anyone interested in the general nature of the relationship between military power and social revolution might usefully refer to the bibliography in J. Ellis, *Armies in Revolution* (see below).

Abd El-Krim, *Memoiren: Mein Krieg Gegen Spanien und Frankreich*, Dresden, 1927

M. Adler-Bresse, 'Témoignages allemands sur la guerre des partisans', *Revue d'Histoire de la Deuxième Guerre Mondiale*, No 53, 1964

African National Congress, *Guerrilla Warfare*, London, 1970

H. Alavi, Peasants and Revolution, in R. Milliband (ed), *Socialist Register*, London, 1965

W. E. D. Allen and P. Muratoff, *Caucasian Battlefields*, London, 1953

J. Amery, *Sons of the Eagle*, London, 1948

Appian (trans H. White), The Wars in Spain, in *Appian's Roman History*, London, 1912, Vol 1

J. A. Armstrong (ed), *Soviet Partisans in World War Two*, Madison (Wisc), 1964

A. Arnold, *The Fateful Pebble: Afghanistan's Role in the Fall of the Soviet Union*, Novato (CA), 1992

G. Arnold, *Wars in the Third World since 1945*, London, 1991

P. Arshinov, *History of the Makhnovist Movement 1918–21*, [1923], Chicago, 1974

R. B. Asprey, *War in the Shadows: The Guerrilla in History*, (rev. ed.), London, 1994

Gen P. Azan (ed), *Par l'épée et par la charrue: écrits et discours de Bugeaud*, Paris, 1948

A. J. Bracevich (*et al*), *American Military Policy in Small Wars: The Case of El Salvador*, New York, 1988

B. Bar-Kochva, *Judas Maccabaeus: The Jewish Struggle Against the Seleucids*, Cambridge, 1990

E. M. Barron, *The Scottish War of Independence* (2nd ed), Inverness, 1935

G. W. S. Barrow, *Robert the Bruce*, London, 1965

T. Barry, *Guerrilla Days in Ireland*, Dublin, 1969

R. D. Bass, *Swamp Fox: the Life and Campaigns of General Francis Marion*, London, 1959

C. Beals, *Great Guerrilla Leaders*, Englewood Cliffs (NJ), 1970

J. Beckett (ed), *The Roots of Counterinsurgency: Armies and Guerrilla Warfare 1900–45*, London, 1988

J. Beeler, *Warfare in Feudal Europe 730–1200*, Ithaca, 1971

G. Benton, *Mountain Fires: The Red Army's Three-Year War in South China 1934–38*, Berkeley, 1992

E. Bickerman, *The Maccabees*, New York, 1947

P. Billingsley, *Bandits in Republican China*, Stanford, 1989

I. R. Blacker (ed), *Irregulars, Partisans, Guerrillas*, New York, 1954

L. Blanch, *The Sabres of Paradise*, London, 1960

H. Blanco, *Land or Death: the Peasant Struggle in Peru*, New York, 1972

D. Blaufarb, *The Counterinsurgency Era*, New York, 1977

M. Blumenthal, *Der Preussische Landsturm von 1813*, Berlin, 1900

W. Blunt, *Desert Hawk: Abd el-Kader and the French Conquest of Algeria*, London, 1947

R. Bonds (ed), *The Vietnam War*, London, 1979

Col G. Bonnet, *Les guerres insurrectionelles de l'antiquité à nos jours*, Paris, 1958

S. G. F. Brandon, *Jesus and the Zealots*, Manchester, 1967

M. Browne, *The New Face of War*, London, 1965

R. S. Brownlee, *Grey Ghosts of the Confederacy*, Baton Rouge (LA), 1958

Capt A. Buchanan, *Three Years of War in East Africa*, London, 1919

H. Buckmaster, *The Seminole Wars*, New York, 1966

R. V. Burks, *The Dynamics of Communism in Eastern Europe*, Princeton, 1961

A. Burton, *Urban Terrorism: Theory, Practice and Response*, London, 1975

J. Buttinger, *Vietnam: a Dragon Embattled*, New York, 1967 (2 vols)

L. E. Cable, *Conflict of Myths: The Development of American Counterinsurgency Doctrine and the Vietnam War*, New York, 1986

J. Caesar (trans J. Warrington), *Gallic Wars*, London, 1953

O. Caroe, *The Pathans 550 BC to AD 1947*, London, 1958

G. Chaliand, *The Palestine Resistance*, Harmondsworth, 1972

G. Chaliand (ed), *Guerrilla Warfare from the Long March to Vietnam*, Berkeley, 1982

D. Charters and M. Tugwell, *Armies in Low-Intensity Conflict*, London, 1989

J. Chen, *Mao and the Chinese Revolution*, London, 1965

J. Chesneaux, *Peasant Revolts in China, 1840–1949*, London, 1973

R. H. Chilcote (ed), *Protest and Resistance in Angola and Brazil*, Los Angeles, 1972

E. Childers, *The Times History of the War in South Africa* (Vol 5), London, 1907

E. Christiansen, *The Northern Crusades: the Baltic and the Catholic Frontier 1100–1525*, London, 1980

S. Christowe, *Heroes and Assassins*, London, 1935

C. C. Clendenen, *Blood on the Border: the United States Army and the Mexican Irregulars*, New York, 1969

M. Clodfelter, *The Limits of Airpower: The American Bombing of North Vietnam*, New York, 1989

R. Clutterbuck, *Guerrillas and Terrorists*, London, 1977

R. Clutterbuck, *The Long, Long War*, London, 1966

J. M. Collins, *America's Small Wars: Lessons for the Future*, New York, 1991

M. Cooper, *The Phantom War: The German Struggle against Soviet Partisans 1941–44*, London, 1979

A. H. Cordesmann and A. R. Wagner, *The Afghan and Falklands Conflicts (Lessons of Modern Conflicts vol.III)*, London, 1990

M. Crowder (ed), *West African Resistance*, London, 1971

D. Dakin, *The Greek Struggle in Macedonia*, Salonika, 1966

D. Dakin, *The Greek Struggle for Independence 1821–33*, London, 1973

J. Dalloz, *The War in Indo-China 1945–54*, Dublin, 1990

C. F. Dalzell, *Mussolini's Enemies*, Princeton, 1961

A. Davidoff, *Essai sur la guerre des partisans*, Paris, 1841

A. B. Davidson, 'African Resistance and Rebellion Against the Imposition of Colonial Rule', in T. O. Ranger (ed), *Emerging Themes in African History*, London, 1968

B. Davidson (*et al.*), *Behind the War in Eritrea*, Nottingham, 1980

B. Davidson, *The Liberation of Guiné*, Harmondsworth, 1969

B. Davidson, *In the Eye of the Storm*, London, 1974

P. B. Davidson, *Vietnam at War 1946–75*, London, 1988

F. W. D. Deakin, *The Embattled Mountain*, London, 1971

R. Debray, *Revolution in the Revolution?*, Harmondsworth, 1968

E. de Cunha (trans S. Putnam), *Revolt in the Backlands*, London, 1947

M. Deeb, *The Lebanese Civil War*, New York, 1980

de Grandmaison, *La Petite Guerre*, Paris, 1756

F. de Jeney, *The Partisan or the Art of Making War in Detachment*, London 1760

de la Croix, *Traité de la Petite Guerre*, Paris, 1752

A. Del Broca, *The Ethiopian War 1935–41*, Chicago, 1969

G. Desroziers, *Combats de partisans ... depuis le XIVième siècle*, Paris, 1883

C. de Wet, *Three Years War*, London, 1902

de Wüst, *L'art militaire de partisan*, La Haye, 1768

J. Dunn, *Modern Revolutions*, Cambridge, 1972

T. N. Dupuy and P. Martell, *Flawed Victory: The Arab-Israeli Conflict and the 1982 War in Lebanon*, Fairfax (VA), 1986

H. Eckstein (ed), *Internal War*, New York, 1964

D. Eeckaute, 'Les brigands en Russie du XVIIième au XIXième siècle', *Revue d'Histoire Moderne et Contemporaine*, July-Sept, 1965

Maj-Gen J. G. Elliott, *The Frontier 1839–1947*, London, 1968

M. Elliott-Bateman, *Defeat in the East; the Mark of Mao Tse-tung on War*, London, 1967

J. Ellis, *Armies in Revolution*, London, 1973

J. F. Elton, *With the French in Mexico*, London, 1867

L. B. and J. E. Elwood, *The Rebellious Welsh*, Los Angeles, 1951

F. Engels, Engels on Guerrilla Warfare, *Labour Monthly*, August, 1943

F. Engels, *Ausgewählte Militärische Schriften* Berlin, 1958 (2 vols)

M. Ereliiska, 'Le mouvement de résistance bulgare', *Revue d'Histoire de la Deuxième Guerre Mondiale*, No 72, 1968

J. Erickson, 'The Origins of the Red Army', in R. Pipes (ed), *Revolutionary Russia*, London, 1968

E. E. Evans-Pritchard, *The Sanusi of Cyrenaica*, London, 1973

G. Fairburn, *Revolutionary Warfare and Communist Strategy*, London, 1968

B. Fall, *Street Without Joy*, London, 1963

B. Fall, *The Two Vietnams*, London, 1967

F. Fanon, *The Wretched of the Earth*, Harmondsworth, 1969

M. Fellman, *Inside War: The Guerrilla Conflict in Missouri During the American Civil War*, London, 1990

First International Conference on the History of Resistance Movements, *European Resistance Movements 1939–45*, Oxford, 1960

R. Fisk, *Pity the Nation: Lebanon at War*, London, 1990

G. Flint, *Marching with Gomez*, New York, 1898

M. R. D. Foot, *SOE: The Special Operations Executive 1940–46*, London, 1984

D. Footman, *The Civil War in Russia*, London, 1961

Frontinus (trans C. E. Bennett), *The Strategems*, London, 1925

R. Furneaux, *Abdel Krim*, London, 1925

C. A. Gabriel and P. I. Savage, *Crisis in Command: Mismanagement in the Army*, New York, 1978

D. Galula, *Counter-insurgency Warfare: Theory and Practice*, New York 1964

M. Gammer, *Muslim Resistance to the Tsar: Shamil and the Conquest of Chechnia and Daghestan*, London, 1994

L. H. Gann, *Guerrillas in History*, Stanford, 1972

B. Gardner, *German East*, London, 1963

P. Gavi, *Le triangle indien: de Bandoeng à Bangladesh*, Paris, 1972

S. Gelder, *The Chinese Communists*, London, 1946

E. Gentilini, 'La guerre des partisans', in M. Bravo (ed), *Les socialistes avant Marx*, Paris, 1970, Vol 3

Geraldus Cambriensis (trans T. Wright), 'Description of Wales', in *The Historical Works of Geraldus Cambriensis*, London, 1863

J. Gerassi (ed), *Towards Revolution*, London, 1972 (2 vols)

M. E. Gettleman, *Vietnam*, Harmondsworth, 1966

Vo Nguyen Giap, *People's War, People's Army* (1961), New York, 1967

Vo Nguyen Giap, *The Military Art of People's War*, New York, 1970

J. S. Girling, *People's War*, London, 1970

D. C. Gordon, *The Passing of French Algeria*, London, 1966

R. Gott, *Rural Guerrillas in Latin America*, Harmondsworth, 1973

J. Gottman, Bugeaud, Galliéni, Lyautey: the 'Development of French Colonial Warfare', in E. M. Earle (ed), *Makers of Modern Strategy*, Princeton, 1941

G. E. Grant, 'Partisan Warfare: Model 1861–65', *Military Review*, No 8, 1958

Lt-Col T. N. Greene (ed), *The Guerrilla and How to Fight Him*, New York, 1962

F. Grenier, *Francs-tireurs and Guerrillas of France*, London, 1944

S. B. Griffiths (trans), *Sun Tzu: the Art of War*, Oxford, 1963

E. Guevara, *Guerrilla Warfare*, New York, 1961

E. Guevara, *Reminiscences of the Cuban Revolutionary War*, Harmondsworth, 1969

J. Guillermaz, *A History of the Chinese Communist Party 1921–49*, London, 1972

C. W. Gwynn, *Imperial Policing*, London, 1934

W. Hahlweg, *Preussische Reformzeit und Revolutionärer Krieg*, Frankfurt, 1962

W. B. Harris, *France, Spain and the Rif*, London, 1927

J. P. Harrison, *A History of the CCP 1921–72: The Long March to Power*, London, 1972

R. Haycock (ed), *Regular Armies and Insurgency*, London, 1979

O. Heilbrunn, 'Guerrillas in the Nineteenth Century', *Journal of the Royal United Services Institution*, 1963

O. Heilbrunn, *Partisan Warfare*, London, 1962

O. Heilbrunn, *Warfare in the Enemy's Rear*, London, 1963

O. Heilbrunn and C. A. Dixon, *Communist Guerrilla Warfare*, London, 1964

W. C. G. Heneker, *Bush Warfare*, London, 1907

C. F. Henningsen, *A Twelve Month's Campaign With Zumalacárregui ...*, London, 1836

A. Heriot, *The French in Italy 1796–99*, London, 1957

Herodotus (trans A. D. Godfrey), London, 1921, Vol 2

H. J. Hewitt, 'The Organisation of War', in K. Fowler (ed), *The Hundred Years' War*, London, 1971

D. Hiro, *Lebanon, Fire and Embers: A History of the Lebanese Civil War*, London, 1993

E. J. Hobsbawm, *Bandits*, Harmondsworth, 1972

E. Holt, *The Carlist Wars in Spain*, London, 1967

W. Hoobergen, *The Boni Maroon War in Suriname*, Leiden, 1990

E. R. Hooton, *The Greatest Tumult: The Chinese Civil War*, London, 1991

A. Horne, *A Savage War of Peace: Algeria 1954–62*, London, 1977

M. Howard, *The Franco-Prussian War*, London, 1967

G. Huitzer, *Peasant Rebellion in Latin America*, Harmondsworth, 1973

A. Humbaraci, *Algeria: the Revolution that Failed*, London, 1966

R. Hunter, *The Palestine Uprising: A War by Other Means*, Berkeley, 1993

D. Hyde, *The Roots of Guerrilla Warfare*, London, 1968

E. H. Jacoby, *Agrarian Unrest in South-east Asia* (2nd ed), London, 1961

M. Jähns, *Geschischte der Kriegswissenschaften*, Leipzig, 1891. See the Bibliography at the end of Vol 3 for a complete listing of books on guerrilla warfare ('little wars') published in the second half of the eighteenth century.

C. L. R. James, *The Black Jacobins*, London, 1938

P. Janke and J. Sim, *Guerrilla and Terrorist Organisations: A World Directory and Bibliography*, Brighton, 1983

C. A. Johnson, *Peasant Nationalism and Communist Power*, Stanford, 1962

R. M. Johnston, *The Napoleonic Empire in Southern Italy*, London, 1904 (2 vols)

A. Jones (trans), *The History of Gruffydd ap Cynan*, Manchester, 1910

V. C. Jones, *Ranger Mosby*, Chapel Hill, 1944

R. Jouet, *La résistance à l'occupation anglaise en Basse-Normandie 1418–50*, Caen, 1969

C.-A. Julien (ed), *Les techniciens de la colonisation (XIXième et XXième siècles)*, Paris, 1947

G. M. Kahin, *Nationalism and Revolution in Indonesia*, Ithaca, 1952

R. K. Kent, Palmares: an African State in Brazil, *Journal of African History*, Vol 6, 1965

M. T. Klare and P. Kornbluh, *Low Intensity Warfare*, London, 1989

K. Knoebel, *Victor Charlie*, London, 1967

G. Kolko, *Vietnam: Anatomy of a War 1940–75*, London, 1985

R. Korngold, *Citizen Toussaint*, London, 1944

H. Kuhnrich, *Der Partisanenkrieg in Europa 1939–45*, (rev ed), Berlin, 1968

A. Labrousse, *The Tupamaros*, Harmondsworth, 1974

J. Laffin, *War Annuals 1–7 (The World in Conflict)*, London, 1986 and annually

S. Landau, *The Guerrilla Wars of Central America*, London, 1993

W. Laqueur, *Guerrilla*, London, 1976

W. Laqueur, *The Guerrilla Reader*, London, 1978

T. E. Lawrence, *Seven Pillars of Wisdom*, London, 1935

T. E. Lawrence, 'Anatomy of a Revolt', in T. Bowden and M. E. Elliott-Bateman, *From Revolt to Revolution*, Manchester, 1974

T. E. Lawrence, 'Guerrilla Warfare', *Encyclopaedia Britannica, 1929*

J. F. A. Le Mière de Corvey, *Des partisans et des coups irreguliers ...*, Paris, 1923

'Yank' Levy, *Guerrilla Warfare*, London, 1942

G. Lewy, *America in Vietnam*, New York, 1978

B. H. Liddell-Hart, *T. E. Lawrence*, London, 1965

E. Lister, 'The Lessons of the Spanish Guerrilla War 1939–51', *World Marxist Review*, 1965

G. Lockhart, *Nation in Arms: The Origins of the People's Army of Vietnam*, London, 1990

P. Longworth, *The Cossacks*, London, 1970

F. P. Lopez, (trans J. D. Harris), *A Guerrilla Diary of the Spanish Civil War*, London, 1972

G. H. Lovett, *Napoleon and the Birth of Modern Spain*, New York, 1965 (2 vols)

H. Lumsden, *Frontier Thoughts and Requirements*, London, 1902
J. Lynch, *The Spanish-American Revolutions, 1808–26*, London, 1973

Col. J. M. MacCarthey, *Limerick's Fighting Story*, Dublin, nd
P. J. MacGarvey, *Visions of Victory: Selected Vietnamese Communist Writings 1964–68*, Stanford, 1969
F. Maclean, *The Battle of Neretva*, London, 1970
T. M. Maguire, *Guerrilla or Partisan Warfare*, London, 1904
J. K. Mahon, Anglo-American Methods of Indian Warfare 1676–1794, *Mississippi Valley Historical Review*, No 45, 1958
M. Malet, *Nestor Makhno in the Russian Civil War*, London, 1982
Mao Tse-tung, *Selected Military Writings*, Peking, 1967
C. Marighela, *For the Liberation of Brazil*, Harmondsworth, 1971
H. Michel, *La guerre de l'ombre*, Paris, 1970
T. R. Mockaitis, *British Counterinsurgency 1919–60*, London, 1990
E. Mondlane, *The Struggle for Mozambique*, Harmondsworth, 1969
P. L. Moorcraft, *African Nemesis: War and Revolution in Southern Africa 1945–2010*
R. Moss, *Urban Guerrillas*, London, 1972
D. J. Mrozek, *Air Power and the Ground War in Vietnam*, London, 1989

A. H. Nasution, *Fundamentals of Guerrilla Warfare*, New York, 1965
L. H. Nelson, *The Normans in South Wales*, Austin (Texas), 1966
A. Neuberg, *L'insurrection armée*, (1931), Paris, 1970
New York Times, *The Pentagon Papers*, New York, 1971
Ngo-van-Chieu, *Journal d'un combattant Viet-Minh*, Paris, 1955
G. L. Niox, *Expédition du Mexique 1861–67*, Paris, 1874

E. O'Ballance, *The Kurdish Revolt 1961–70*, London, 1973
W. E. Odon, *On Internal War: American and Soviet Approaches to Third World Clients and Insurgents*, Durham (NC), 1992
B. A. Ogot (ed), *War and Society in Africa*, London, 1972
D. E. Omissi, *Air Power and Colonial Control: The RAF 1919–39*, Manchester, 1990
M. Oppenheimer, *Urban Guerrilla*, Harmondsworth, 1970
F. M. Osanka (ed), *Modern Guerrilla Warfare*, Glencoe, 1962
M. Osborne, *Region of Revolt: Focus on South East Asia*, Harmondsworth, 1971
R. Osgood, *Limited War Revisited*, Boulder (CL), 1979

J. Paget, *Counter-insurgency Campaigning*, London, 1967
P. Paret, 'Colonial Experience and European Military Reform at the End of the Eighteenth Century', *Bulletin of the Institute for Historical Research*, 1964
P. Paret, *French Revolutionary Warfare*, London, 1964
P. Paret and J. Shy, *Guerrillas in the 60s*, (rev. ed.), New York, 1965
J. S. Paul, 'Frelimo and the Mozambique Revolution', in C. Arrighi and J. S. Paul (eds), *Essays on the Political Economy of Africa*, New York, 1973
M. Pavlovich, 'Zelim Khan ...', *Revue du monde musulman*, 1912

M. Pearlman, *The Maccabees*, London, 1973

D. Pike, *The Organisation and Techniques of the National Liberation Front of South Vietnam*, London, 1966

Plutarch (trans A. H. Clough), Sertorius, in *Lives*, London, nd, Vol 2

W. J. Pomeroy, *The Forest*, New York, 1963

W. J. Pomeroy, *Guerrilla and Counter-guerrilla Warfare*, New York, 1964

W. J. Pomeroy (ed), *Guerrilla Warfare and Marxism*, London, 1969

M. W. Potter, (trans), *Zachary Stoyonoff: Pages from the Autobiography of a Bulgarian Insurgent*, London, 1913

J. C. Pratt (ed), *Vietnam Voices*, New York, 1984

Maj-Gen J. S. Pustay, *Counter-insurgency Warfare*, New York, 1965

I. Rácz, *Couches militaires issues de la paysannerie libre en Europe orientale du 15ième au 17ième siècles*, Debreczen, 1964

D. V. Rattan, Anti-guerrilla operations: a Case-study from History, *Military Review*, May, 1960

S. Raven, *Rome in Africa*, London, 1993

N. Reed, *The Caste War in Yucatan*, Stanford, 1964

D. Reitz, *Commando*, London, 1929

D. G. Reporaz, *The War in Cuba*, London, 1898

C. Robinson, *The Fighting Maroons of Jamaica*, Jamaica, 1969

E. Robson, *The American Revolution 1763–83*, London, 1955

A. J. Roderick (ed), *Wales through the Ages*, Llanybie, 1959, Vol 1

B. J. H. Rowe, John Duke of Bedford and the Norman Brigands, *English Historical Review*, October 1932

O. Roy, *The Lessons of the Soviet–Afghan War*, (IISS Adelphi Paper 259), London, 1994

C. W. Russell (ed), *The Memoirs of Colonel John S. Mosby*, Bloomington (Indiana), 1959

H. Salisbury, *The Long March*, New York, 1985

O. Sarin and L. Dvoretsky, *The Afghan Syndrome: The Soviet Union's Vietnam*, Novato (CA), 1993

S. Schram, *Mao Tse-tung*, (rev. ed.), Harmondsworth, 1967

T. Shanin (ed), *Peasants and Peasant Societies*, Harmondsworth, 1971

W. Shawcross, *Sideshow: Kissinger, Nixon and the Destruction of Cambodia*, London, 1979

N. Sheehan, *A Bright Shining Lie: John Paul Vann and America in Vietnam*, New York, 1988

A. Short, *The Communist Insurrection in Malaya*, London, 1975

Major J. R. Sibley, *Tanganyikan Guerrilla*, London, 1973

A. D. H. Smith, *Fighting the Turk in the Balkans*, New York, 1908

E. Snow, *Red Star Over China*, London, 1937; (rev. ed.), New York, 1939

J. Šolc, 'Le mouvement slovaque des partisanes', *Revue d'histoire de la Deuxième Guerre Mondiale*, No 52, 1963

P. C. Standing, *Guerrilla Leaders of the World*, London, 1913

S. Stanton, *The Rise and Fall of an American Army: US Ground Forces in Vietnam 1965–73*, Novato, CA, 1989

R. Stubbs, *Hearts and Minds in Guerrilla Warfare: The Malayan Emergency 1948–60*, London, 1989

F. Sully, *The Age of the Guerrilla*, New York, 1968

H. G. Summers, *On Strategy: A Critical Analysis of the Vietnam War*, Novato (CA), 1983

H. G. Summers, *Vietnam War Almanac*, New York, 1985

S. Swarup, *A Study of the Chinese Communist Movement*, Oxford, 1966

A. Swinson, *The North West Frontier*, London, 1967

J. Swire, *Bulgarian Conspiracy*, London, 1939

R. Taber, *The War of the Flea*, London, 1970

Tacitus (trans M. Grant), *Annals of Imperial Rome*, Harmondsworth, 1971

G. K. Tanham, *Communist Revolutionary Warfare*, London, 1962

E. Tarle, *Napoleon's Invasion of Russia*, London, 1942

L. Taruc, *He Who Rides the Tiger*, London, 1967

D. J. M. Tate, *The Making of Modern South East Asia*, Kuala Lumpur, 1971, Vol 1

I. A. Taylor, *The Tragedy of an Army: La Vendée 1793*, London, 1913

H. Thomas, *Cuba or the Pursuit of Freedom*, London, 1971

E. A. Thompson, *The Early Germans*, Oxford, 1965

R. Thompson, *Defeating Communist Insurgency*, London, 1966

C. Tilly, *La Vendée*, London, 1964

J. Tito, *Selected Military Works*, Belgrade, 1969

C. Townshend, *Britain's Civil Wars: Counterinsurgency in the 20th Century*, London, 1986

Col R. Trinquier, *Modern Warfare: a French View of Counter-insurgency*, New York, 1964

L. Trotsky, *Ecrits militaires*, Paris, 1970, Vol 1

Truong Chinh, *The Resistance Will Win*, (1947), Hanoi, 1960

N. Urban, *War in Afghanistan*, London, 1990

N. D. Valeriano and C. T. R. Bohannan, *Counter-guerrilla Operations*, London, 1962

J. M. van Der Kroef, 'Prince Diponegoro ...', *Far Eastern Quarterly*, August, 1949

L. M. Vega, *Guerrillas in Latin America*, London, 1969

L. Villari, *The Liberation of Italy*, Appleton (Wisc), 1959

Voline, *The Unknown Revolution*, London, 1955, (Part II)

C. von Clausewitz, *On War*, London, 1966, (Vol 2, Bk 6, Ch 26)

P. von Lettow-Vorbeck, *My Reminiscences of East Africa*, London, 1920

Col G. C. von Widdern, 'The Guerrilla Warfare in the Districts in the Rear of the German Armies', in Maj-Gen J. F. Maurice, (ed), *The Franco-German War 1870–71*, London, 1900

R. F. Weighly, *The Partisan War: The South Carolina Campaign 1780–82*, Columbia (S. Carolina), 1970

J. Weller, 'Irregular but Effective . . .', *Military Affairs*, Fall, 1957

J. Weller, 'The Irregular War in the South', *Military Affairs*, Fall, 1960

J. Weller, 'Wellington's Use of Guerrillas', *Journal of the Royal United Services Institution*, May, 1963

T. P. Wickham-Crawley, *Guerrillas and Insurgents in Latin America: A Comparative Study of Regions and Insurgents since 1956*, Princeton, 1992

D. Williams (ed), *The Irish Struggle 1916–26*, London, 1966

T. Wintringham, *People's War*, Harmondsworth, 1943

E. R. Wolf, *Peasant Wars of the Twentieth Century*, London, 1971

J. Womack Jr, *Zapata and the Mexican Revolution*, Harmondsworth, 1972

M. M. Wood, 'From Gaucho to Guerrilla', *Americas*, January 1961

C. M. Woodhouse, *The Struggle for Greece 1941–49*, London, 1976

D. Woodman, *The Making of Burma*, London, 1962

D. S. Woolman, *Rebels in the Rif*, London, 1969

Y. Yadin, *Bar-Kokhba*, London, 1971

B. Yang, *From Revolution to Politics: Chinese Communists on the Long March*, Oxford, 1990

Sir W. Young, *An Account of the Black Charaibs in the Island of Saint Vincent's, (1795)*, London, 1972

C. Younger, *Ireland's Civil War*, London, 1970

J. K. Zawodny (ed), *Annals of the American Academy of Political and Social Science*, (special issue on 'Unconventional Warfare'), Vol 341, May 1962

Index